LANFRANC

LANFRANC

SCHOLAR, MONK, AND ARCHBISHOP

H. E. J. COWDREY

OXFORD
UNIVERSITY PRESS

This book has been printed digitally and produced in a standard specification in order to ensure its continuing availability

OXFORD
UNIVERSITY PRESS

Great Clarendon Street, Oxford OX2 6DP

Oxford University Press is a department of the University of Oxford.
It furthers the University's objective of excellence in research, scholarship,
and education by publishing worldwide in

Oxford New York

Auckland Cape Town Dar es Salaam Hong Kong Karachi
Kuala Lumpur Madrid Melbourne Mexico City Nairobi
New Delhi Shanghai Taipei Toronto
With offices in
Argentina Austria Brazil Chile Czech Republic France Greece
Guatemala Hungary Italy Japan South Korea Poland Portugal
Singapore Switzerland Thailand Turkey Ukraine Vietnam

Oxford is a registered trade mark of Oxford University Press
in the UK and in certain other countries

Published in the United States
by Oxford University Press Inc., New York

© H. E. J. Cowdrey, 2003

The moral rights of the author have been asserted

Database right Oxford University Press (maker)

Reprinted 2007

All rights reserved. No part of this publication may be reproduced,
stored in a retrieval system, or transmitted, in any form or by any means,
without the prior permission in writing of Oxford University Press,
or as expressly permitted by law, or under terms agreed with the appropriate
reprographics rights organization. Enquiries concerning reproduction
outside the scope of the above should be sent to the Rights Department,
Oxford University Press, at the address above

You must not circulate this book in any other binding or cover
And you must impose this same condition on any acquirer

ISBN 978-0-19-925960-1

Preface

ANOTHER STUDY OF LANFRANC calls for justification in view of the availability of those by A. J. Macdonald and Margaret Gibson. Despite its age, Macdonald's biography offers a reliable account of Lanfranc's career which is well grounded in the sources; Gibson's remains authoritative as an exposition and appraisal of Lanfranc the scholar which is complemented by a full description of the sources for his life and activity, both in his own writings and in contemporary literature. But, some seventy-seven years since Macdonald's first edition, it is possible to set Lanfranc and his work more fully in the context of the intellectual, religious, and political life of the eleventh century. Excellent though Gibson's book is, particularly on Lanfranc's scholarship, there are large areas of his work and achievement as archbishop with which she dealt only lightly. Moreover, his work and achievement have been overshadowed by the figure of his successor as archbishop, St Anselm, not least on account of the consummate scholarship and artistry of Sir Richard Southern's depiction of him. Thus, there appears to be room for a fresh appraisal of Lanfranc upon which the shadow of Anselm is not too heavily cast. Each stage of his long and varied career calls for consideration in the light of the momentous developments that were taking place both in the Latin Christendom and in the England of his time; and some estimate is called for of his place and achievement in the line of the archbishops of Canterbury from Augustine to the present day.

In the process of writing this book I have incurred many debts, and particularly to the Oxford University Press. I am especially grateful to Ruth Parr for her sustaining confidence and ready counsel at all stages, to Anne Gelling for overseeing its production, to my sub-editor Jeff New, and to the anonymous readers of my typescript for many corrections and suggested improvements. And I am once more deeply indebted to the principal and fellows of St Edmund Hall for permitting a long-since retired fellow the use of college facilities and for their encouragement and readiness to answer my questions.

Contents

Abbreviations   x

1. EARLY LIFE   1
1.1 Pavia   1
1.2 Family, Education, and Early Career   5
1.3 From Pavia to Bec   9

2. MONK AND ABBOT   11
2.1 Conversion of Life   11
2.2 Prior of Bec   15
2.3 Abbot of Saint-Étienne at Caen   24

3. SERVICE OUTSIDE THE CLOISTER, c.1042–1070   29
3.1 To the Duke of Normandy   29
3.2 Lanfranc and the Reform Papacy   38

4. SCHOLAR AND TEACHER   46
4.1 The Liberal Arts   47
4.2 The Bible and the Christian Fathers   50
4.3 Berengar and the Eucharist   59

5. RETROSPECT   75

6. THE MOVE TO CANTERBURY   78

7. THE PRIMACY OF CANTERBURY   87

8. THE CHURCH OF CANTERBURY   104
8.1 The Buildings of the Cathedral and Cathedral Monastery   104
8.2 Lanfranc's Charitable Foundations at Canterbury   107
8.3 The Securing of Christ Church's Lands and Privileges   109

8.4 The Administration of Canterbury's Lands and Income	115
8.5 The See of Rochester	117

9. THE ORDERING OF THE ENGLISH CHURCH — 120

9.1 Lanfranc's Primatial Councils	120
9.2 The Dioceses and Diocesan Synods	129
9.3 The Separation of Ecclesiastical Jurisdiction	132
9.4 Archdeacons	134
9.5 Parishes and Deaneries	136
9.6 Canon Law	138
9.7 Conclusion	143

10. THE WIDER PRIMACY — 144

10.1 Ireland	144
10.2 Scotland	147
10.3 Wales	148

11. THE MONASTIC ORDER — 149

11.1 Christ Church, Canterbury	149
11.2 Lanfranc's Monastic Constitutions	154
11.3 Other Cathedral and Episcopal Monasteries	160
11.4 Three Abbeys	163
11.4.1 St Albans	164
11.4.2 Bury St Edmunds	164
11.4.3 St Augustine's at Canterbury	167
11.5 Severity and Mercy	172

12. LANFRANC AND THE ENGLISH — 175

13. LANFRANC AND KING WILLIAM I — 185

13.1 Archbishop and King	186
13.2 Lanfranc as Royal Deputy and Royal Justice	188

14. LANFRANC AND THE GREGORIAN PAPACY — 197

14.1 Lanfranc and Pope Gregory VII	197
14.2 Lanfranc and the Anti-pope	202

15. EXTERNAL CONCERNS — 206

15.1 Lanfranc and Normandy — 206
15.2 Lanfranc and the French Church — 215

16. THE LAST YEARS — 217

16.1 The Succession of King William II — 217
16.2 The Trial of William of Saint-Calais — 219
16.3 Death and Burial — 225

17. CONCLUSION — 226

Bibliography — 232

Index — 247

Abbreviations

This list contains abbreviations of periodicals and series. Abbreviations of sources may be found in the Bibliography.

AB	*Analecta Bollandiana*
ANS	*Anglo-Norman Studies* (Until vol. 4 (1981): *Proceedings of the Battle Abbey Conference*)
AQ	*Ausgewählte Quellen zur deutschen Geschichte des Mittelalters*
BIHR	*Bulletin of the Institute of Historical Research*
CC	*Corpus christianorum*
CCM	*Corpus christianorum, continuatio medievalis*
CCMon.	*Corpus consuetudinum monasticarum*
CSEL	*Corpus scriptorum ecclesiasticorum Latinorum*
CSer.	Camden Series
DBI	*Dizionario biografico degli Italiani*
EHR	*The English Historical Review*
FMS	*Frühmittelalterliche Studien*
HBS	The Henry Bradshaw Society
Hefele–Leclercq	C. J. von Hefele, continued by H. Leclercq, *Histoire des conciles*, 8 parts in 16 vols. (Paris, 1907–21)
HSJ	*The Haskins Society Journal*
JEH	*The Journal of Ecclesiastical History*
JL	P. Jaffé, *Regesta pontificum Romanorum*, 2 vols. (2nd edn. by S. Loewenfeld, F. Kaltenbrunner, and P. Ewald, Leipzig, 1885–8)
JTS	*The Journal of Theological Studies*
Manaresi	*I placiti del 'Regnum Italiae'*, ed. C. Manaresi, 3 vols. (Rome, 1955–60)
Mansi	*Sacrorum conciliorum nova et amplissima collectio*, ed. J. D. Mansi, 20 vols. (Florence and Venice, 1755–75)
MARS	*Mediaeval and Renaissance Studies*
MGH	*Monumenta Germaniae Historica*
AA	*Auctores antiquissimi*
Briefe	*Die Briefe der deutschen Kaiserzeit*
Const.	*Constitutiones et acta publica imperatorum et regum*
DD	*Diplomata regum et imperatorum Germaniae*
HII	Henry II
Epp. sel.	*Epistolae selectae*
LL	*Leges (in Folio)*
Libelli	*Libelli de lite imperatorum et pontificum*
OCC	*Ordines celebrando concilio*
Schriften	*Schriften der MGH*
SRG	*Scriptores rerum Germanicarum in usum scholarum separatim editi*

SS	*Scriptores*
S. and T.	*Studien und Texte*
PL	*Patrologia Latina*, ed. J. P. Migne
RS	Rolls Series
RSR	*Revue des sciences religieuses*
RTAM	*Recherches de théologie ancienne et médiévale*
SC	*Sources chrétiennes*
SG	*Studi Gregoriani*
SM	*Studi medievali*
SMon.	*Studia monastica*
SS	Surtees Society
ST	*Studi e testi*

1

Early Life

1.1 PAVIA

Lanfranc's birthplace, Pavia, had its origin in the Roman *municipium* of Ticinum which was established before the Christian era on the River Ticino, just north of its confluence with the River Po.[1] After the fall of the Roman Empire in the west, it continued to be a royal and administrative centre. Its importance was increased because it lay between Vercelli and Piacenza on the main line of communication that ran from Burgundy through the Great St Bernard Pass on the way to Rome. For pilgrims, in particular, it was a much-frequented city which they in turn familiarized with the lands from which they came and with the centre of Latin Christendom to which they travelled. To be born at Pavia brought a heritage of awareness both of past history and of the present political configuration of the Christian west.

In terms of its own topography, from Roman times Pavia was an example of the duality of *civitas*, or major city which was a place of regional authority, and *palatium*, the administrative centre at the heart of the city which, whether or not it was currently a regular or occasional royal residence, symbolized royal authority and which, with its staff of officials, served as a legal and administrative centre for the city and for its surrounding countryside. In the course of the centuries, Pavia, as Ticinum came increasingly to be called from the seventh century, received the imprint of successive masters of north Italy. After the Ostrogoth Theodoric in 493 captured Ravenna, he restored the *palatium* at Pavia. Throughout the middle ages, a statue, popularly known as the *regisole*, which was in fact of a Roman emperor, was believed to represent Theodoric; it perpetuated his memory. In 572 Pavia fell to the Lombard invaders; from 626 it was the capital of Lombard Italy. The *palatium* was a royal residence as well as a legal and administrative centre. The prologues to the laws of Kings Rothari and Aistulf, written respectively in 644 and 740, referred to their association with the *palatium* at Pavia.[2]

In 774 Charlemagne's capture of the Lombard kingdom led to its annexation to the Frankish domains after a siege and capture of Pavia, where he crowned himself king of Italy. If visits by the kings became occasional, Pavia retained its administrative importance not only under the Carolingians but also under the 'national kings' who from 887 followed them and often resided there, and thereafter under the German Ottonians. The *comes palatii* emerged as the holder of a lay office which

---

[1] For Pavia, see esp. Bullough, 'Urban Change', and Brühl, 'Das "Palatium"'. Jones, *The Italian City-State*, esp. 73–151, provides an indispensable survey of the wider background.
[2] *Liber legis Langobardorum*, 1, 195.

became virtually hereditary in the family of Lomello, who lived outside the city. Pavia recovered quickly from a sacking by the Hungarians in 924, and the *palatium* was rebuilt.

During Lanfranc's early lifetime, the German ruler was the Emperor Henry II (1002–24).[3] His visits to Italy were occasional, but he sought strenuously to assert his authority, not least at Pavia. His first Italian expedition was in 1004, when he defeated the Italian king Arduin. He was himself elected Italian king at Pavia in the ancient church of S. Michele and was crowned there by Archbishop Arnulf of Milan. But on the very evening of his coronation, an insurrection of the citizens led to the burning down of the royal palace that his predecessor Otto III had restored. It was rebuilt. During Henry's second Italian expedition of 1013–14, when Arduin at last finally submitted to him, he received imperial coronation at Rome from Pope Benedict VIII. In December 1013 he stayed at Pavia and did so again in May 1014 as he returned from Rome. In 1014 the record of a *placitum* held in the public loggia newly built near the palace affords a sharp picture of the exercise of authority in the city. In his dignity as *serenissimus imperator*, Henry was, exceptionally, personally present. Otto of Lomello, described as *comes palacii et comes uius* (sic) *comitatus*, sat with, as his assessors, three bishops including Reynald of Pavia, two marquises, Alberic *iudex et missus domni imperatoris*, twelve named *iudices sacri palacii*, and many others who were not named. They confirmed as genuine a privilege of the Emperor Otto III for the monastery of S. Salvatore and vindicated its abbess against local challenges to its possessions.[4] Under Henry, imperial *missi* became increasingly important in Italy, while the powers and jurisdiction of the local *comes* were diminished.

Henry's third Italian expedition of 1021–2 witnessed the holding at Pavia of a synod in which Pope Benedict VIII sought to promote certain quite radical reforms of the secular church.[5] Although Benedict was a member of the Tusculan family at Rome and was by no means a strong pope, he was genuinely concerned to promote measures that foreshadowed some of those adopted by the later eleventh-century reform popes.[6] The copious record of the synod begins with a papal allocution, perhaps in its present form drafted by Bishop Leo of Vercelli (999–1026) who was a staunch supporter of the emperors of his day. The pope deplored the alienation from churches of the generous endowments made by Christian kings and emperors. Conspicuous as culprits were the unfree clerks who married free-born women through whom church lands were alienated to their progeny. Benedict enacted stringently worded canons which forbade those in major orders—priests, deacons, or subdeacons—to keep wives or concubines and which required the sons and daughters of the clergy to remain the unfree subjects of their churches. Henry II confirmed and repeated Benedict's legislation, having made a clear statement of an emperor's duty to reinforce papal initiatives:

[3] For the events of his reign, see esp. Hirsch, *Jahrbücher*, and Holtzmann, *Geschichte*, 440–87.
[4] *MGH DD HII* no. 299, cf. 301–2; no. 302 = Manaresi, no. 283.
[5] *MGH Conc.* 1, no. 34, pp. 70–8.
[6] For Benedict, see Herrmann, *Das Tuskulanerpapsttum*, esp. 169–78.

The emperor's reply. I can deny you nothing, most holy Pope Benedict, to whom under God I owe everything, especially because what you ask is just, because in concert with just brothers you propose things that are fitting, and because you so summon me to a share in your pastoral charge that as we shall be sharers in the toil so we shall be sharers in the glory.... Therefore, father, all that you have synodically proposed and made new for the necessary repair of the church, as a son I applaud, confirm, and approve; and so that everyone may be the more servicable, I promise with God's help that I will inviolably observe these measures, and by this our authority, with the elders of the land, with the domestics of the palace, and with the friends of the public good, we confirm that they shall stand for ever and be solemnly written among human laws.[7]

At least in the rhetoric of the occasion, in 1022 Henry II thus committed himself and his Italian subjects to support the pope in enforcing the chastity of the clergy and in safeguarding churches in the free and inalienable possession of the endowments that pious rulers had bestowed.

Even in the form of a programmatic statement, however, such an expression of concordant and mutual reforming intentions of pope and emperor was only conceivable in the rare event of the presence in Italy of a strong and well-motivated German ruler. At Pavia, the fragility of royal authority in the ruler's absence was quickly apparent when, in 1024, Henry II died. The citizens at once razed to the ground the walls and buildings of the *palatium* with the intention that no future king should be able to restore them. Alone among the Lombard cities, Pavia refused to acknowledge as king the new German ruler, Conrad II. Conrad rejected the citizens' ingenious excuses for the destruction of the palace. In 1026 he began a two-year investing of the city which, despite severe damage to its buildings, agriculture, and trade, did not lead then or at any future time to the rebuilding of the palace.[8]

Notwithstanding this bold challenge to royal authority, Pavia retained considerable importance as a legal and administrative centre. In 1037, when Conrad II was confronted with a tumult of the archbishop and people of Milan, it was at Pavia that he speedily convened a general assembly (*generale colloquium*) of the kingdom at which he confronted the archbishop.[9] The place of the assembly is not known; it may have been in the monastery of S. Pietro in Ciel d'Oro, founded in 727 by the Lombard king Liutprand and the resting-place of the remains of St Augustine of Hippo and of the philosopher and statesman of Theodoric's reign, Boethius. Together with the monastery of S. Salvatore, founded in 972 by the Empress Adelaide, it was a monument at Pavia to royal piety and benevolence.[10] Later in the eleventh century it seems to have housed a royal treasury.[11]

The see of Pavia had once been a suffragan see of the archbishopric of Milan, but since the eighth century it had become an exempt bishopric which depended directly upon the apostolic see of Rome and which enjoyed considerable privileges and prestige.[12] The early eleventh century saw the long episcopate of Reynald

---

[7] *MGH Conc.* 1, no. 34, pp. 76–7.   [8] Wipo, *Gesta Chuonradi*, caps. 7, 12, pp. 558–61, 566–7.
[9] Wipo, cap. 35, pp. 600–1. For the background, see Cowdrey, 'Archbishop Aribert II'.
[10] Benzo of Alba, *Ad Heinricum*, 7.7, pp. 648–9.   [11] Benzo of Alba, 1.1, pp. 108–11.
[12] For examples, see Pope John VIII's letters of 877–9: *Epp.* 90, 167–8, *PL* 126.739–42, 806–7, 815.

(1008/14–46). Very little is known about him, but a reference to him as 'chariot of the empire, peace of the Pavians' suggests that he was an active servant of the royal power and protector of the citizens.[13]

Neither Lanfranc's own writings nor anything written about him gives any positive evidence for the impact upon his mind of Pavia's long history or of the events there in his childhood and youth. Yet the environment in which he grew up should be remembered when his later career is studied, most of all in the years during which he was actively engaged in the religious and secular affairs of the Anglo-Norman kingdom. The impressions that may have been left upon his mind are, first, of the beneficent results for the church of royal authority as exercised by lay rulers from Theodoric to Henry II. From the Lombard kings, in particular, there had come down a body of legislation which brought home not only to expert lawyers but also to the intelligent public the prestige and scope of the law as a matter of debate and practical application. Yet, second, Lanfranc can scarcely have failed to note the fragility of public order. In 1004 and, still more, in 1024, popular risings against the visible symbols and the implementation of royal authority provided object-lessons in the damage that could be caused to the fabric of society by tumultuous and unrestrained subjects. Third, in ecclesiastical affairs, Lanfranc grew up in a city that was rich in churches and monasteries which familiarized its citizens with the ways of both the secular and the monastic orders of the church. As an exempt see, Pavia provided an example of episcopal authority that was in practice largely independent as well as, so far as can be seen, effective. Finally, and perhaps not least important, the joint endeavour of Pope Benedict VIII and the Emperor Henry II in 1022 to initiate the reform of the clergy was an early example of papal reforming aspirations which were expressed in coherent propaganda and legislation and directed to well-defined issues. Benedict secured the recognition by the emperor of the already burgeoning claims of the apostolic see to authority and leadership.

But, on the other hand, the weakness and worse of many tenth-century popes and the renewed shortcomings of Pope Benedict IX (1032–44) may well have helped to form the opinion that Lanfranc later expressed about the vesting of Petrine authority and leadership. He held that Christ's words to St Peter about the power of the keys (Matt. 16: 18–19) were addressed more to the Roman church than to its individual pontiffs.[14] The *sedes*, not the *sedens*, was the principal recipient of Christ's commission. Such a view, which had the powerful endorsement of Cardinal Humbert of Silva Candida,[15] casts a strong shadow forward upon the entire course of Lanfranc's dealings with the papacy.

Lanfranc thus grew up in a city and church that are likely to have left him with many, and perhaps conflicting, impressions about the principles and issues of public and private life, both ecclesiastical and secular.

---

[13] Benzo of Alba, 4.30 (1), pp. 362–3; for the phrase *currus regni*, cf. 2 Kgs 2: 12; 13: 14. For the bishops of Pavia, see esp. Pauler, *Das Regnum Italiae*, 117–23.
[14] *DCSD* cap. 16, col. 426CD, cited below, p. 43.
[15] See Ullmann, 'Cardinal Humbert and the Ecclesia Romana', esp. 121–3.

1.2 FAMILY, EDUCATION, AND EARLY CAREER

The scantiness, the lateness, and the manner of presentation of the sources for Lanfranc's family and youth present severe difficulties to an understanding of them.[16] Lanfranc himself always lived in the present and tended to discard whatever in the past did not bear upon his current responsibilities and manner of life. One of his letters while archbishop of Canterbury shows that he eventually put behind him his early concern with the liberal arts. When, in 1080/1, an Irish bishop put to him some problems of secular learning, he curtly declined to consider them. Such preoccupations did not fit the true concerns of a bishop; long ago in his youth he had been involved with them, but when he assumed the cure of souls—he did not make clear whether as monastic prior or abbot or as archbishop—he had renounced them.[17]

Lanfranc's own playing down of his past concern with secular learning stands in line with what seems to have been the predominant tradition of his Norman abbey of Bec as later written down in Gilbert Crispin, abbot of Westminster's *Life* of his abbot there, Herluin, written in 1109/17, and the *Vita Lanfranci* which is attributed to Milo Crispin and dates from *c*.1140/56. This tradition honoured Lanfranc for the skill as a teacher of the liberal arts that he brought to Bec from Italy. But it was still more concerned with Lanfranc the exemplary monk who had put the world behind him upon embracing a monastic vocation: from the first he had shown a tendency to renounce the world and to eschew a secular career.

Thus, there is no direct evidence for the date of Lanfranc's birth and no certain picture of the stages of his early life. It is likely that he was born *c*.1010, but this is only an inference from his having entered Bec in 1042 as an established scholar and teacher and from his having died in 1089 while still in full possession of his powers. A late Canterbury tradition, perhaps based upon entries in a Necrology, now lost, gave his parents' names as Heribald and Roza;[18] they cannot be identified in any Pavian source.

The Bec tradition has a little more to say.[19] According to the *Vita Lanfranci*, his parents were prominent and respected citizens, for according to a hearsay account (*ut fertur*), his father 'belonged to the order of those who watched over the rights and laws of the city' of Pavia (*pater eius de ordine illorum qui iura et leges civitatis asservabant fuit*). This passage seems to evoke the circle of the *iudices sacri palatii* of Pavian *placita* and of the assessors who sat with them when doing justice.[20] According to this tradition, Lanfranc's father died while he was still a child. When Lanfranc was of age to succeed him in his public position (*et in honorem et dignitatem*), he chose to leave the city and to study the arts elsewhere (*relicta civitate amore discendi*

---

[16] For the sources, see esp. Gibson, *Lanfranc*, 195–225 and, for the Bec historical tradition, eadem, 'History at Bec'.

[17] Lanfranc, *Letters*, no. 49, pp. 158–61.

[18] Gervase of Canterbury, *Act. pont.* 363–4. Gervase said only that Lanfranc was born to 'civibus egregiis et honesta conditione'.

[19] *VH* cap. 55, pp. 95/195 (page references to *VH* will be given in this way to both Armitage Robinson's and Evans's editions); *VL* cap. 1, p. 668.

[20] Above, Ch. 1.1.

ad studia litterarum perrexit). Only after a long absence during which he became fully versed in secular learning (*omni scientia seculari perfecte imbutus*) did he return to Pavia, apparently quite soon afterwards to leave the city for ever.[21] In harmony with such an early turning away from an active to a studious course, the *Lives* of Herluin and of Lanfranc both open with a rhetorical introduction exhibiting Lanfranc as at first the master who completely restored Latin culture (*Latinitas*) to its ancient level while (in an unexplained phrase) Greece herself, mistress of the world in liberal studies, gladly heard and admired his disciples. It was upon such studies, undertaken from love of them, that this presentation of the young Lanfranc concentrated; there was no mention of special expertise in, let alone practice of, the law. Conformably with this view, when he left Italy he did so with other scholars, evidently in the arts.[22] Later on, the *Vita Lanfranci* digressed (as it was said) to make good some gaps in its account of Lanfranc's early years. In so doing, it may have drawn upon the lost portion of William of Poitiers's *Life* of William the Conqueror, written by 1074.[23] Here, Lanfranc was educated in the schools of the liberal arts and also of the secular laws according to the custom of his country (it is not specified whether at Pavia or elsewhere). As a young man, he was a successful advocate in the Pavian law-courts; one recalls the *advocati* who spoke for litigants in the Pavian *placita*.[24] By his eloquence he frequently overcame senior and experienced lawyers, and his deliverances were accepted in Pavia as authoritative. Whether the comment that 'Pavia remembers these things (*meminit horum Papia*)' alludes to genuine oral or written memory or whether it is merely a rhetorical flourish is not clear. But, for this tradition, Lanfranc pursued a successful if perhaps brief legal career at Pavia which he abandoned for the true wisdom (*amor vere sapientie*) of sacred study after leaving Italy.

These traditions leave no room for doubting that, while still in Italy, Lanfranc studied the liberal arts, although they do not conclusively establish that he did so in

---

[21] The Latin of *VL* allows for different translations that are contradictory. The translation here adopted is that 'Lanfranc was bereaved of his father at a very tender age. *When he should have* succeeded him in both office and rank, he *instead* left the city and from love of learning turned to the study of letters. When he had remained away for a very long time and was fully steeped in all secular knowledge, he returned. Then he left his own country and crossed the Alps.' The alternative translation is that: '... *since he must succeed* him both in both office and rank, he *therefore* left the city and from love of learning turned to the study of letters....' Against the second translation, it can be urged that it would have been strange for Lanfranc to have left Pavia at a critical point of his early adult life if he had wished to have established himself in its public affairs, that it leaves little time for Lanfranc to have had a public career before his second departure from Pavia, and that the first translation offers a more consistent and credible sequence of events.

[22] *VH* cap. 55, pp. 95/195; *VL* cap. 1, p. 668. So, too, the anonymous Bec compilation of c.1140, the *Miracula sancti Nicholai*, states that Lanfranc taught the arts in Italy: 'nam plures in sua patria scholas tenuerant de grammatica et rhetorica et maxime dialectica': *MSN* cap. 7, p. 409. William of Malmesbury made no reference to Lanfranc's early legal skills: *GP* 1.24, pp. 27–8. It remained for Orderic Vitalis to say both that Lanfranc was schooled in the liberal arts and that he became skilled in secular law (*saecularium legum peritiam ad patriae suae morem intentione laica fervidus edidicit*): 4, vol. 2.248–9. Orderic was possibly following William of Poitiers, but there is no certainty that he derived this phrase from him.

[23] *VL* cap. 5, p. 681. For the lost part of William of Poitiers, see Orderic Vitalis, 2.xviii–xxi, 248; William of Poitiers, pp. xxxv–xxxix.

[24] *MGH DD HII* no. 299; cf. Manaresi, no. 301.

his native Pavia. As regards whether he also made a special study of the law which he practised at Pavia with conspicuous success, they contradict each other: according to the first, Lanfranc from the first shunned the law; according to the second, he became expert in it.

Italian sources provide some additional evidence but do not provide material for a certain resolution of the problem. Undoubtedly the law was assiduously studied, debated, and practised in eleventh-century Pavia, but it is hard to assess how much this was the case in the troubled 1020s before Lanfranc left for France. Two especially noteworthy legal compilations survive.[25] The first is the *Liber Papiensis*, or *Liber legis Langobardorum*; surviving in several recensions, it offers a chronological body of Lombard laws from 643 to the early eleventh century.[26] It is certainly an eleventh-century complilation, but there is no indication of the time at which work was begun. A second book, the *Lombarda*, or *Lex langobarda*, covered much the same ground, but systematically; it is of late eleventh- to early twelfth-century date.[27]

The gathering amount of legal debate at Pavia is further illustrated by the *Expositiones*, or arguments about points of law, that were intercalated with the texts of the *Liber Papiensis*; they illustrate debates that arose between *antiqui*, who adhered to the letter of the law, and *moderni*, who drew creatively upon case law to interpret and adapt it.[28] They also preserve the names of some of those learned in the law who took part, one of whom was a *Lanfrancus*.

In a debate about inheritance, *Lanfrancus* is introduced as 'Archbishop Lanfranc (*archiepiscopus Lanfrancus*)', who put a question to a *iudex* named Bonfilius, a jurist attested at Pavia between 1014 and 1055.[29] The point at issue was whether, if a charter had no living witnesses, its validity could be challenged. Bonfilius claimed that by custom it could be defended by calling twelve oath-helpers and by comparison with two other charters by the same notary. Lanfranc, however, silenced him by alleging such custom to be counter to the law as declared by the Emperor Otto I. But then a third disputant, named William, successfully challenged Lanfranc's interpretation of Otto's ruling: Otto had not condemned the custom itself but only its abuse, and he left to the challenger the option of trial by battle.[30] Whoever wrote the words 'Archbishop Lanfranc' must have had Lanfranc of Canterbury in mind, for there was no other eleventh-century archbishop of that name. If the attributions of the *Expositio* are in all respects correct, Lanfranc was, indeed, a learned participant in legal debates at Pavia, although not an invariably triumphant one.

But some reservations may be made. In two other *Expositiones* Lanfranc appears in debate with the disciples of Bonfilius; using the skills of the *moderni*

---

[25] For further details, see Calasso, *Medio evo del diritto*, 307–14.
[26] *MGH LL* 4.289–585.   [27] Ibid. 4.607–38.
[28] For the study of law at Pavia, see further Radding, *The Origins*, esp. 37–112. For the *Expositiones*, see Diurni, *L'Expositio ad Librum Papiensem*.
[29] For his career, see Moschetti, 'Bonfiglio'.
[30] *Expositio* to Guy, 6.23, *MGH LL* 4.566–7. The sole source is Naples, Biblioteca nazionale, MS Brancacci I B 12, listed in Loew, *The Beveventan Script*, 2.105; it probably dates from the second half of the twelfth century.

he defeated them, but he was not referred to as archbishop.[31] Furthermore, the reference to Lanfranc as archbishop cannot pre-date 1070 and may be up to fifty years or so later; there is room for confusion on a compiler's or a scribe's part with some other Lanfranc, which was a common name. And the *Expositio* is the sole piece of evidence which exhibits Lanfranc as certainly a practising master of Lombard law.

In his own later writings Lanfranc left little trace of an acquaintance with, or a training in, secular law.[32] The only significant apparent exception is in a biblical commentary, when he glossed the word *parentibus*, in 1 Tim. 5: 4: to establish the extent of a person's kindred, he alluded to a principle found in secular law (*in mundana lege*) which has a close parallel in the laws of the Lombard king Rothari.[33] But there was much discussion in North Italy during the early eleventh century of the extent of a kindred, especially in connection with the prohibited degrees of marriage, a matter in which Roman law was more accommodating than Lombard law.[34] Lanfranc's passing reference to Rothari does not necessarily imply a closer or more professional knowledge of Lombard law than is likely to have been possessed by many an educated man of his generation.

The direct evidence for Lanfranc's early professional concern with secular law is thus not great, although it cannot be simply dismissed or ignored. How it is assessed must depend upon how the contradictory evidence of later traditions about Lanfranc is to be construed. Lanfranc himself was later concerned to dissociate himself from whatever in his past did not directly relate to his monastic vocation, while the predominant Bec view of his early life was that he was from the first guided by an aversion to secular life and activities which included his turning from his father's legal avocation. Was this picture of continuity and consistency in Lanfranc's career presented at the cost of deliberately suppressing his early successes as a lawyer which are reflected in the *Expositiones*? Or do the *Expositiones* lend credibility to another Norman tradition, which may be at least as old as William of Poitiers's encomium of the Conqueror, that Lanfranc had once begun a successful legal career? On the available evidence, it is perhaps wise to suspend judgement and to keep both possibilities alive. It is not, however, open to doubt that, if Lanfranc had once practised as a trained lawyer, both he himself and the predominant tradition at Bec were at pains to set it aside as if it had never been. With this in mind, the legal cast of Lanfranc's mature thinking should not be exaggerated.

---

[31] *Expositiones* to Grimoald, 8, and to Liutprand, 3, *MGH LL* 4.402–3, 404.

[32] See esp. Tamassia, 'Lanfranco arcivescovo di Canterbury'.

[33] 'Parentes vocat quos superius filios et nepotes. Tota enim progenies parentela dicitur, unde et in mundana lege parens parenti per gradum et parentelam succedere iubetur': *PL* 150.355B, as corrected by Gibson, *Lanfranc*, p. 9 n. 4; cf. the phrase 'parens parenti per gradum et parentillam heres succedat': *Edictus Rothari*, cap. 153, *MGH LL* 4.35. It should be noticed that Lanfranc did not make a verbatim citation.

[34] *Die Briefe des Petrus Damiani*, nos. 19, 36, vol. 1.179–99, 339–45.

1.3 FROM PAVIA TO BEC

In the early eleventh century, the roads from Lombardy to France were well trodden in both directions. Pavia itself lay on the pilgrims' route which led across the Great St Bernard Pass to St Peter and St Paul at Rome;[35] travellers from and to Normandy and also England must have been a familiar sight to Lanfranc in his early years. Moreover, so far as Normandy is concerned, monks from North Italy played a major role in the reform and foundation of Norman monasteries which made the duchy conspicuous for the flourishing of the monastic order there. The key figure was William of Volpiano, an Italian born c.960 near Turin who, having become a monk and having transferred to Cluny, was in 989 sent to reform the Burgundian monastery of Saint-Bénigne at Dijon. He remained its abbot until his death in 1031. In 1001 Duke Richard II of Normandy invited him to reform the monasteries of the duchy. The centre of his activity was Fécamp, where he also held the office of abbot. From it, he reformed the older houses of Normandy such as Jumièges, Mont-Saint-Michel, and Saint-Ouen at Rouen; towards the end of his life he also prompted the foundation of a number of new houses.[36] William kept in touch with his native Italy, which he revisited on a number of occasions. He also attracted to Normandy so significant a figure as his nephew and favourite disciple John, a spiritual writer who was his successor as abbot of Fécamp, which he ruled for fifty years (1028–78).[37] Another Italian, Suppo, was abbot of Mont-Saint-Michel from 1033 to 1048.[38] Italians also travelled to other parts of France, for example Benedict of Chiusa, *grammaticus perfectus*, a monk well trained in the arts who in 1029 disputed at Limoges with Adhemar of Chabannes about the apostolicity of St Martial.[39]

Lanfranc himself left Italy early in the 1030s,[40] perhaps more impelled by the political instability of Lombardy than attracted by either the schools or the monasteries to be found beyond the Alps. He and the followers who may have accompanied him came as students of the arts; there is little likelihood that his thoughts were already turning towards the monastic life. He seems to have progressed slowly through Burgundy to the Loire valley, teaching the arts.[41] A late tradition has it that he heard incognito the teaching of Berengar of Tours; he found little in it that was profitable, and when he left Berengar Lanfranc was already convinced of the unsoundness of his teaching.[42] There is a single slight and indirect piece of evidence for

---

[35] Barlow, *The English Church, 1000–1066*, 12–13, 20–2.
[36] William of Dijon's work is well summarized by Knowles, *The Monastic Order*, 84–8. See also the texts and discussion in Rodulfus Glaber, *Historiarum*, esp. pp. lxx–lxxxii, 120–3, 186–7, 254–99.
[37] See Leclercq and Bonnes, *Un Maître*.
[38] Bazin, *Le Mont-Saint-Michel*, 22, 43; Alexander, *Norman Illumination*, 8–15.
[39] Adhemar of Chabannes, *Epistola*, esp. cols. 90–1, 97–8, 107. For Benedict's career, see Rossi, 'Benedetto'.
[40] According to the *VL*, Lanfranc came to France (*in Gallias venit*) in the time of King Henry I of France (1031–60) and of Duke William II of Normandy (1035–87): cap. 1, p. 668. In view of the general terms of the chapter, it does not necessarily follow that Lanfranc came to France only after 1035.
[41] *MSN* cap. 7, p. 409.
[42] Ibid. Guitmund of Aversa wrote of Lanfranc's shaming defeat of Berengar on a point of dialectic: *De corp. et sang. Christi*, 1, col. 1428B.

his contact with Chartres, which he may have visited. Writing to Lanfranc in 1049, Berengar of Tours referred to Ingelrannus, master of the schools at Chartres, as the intermediary through whom he heard of Lanfranc's views on the eucharist.[43] A more reliable, but late, record states that he for some time stayed and taught at Avranches, in Lower Normandy.[44] Academic activity is likely to have been on a modest scale. But Lanfranc's time there, probably at the end of the 1030s, offered the possibility of contact with the abbey of Mont-Saint-Michel, with its Lombard abbot Suppo and its vigorous literary and artistic tradition.[45] Except for the assured fact of his progress from Pavia to the border of Normandy, the 1030s are the most obscure decade of Lanfranc's life.

[43] Huygens, 'Textes latins', 459.
[44] *VL* cap. 1, p. 668. This detail is here added to the account of Lanfranc's early life in *VH* cap. 55, pp. 95/195. For Anselm of Aosta's later stay at Avranches on his way to Bec, see *VA* 1.5, p. 8; this source does not expressly confirm that Avranches was already a centre of teaching.
[45] Alexander, *Norman Illumination*, esp. 1–21.

2

Monk and Abbot

2.1 CONVERSION OF LIFE

Discussion of Lanfranc's entry into the monastic order and of his life as monk, prior, and abbot at Bec and Caen is made difficult by the nature of the evidence. Most of it comes from a Bec tradition which was written down much later by monks who were associated with Bec and thus concerned to present him in terms of the prevailing image of a good monk. Whatever he had in common with other monks was, therefore, stereotyped; whatever differentiated him from them tended to be passed over. With this in mind, it is instructive to compare the accounts of Lanfranc's becoming a monk in the *Vita Herluini* and the *Vita Lanfranci* with that of Anselm of Aosta's taking the same step in his *Life* by Eadmer of Canterbury. The current estimate of entering a monastery as a fundamental conversion of life caused both men to be presented as exemplifying the biblical topos of someone 'coming to himself' (*reversus ad se*—cf. the prodigal son in Luke 15: 17); undertones of a sudden and radical change were necessarily imported. Both men were concerned to turn from the vanity of the world and its concerns, including secular studies, and to become pleasing only to God. Both men at about the time of their conversion considered an eremitical way of life but opted for a monastic one. Both deliberately became monks at Bec because there, if for partly differing reasons, they might become insignificant and might shun human esteem.[1]

Despite the stereotype in which it is cast, there is no positive reason to doubt that Lanfranc's decision to change his manner of life came quite suddenly.[2] He seems to have taken it alone; the companions with whom he may have come from Italy seem long since to have gone their own ways, and there is no suggestion that anyone else changed with him. According to a story which is not attested earlier than the *Vita Lanfranci*, his decision came when he was travelling alone towards Rouen by the bank of the River Risle, when robbers seized him and left him overnight tied to a tree. Knowing by heart no such words in which to pray as the divine office would have afforded him, he turned to the Lord (*conversus ad Dominum*), deciding there and then no longer to waste his time in the teaching and study of letters. He asked the chance passers-by who eventually freed him for directions to the humblest and poorest monastery of the neighbourhood; they referred him to the nearby

---

[1] *VH* caps. 55–61, pp. 95–7/195–7; *VL* caps. 1–2, pp. 668–75; *VA* 1.5–6, pp. 8–10.
[2] As emphasized by Orderic Vitalis, 4, vol. 2.248–51. In *VL*, the second account of Lanfranc's entry into Bec says that he took the monastic habit 'repentino ... animi motu se abnegans': cap. 5, p. 681.

monastery of Bec.[3] In detail, the story must be regarded with reserve. But it correctly indicates that, although he had recently lived near Mont-Saint-Michel, Lanfranc deliberately chose to enter none of the large, prosperous, and often observant Norman monasteries; instead, he sought a newly founded and still struggling house which was unconnected with them and which could fairly be described as 'small in its buildings, poor in its circumstances, and poorer still in its level of religious life'.[4] Lanfranc's decision should not be construed as if implying an adverse judgement upon the other Norman monasteries. It reflected an inner desire for the abject austerity of a rigorously eremitical way of life which he shared with other young Italians of his day when they embarked upon a monastic commitment.[5]

Lanfranc became a monk at a date that cannot be precisely established, although in the light of the general development of his career it is likely to have been c.1042. Bec, to which he resorted, had been founded some eight years earlier by Herluin, a Norman knight. After living as an exemplary layman, at the age of more than 37 years Herluin decided to become a monk. Repelled by the worldliness of the monks of a monastery that he visited (it may not have been a Norman monastery), he built a church of his own, became a monk, and having recruited some followers, became their abbot. The unsuitability of his original site led him to transfer to another near a stream at Bec. Lanfranc's name stands thirty-fifth in the profession list of Bec. This suggests that, by the time of his arrival, the community had been successful in recruiting members; indeed, not until the 1070s did Bec again reach the number of professions that there had been in its first ten years.[6] Against the background of the simple life of the new monastery, Herluin provided an example of piety and of sharing in the manual work of his monks. After transferring to Bec, he built a church of adequate size with adjacent conventual buildings. But he suffered a setback in the collapse of the monks' dormitory roof, and he experienced problems with local laity. Lanfranc's arrival seemed to provide him with assistance that he needed in the form of one who, as a Lombard, had no commitment to other Norman interests and who had the personal skills to reinforce his own rule as abbot.[7]

Upon arriving at Bec, Lanfranc found Herluin occupied with his hands in building an oven. The *Vita Lanfranci* expands the brief account in the *Vita Herluini* by reconstructing their conversation. Herluin's first inquiry was whether Lanfranc was a Lombard. Upon learning that he was, Herluin elicited his wish to become a monk, and he deputed a monk named Roger to show him the Rule.[8] Having read it and promised to observe it fully, Lanfranc was admitted to become a monk.[9]

---

[3] *VL* cap. 1, p. 668; see also *MSN* cap. 8, pp. 409–10.
[4] 'aedificiis parvus, pauper fortuna, pauperior religionis norma': letter of Abbot William of Cormeilles to Abbot William of Bec (1093/1109), *PL* 158.1198D–1202D, at col. 1199C.
[5] For Anselm's thinking about the eremitical life, see *VA* 1.6, p. 10; for Archbishop Maurilius of Rouen as a solitary, see *Acta archiep. Roth.*, col. 278B; for Abbot Desiderius of Montecassino's early austerities, see *Chron. mon. Cass.*, 2.2–7, pp. 364–9.
[6] For the profession list, see Porée, *Histoire*, 2.629–42; for recruitment, also Gibson, *Lanfranc*, 201.
[7] *VH* caps. 1–54, pp. 87–95/185–95.
[8] Roger's name stands tenth in the Bec profession list; he became abbot of Lessay, and died in 1106.
[9] *VH* cap. 57, pp. 96/196; *VL* cap. 1, pp. 669–70.

The *Lives* present Lanfranc's first three years at Bec as a period during which, as Herluin had long hoped, the two men complemented each other in the life of the monastery. Herluin, whom Lanfranc admired for his humility of soul and elevation of speech, attended to matters of internal and external business. Lanfranc had little to do with such things; he humbly obeyed Herluin within the monastery and devoted much time to studying and expounding the scriptures. He was abundantly granted the grace of tears which contemporaries regarded as an indication of deep spirituality. Lanfranc made nothing of his scholarly eminence. He humbly submitted to the correction of his Latin by an ignorant prior who, when Lanfranc read in the refectory, insisted wrongly that he pronounce the word *docere* with a short not a long *e*; to mispronounce one syllable was not a capital offence, while disobedience to a superior who commanded him *ex parte Dei* was no light fault. Overall, both Herluin and Lanfranc were examples for the monastic flock at Bec to follow—the abbot of the active life, but Lanfranc of the contemplative. It is particularly noteworthy that, according to the Bec tradition as here expressed, it was Herluin, not Lanfranc, who was expert in customary law and in transacting external business and external affairs.[10] It is impossible to determine whether this tradition tacitly followed Lanfranc's own rejection of a legal career that he had once pursued at Pavia, or whether it correctly represented his pre-monastic life as essentially one of a scholar and teacher. But the depiction of his conversion of life would have been the sharper if he had been shown as turning from a legal as well as from a scholarly past; the silence in the Bec sources tells somewhat, but not decisively, against his having done so.

According to the passages in the Bec tradition that exhibit Lanfranc in this way, his first three years at Bec were, for him, a happy time of monastic withdrawal:

Now this most eminent teacher devoted his entire concern to peace (*quies*) and silence, cultivating the fields of his heart by the assiduous reading of the scriptures and watering them by the sweet compunction of tears which he used frequently to obtain.[11]

But two stories indicate that, even upon the evidence of this tradition, this picture must be qualified. First, in an anecdote that was intended to point his humility as evidenced in his submission to the monastic life, he was sent to attend to (*ut . . . servaret et instauraret*) a piece of land which a laymen gave to Bec; he returned there with a cat tied in a cloth to his saddle in order to control the mice and rats with which Bec was infested.[12] If, as seems the case, this story relates to his earliest monastic years, he was given some involvement in the this-worldly and external affairs of Bec.

A second story discloses that Lanfranc quickly became somewhat disenchanted with monastic life at Bec. He found that there were few literate monks; too many in the community were lax in their personal lives and monastic observance; some

---

[10] *VH* caps. 57–61, pp. 96–7/196–7; *VL* caps. 1–2 , pp. 670–1.
[11] *VH* cap. 61, pp. 96–7/197; *VL* cap. 2, p. 671.
[12] *VL* cap. 2, p. 672. It needs hardly be said that this story implies no special legal knowledge or training.

feared Lanfranc as a future office-holder who would seek to correct their ways. Bec, as Lanfranc at first experienced its life, had not as yet found a sure direction. Upon the evidence of its profession list, it was already too large and diluted by monks with a low view of their vocation to facilitate the contemplative life to which Lanfranc currently aspired.[13] Yet, despite Abbot Herluin's personal sanctity and practical acumen, it had not settled down to the ordered and confident observance of a mature cenobitic house. Its unformed state was well illustrated when Lanfranc resolved to escape to the life of a solitary. Feigning sickness, he requested the gardener, Fulcrannus,[14] to bring him thistle-roots, ostensibly as a medicine but in fact to prepare his digestion for the rigours of life in the wild. Lanfranc's intention to escape was frustrated at the last minute when Herluin experienced a vision: his recently deceased nephew Hugh, an exemplary monk who was the son of his brother Baldric of Servaville,[15] informed him of Lanfranc's intention and also of the need for swift remedial action at Bec. When Herluin next day challenged Lanfranc about his intention, Lanfranc admitted it and, having accepted penance, was absolved; he promised never to desert Herluin and to obey his commands absolutely. Herluin speedily appointed Lanfranc to be prior, committing to his oversight both the internal and the external affairs of Bec.

This story is based upon exceptionally good authority. Lanfranc confided it to a monk of Bec, William, enjoining secrecy during his lifetime. After Lanfranc's death, William, by then abbot of Cormeilles, communicated it by letter to Abbot William of Bec and his monks.[16] The question arises why Lanfranc cherished this story and envisaged its eventual publication. In form, it follows a familiar pattern of anecdotes which were intended to reinforce the authority of abbots within their communities. With circumstantial detail, an abbot was represented as receiving information about a disciplinary matter by a vision of a lately deceased monk or other dependant of a monastery who was well known and respected. Such anecdotes made clear the wisdom and also the prudence of showing obedience and humility to an abbot within the life of his community. This was the message that the mature Lanfranc was concerned to convey to monks. It seems to have been formed in his mind by his own initial struggle with the as yet imperfectly ordered life of Bec. The fairly speedy outcome of that struggle seems to have been that Lanfranc abandoned his desire for an eremitical life for a following of the Rule of St Benedict in a cenobitic community over which the abbot exercised the fatherly authority, matched by obedience on the part of the monks, which the Rule envisaged.[17] As a

[13] It may be recalled that the early Carthusians envisaged thirteen, or fourteen at most, as the desirable number of monks for their kind of eremitical association: Guigo I, *Coutumes*, cap. 78, pp. 284–5.

[14] Fulcrannus is thirteenth in the Bec profession list.

[15] Hugh and Baldric are respectively eighth and fourth in the profession list.

[16] As n. 4; *VL* cap. 2, pp. 672–5. William of Cormeilles is nineteenth in the Bec profession list. The evidence of the sources that Lanfranc 'ipse a puero nutrierat et docuerat plurimumque amabat' William shows that Lanfranc had educated him before he himself entered Bec.

[17] For an example of a considered view at Bec of the monastic obligations of stability and growth in the cenobitic life, see Anselm, *Epp.* 37–8, vol. 3.144–9. For approval of the life of a hermit, cf. ibid. 45, 112, vol. 3.158, 244–6.

stage in Lanfranc's development, it opened the way to a period of more than twenty-five years during which he was committed to such a life in a community in which he himself exercised authority, first as prior of Bec and then as abbot of Saint-Étienne at Caen.

2.2 PRIOR OF BEC

Herluin appointed Lanfranc to be his prior *c.*1045; Lanfranc retained the office until his departure for Caen in 1063. Herluin and Lanfranc established a working relationship which remained harmonious and fruitful; different though the two men were in background and temperament, it was clearly based upon mutual affection and respect. This was signally apparent in 1077, when Lanfranc returned to Bec from Canterbury and was welcomed by the aged Herluin at the consecration of the abbey church.[18] In the meantime, Bec could remember a time of stability, observance, and material consolidation. During Lanfranc's years as prior there was no dramatic rise in numbers; professions were stabilized at about two a year.[19] But, as Lanfranc's presence became more generally known to clergy, laity, and other scholars, Bec won public recognition and respect; it secured property and endowments; and it achieved a fair balance between safeguarding the proper internal concerns of the monastic life and promoting a fruitful interaction with surrounding society. It established the limits of its own enclosure for a mile around and became equipped with the necessary offices and cultivated lands.[20] The brief summaries of the Bec tradition undoubtedly leave much unsaid about the abbey's vicissitudes in the politics and strife of the Norman duchy.[21] But they make clear the paradoxical result of Lanfranc's presence at Bec in assisting the transformation of the new, poor, and unregarded house to which he deliberately came into one which was assured, well provided, and prosperous; by the time that he left, it was no longer distinguishable from the great and famous monasteries of Normandy.

Lanfranc himself pressed strongly for Bec's physical development. At an uncertain date, but probably *c.*1060, the original situation of the monastery, however much improved, was recognized to be inadequate on account both of the number of the monks and of their well-being and safety. Lanfranc urged upon Herluin the need for an enlarged monastery and monastic offices, but Herluin, who was approaching his seventies, was reluctant to make radical changes. Then a sudden collapse of the choir of the church made action imperative. Lanfranc seized his opportunity; relying upon his help, Herluin agreed to the construction of new buildings on a more salubrious site. When Lanfranc left Bec for Caen, the reconstruction

---

[18] *VH* caps. 109–27, pp. 104–8/206–9; *VL* cap. 8, pp. 690–2; cf. the stories of Herluin's earlier visit to Lanfranc in England: *VH* caps. 91–4, pp. 101–2/202–3; *VL* cap. 1, pp. 688–9.
[19] Gibson, *Lanfranc*, 201.
[20] *VH* caps. 61–3, 71, pp. 97/197, 98/198; *VL* cap. 2, p. 671. For ducal charters in favour of Bec, see Fauroux, nos. 178–9, 181, 189, pp. 364–5, 371–2.
[21] See below, pp. 32–4.

was complete except for the church; work on it was briefly delayed, but it was finished by 1073, although not consecrated until Lanfranc came from Canterbury in 1077 to perform the ceremony. The *Vita Herluini* described the new monastery as 'a very large and appropriate work, to the impressiveness of which many richer abbeys did not attain (*opus pergrande, dignum, cuius dignitati ditiores multae non accedunt abbatiae*)'.[22] Lanfranc would build no less impressively at Caen and at Canterbury; his building programmes illustrate the change in monastic outlook that experience brought about in him during his years at Bec.

While Lanfranc was prior of Bec there is some evidence for his concern with monastic life elsewhere in the Norman duchy. It comes from the pages of Orderic Vitalis, who became a monk of Saint-Évroult in 1085 and in the next century wrote about the early history of his monastery. Saint-Évroult had its origins just before 1050 in the forest of Ouche on the southern frontier of the duchy. As it developed, Saint-Évroult differed from Bec in two major respects. First, it was established by two local families, those of Giroie and Grandmesnil, which, however, quickly suffered eclipse in its region. Second, and partly because of the troubles which ensued, the duke of Normandy was greatly concerned with its affairs. He was particularly concerned with the choice of abbots, of whom there were four during Lanfranc's years in the duchy (Thierry, 1050–8; Robert of Grandmesnil, 1059–61; Osbern, 1061–6; and Mainer, 1066–89).[23] In his dealings with Saint-Évroult, Lanfranc was brought into the mainstream of the ecclesiastical and political life of Normandy.

He was brought in gradually. Saint-Évroult had its origin when a pious knight, William Giroie, who was somewhat after the stamp of Abbot Herluin, became a monk at Bec and endowed it with lands in the forest of Ouche which included a church dedicated to St Peter. To it, Herluin sent Lanfranc with three other monks to restore religious life; they found there to be their companions only two elderly clerks. Orderic Vitalis's comment that 'in such a wilderness they served God as best they could in poverty of life (*in tanta heremo sub paupere vita Deo pro posse suo famulabantur*)' suggests that he encountered a manner of life akin to what he had initially sought at Bec. But William Giroie heard of the intention of his nephews Hugh and Robert Grandmesnil to found an abbey; by agreement with the monks of Bec, the nephews did so in the church that Lanfranc and his companions occupied. With the agreement of Duke William and of Archbishop Mauger of Rouen, the abbey of Saint-Évroult was there founded in 1050, and its first abbot, Thierry, was appointed from Jumièges.[24] Lanfranc had already returned to Bec.[25]

In Orderic Vitalis's account of the troubled early years of Saint-Évroult, Lanfranc twice appears in connection with its affairs. The first occasion was towards the end of the rule of Abbot Thierry. Thierry was a man of austerity and religious strictness who was a strong disciplinarian; but he lacked the tastes and skills of an

---

[22] *VH* caps. 72–6, pp. 98–9/199; *VL* cap. 4, pp. 679–80; Robert of Torigny, *a*. 1073, p. 40.
[23] For the early history of Saint-Évroult, see esp. Chibnall, *The World*, 17–26.
[24] Orderic Vitalis, 3, vol. 2.12–19; Fauroux, no. 122, pp. 287–92.
[25] He evidently returned to Bec before Oct. 1049, when he was with Pope Leo IX at, or soon after, the council of Rheims: see below, pp. 38–40.

administrator. He encountered the opposition of his prior, Robert of Grandmesnil, and of some of his monks. The resulting division led, in 1056, to a visitation of the abbey by a numerous group led by Maurilius, now the archbishop of Rouen, and which included Bishop Hugh of Lisieux, Abbot Ansfrid of Préaux, and Lanfranc. They confirmed the authority of Abbot Thierry and admonished Prior Robert to imitate the poverty of Christ and in all things to obey his abbot. But within a year Thierry withdrew from the abbey, and in 1059 the monks elected Robert as his successor.[26] Lanfranc's concern to uphold the authority of an abbot and to secure the obedience of subjects both reflect the lesson that he seems to have learnt during his early years at Bec and foreshadow an insistence of his later years.[27] In the short term, however, Robert, who had been the subject of Lanfranc's censure, became abbot of Saint-Évroult.

Robert ruled with energy and success so far as the abbey was concerned; but, against a background of external strife between Duke William and his subjects, Robert was summoned to the ducal court to answer charges laid against him by his own prior, Rainer. Being aware of the duke's fury against his kindred, he took the advice of Bishop Hugh of Lisieux to flee; on 27 January 1061 he left Saint-Évroult to lay his case before Pope Nicholas II. Upon the advice of a number of ecclesiastical persons, who included Abbot Ansfrid of Préaux and Prior Lanfranc of Bec, Duke William asked Abbot Rainer of la Trinité-du-Mont at Rouen to send for Osbern, prior of Cormeilles. In a synod at Rouen, Duke William appointed the unsuspecting Osbern to be abbot of Saint-Évroult, using the pastoral staff of Archbishop Maurilius for his investiture. At the duke's command, Bishop Hugh of Lisieux took him to Préaux where, without the knowledge of the monks of Saint-Évroult, he consecrated him abbot, subsequently leading him to Saint-Évroult.[28] Lanfranc's part in events at and following the synod of Rouen does not emerge, but in what seems to be a retrospect to the circumstances of Abbot Robert's departure in 1061, Orderic Vitalis gave a further hint about Lanfranc's part in them. Before leaving for Rome, Robert had appointed Mainer, a monk whom he had recently professed, to be his claustral prior. Soon after being thus appointed, Mainer travelled to Bec and was first among the monks of Saint-Évroult to discuss with Lanfranc the appointment of a new abbot. The way was thus prepared for Duke William's appointment of Osbern. There is no indication of what advice Lanfranc gave, but the very fact of Mainer's journey to Bec suggests that he expected Lanfranc to be sympathetic. Mainer's own future career was eventually a distinguished one. In the short term, the threats and reproaches of Abbot Robert's supporters and kinsmen led him, with Abbot Osbern's permission, to withdraw for a year to Cluny; but in 1066 he succeeded Osbern as abbot.[29]

---

[26] Orderic Vitalis, 3, vol. 2.66–75.   [27] See below, pp. 172–4.

[28] Orderic Vitalis, 3, vol. 2.90–3. For a note on investiture in the duchy, see Cowdrey, 'Lanfranc, the Papacy, and the See of Canterbury', 497–500.

[29] Orderic Vitalis, 3, vol. 2.96, cf. 146–51. I differ from Dr Chibnall's interpretation of this passage as implied by her translation by taking fuller account of the pluperfect tense; *porro* may be translated 'furthermore' rather than 'when'; 'Beccum perrexerat' scarcely warrants the translation 'breaking his journey at Bec' rather than simply going there; *primusque* calls for notice.

The meagre information that Orderic Vitalis provides for Lanfranc's part in events concerning Saint-Évroult prompts three observations. First, there is a similarity in the dramatis personae of the events of 1056 and 1061 in which Lanfranc was expressly involved: there appeared the archbishop of Rouen together with Bishop Hugh of Lisieux and Abbot Ansfrid of Préaux among others; they acted in concert with Duke William and habitually conformed to his wishes, making it a prime concern to counsel others to act similarly.

Second, this led Lanfranc, in particular, into opposition at Saint-Évroult to its founder and abbot, Robert of Grandmesnil. Such opposition ranged Lanfranc, at least potentially, against the popes of the time. For in 1061, upon his first recourse to Rome, Robert was welcomed by Pope Nicholas II who eventually sent him back to Normandy with two cardinals in order to claim back the abbey and to arraign as a usurper the ducal candidate, Osbern, whose promotion Lanfranc had advised. Duke William responded with fierce anger, saying that he would willingly receive legates of the pope as universal father in matters of faith and of the Christian religion; but if any Norman monk lodged a plea against his interest he would unceremoniously hang him by his cowl from the highest oak tree nearby. Abbot Robert deferred to Bishop Hugh of Lisieux's suggestion that he should keep at a safe distance. But when Abbot Osbern later evaded a summons to submit the question of the abbacy to the canonical judgement of the cardinals on neutral ground, Robert secured his excommunication and also the secession of a number of the monks.[30] The next pope, Alexander II, welcomed Robert at Rome with eleven monks of Saint-Évroult and gave them temporary hospitality in the Roman monastery of St Paul-without-the-Walls.[31] Lanfranc's prolonged opposition to Abbot Robert must inevitably have placed him at risk of incurring papal displeasure.

But, third, such displeasure was circumvented in the cases both of Lanfranc and of the duke. Abbot Osbern was at pains quickly to repair bridges with the papacy. According to Orderic Vitalis, he recalled from Cluny Lanfranc's contact Mainer in order to make him prior in place of Robert's nominee Fulk; but he also sent to Pope Alexander II a submissive letter in response to which the pope absolved him from the excommunication that Robert had secured from his legates. Alexander did so at the request of Robert himself, who by now had been made abbot of S. Eufemia in Calabria. Thus, a general reconciliation was achieved which restored prosperity to Saint-Évroult and left the duke, and presumably Lanfranc, with no loss of papal favour.[32]

Lanfranc's involvement in the troubled affairs of Saint-Évroult provided him with experience in relations with Duke William, who was well disposed towards the church in his duchy and to the papacy in spiritual matters but who was nevertheless determined to be master in his own domains. His wrath against churchmen, as others, who resisted his will was to be avoided. But the most important lesson of events at Saint-Évroult was probably that, with the exercise of prudence, a balance of interests could be achieved.

---

[30] Orderic Vitalis, 3, vol. 2.94–7.   [31] Ibid. 98–9.   [32] Ibid. 106–15.

The first respect in which such experiences modified Lanfranc's intention when he entered Bec was that he perforce came to learn the value of Benedictine monasticism according to the Rule in a monastery which was prosperous both spiritually and materially and which also found its place in the ecclesiastical and political structures of the Norman duchy. A second, and no less important, respect was that he was drawn back to the study and teaching that he had aspired to abandon; he did so with a renewed zeal that was registered both at Bec and in the western church at large.

According to the Bec tradition, Lanfranc's time of solitude and seclusion lasted for only some three years. His presence there became widely known, and in the rhetorical language of Gilbert Crispin there hastened to Bec 'clerks, the sons of dukes, and the most celebrated masters of the schools of Latin learning'.[33] It is, however, not easy to perceive in detail how Lanfranc's scholarly activity developed. The general fame that his teaching at Bec had won by c.1060 can hardly have been established only in recent years; yet not only his duties as prior but also his prolonged absences from Bec, notably his time at Saint-Évroult which was quickly followed by more than a year of travelling in the entourage of Pope Leo IX, must have involved times when he cannot himself have taught at Bec or elsewhere. Bec must, indeed, have had a claustral school in which, for example, Gilbert Crispin who entered Bec at a tender age, perhaps c.1055, received his early education.[34] But it is not likely to have called for Lanfranc's continual presence as a teacher. So far as can be seen, early recruitment to Bec was largely of adult men who, if capable of study—in Lanfranc's early days even the prior was *non litteratus*[35]—had received elementary education in the arts before coming to Bec. In any case, recruitment remained numerically low until Lanfranc had left for Caen and Canterbury. His teaching at Bec seems to have been predominantly of external pupils. It may also have been sporadic. It was in part necessitated by the need to raise money by fees for the building and development of the abbey. Thus, Gilbert Crispin by implication connected Lanfranc's earliest teaching with the increase in Bec's monastic facilities.[36] When Lanfranc eventually persuaded Abbot Herluin to embark upon new buildings, Gilbert Crispin implied that funds appeared somewhat miraculously; the *Vita Lanfranci* explained that, with Herluin's permission, Lanfranc again kept a school. This suggests that, although Lanfranc had formerly taken external pupils, he had not done so recently; Lanfranc now gave his fees to the abbot in order to pay the workmen.[37]

There is a consensus in later sources that, as a student and teacher of the arts, both before and after he entered Bec Lanfranc was above all a dialectician.[38] That is, among the subjects that comprised the *trivium*, he was most skilled in that which concerned logical argument, rather than grammar which concerned the meaning

---

[33] *VH* cap. 62, pp. 97/197; *VL* cap. 2, p. 671.
[34] *De nob. Crisp. gen.* col. 738BC; cf. Fauroux, pp. 34–5.
[35] *VL* cap. 2, p. 672.   [36] *VH* caps. 62–3, pp. 97/197; *VL* cap. 2, p. 671.
[37] *VH* cap. 75, pp. 99/199; *VL* cap. 4, p. 679.
[38] See esp. William of Malmesbury, *GP* 1.24, 2.74, pp. 38, 150; Sigebert of Gembloux, *DVI* pp. 97–8, no. 156; *MSN* cap. 7, pp. 408–9.

of words or rhetoric which concerned how best to persuade others, although in Lanfranc's time, the distinction between grammar and dialectic, in particular, was not strictly drawn. Lanfranc was praised for having ability in all the liberal arts, including those of the *quadrivium*—arithmetic, music, geometry, and astronomy[39]—although the *trivium* was his especial field.

There is, however, evidence to establish that, by c.1060 when Lanfranc was constrained by economic necessity to reopen his school at Bec, he had increasingly made the study of the Bible his overriding scholarly concern. This is especially apparent in a letter which Pope Nicholas II sent in 1059 to Lanfranc.[40] The pope dispatched to Bec some favoured imperial and papal chaplains whom he wished Lanfranc to instruct in the arts of dialectic and rhetoric, in which he understood Lanfranc to be pre-eminent. He had also heard that the study of scripture (*divina pagina*) had diverted Lanfranc from studies of that kind; if so, Nicholas charged Lanfranc under obedience to give the clerks the instruction in the arts of which they were in need. It is a reminder of the growing demand in the mid-eleventh century for clerks thoroughly schooled in the arts to be available for the service of both ecclesiastical and lay rulers; it was this demand that caused Lanfranc's school to prosper financially as well as educationally.

Other evidence from papal sources confirms such a view of Lanfranc's activities during his last years at Bec. Probably not long before he left for Caen, Pope Alexander II asked him to accept a favourite nephew as a pupil in the arts; he promised him a generous reward both spiritually and materially. Alexander saluted Lanfranc as 'filled with both kinds of wisdom (*utriusque sapientiae gratia repleto*)', that is, as being skilled both in the liberal arts and in sacred study; he went on to say that, having become learned in this world's wisdom, he had transferred to the study of the true, biblical wisdom. But both wisdoms came from the Holy Spirit. Alexander's nephew was already well versed in grammar and had made a good start with dialectic; it was upon this that Lanfranc was clearly expected to build.[41] A generation later, the anti-pope Clement III would recall that Lanfranc, who taught the arts to the Latin west, had also been its pre-eminent master and doctor in the Old and New Testaments.[42]

Despite such papal recognition of the intrinsic value of an education in the arts as an instrument of government, the internal and external pressures upon a monk such as Lanfranc to turn decisively to sacred study as his proper concern were strong. They are illustrated by the preface which a German monk, Abbot Williram of Ebersberg, who had heard Lanfranc teaching at Bec, wrote c.1060 for his own *Exposition of the Song of Songs*.[43] He began by conventionally disparaging the study of the liberal arts save in so far as they were propaedeutic to that of the sacred page.

---

[39] Orderic Vitalis, 3, vol. 2.248–53, which probably follows the lost portion of William of Poitiers; the anti-pope Clement III's letter to Lanfranc: Liebermann, 'Lanfranc and the Antipope', p. 331, no. 3.

[40] For the best text, see Southern, *Saint Anselm: A Portrait*, 32–3; for an English translation and discussion of the date, see ibid. 20–3.

[41] Alexander II, *Ep.* 70, *PL* 146.1353; the date must be after Alexander's accession to the papacy in 1061, and the lack of reference to Lanfranc as abbot points to a date before 1063.

[42] As above, n. 39.   [43] The '*Expositio*', 1; for the date, see p. xi.

He then praised Lanfranc who had formerly excelled in dialectic but who had now devoted himself to studies proper for a churchman: he was giving his mind to the Pauline epistles and to the Psalms. Would that many of the Germans who went to hear him would follow suit when they returned to Germany! The picture is one of Lanfranc turning increasingly to the study and teaching of the sacred page, while both the economic necessity of his abbey and the needs of rulers in church and lay society compelled him nevertheless to resume the teaching of the arts for their own sake.

Lanfranc's dual concern as prior and as scholar contributed to his having at Bec a roll-call of pupils which was well remembered there as distinguished.[44] First in importance was Anselm of Aosta, whose association with Bec most fully illustrates Lanfranc's impact upon other people while prior. According to his biographer Eadmer, Anselm had as a boy thought of becoming a monk, but his intention had faded.[45] It was after wanderings in Burgundy and France that he was drawn to Normandy by Lanfranc's reputation. He is likely to have reached Bec in 1059. He quickly became Lanfranc's most favoured pupil in the study of letters (*in litterarum studio*); he also assisted as a teacher of others, thus witnessing to the significant size of Lanfranc's school at this time. Within a year Anselm's sense of a monastic vocation gradually revived, and he adopted Lanfranc as his counsellor. At this juncture, according to Eadmer, Anselm so hung upon Lanfranc's advice that if, while travelling through the woods between Bec and Rouen, Lanfranc had directed him to settle in them for the remainder of his life, he would have done so. In fact, Anselm laid before Lanfranc three possibilities: that he should become a monk, or settle as a hermit, or return to his family estate and there minister to the poor. Lanfranc postponed giving an opinion, and he travelled with Anselm to Archbishop Maurilius of Rouen; the archbishop directed Anselm to become a monk at Bec. The incident shows how far Lanfranc had progressed from his presumption upon entering Bec that a monk might follow his own path, how highly he valued the taking of counsel as St Benedict enjoined,[46] and how close he stood to the monk-archbishop Maurilius of Rouen.[47] In due course, Anselm would succeed Lanfranc as prior of Bec and as archbishop of Canterbury, and however much their outlooks may have been modified they remained close in sympathy and commitment.

Others who came under Lanfranc's influence as monks of Bec and who were destined to play major roles in the Anglo-Norman church included the successive bishops of Rochester Ernost (1076) and Gundulf (1077–1108). As described in his *Life*, Gundulf's years at Bec provide insights into monastic life there while Lanfranc was prior and in the circle of monks that gathered around him. Gundulf was originally a clerk of Rouen and a friend of its archdeacon, William, who became a monk at Caen during Lanfranc's abbacy; in 1070 William succeeded Lanfranc as abbot, and from 1079 to 1110 he was archbishop of Rouen. The young Gundulf belonged to the circle of Archbishop Maurilius. Hardships endured while on pilgrimage

---

[44] See the accounts of Herluin's dream before Lanfranc's departure for Canterbury: *VH* caps. 79–82, 97–102, pp. 100–1/200–1, 103/203–4; *VL* caps. 6, 7, pp. 686, 689.
[45] *VA* 1.3–4, pp. 5–7.   [46] *RSB* cap. 3, vol. 1.452–5.   [47] *VA* 1.5–6, pp. 8–11.

together to Jerusalem led William and Gundulf to vow to become monks. Probably in 1057 Gundulf entered Bec where he became an exemplary monk; his devotional life, which illustrates the standards of monasticism that were approved there, was especially characterized by the grace of tears and by a devotion to the Virgin which was nourished by his soon becoming sacrist of the monastic church that was dedicated to her. Gundulf and his near-contemporary Anselm were joined in close friendship; Anselm's scriptural learning and Gundulf's contemplative devotion led to comparison with the biblical sisters Martha and Mary. Gundulf was also closely attached to Lanfranc as prior; he accompanied Lanfranc to Caen in 1063 and evidently became prior of Saint-Étienne.[48] Amongst abbots, besides Gilbert Crispin, abbot of Westminster (?1085–1117/18), Henry, abbot of Battle (1096–1102) was a monk of Bec; he was also prior of Christ Church, Canterbury (c.1074–96).[49]

A list of the leading persons whom Lanfranc taught at Bec without their becoming monks there is more difficult to draw up with certainty. According to a late York tradition, Archbishop Thomas I (1070–1100) was among the large number of persons of reputation in letters in France, Germany, and Italy who were instructed by Lanfranc, 'famous for learning and piety'.[50] In France, Guitmund, of la-Croix-Saint-Leofroy (dioc. Évreux) and, in the time of Pope Urban II, bishop of Aversa in south Italy, wrote in his anti-Berengarian treatise on the eucharist of Lanfranc as being his master.[51] According to the very late testimony of the chronicler Robert of Torigny, Bishop Ivo of Chartres (1090–1115), the eminent canon lawyer, heard Lanfranc's teaching at Bec in both secular and sacred subjects.[52] Abbot Williram of Ebersberg was a German monk whose reference to Lanfranc suggests that he was not alone amongst his countrymen in hearing him at Bec.[53] Some manuscripts of Lanfranc's *De corpore et sanguine Domini* state in the title that he wrote at the request of a German pupil, Theodoric, canon of Paderborn, whom he presumably taught at Bec.[54]

As regards pupils from Italy, Lanfranc himself testified to his having while at Bec and Caen instructed in sacred and profane subjects a number of men, including relatives of Pope Alexander II, who came with testimonials from Rome.[55] There is some suggestion that they may have included Alexander himself, who as Anselm da Baggio was from 1056 to 1073 bishop of Lucca as well as being pope from 1061; another possibility is his nephew Anselm, who was bishop of Lucca from 1073/4 to 1086.[56] In the former case, the suggestion arises from later accounts of Lanfranc's visit to Rome in 1071 in order to receive his *pallium* as archbishop of Canterbury.

---

[48] *VH* cap. 100, pp. 103/204; *VL* caps. 7, 13, pp. 689, 709; *The Life of Gundulf*, caps. 3–9, pp. 26–31.
[49] *VH* cap. 100, pp. 103/204; *VL* cap. 7, p. 689; *The Chron. of Battle Abbey*, 100–3.
[50] Hugh the Chanter, *History*, 4–5.
[51] *De corp. et sang. Christi*, 2, cols. 1449D–1450A.
[52] Robert of Torigny, a. 1117, pp. 100–1. On Ivo, see Barker, 'Ivo of Chartres', esp. 17–18.
[53] As above, n. 43.   [54] Huygens, 'Bérenger', 363–7; cf. Gibson, *Lanfranc*, 103.
[55] Lanfranc, *Letters*, no. 1, pp. 32–3; they no doubt include any who came in pursuance of Pope Nicholas II's letter to Lanfranc: Southern, *Saint Anselm*, 32–3.
[56] The evidence has been much discussed. For the case that Alexander is unlikely to have been Lanfranc's pupil, see esp. Schmidt, *Alexander II.*, 10–30; the contrary case is presented by Vaughn, *Anselm of Bec*, 33–4.

According to the Canterbury monk Eadmer, Alexander surprised his entourage by rising to greet Lanfranc. Eadmer gave the pope's explanation in direct speech: 'We have shown an honour that we owed, not to your archiepiscopate, but to the master by whose zeal we have been versed the things that we know. Hence it is reasonable for you to receive what is due to you from reverence for blessed Peter.'[57] In his *Gesta pontificum*, William of Malmesbury recorded the pope's explanation similarly but in reported speech and with no allusion to himself as having been Lanfranc's pupil: he paid his respect to Lanfranc not as archbishop, but as a master of letters. However, in his *Life* of Bishop Wulfstan of Worcester, William commented upon Alexander's ruling in Lanfranc's dispute about primacy with the archbishop of York that the pope predictably would not offend Lanfranc as his former master (*ut pote magistrum suum quondam*).[58] It was left for the *Vita Lanfranci* to specify that Alexander had been Lanfranc's pupil at Bec. It did so in an interpolation into the account of the archbishops' visit to Rome in the Canterbury memorandum on the primacy.[59] It first gave three reported (*dicitur*) reasons why the pope rose to greet Lanfranc: first, Lanfranc's great religion and outstanding knowledge; second, while still in Normandy Lanfranc had honourably received agents of the Roman church; and third, Lanfranc had zealously taught certain of the pope's relations (*consanguineos*). Then, using direct speech, it added a remark that Alexander was said (*fertur*) also to have passed: 'I do not rise to him because he is archbishop of Canterbury but because I was at Bec in his school and sat at his feet as a hearer with others.'[60] This remark, from a hearsay source, is the sole evidence for Alexander's having studied at Bec.[61]

Like all the statements that Alexander was Lanfranc's pupil, this evidence is of late date. There is silence upon the subject in all the earlier sources in which references might be expected. No hint is given in the dossier of documents in Lanfranc's letter-collection that record the events of 1070–2. Nor did Lanfranc afterwards allude to it in his letter to Alexander of 1072/3 in which he stated his claim upon the pope to be released from his office of archbishop; he expressly referred only to his having taught Alexander's relations.[62] Alexander's letters to Lanfranc are similarly silent, even though a reference would have been particularly appropriate in his letter, evidently written while Lanfranc was still at Bec, in which he asked him to undertake the further education of a kinsman (*fratuelis*).[63] Thus, while the assertion in a Bec source such as the *Vita Lanfranci* cannot be dismissed, it is nowhere

---

[57] *Hist. nov.* 1, pp. 10–11.   [58] *GP* 1.42, p. 65; *VW* 2.1, pp. 24–5.

[59] Lanfranc, *Letters*, no. 3/ii, pp. 42–3.

[60] *VL* cap. 11, p. 697. The second and third points may be based on Lanfranc, *Letters*, no. 1, p. 30–3, esp. lines 9–20, 37–41.

[61] It should perhaps be borne in mind that, if Lanfranc was by a few years Alexander's senior, he could have taught him before he left Italy; furthermore, he may have undertaken some teaching in Italy in 1049–50 in order to support his travels. But there is no positive suggestion of such early contact between the two men.

[62] Lanfranc, *Letters*, nos. 3–4, pp. 38–57, esp. 3/ii, pp. 42–3 and 4, pp. 54–7; no. 1, pp. 32–3.

[63] *Ep.* 70, *PL* 146.1353. For the date, which is probably 1063, see Schmidt, *Alexander II.*, 21 n. 85, 27 n. 108.

expressly confirmed, and there is silence in the earliest evidence.[64] In default of further evidence, it must be regarded as unproven.

The case for Bishop Anselm II of Lucca's having been Lanfranc's pupil depends on his having been the *fratuelis* of his uncle's letter. But Alexander II had a large kindred about which little is known, and while the noun *fratuelis* normally means nephew it does not necessarily do so.[65] There is no further hint that Anselm II was ever in Normandy as a pupil of Lanfranc.[66] It is unlikely that he had been such.

During his twenty years or so as prior of Bec, Lanfranc evidently continued to be a teacher of both internal and external pupils in both secular and sacred subjects. Indeed, his teaching seems to have been at its most intensive during the final years before his departure for Caen. Despite these calls upon his time and despite external commitments in the service of the pope and the duke of Normandy which have yet to be studied, he also worked closely and harmoniously with his abbot, Herluin, in training monks and in attending to the internal and external business of the monastery. Moreover, he impressed other people as an exemplary monk according to the expectations of his day. Whatever his purpose upon entering Bec, he had identified himself with the cenobitic life according to the Rule of St Benedict; he also manifested a deep personal piety, significantly expressed in the compunction, or grace of tears, which was the mark of a dedicated monk. As such he was remembered in the traditions of Bec.[67]

2.3 ABBOT OF SAINT-ÉTIENNE AT CAEN

Lanfranc became abbot of Saint-Étienne at Caen in 1063,[68] and ruled the newly founded abbey until he became archbishop of Canterbury in 1070. When he moved to Caen he is likely to have been already some fifty years of age. His seniority, and therefore his experience and proven loyalty, are likely to have commended him to Duke William, who for political as well as for ecclesiastical reasons was seeking to establish the town of Caen as a centre of ducal authority.

For it was only by c.1060 that William had achieved something like mastery over his entire duchy; along with the consolidation of ducal power and with achieving

---

[64] As n. 63; Alexander II's wish at about this time to send a *cognatus* to France for education is confirmed by a letter of Berengar of Tours: *Die Hannoversche Briefsammlung, 3: Briefe Berengars von Tours*, no. 100, in *Briefsammlungen, MGH Briefe*, 1.168.

[65] See Schmidt, *Alexander II.*, 30.

[66] For Anselm II, see Violante, 'Anselmo da Baggio'. Anselm's declaration in 1084/5 to King William I that he was mindful of the benefits (*memor beneficiorum*) that the king had conferred upon him creates a possibility that he had visited the Anglo-Norman lands: *Die Hannoversche Briefsammlung, 1: Die Hildesheimer Briefe*, no. 1, in *Briefsammlungen, MGH Briefe*, 5.16.

[67] e.g. *VL* cap. 6, pp. 684–5.

[68] The date of Lanfranc's transfer to Caen is not directly attested, but 1063 is highly probable. Apart from the improbability that Duke William would have delayed for long in founding Saint-Étienne when progress was being made with la Trinité, the following arguments support 1063: (i) Lanfranc's successor as prior of Bec, Anselm, later testified that, after three years as an ordinary monk at Bec, he was prior for fifteen years. Since he succeeded as abbot in 1078, this means that he became prior in 1063: *Ep.* 156, *Opera*, ed. Schmitt, 4.15; cf. Orderic Vitalis, 5.2, vol. 3.12–13; (ii) Pope Alexander II's privilege of 1068 referred to

control of a turbulent aristocracy, the building up of a reformed but obedient secular and monastic church had been a means by which he had done so. But even the strongest of the dukes who had preceded him had done little to consolidate their power in Lower Normandy; the time had come for William to take this task in hand. The town of Caen became of critical importance for him.

In Roman times, Bayeux (Augustodunum), which lay on a road running from Rouen to the northern shore of the Cotentin peninsula, was established as the principal town of the region. In the eleventh century it remained the site of a bishopric which in 1049/50 William gave to his young half-brother Odo, as in 1048 he gave the see of Coutances, in the Cotentin, to the warlike Geoffrey of Mowbray. But control of the Cotentin did little to meet the problems of the south-west of the duchy. It was, therefore, important for the future that, early in the eleventh century, a town began to develop at Caen; it was first mentioned as a *villa* c.1025.[69] From the point of view of communications, it was better situated than Bayeux to give access to the south-west; a spur of rock rising above the River Orne provided a site for a castle and ducal residence; with its ready access by river to the sea, Caen was early a trading as well as an agricultural centre; good stone quarries provided material for building as well as a commodity for export.

Duke William, therefore, set it upon the way to becoming, after Rouen, the second town of the duchy; it would be a centre of control for Lower Normandy as Rouen was for Upper Normandy. He established a castle with an ample precinct, providing it with the public and private apartments and the chapel (*aula, camera, capella*) which were the essential buildings, and he probably initiated its fortification by a keep.[70] From an ecclesiastical point of view, there was never a question of transferring the see of Bayeux to Caen or of establishing a new diocese. But the duke and his wife, Matilda, decided upon the foundation of twin abbeys at opposite ends of the town—the abbey of la Trinité for women, consecrated as early as 18 June 1066, and that of Saint-Étienne for men; in due course they became the burial-places of their respective founders. Their foundation, and especially that of Saint-Étienne, also reflected the duke's desire for monastic intercessory support in the major military and political contingencies of his rule.[71] In a town which lacked a cathedral and a cathedral establishment, the abbeys were essential for the spiritual life and the temporal impressiveness of Caen as Duke William developed it.

In view of the manifold importance of Saint-Étienne, Lanfranc was an obvious choice for William and advisers in appointing the first abbot. Lanfranc had recently

---

the buildings and endowments of Saint-Étienne as being by then well advanced: *Ep.* 57, *PL* 146.1540AB; (iii) Lanfranc is likely to have been abbot for an appreciable time before he was asked to succeed Maurilius as archbishop of Rouen upon his death in 1067: *VL* cap. 5, p. 682. There is, however, some suggestion that Lanfranc became abbot in 1066. Orderic Vitalis elsewhere states that Lanfranc was chosen on the same day, 16 July 1066, that Mainer became abbot of Saint-Évroult: 3, vol. 3.144–7; this would account for the otherwise unexplained absence of Lanfranc's name from the witnesses of the ducal charter for la Trinité on its dedication day, 18 June 1066: Musset, 'Les Actes', no. 2, p. 57. The conflicting evidence cannot be satisfactorily explained,

[69] Fauroux, no. 58, p. 182 (*villa que dicitur Cathim*).
[70] Boüard, *Le Chateau*, esp. 10–11, 30, 63–7.   [71] William of Poitiers, 1.52, pp. 84–7.

shown resolution and skill in promoting the rebuilding of Bec. He had become well versed in the ecclesiastical and political affairs of the duchy; the next chapter will show him to have been both a valued adviser of the duke and a churchman held in the highest regard by the papacy under Alexander II. Not only was he widely known as a scholar and teacher but he was esteemed for his qualities as a monk. When chosen to be abbot, he expressed a reluctance to accept a position of authority that was certainly conscientious and not merely formal. But he soon yielded to the pressure to accept the burden that was laid upon him.[72]

As abbot, Lanfranc maintained his links with Bec in a way that assisted the formation of his new community at Caen. He brought with him the exemplary monk Gundulf who, it appears, became his first prior.[73] An important early recruit was Gundulf's former companion in pilgrimage, William Bona Anima, archdeacon of Rouen. He was sent to Bec for his noviciate, but after profession at Caen he so commended himself as to become claustral prior and to succeed Lanfranc as abbot.[74] Another monk who accompanied Lanfranc from Bec was the as yet unprofessed Ralph, who in due course became prior of Saint-Étienne, prior of Rochester, and, from 1107 to 1124, abbot of Battle.[75] From the start, Lanfranc had about him a nucleus of outstanding monks, and he was remembered as having instituted a large and enduring community.[76] William Bona Anima was in due course given oversight of the increasing number of novices at Caen.[77]

Of the material growth of the abbey under Lanfranc only a little can be said, and that but tentatively. It has become increasingly apparent that the construction of the church and the monastic buildings was a prolonged process, despite the wealth that became available after the Norman conquest of England in 1066.[78] Pope Alexander II's privilege of 1068 makes clear that by then the building of the church had made progress.[79] But recent archaeological investigation indicates that, during Lanfranc's abbacy, construction of the church did not proceed beyond the choir, which was itself rebuilt in the thirteenth century so that very little of Lanfranc's work now remains.[80] A first consecration of the church, probably restricted to its east end, is recorded in 1073; Lanfranc was himself present for the greater ceremony of 1077.[81] While he was abbot, Lanfranc like his successors was concerned to acquire property which would increase the abbey's lands and endowments.[82]

---

[72] *VH* cap. 3, pp. 99/199; *VL* caps. 4–5, pp. 679–80, 682; William of Poitiers, 1.52, pp. 84–5, where William appointed Lanfranc abbot 'as it were by an act of pious violence'.

[73] *The Life of Gundulf*, cap. 9, p. 31. Lanfranc is said to have had Gundulf as 'in eiusdem coenobii gubernatione coadiutorem'.

[74] *VL* cap. 4, p. 680; for William, see Spear, 'William Bona Anima'.

[75] *VL* cap. 4, p. 680; see also *The Chron. of Battle Abbey*, 116–33.   [76] *VL* cap. 4, p. 680.

[77] For William's responsibility at Caen 'ad instructionem neophitorum', see Orderic Vitalis, 3, vol. 2.254–5.

[78] William of Poitiers, 1. 52, 2.42, pp. 84–7, 176–9.   [79] As n. 68.

[80] See Carlson, 'Excavations'; Baylé, 'Les Ateliers', 1–4.

[81] For 1073, see *Historia brevis, a.* 1073, p. 1018: 'Hoc anno dedicata est Basilica S. Stephani Cadomi'; for 1077, see Orderic Vitalis, 3, 5.12–16, vols. 2.148–9, 3.10–13, 158–61; cf. Musset, 'Les Actes', 14–15.

[82] Musset, 'Les Actes', no. 20, pp. 226–8 (the date seems to be before 1070; seventeen transactions are noticed); cf. no. 14, pp. 103–11 = *Regesta WI*, no. 53, pp. 248–57; and see comment by Musset, pp. 32–3.

The most important surviving document of Lanfranc's abbacy is the papal privilege of exemption which regulated the relationship between Saint-Étienne and the ecclesiastical structures of the province of Rouen.[83] It may reasonably be dated to 1068, and Lanfranc may have discussed its terms with Pope Alexander II during his visit to Rome in 1067 about the archiepiscopal succession at Rouen. The privilege was carefully drafted, and it sheds light upon the Norman perception of papal authority in Alexander's time and in the immediate aftermath of the Norman conquest of England. It opened by setting Saint-Étienne under papal protection (*sub tutela et defensione sanctae sedis apostolicae*) and by excluding every ecclesiastical and secular authority from power over the monastery and its possessions; such power was reserved for the abbot. If he were troubled by any bishop, the abbot had a right of direct approach to the apostolic see. The relationship to it of the bishop of Bayeux as diocesan was recognized but strictly limited. In view of its exemption, the bishop was denied any coercive power: he might not excommunicate the abbot or monks for any fault, nor might he prohibit the performance of divine service. However, he had a pastoral role: if the abbot or the community were at fault, he might admonish the abbot privately and amicably correct his conduct and that of his monks. But if the abbot were contumacious, the bishop might not summon the matter at issue before his episcopal synod, but it should be referred to the archbishop of Rouen at a council of his whole province; in the gravest cases, a decision was reserved to the apostolic see. In sacramental matters, the bishop of Bayeux was stated to have no rights save for the considerable exceptions that he might ordain the abbot and monks of the abbey and that, for its lands and estates, he might consecrate chrism, dedicate churches, and give penance to laymen. If the bishop of Bayeux should be a simoniac or if he were excommunicated by the apostolic see, or if he maliciously postponed ordinations for more than a month, the abbot might instead have recourse to the apostolic see or to any religious bishop of his choice.

Alexander's privilege was characterized by moderation and was formulated, it may be suspected, after much consultation amongst the interested parties. The abbey was built into the ecclesiastical structure of the province of Rouen. There was ample recognition of the authority of the papacy, although the abbey was not specially commended to St Peter or the apostolic see; it was entrusted to papal protection. It cannot be argued that the terms of the privilege were in any special way directed against the bishop of Bayeux, whether understood officially of him as diocesan or personally as Odo, the bishop for the time being. There is no suggestion that Odo was other than well-disposed towards Saint-Étienne. A *pancarte* of King William and Queen Matilda which dates from before 1083 shows that, like Archbishop William of Rouen and Bishop Geoffrey of Coutances, Odo had agreed to an extended exercise by the abbey of archidiaconal rights over its

---

For William I's confirmation of the lands of Saint-Étienne (1066/77), see Musset, no. 4, pp. 59–65 = *Regesta WI*, no. 45, pp. 216–19, with Musset's discussion at pp. 26–8.

[83] *Ep.* 57, *PL* 146.1339–41.

possessions.[84] There evidently remained a certain flexibility in the abbey's position, with room for amicable negotiation.[85]

All in all, by the time that Lanfranc left it for Canterbury the abbey of Saint-Étienne seems to have been well established in the position in the Norman duchy that was intended for it, without there being evidence of serious conflict with external authorities, whether in matters of principle or of practice. Relations with the pope, the diocesan bishop, and the duke were all well defined and a noteworthy harmony was established.

---

[84] Musset, 'Les Actes', no. 19, pp. 122–5 = *Regesta WI*, no. 57, pp. 266–9. For discussion, see Lemarignier, *Étude*, 162–76.

[85] For evidence of negotiations in 1074, see Gregory VII, *Reg.* 1.70, p. 102.

3

Service Outside the Cloister, c.1042–1070

3.1 TO THE DUKE OF NORMANDY

William II, duke of Normandy, succeeded to the duchy of Normandy in 1035 as a boy aged only some 7 years. It was not until c.1060 that he had won effective control over most parts of his turbulent duchy and could, therefore, develop Caen as a centre of his authority in Lower Normandy. Such building up of ducal power by direct means was complemented by two further lines of endeavour: that of holding in loyalty and serviceability a restless lay aristocracy, and that of fostering a well-organized and spiritually effective church which, being strong alike in its monastic and secular aspects, served the duke's purposes as ruler of the duchy.[1] The texts of the liturgical *laudes* which were sung on major festivals in the Norman duchy and in the Anglo-Norman kingdom of England graphically set out current ideas of order and hierarchy in a conceptually unitary society in which the resources of its spiritual and lay aspects blended together to promote welfare and prosperity.[2]

So far as Lanfranc's place in the affairs of the Norman duchy is concerned, the continuing effects of the monastic expansion and development that were inaugurated in the early years of the eleventh century by Abbot William of Dijon and Fécamp must be kept in mind.[3] Four further features of the Norman church under Duke William are particularly relevant when considering the position of Lanfranc.

First, and of especial importance, was the series of church councils which were held in the duchy, perhaps beginning in 1042; between that year and 1070 there were some thirteen councils, and seven more followed there before Duke William's death.[4] The councils were attended by the bishops of the province of Rouen which was almost coterminous with the duchy. A number of abbots attended, especially from the monasteries of Upper Normandy where most of the councils were held. There was also a considerable lay attendance, and the business often concerned the good order of the lay as well as of the ecclesiastical order of society. Upon rare occasions when the nature of the principal business so demanded, councils might be under the presidency of a papal legate, as when Bishop Ermenfrid of Sion presided at councils such as Lisieux (1054) and Rouen (1069) which were concerned with the

---

[1] For a general survey of the church in the duchy, see Bates, *Normandy Before 1066*, 189–235.
[2] Cowdrey, 'The Anglo-Norman *Laudes Regiae*', esp. 48–55, 68–73.
[3] See above, pp. 9–10.
[4] On the Norman councils, see esp. Foreville, 'The Synod of the Province of Rouen' (with a list on p. 22); Pontal, *Les Conciles*. Many of the relevant texts are collected in Bessin, *Concilia*.

disposal of the see of Rouen. But a characteristic of the Norman councils was the strict and direct control of their summons and proceedings by the duke himself. Duke William's panegyrist William of Poitiers, who was for some years a ducal chaplain and then archdeacon of Lisieux, commented with admiration upon the duke's employment of councils to keep the higher clergy up to the mark:

> The ruling prince, although a layman, acutely advised, constantly exhorted, and severely castigated abbots and bishops in respect of ecclesiastical discipline. As often as by his order and encouragement the bishops—the metropolitan with his suffragans—assembled to take action for the state of religion, the clergy, the monks, and the laity, he was unwilling not to be the controller of those synods, since by his presence he might augment the zeal of the zealous and the caution of the cautious. For he did not wish to rely upon testimony at second hand in order to learn how affairs had been conducted which he desired himself to attended to reasonably, in good order, and according to religion.[5]

In practice, the Norman councils varied in respect of their purpose and concerns, but the surviving canons of Lisieux (1064), Rouen (1072), and Lillebonne (1080) demonstrate the range and depth of business that could be discharged.[6] In reading them, it should be borne in mind that the councils were not only administrative and juridical occasions; they were also intended to be occasions of corporate devotion, of the affirmation of Catholic orthodoxy, and of general and individual penitence and amendment.[7] In respect of the church at large, they had much in common with the daily chapter within the monasteries. Through their influence, what may, perhaps, be called a conciliar culture was part of the Norman church with which Lanfranc became familiar.

Second, the Norman church was open to currents of reform which were widely current in the west, and not least through the reform papacy of Pope Leo IX (1049–54) and his successors. Some of these currents are to be seen in the legislation of the Norman councils. Canons against simony—the buying and selling of ecclesiastical orders and offices—began as early as c.1045 in Archbishop Mauger's council at Rouen; the practice came to be proscribed as the 'simoniac heresy' in a phrase going back to Pope Gregory the Great and adopted by the reform popes.[8] From Archbishop Maurilius's council of 1063 there followed strict legislation about the continence of the clergy.[9] At Lisieux in the following year, all those in major orders were to put away their wives, while those in minor orders were not to be deprived of their wives by force (*violenter*) but were to be urged voluntarily to put them away.[10] Such stringent legislation remained a feature of councils held in the duchy.[11] The regulation of clerical and lay morality as well as the promotion of public peace

---

[5] William of Poitiers, 1.51, pp. 82–3.
[6] Lisieux (1064): Delisle, 'Canons du concile', whence Hefele–Leclercq, 4.1420–3. Rouen (1072): Orderic Vitalis, 4, vol. 2.284–93. Lillebonne (1080): ibid. 5.5, vol. 3.24–35.
[7] See the order for holding a council as given in the Pseudo-Isidorian decrees: Hinschius, pp. 22–4; also the Norman texts in *The Benedictional of Archbishop Robert*, 152–7; and *Die Konzilsordines*, no. 26, pp. 568–74.
[8] Esp. canons 6–7: Bessin, *Concilia*, 40–2.   [9] Bessin, *Concilia*, 47.
[10] Canons 2–3, Hefele–Leclercq, 4.1121.
[11] See esp. Rouen (1072): Orderic Vitalis, 4, vol. 2.290–1; Lillebonne (1080), ibid. 5.5, vol. 3.26–7.

and social order was attempted with increasing strenuousness. As is illustrated by Pope Alexander II's privilege of 1068 for Saint-Étienne at Caen, the provincial councils were complemented in the dioceses by episcopal synods;[12] by about this time the Norman dioceses were developing a staff of archdeacons who were concerned at a local level with the spiritual and moral condition of the clergy and laity.[13]

Third, the extent to which the Norman church and duchy were in touch with the reform papacy calls for a balanced assessment. The prestige with which the reform popes were invested should not be underestimated. William of Poitiers spoke warmly of Alexander II, in particular, in the course of his eulogy of William the Conqueror. Alexander was a pope who deserved the obedience and trust of the universal church. Significantly, he was expected to respond to rather than to take initiatives in matters of business: his responses to approachs that were made to him were just and salutary, and he was rightly to be regarded as the head and master of all bishops. Wherever in the world he had the power, he uncompromisingly corrected what was evil. By such words, William of Poitiers introduced the papacy's greatest act of usefulness to Duke William, when he supported the invasion of England in 1066 and sent him a banner of St Peter to bear at the head of his army. The genuine regard in which the papacy was held was balanced by the expectation that popes would act in response to ducal needs and to fulfil ducal requirements; papal authority, however venerable, must not challenge that of the duke in his duchy.[14]

Within such parameters which were communicated to the clergy and monks of the duchy, Norman contacts with the papacy were neither infrequent nor unimportant. Thus, for example, in 1049 five Norman bishops—Geoffrey of Coutances, Ivo of Sées, Herbert of Lisieux, Hugh of Bayeux, and Hugh of Avranches—were present at Pope Leo IX's council of Rheims; during this council, Geoffrey of Coutances confessed that his brother had bought his see for him but without his knowledge, and he was adjudged to be guiltless of the simoniac heresy.[15] Geoffrey also attended Leo's council at the Lateran in April 1050.[16] At about the same time, Abbot John of Fécamp served Leo as a papal legate in South Italy.[17] Such a continuing tradition makes unsurprising the desire for papal sanction that led to Pope Alexander II's granting of his privilege of exemption in 1068 to Lanfranc's abbey of Saint-Étienne at Caen.[18] St Peter and his vicar at Rome were a strong factor in Norman calculations.

Nevertheless, no story better epitomizes both the cordiality and the limits of Duke William's attitude to the papacy than Orderic Vitalis's report of his fierce reply to the supporters of Abbot Robert of Grantmesnil at Saint-Évroult: he would willingly receive the legates of the pope as universal father in matters of faith and religion; but a monk who lodged a plea at Rome against the ducal interest would be hanged by his cowl from the nearest tall oak-tree.[19]

---

[12] See above, pp. 27–8.   [13] For archdeacons, see Bates, *Normandy Before 1066*, 215–16.
[14] William of Poitiers, 2.3, pp. 104–5, cf. 2.31, pp. 152–5.
[15] Anselme de Saint-Remi, caps. 26, 33, pp. 236, 248.   [16] Leo IX, *Ep.* 38, *PL* 143.647B.
[17] *PL* 143.797–800. The eulogy of Leo IX may be noted.   [18] See above, pp. 27–8.
[19] See above, p. 18.

Fourth, and against the background of all these features of the Norman church, the 1060s and 1070s in particular witnessed an advance in the standards of the Norman episcopate.[20] This amelioration was most apparent in the three archbishops of Rouen who followed the unsatisfactory Mauger (1037–54)—Maurilius (1054–67), John (1068–79), and William Bona Anima (1079–1102). The first and the last of these had, like Lanfranc, been monks. While working in close concert with the duke, they were energetic in their zeal for the reform of the church and for the amendment of moral and social abuses. To these ends they were concerned to work through their provincial councils and through a well-articulated ecclesiastical structure. They provided Lanfranc with models of what a good archbishop might be and do.

In general terms, Lanfranc was later acknowledged to have been Duke William's close adviser in the affairs of the duchy. According to William of Poitiers, the duke honoured Lanfranc as a trusted counsellor, 'reverencing him as a father, respecting him as an instructor, and cherishing him as a brother or son'. Lanfranc was at once the duke's spiritual director and, on his behalf, the overseer of the ecclesiastical establishment throughout Normandy; in his capacity as an exemplary monk, Lanfranc was reverenced by William as a 'holy man' who in word and deed reflected the spirit of God.[21] More tersely, Gilbert Crispin commented that the duke made him his principal counsellor in respect of the business of the whole of the duchy.[22]

However, in evidence dating from before Lanfranc left Normandy in 1070, there is surprisingly little trace of Lanfranc's participation in Norman ecclesiastical councils, although especially while he was abbot of Saint-Étienne his presence at some of them is likely. His only attested presence was at Brionne in 1050, when he had a subordinate part in a debate amongst scholars which the duke arranged to discuss eucharistic doctrine and at which Berengar of Tours was present.[23]

Furthermore, at an unestablishable date but apparently during Lanfranc's earlier years as prior, he suffered a temporary but sharp loss of ducal favour which calls for detailed examination. Gilbert Crispin gave the earliest account of it in terms that had become stylized in the course of long tradition.[24] According to Gilbert, Duke William was bitterly angered against Lanfranc upon unspecified accusations made by unnamed accusers.[25] William ordered his expulsion from Bec and in his anger caused one of Bec's vills, named Parc, to be burnt down. Lanfranc left Bec with a single servant and with a lame and (as it later emerges) unrideable horse, leaving the bereft monks at prayer 'in expectation of the salvation of the Lord' (Lam. 3: 26). Upon leaving Lanfranc met the duke, who at first averted his eyes but who soon allowed him to speak. Lanfranc then turned the duke's anger by a jest: 'At your command, I am leaving your lands on foot, but I am hampered by this useless

---

[20] See Bates, *Normandy Before 1066*, 213–18.
[21] William of Poitiers, 1.52, pp. 84–5, cited in *VL* cap. 6, p. 684.
[22] 'Ad administranda quoque totius regni negotia summus ab ipso Normanniae duce Willelmo consiliarius assumitur': *VH* cap. 64, pp. 97/197; *VL* caps. 3, 5, pp. 675, 682.
[23] *RCL* lines 300–4, 433–5, pp. 44, 48; Durand of Troarn, *De corpore*, 9.33, col. 1422A.
[24] *VH* caps. 64–70, pp. 97–8/197–8.
[25] For a story that his accuser was the duke's chaplain Herfast, later bishop of Elmham, whose ignorance Lanfranc exposed, see William of Malmesbury, *GP* 2.74, pp. 150–4, cf. 1.24, p. 38.

quadruped; in order that I can comply with your order, at least give me a better horse.' Moved to laughter, the duke asked: 'Whoever asks for gifts from an offended judge while his offence remains unpurged?' The ice was broken: Lanfranc pleaded his case and, supported by the monks' prayers, he was returned to the favour of the duke, who also made restitution to the monks for their ravaged estate and confirmed their possessions.

As told by Gilbert Crispin in a *Life* of Abbot Herluin, a main purpose of this story was to demonstrate the efficacy of his monks' prayers; he also provided an example of how, by using his prerogative of boldness of speech, a 'holy man' like Herluin's prior could by a jest turn the wrath of a ruler, repair fractured human relationships, and secure the just resolution of a situation of discord.[26] It was not germane to Gilbert's didactic purpose to indicate what was at issue between Lanfranc and the duke; rather, he provided an edifying example of how, according to prevailing conventions, a dispute might best be resolved.

Several points in Gilbert Crispin's account deserve notice. First, the 'clouding over' of relations happened suddenly (*repente*), just as by act of God fair weather returned unexpectedly but without delay (*confestim*).[27] Second, however, Lanfranc's encounter with the duke seems to have been not fortuitous but contrived with a view to restoring relationships. It is barely conceivable that Bec would, without good reason, have provided its revered prior with a useless horse; Lanfranc met the duke forthwith (*protinus*) upon leaving the abbey. Third, being conscious of his innocence, Lanfranc was confident of winning his case, given an opportunity to speak to the duke in person.[28] It is a clear example of how, by the setting up of an almost ritual procedure, a dispute might be resolved to the general advantage, but especially to that of the monastery concerned. At the same time, the incident may well have served to bring Lanfranc decisively to the duke's notice as a counsellor in personal and official matters.

Later tradition at Bec as exemplified in the *Vita Lanfranci* sought an explanation for the ducal order of banishment.[29] According to this source, it was said that the reason for this ill-judged order[30] was that Lanfranc had spoken against the marriage that William had contracted within the prohibited degrees of kinship with Matilda of Flanders, for which the pope had placed all Normandy (*tota Neustria*) under interdict. There are grounds for being doubtful about this explanation. The *Vita Lanfranci* probably exaggerated the effects and the duration of the problems to which the duke's marriage gave rise.[31] Moreover, it is not likely that the breach between the duke and Lanfranc could have been healed so easily and quickly as Gilbert Crispin indicates if Lanfranc's stance had the drastic consequences for the duchy that the *Vita Lanfranci* claims.

[26] Cf. Bishop Hugh of Lincoln's jest to the aggrieved King Henry II: *Vita magna Sancti Hugonis*, 1.116–18.
[27] 'Cuius gratiae nimiam quae una die irruit repente obnubilationem, insperato Deus confestim laetificavit sereno...'
[28] 'Innocentiae quidem conscius, si locus dicendi daretur, non diffidebat causae.'
[29] *VL* cap. 3, p. 676; the *Vita* appends its explanation to an almost verbatim citation of *VH*: 675–6.
[30] 'Huius tam improvide iussionis causam fuisse aiunt...'   [31] See below, pp. 34–7.

Issues other than the duke's marriage may have aroused Duke William's wrath. Attention has been drawn to the possible background in his struggle with Guy 'of Burgundy', count of Brionne and Vernon.[32] Guy was a grandson of Duke Richard II and thus William's close kinsman. Upon the death, perhaps c.1040, of Count Gilbert of Brionne, he had secured control of the castle there; in 1047 he headed the revolt against Duke William which was defeated at the battle of Val-ès-Dunes, although he thereafter for some time resisted a siege by William.[33] Control of the castle of Brionne was critical for the local interests of the abbey of Bec; thus, when in 1041 Duke William had issued a charter for it, he included a confirmation of gifts by Count Gilbert that Guy had himself confirmed.[34] During the siege that followed the battle of Val-ès-Dunes, Lanfranc may well have fallen foul of accusations that he had been in touch with the duke's enemies; they would account for the reported ravaging of Bec's property at Parc, and also for the duke's known proximity to Bec when Lanfranc left it for exile.

A further possibility is that an accusation was made against Lanfranc in relation to the Berengarian controversy, which was in the duke's mind during the period leading to the council of Brionne in 1050. During this period Lanfranc came under suspicion of sharing opinions of Berengar, at whose feet he was said to have sat; he had to defend himself at Rome.[35] It is conceivable that allegations were made to the duke while he was in the vicinity of Bec. This could account for both the sudden emergence and the speedy resolution of the matter when Lanfranc gained access to the ducal ear. The ravaging of Parc could be a warning to the monks against any association with Berengar, who was a clerk of Duke William's rival, Count Geoffrey of Anjou.[36]

Any one of these matters—the duke's marriage, the hostility to him of Guy 'of Burgundy', and the Berengarian controversy—may lie behind Lanfranc's loss of ducal favour. It is not possible to decide which of them it may have been, although the second and third are at least as likely as the first. In any case, the duke's anger was speedily allayed.

During Lanfranc's years at Bec his active participation in ducal affairs is surprisingly difficult to establish, even in the matter of the duke's marriage. The canonical problem to which it gave rise on account of alleged consanguinity and Lanfranc's role in overcoming it remain almost impenetrably obscure. By 1051, and probably in the previous year, William married Matilda, daughter of Count Baldwin V of Flanders and his wife Adela, daughter of the Capetian king Robert the Pious.[37] The marriage brought the duke the double advantage of alliance with a powerful neighbour and the infusion into his family of royal blood.[38] As to the canonical problem,

---

[32] Gibson, *Lanfranc*, 30–1.
[33] William of Poitiers, 1.7–9, pp. 8–13; William of Jumièges, 7.7, vol. 2.120–3; Orderic Vitalis, 7.15, vol. 4.82–5.
[34] Fauroux, no. 98, pp. 249–54.   [35] See below, p. 61.
[36] William of Poitiers, 1.11, 15–16, pp. 14–15, 20–3; William of Jumièges, 7.8, vol. 2.122–7.
[37] In 1051 Matilda attested as *comitissa*: Fauroux, nos. 124, 126, pp. 293–5, 296–7. The subscription of Robert *iunior comes* indicates a marriage in 1050 or very early 1051.
[38] William of Jumièges, 7.9, vol. 2.128–31. For the view that William wrote the earlier part of the *Gesta* before 1060, see vol. 1.xxiii–xxxv.

the one certain piece of evidence arose from Pope Leo IX's council at Rheims in the autumn of 1049, at which, having legislated against incestuous unions, the pope forbade Count Baldwin from giving his daughter to Duke William and the duke from taking her as his wife.[39] The relationship between William and Matilda is far from clear, although it must have fallen inside the degrees within which marriage was canonically prohibited; the most likely supposition is that it arose because Matilda was the granddaughter of Count Baldwin IV of Flanders whose second wife is said to have been a sister of William's father, Duke Robert I.[40]

According to twelfth-century sources, but solely to them, the prolonged difficulties that ensued were overcome only after papal goodwill for the marriage was secured by the ducal pair's foundation of the abbeys of la Trinité and Saint-Étienne at Caen. Thus, in an addition to the chronicle of William of Jumièges, Orderic Vitalis placed papal involvement after, not before, the marriage. Responding to repeated allegations by unnamed churchmen that he had married a kinswoman, William sent envoys to an unnamed pope at Rome in order to secure his advice. The pope realistically pointed out that a separation might lead to damaging hostilities between Flanders and Normandy. Therefore he absolved William and Matilda of any guilt and, by way of penance, ordered each to found a monastery.[41] William of Malmesbury next referred to current stories—of manifest improbability—which ascribed the initial Norman criticism of the marriage to religious zeal on the part of Archbishop Mauger of Rouen, who threatened the pair with excommunication. This was a reason for Mauger's deposition in 1054. Only after Duke William had grown older and wiser did the ducal couple see the need to expiate their offence and to found the two abbeys.[42] Only with the *Vita Lanfranci* did Lanfranc come into the picture. Its author tacked on to Gilbert Crispin's account of Lanfranc's temporary loss of ducal favour the hearsay story that he had taken an initiative in opposing the duke's marriage, but had gone to Rome in 1059 with the express purpose of pleading the duke's case in the matter. This he did by pointing out that an adverse sentence would only bring ducal wrath upon churchmen who had neither married the couple nor had power to separate them, since nothing would bring the duke to part with his wife. Persuaded by this practical argument, Pope Nicholas II agreed to a dispensation, requiring the construction of the two monasteries rather as a condition of the dispensation than as a penance for an offence.[43]

Serious doubts arise about the twelfth-century accounts of the marriage problem, as about Lanfranc's having played a leading part in resolving it.[44] As regards the problem in general, there is no doubt about the concern of the early reform popes to publicize the rule that no one might marry another person until the seventh degree of relatedness; Pope Leo IX's canon at the council of Rheims was followed by one of Pope Nicholas II at his Lateran synod of 1059 which Pope Alexander II

---

[39] Anselme de Saint-Remy, cap. 34, pp. 252–3.
[40] William of Jumièges, 5.13, vol. 2.28–9. For a fuller discussion, see Douglas, *William*, 391–5.
[41] William of Jumièges, 7.26, vol. 2.146–9.   [42] *GR* 3.267, vol. 1.492–35.
[43] *VL* caps. 3, 4, pp. 676, 678, 684. For a still later source, see Wace, lines 4525–40, vol. 2.55–6.
[44] I am indebted to the perceptive discussion by Bates, *Normandy Before 1066*, 199–201.

renewed in 1063.⁴⁵ Alexander was energetically concerned to enforce this regulation in Italy against the less stringent principles which were based upon Roman civil law.⁴⁶ Nevertheless, in the case of kings and princes the letter of the law was by no means rigorously applied. An example is the marriage in 1043 of the Emperor Henry III (1039–56) to Agnes of Poitou. They had a great-grandparent in common, and there were, and continued to be, shrill protests from strict churchmen, especially in Lotharingia. Yet the reform popes accepted the marriage; the predominating view was that Henry and Agnes were exemplary figures in respect of both their personal and their public lives.⁴⁷ Their good reputation extended to Normandy: Abbot John of Fécamp addressed Agnes in her widowhood as someone who had been a true Christian woman throughout her life.⁴⁸

When Duke William married, it is hardly credible that the papacy, let alone Norman churchmen, should have taken a harder line than emerged in the case of the Emperor Henry III, which was recent history at the time of the council of Rheims. William of Jumièges may have presented a general opinion in writing that, upon first meeting his bride at Eu, William contracted a fully legal betrothal to her (*illam sibi despondit iure coniugali*).⁴⁹ The late and hearsay story retailed only in the *Vita Lanfranci* that a papal regularization of the marriage was postponed until 1059 is improbable, not least in the light of Pope Nicholas II's letter of early in that year to Lanfranc in which the pope described William as his friend who followed Lanfranc's advice in all things and in whom the pope had confidence (*Confido enim bene de eo*).⁵⁰ Such words do not suggest a nine-year persistence in an irregular marriage. In view of this letter, it is significant that the ducal documents associated with the abbeys of la Trinité and Saint-Étienne at Caen say not a word about their being founded either in penance for an irregular marriage or as a condition of dispensation.⁵¹ Nor does the correspondence of Alexander II about Norman matters, including his privilege of exemption for Saint-Étienne,⁵² allude to the matter. Finally, the delay after 1059 in founding Saint-Étienne, though not la Trinité, is hard to explain if the rectification of the duke's marriage were involved. All in all, it is highly questionable whether the marriage remained in any way a problem after it was contracted in 1050/1.

Nor is Lanfranc's part at any stage in dealing with the matter likely to have been a significant one. It is far from certain that he was present at the council of Rheims,

---

⁴⁵ cap. 11, Schieffer, *Die Entstehung*, 222–3.
⁴⁶ *Epp.* 92, 113, 221, *PL* 146.1374–83, 1402–3, 1406.
⁴⁷ For the marriage and for criticism of it, see Steindorff, *Jahrbücher*, 1.187–93; also *De ordinando pontifice*, lines 262–5, in: Frauenknecht, *Der Traktat*, 94. The rapid resolution by Pope Gregory VII of the crisis which arose in 1080 after the marriage of King Alphonso VI of León-Castile to Constance of Burgundy may also be noticed: Cowdrey, *Pope Gregory VII*, 477–9.
⁴⁸ Letter to Empress Agnes: Leclercq and Bonnes, *Un Maître*, 211–17, esp. cap. 2, p. 212.
⁴⁹ As n. 17.   ⁵⁰ Southern, *Saint Anselm: A Portrait*, 32–3.
⁵¹ Musset, 'Les Actes'; see esp. the confirmation of the possessions of la Trinité at its consecration (18 June 1066) in which William referred to Matilda as his *honestissima coniunx*: no. 2, pp. 52–7, and his confirmation of the possessions of Saint-Étienne: no. 4, pp. 59–65 = *Regesta WI*, no. 45, pp. 215–19.
⁵² *Ep.* 57, *PL* 146.1339–41. Pope Gregory VII's opaque phrase in a letter to William I in 1074: 'Privilegium vero sancti Stephani, de quo mandasti, animę tuę salus est', does not appear to be specifically a reference to the marriage issue: *Reg.* 1.70, p. 102.

where it was certainly at issue.[53] Even if he was, his subsequent travels with Pope Leo IX tell against his having represented ducal interests; had he done so, he would surely have at once reported back to the duke in Normandy. In fact, one or more of the five Norman bishops who were present would have carried more weight on the duke's behalf, and Bishop Geoffrey of Coutances's presence in Rome early in 1050 suggests him as a more likely intermediary than Lanfranc for the transmission of a papal ruling.[54] If Lanfranc were himself at Rome in 1059,[55] the unsupported evidence of the *Vita Lanfranci* is insufficient to establish that he was then involved in negotiations about the marriage which are rendered unlikely by the pope's earlier letter to him. It must be concluded that it is far from established that Lanfranc had any part in business concerning the duke's marriage.

Hard evidence for Lanfranc's involvement in ducal business while he was prior of Bec is, in fact, very meagre indeed. Apart from his association with Archbishop Maurilius,[56] the principal support for the assertions of William of Poitiers and the *Vita Lanfranci* that he was the duke's counsellor is Pope Nicholas II's letter. According to it, the duke already made Lanfranc a regular and trusted adviser in all things in the course of counsel and association, which the pope wished to continue for the benefit of the clergy and the savage people of the duchy.[57]

As abbot of Saint-Étienne at Caen, Lanfranc gained rather more prominence in the affairs of the duchy. In 1066 he played no discernible part in the duke's preparations for the invasion of England, despite his standing with Pope Alexander II.[58] But when Archbishop Maurilius of Rouen died in the summer of 1067, according to the *Vita Lanfranci* the entire clergy and people of the city wished to elect Lanfranc to succeed him; nevertheless, having only reluctantly accepted the office of abbot, Lanfranc strenuously and effectively resisted. Still according to the *Vita*, when the duke heard of this he decided upon the translation of Bishop John of Avranches. Because such a translation canonically required papal sanction,[59] William dispatched Lanfranc to Rome in order to secure it; since he desired to be serviceable to the churches (*sicut ecclesiis cupiebat esse consultum*), Lanfranc responded with alacrity and brought back from Rome both Pope Alexander II's permission and the archbishop's *pallium*.[60] Alexander's letter to John of Avranches discloses that the papal legate to Normandy, Bishop Ermenfrid of Sion, was associated with Lanfranc in his mission to the pope who, when signifying his willing permission, noted that John had been promoted by the duke's choice (*ex electione principis*).[61] Since the duke was in Normandy when Maurilius died, he must certainly have been more

---

[53] See below, pp. 39–40.   [54] See above, p. 31.   [55] See below, p. 42.
[56] See above, pp. 17, 21.   [57] As n. 50.
[58] The absence of Lanfranc's name from the list of those attending the consecration in June 1066 of the abbey of la Trinité at Caen suggests that Lanfranc may have been sick during this summer: Musset, 'Les Actes', no. 2, p. 57.
[59] It did so the more pressingly because Archbishop Mauger's council of Rouen c.1045 had legislated against the translation of bishops from see to see: canon 3, Bessin, *Concilia*, 40–2.
[60] *VL* cap. 5, p. 682; cf. *Acta archiep. Roth.*, col. 279–80; Orderic Vitalis, 4, vol. 2.200–1.
[61] Alexander II, *Ep.* 56, *PL* 146.1339. Alexander committed more secret instructions to be transmitted verbally by his envoys—presumably Ermenfrid and Lanfranc.

concerned about the succession to the see than the *Vita Lanfranci* implies; possibly he resisted the local desire at Rouen that Lanfranc should succeed in order to reserve him for office in England, and possibly he did not wish him so soon to vacate his abbacy at Caen.

At all events, William returned to England in December 1067 and Lanfranc did not again meet him until he had been appointed archbishop of Canterbury. In the meantime there is no record of his activities in Normandy, although he may well have been left with such a duty of oversight as is implied by William of Poitiers's imagery of Saint-Étienne as a watchtower in the duchy.[62] This is reminiscent of Lanfranc's own comment upon St Paul's exhortation that prayer should be offered for kings and for all in high position, 'that we may lead a quiet and tranquil life in all religion and chastity' (1 Tim. 2: 1–2). It is eloquent of his support for a strong prince both as a source of peace and order and as a guarantor of moral righteousness:

Ut quietam: in the peace of princes are preserved the quiet and good estate (*regimen*) of churches; for in wars and discords their tranquillity is shattered, religion grows cold, deference (*distinctio*) is destroyed, and where deference is destroyed chastity of living (*morum castitas*) is violated.[63]

This comment makes plain both Lanfranc's commitment to ducal authority as exercised in Normandy and his preparedness to be its active and loyal proponent.

It must, however, be concluded that the evidence for Lanfranc's activity on behalf of the duke and the duchy while he was at Bec and at Caen is scanty. But the contemporary and later testimony to it is considerable, and William would not have chosen him to be archbishop of Canterbury had not his loyalty and his competence been established by thorough testing.

3.2 LANFRANC AND THE REFORM PAPACY

There can be no doubt that both contemporary and later sources understate Lanfranc's contacts and association during his monastic years with the reform papacy which was ushered in by the Emperor Henry III's intervention at Rome in 1046 and especially by the energetic pontificate of Leo IX (1049–54).[64] In particular, they largely ignore Lanfranc's travels in the year or so after Leo's council of Rheims in October 1049. The duration of these travels is surprising in view of Lanfranc's position at Bec as prior and teacher. The Bec historical tradition passed over them in complete silence.

It is uncertain whether or not Lanfranc was present at Rheims for the whole or part of Leo's council. The problem turns upon a letter that Berengar of Tours

---

[62] As n. 22. If the *Carmen de Hastingae proelio* is indeed by Bishop Guy of Amiens and is to be dated before Lanfranc went to Canterbury, and if it is dedicated to him while abbot of Caen, it suggests that Lanfranc was perceived to favour the military conquest of England in 1066: *The Carmen*, lines 1–14, pp. 2–3.
[63] Lanfranc, *In omnes*, col. 349B. [64] See Cowdrey, *Pope Gregory VII*, 21–6.

sent to him in Normandy just before or just after it met.⁶⁵ In view of its manifold importance and difficult Latin, a full translation may be given:⁶⁶

Berengar to brother Lanfranc.
There has reached me, brother Lanfranc, a certain report from Ingelrannus of Chartres with regard to which I should not neglect to issue a warning to you as a dear friend (*ammonere dilectionem tuam*). Now, it is this: that the propositions (*sententias*) of John the Scot concerning the sacrament of the altar in which he differs from Paschasius, with whom you associate yourself, are displeasing to you—indeed, you have held them to be heretical.⁶⁷ Therefore in this matter, if it be so, brother, you have acted unworthily of the intelligence that God has conferred upon you in no negligible degree by pronouncing too hasty a judgement. For you are not yet sufficiently well versed in divine scripture (*divina scriptura*)⁶⁸ nor have you much conferred with those more attentive than yourself. And now, therefore, brother, being somewhat unversed myself in this scripture, I should like just to hear about this (*tantum audire de eo*), if an opportunity should arise for us, there being gathered together whomever you may wish as competent judges or as hearers. For so long as this does not happen, do not regard with contempt what I say: if you hold to be a heretic John, whose pronouncements about the eucharist we approve, there must also be held by you to be heretical Ambrose, Jerome, and Augustine, not to mention others.

We earnestly desire in the Lord that you will enjoy good health and think with sober judgement (*sobrium esse*).⁶⁹

When writing more than ten years later to Berengar about this letter in the context of a discussion of Leo IX's Lateran synod of 1050, Lanfranc enlarged upon its effect on his own fortunes before it came to be read out to that synod.⁷⁰ Berengar's messenger, he wrote, had not found Lanfranc in Normandy when he arrived, but he showed it to 'certain clerks' unnamed, evidently in the duchy. Having read it, they were shocked by its contents, and debate ensued which placed Lanfranc under suspicion of being compromised by his favouring Berengar and countenancing some of his opinions. A clerk of Rheims took the letter to Rome, where it was read to the Lateran synod in the first week of May 1050.

Lanfranc's presence at the council of Rheims is suggested, but far from proved, by the facts, first, that he was not in Normandy when Berengar's letter arrived

---

⁶⁵ The best text is in Huygens, 'Textes latins', 456, with discussion by Huygens and Montclos, 451–9; see also Montclos, *Lanfranc et Bérenger*, 53–6; id., 'Lanfranc et Bérenger', 298–9.

⁶⁶ In the light of Montclos's discussions (as n. 65), this translation differs somewhat from that of Gibson, *Lanfranc*, 66.

⁶⁷ Here and elsewhere Berengar referred to 'John the Scot' in error for the ninth-century monk of Corbie, Ratramnus; Paschasius is Ratramnus's contemporary at Corbie, Paschasius Radbertus: see Gibson, *Lanfranc*, 74–6.

⁶⁸ It is clear from the letter that the reference is not limited to biblical studies but includes, and indeed mainly envisages, the Christian fathers.

⁶⁹ Cf. Rom. 12: 3.

⁷⁰ *DCSD* cap. 4, col. 413 = Huygens, 'Bérenger', 375–6; id., 'Textes latins', 451–9, text at p. 456. It appears at first sight improbable that the letter read at Rome was indeed Berengar's extant letter to Lanfranc, in which a doctrinal distance between them is apparent. But other evidence, including Berengar's own testimony, makes the identification virtually certain: Letter of Ascelin of Chartres to Berengar, in: Huygens, 'Les Lettres', no. 1, lines 15–21, p. 19; Berengar, *DSC* 1.259–60, 300–4, pp. 42, 44. By 'John the Scot', Berengar meant Ratramnus of Corbie: see below, p. 60.

there; second, that a clerk of Rheims took the letter to Rome; and third, that on 14 November Lanfranc was by his own later testimony in Leo IX's entourage at Remiremont, in the Vosges, when the pope consecrated the church of Saint-Pierre-les-Dames.[71] In any case, for most of the winter and early spring of 1049–50, Lanfranc was in company with Leo. The pope had left Rheims on 5 October and travelled through Verdun and Metz to Mainz.[72] There, on 19 October, in the presence of the Emperor Henry III, he held a reforming synod attended by forty bishops which strongly condemned the simoniacal heresy.[73] Leo returned by way of Verdun to Alsace; on 14 November Lanfranc was certainly present when he dedicated the church at Remiremont.[74] Thence, Leo's itinerary took him to Reichenau and onwards to Bavaria; he kept Christmas at Verona. The spring of 1050 saw him travelling widely in South Italy; in April he held a synod at Siponto. He was back in Rome to hold a synod on 29 April in advance of the larger assembly in the Lateran basilica, which began on 2 May and which Lanfranc attended. On Lanfranc's own testimony, Leo then called upon Lanfranc 'by his command and by his pleas (*precepto ac precibus*)' to remain with him until another synod which met at Vercelli in early September.[75] If Lanfranc indeed remained in the pope's company throughout the summer, his travels will have included Benevento, Florence, and Fiesole.

Except for the dedication at Remiremont and for the Roman synod of May 1050, it is impossible to know for just how long Lanfranc attended Leo IX between the councils of Rheims in October 1049 and Vercelli in September 1050. His attendance may have been continuous, although there would be time for him to have returned briefly to Normandy between the established points of Remiremont and Rome. However, it is clear that, at least in the spring and summer of 1050, he spent a considerable time in Leo's proximity and thus had the opportunity of witnessing at first hand an outstanding reforming pope in action. The reasons for Lanfranc's presence with him are not clear. They are unlikely to have had much, if anything, to do with the marriage of the duke of Normandy.[76] At least from the time that Berengar's letter reached Lanfranc and was publicly read out at Rome, the eucharistic controversy was prominent amongst Lanfranc's concerns.[77] But Leo's wish that, after May 1050, Lanfranc should remain with him may indicate that he was already marked out as one of the men of religion and ability from north of the Alps whom Leo wished to join him in service at the apostolic see itself.

---

[71] Lanfranc, *Letters*, no. 14, pp. 84–5. Lanfranc's memory of Leo's pontifical vesture at Remiremont rather than at the more important dedication of Saint-Remi at Rheims or at other, also earlier dedications at Verdun and Metz, casts some, but not decisive, doubt upon his presence at Rheims.

[72] Leo's travels in 1049–50 are mostly recorded in JL 1 532–9.

[73] *MGH Const.* 1. 97–100, no. 51.   [74] As n. 71.

[75] As n. 70. From Vercelli, Leo travelled by way of Agaune, Romans, Besançon, and Langres to his Lotharingian see of Toul, where he was by 21 Oct. It is possible that Lanfranc accompanied him for some part of the journey as he returned to Normandy.

[76] See above, pp. 34–7.

[77] As n. 70. It is not clear whether Berengar was among the *novi haeretici* who *in Gallicanis partibus emerserant* and whom Leo IX excommunicated at Rheims: Anselme de Saint-Remy, cap. 34, canon 13, pp. 252–3. Since neither Berengar nor any other author refers to his excommunication at Rheims, it is, however, unlikely that he was included.

It may, therefore, be suggested that Lanfranc's travels had a threefold importance. First, whether by direct observation or whether by moving in circles in which the crowded events of Leo's pontificate were much discussed, Lanfranc became acquainted with the energy, objectives, and methods of Leo's reforming zeal and with the ideas that directed and commended it, including those about the relations of *sacerdotium* and *regnum*. At the council of Rheims Leo laid emphasis upon papal authority in theory and practice, and he pursued reforming purposes which were especially directed to the French church of which the province of Rouen formed a part. At Mainz he was associated with the godly Emperor Henry III in presiding over a reforming council of the German church. Lanfranc may have recalled the reforming collaboration of Pope Benedict VIII and the Emperor Henry II in the Lombardy of his earliest years.[78] There was manifestly a rising tide of reform in which the collaboration of churchmen and kings was a decisive force.

Second, Lanfranc had opportunities for acquaintance with men who would be prominent for the rest of his lifetime but who now belonged to the circle of churchmen, drawn from many parts of Europe, whom Leo gathered about himself.[79] Those who were to be particularly significant were Cardinal-bishop Humbert of Silva Candida, the cardinal-priest Hugh Candidus of S. Clemente, and the Roman monk and clerk Hildebrand. Humbert appears to have been by birth a Burgundian, who became a monk in the Lotharingian abbey of Moyenmoutier. Leo IX had in 1049 brought him to Rome and had ordained him to be archbishop of the as yet unconquered Sicily. He was present at the Lateran synod of 1050. Soon after he became cardinal-bishop of Silva Candida, where he remained until his death in 1061. He was a reforming enthusiast with uncompromising and extreme views about papal authority and the need to extirpate simony which, in the latter years of his life, he developed in his *Libri tres adversus simoniacos*.[80] Hugh Candidus appears to have attracted Leo's notice during his visit in 1049 to Remiremont, where Hugh was a clerk. In the course of a long, eventful, and tumultuous career, he at first supported the election to the papacy in 1073 of Archdeacon Hildebrand (Gregory VII), but he quickly became virulently hostile to him; in 1080 he was to the fore in the German king Henry IV's choice of Archbishop Guibert of Ravenna as anti-pope; from 1084 he was a staunch adherent of Guibert as the anti-pope Clement III.[81] Hildebrand himself became well known to Lanfranc at this time. Early in 1049 Leo IX had brought him back to Rome from the exile in Germany into which he had gone in 1046 with his early patron Pope Gregory VI. In 1079 Gregory VII almost certainly looked back to an association with Lanfranc in 1050 when, in urging him at last to pay an *ad limina* visit, he appealed to the recollection of their former love (*prisci amoris memoria*).[82]

Third, Lanfranc's prolonged association with Leo IX seems to have impressed upon papal circles Lanfranc's capabilities and potential for service, whether performed at Rome or in the domains of the duke of Normandy. This was made

---

[78] Above, pp. 2–3.   [79] As n. 71.   [80] For Humbert, see Hüls, *Kardinäle*, 131–4.
[81] For Hugh Candidus, see ibid. 111, 158–60.   [82] *Reg.* 6.30, p. 443.

especially apparent when the chance arrival of Berengar's letter before the Roman synod of 1050 provided an occasion at Rome and then at Vercelli for him to rebut Berengar's position about the eucharist. The result was that Lanfranc left behind at Rome a high estimate of his qualities as scholar, teacher, and public figure.

Such an estimate was apparent in the mind of the next pope whose surviving correspondence includes a reference to Lanfranc. Evidently at the outset of his pontificate in the early months of 1059, Nicholas II began a letter to Lanfranc by saying how much he desired his presence at Rome and the benefit of his counsels, because he had heard how useful Lanfranc was in Roman and papal business (*quem in Romanis et apostolicis servitiis satis opportunum audivimus*). He acknowledged that an early visit to Rome by Lanfranc might not be possible (*quia tam facile nunc forsan fieri non potest*). But in sending some imperial and papal chaplains to Lanfranc at Bec for education in dialectic and rhetoric, he hoped that the benefit to the Roman church of Lanfranc's being there might foreshadow that of his coming to Rome; he hoped that very soon (*quam cito*) he might see Lanfranc there with the chaplains.[83] Nicholas's expectations of service from Lanfranc and his wish soon to have him at Rome for a longer or shorter time are apparent.

No less certainly, however, Nicholas did not summon Lanfranc to the Lateran synod that he purposed to hold in April 1059, nor did he expect him to come. It cannot be ruled out that Lanfranc then travelled to Rome in connection with the duke of Normandy's marriage, but the unsupported hearsay evidence of the *Vita Lanfranci* is not sufficient to establish that he did so.[84] It is more likely that, if Lanfranc attended, he did so as his own response to Nicholas's letter and perhaps to oral reports that came with it about Nicholas's intention to deal with Berengar of Tours. His own dealings over Berengar in 1050 at Rome, Vercelli, and Brionne may have persuaded him that he must look to his own position in so august a forum as a Roman synod. The evidence for the synod, including that in the subsequent writings of Berengar and Lanfranc, may be scanned in vain for any clear evidence for or against Lanfranc's presence, although the clarity of his own account of what happened suggests that he was a first-hand witness.[85] Although by no means certain, his presence at Rome in 1059 is perhaps, on balance, more likely than not.

---

[83] Southern, *Saint Anselm: A Portrait*, 32.   [84] See above, p. 37.

[85] Scholarly opinion is divided about whether or not Lanfranc was present. Southern, *Saint Anselm: A Portrait*, 25–8, strongly defends his presence, but partly upon the grounds of his settling then the problem of the ducal marriage. It is denied by Montclos, *Lanfranc et Bérenger*, 43–4; Gibson, *Lanfranc*, 69–70, and Bates, *Normandy Before 1066*, 201. In face of the express statement in the widely publicized profession of faith which was prepared by Cardinal Humbert for Berengar to make at the synod that the latter signed it, *Lecto et perlecto sponte subscripsi*: DCSD cap. 2, col. 411 = Huygens, 'Bérenger', 373, Berengar's protestation to Lanfranc that he had not signed it must be treated with caution. Berengar was concerned to argue that *ego in corde errori non adquievi* and that such adherence as he gave was made under duress. His express denial that he had signed it, for he had only taken it into his hands, is placed in question by his own implausible explanation: *nam ut de consensu pronunciarem meo nullus exegit*. His account is further weakened by his no less implausible comment that he took the profession into his hands only from fear of imminent death. Lanfranc's confident and circumstantial reply suggests, but does not establish, that he was a witness of the events described: RCL 1.10–18, p. 35; DCSD cap. 2, cols. 410–12 = Huygens, 'Bérenger', 372–5, omitting the interpolated material about the Lateran synod of 1079; see also caps. 15–16, cols. 414–16, 426.

Under Pope Alexander II, Lanfranc certainly visited Rome in 1067 in order to secure on the duke of Normandy's behalf that the translation to Rouen of Bishop John of Avranches took place with the papal leave that canonical propriety demanded.[86] When Alexander asked Lanfranc to receive his own nephew as a pupil, he expressed admiration for Lanfranc's learning in both secular and sacred studies, citing with regard to him the biblical text 'Blessed is the man who finds wisdom and who is rich in prudence' (Prov. 3: 13).[87] Such an estimate of Lanfranc on the pope's part prepared the way for the harmony of outlook and purpose that was to characterize their dealings when Lanfranc became archbishop of Canterbury.[88]

Such harmony was further fostered by the strong and positive, if also traditional and conventional, view of the Roman see and of its authority that Lanfranc manifested in his writings of this period. He prefaced his commentary on the Pauline epistles by observing that in the Bible Romans 'is put first on account of the honour of the city in which God has willed the primacy of the entire holy church to be'.[89] His reply to Berengar's eucharistic teaching in his *Liber de corpore et sanguine Domini*, completed during his years at Caen, was not undertaken with the knowledge of the apostolic see, still less upon Roman prompting.[90] But he strongly insisted upon the authority of the Roman see as the custodian and guarantor of Christian truth. According to the true tradition of the church, everyone who was at odds with the Roman and universal church about a matter of faith was heretical. When Berengar stigmatized the Roman church as 'a church of the malignant, a council of vanities, and the seat of Satan', Lanfranc rejoined that others, however far they had erred from the faith, had never uttered such words:

> They have splendidly honoured the see of St Peter the apostle and have not presumed to speak or to write any such blasphemy against it. . . . Christ himself spoke of it in the gospels [Lanfranc cited Matt. 16: 18–19]; even if these words are held to have been spoken of the pastors of the church as some catholics expounded them, yet the sacred canons and the decrees of the pontiffs testify that they are especially to be understood of the Roman church.[91]

Lanfranc wrote with deep respect of the individual reform popes. Leo IX was *sanctus Leo*; Victor II (1055–7) was *felicis memoriae papa*; Nicholas II was *beatae memoriae . . . totius christianae nominis summus pontifex*.[92] His regard for Cardinal Humbert, the principal opponent of Berengar at the Roman synod of 1059, was warmly expressed. Humbert was *venerabilis*, and Lanfranc indignantly rebutted Berengar's derogatory assertion that he was a Burgundian (Berengar seemed to imply that God could have no servants in Burgundy!), rather than a Lotharingian. In his contest with Berengar, Humbert was David to Berengar's Goliath; as the true David, he lived humbly, taught humbly, was a member of the church, and fought for the church, taking for himself the shield of faith and the sword of the Spirit,

---

[86] See above, p. 37. [87] *Ep.* 70, *PL* 146. 1353.
[88] See below, pp. 88–90. [89] For the best text, see Gibson, 'Lanfranc's "Commentary"', 108.
[90] See below, pp. 64–5. [91] *DCSD* caps. 2, 16, cols. 409–12, 426.
[92] Leo IX: *DCSD* caps. 2, 4, cols. 409–12, 418 = Huygens, 'Bérenger', 375–6. Victor II: *DCSD* cap. 4, col. 413 = Huygens, 'Bérenger', 376. Nicholas II: *DCSD* cap. 1, col. 409 = Huygens, 'Bérenger', 371.

which is the word of God. Lanfranc extended his eulogy to embrace wider aspects of Humbert's ten years as a cardinal-bishop:

When established in this office he so lived and taught that not the slightest breath of suspicion arose about his faith and doctrine. Witness to this is borne by practically all of Latin Christendom, which, given the pre-eminence of the apostolic see in whose councils and counsels he was always present and predominant, could not fail to recognize them.[93]

Both for what he was and for what he taught, Cardinal Humbert must be accounted a major and a direct influence upon Lanfranc during his middle years.

Lanfranc's attachment to the early reform papacy is also illustrated by the preservation of documents that emanated from it in Lanfranc's own master copy, now Cambridge, Trinity College, MS B 16 44 (405), of the canonical collection that he caused to be brought from Bec to England and there disseminated widely.[94] Especially noteworthy is the copying in full of the encyclical letter *Vigilantia universalis*, in which Nicholas II gave wide publicity to the decrees of his synod of 1059. After proclaiming the universality of the papal duty of watchfulness over the church and summarizing the papal election decree of 1059, Nicholas made a comprehensive statement of the requirements of the reform papacy for strict clerical chastity and the living of a common life by the clergy, the surrender by the laity of tithes and other church revenues, the elimination of simony, and the imposition upon the laity of a strict marriage discipline which included the prohibition of marriages within the seventh degree of relationship. After the encyclical letter, there was copied a further series of canons against simony and concerning papal elections, and then a full text of Berengar's oath at the synod of 1059 as drafted by Cardinal Humbert. Since Nicholas II was at pains to secure the wide dissemination of these documents,[95] Lanfranc's possession of them does nothing to prove his presence at the synod, although he may have owed his familiarity with them to his having witnessed their promulgation. But the store that he evidently set by them establishes his keen awareness of and commitment to the purposes and programme of the early reform popes.

From the popes' side, there is some suggestion that there was a hope that Lanfranc might be persuaded to be added to the numerous clerks from distant churches who, like Humbert, became attached to the papal household or took office in the Roman church. When noticing that a number of churches sought to recruit Lanfranc as abbot or bishop, the *Vita Lanfranci* commented that even Rome, the head of the Christian world, sought to secure his service there by letters and that it

---

[93] For Humbert, see *DCSD* caps. 2, cols. 409–12 = Huygens, 'Bérenger', 372–5, 3, 16, cols. 412–13. For Lanfranc's echoing in the *DCSD* of Humbert's view of the authority of the Roman church, see above, p. 000.

[94] Items appear in the MS on the following pages: 1. p. 209, Nicholas II's encyclical *Vigilantia universalis*: Schieffer, *Die Entstehung des päpstlichen Investiturverbots*, 208–25. 2. pp. 209–10, canons on simony and papal elections, probably of 1059: *MGH Conc.* 1.549–54, no. 386, canons 1–4 (for the date, see Schieffer, 64–6). 3. p. 210, Berengar's oath of 1059: *DCSD* cap. 2, cols. 410–11 = Huygens, 'Bérenger', 372–3. 4. p. 211, Nicholas II's letter to Lanfranc: Southern, *Saint Anselm: A Portrait*, 32–3. 5. p. 407, Alexander II's letter to Lanfranc: *Ep.* 70, *PL* 146.1353.

[95] For the dissemination of Berengar's oath, see *DCSD* cap. 2, cols. 411–12 = Huygens, 'Bérenger', 374.

did so both by entreaty and by coercion; the latter phrase suggests direct negotiation while Lanfranc was visiting Italy.[96] No evidence survives for an invitation to assume a specific office, but his long stay with Pope Leo IX, and Pope Alexander II's wish when he visited Rome as archbishop in 1071 that he might return in the following year and spend three months or longer in the Lateran palace as the pope's guest, indicate the value that the popes set upon his counsel.[97]

All the evidence suggests that Lanfranc was to the core a man of the early reform papacy from Leo IX to Alexander II. He knew and was known by its leading Roman personalities, sharing their principles and purposes. It was agreeable to Duke William of Normandy that this should have been so.

[96] *VL* cap. 5, pp. 681–2, followed by Orderic Vitalis, 4, vol. 2.252–3.
[97] Lanfranc, *Letters*, no. 1, pp. 32–5.

4

Scholar and Teacher

A consideration of Lanfranc as scholar and teacher must inevitably be the subject of a separate chapter. His intellectual concerns extended over his lifetime, but they also underwent changes so far as his priorities were concerned. He came to Normandy as a teacher of the liberal arts, and the financial needs of the abbey of Bec led him to continue as such during his long service as its prior. Nevertheless, as he grew to maturity in the life of a monk, he wished to devote himself increasingly to the study of scripture as an aspect of monastic discipline; his determination led, in particular, to his commentaries on the Psalms and the Pauline epistles.[1] But even as abbot of Saint-Étienne at Caen, he continued to give instruction in both sacred and secular subjects.[2] As archbishop of Canterbury, Lanfranc was able to disclaim concern with secular letters on the grounds that they were not befitting an episcopal vocation; they were to be renounced by one who had undertaken the pastoral care.[3] As for sacred study (*lectio*), the *Vita Lanfranci* recalled that he applied himself to it not only before he became archbishop but also, so far as he could, afterwards; he was especially concerned with the correction of the text of biblical and patristic writers as well as of monastic service-books; he directed to this task the labours of his entourage as well as his own.[4] There was thus a continuity in Lanfranc's scholarly work and instruction that enforces its study across all stages of his career.

At the same time, especially during the critical years of Lanfranc's monastic experience at Bec, his immediate circumstances and role at particular junctures profoundly affected the subjects and the character of his scholarly work. Owing to the accident of Lanfranc's presence there and to its consequence in causing his pupil Anselm to join him as a monk, the Bec of Abbot Herluin with its high standard of monastic observance has been described as the last of the great monastic schools.[5] Lanfranc there encountered, came to terms with, and absorbed the discipline and practice of the Rule of St Benedict as currently understood. Alongside the continuity of Lanfranc's scholarly concerns during his lifetime must be set the immediate background against which each part of his work was performed. Much will depend upon how this balance is made. To give an example, a commentary which is probably based on Lanfranc's own notes upon the penitential Psalm 50 (the *Miserere*) is patient of interpretation in the light of one view of Lanfranc's long-term career as

---

[1] See esp. the evidence of Abbot Williram of Ebersberg: 'The "Expositio"', ed. Bartelmez, Pref. p. 1; and Pope Alexander II's letter to Lanfranc: Southern, *Saint Anselm: A Portrait*, 32.
[2] Lanfranc, *Letters*, no. 1, pp. 32–3.   [3] Ibid., no. 49, pp. 158–61.
[4] *VL* cap. 15, p. 711. Lanfranc sent from Canterbury to Bec for his commentaries on the Pauline epistles: Anselm, *Ep.* 66, vol. 3.186–7.
[5] Smalley, *The Study*, 77.

revealing a logical and legalistic cast of mind; it breathes the atmosphere of the law-court and is the statement of a knowledgeable but contrite prisoner-at-the-bar. But a very different interpretation of the commentary, with its concern for washing and cleansing from both actual and original sin and with its plea, 'I do not grieve momentarily for my sin but constantly', is suggested by Lanfranc's reputation at Bec as an exemplary monk who was known for his grace of tears.[6] A true reading of Lanfranc's words may depend rather upon their monastic than upon their scholarly, let alone their forensic, significance.

4.1 THE LIBERAL ARTS

According to the eulogy that Orderic Vitalis pronounced upon Lanfranc's scholarly eminence, his aptitudes and achievements would have won admiration from Herodian in grammar, from Aristotle in dialectic, and from Cicero in rhetoric.[7] These were the subjects of the *trivium* which constituted the first part of the academic programme which had come down from late antiquity: grammar was the study of the meaning and use of words; dialectic, or logic, that of discussion and disputation; and rhetoric that of eloquence, argument, and persuasion. They led up to the four subjects of the *quadrivium*: geometry, arithmetic, astronomy, and music; but neither by reputation nor upon the evidence of his writings was Lanfranc more than occasionally concerned with these as academic disciplines.[8] So far as the *trivium* is concerned, during the early medieval period there was no clear delineation between its subjects and the ways in which they were studied and taught. A figure of Lanfranc's standing and reputation needed to be skilled in all three and to draw upon them all in the course of his instruction. Nevertheless, he was likely to be, and to be recognized as being, pre-eminently concerned with one of the three subjects.

Throughout the eleventh century the subjects of the *trivium* were undergoing a process of rediscovery and exploration which would reach its clarification and consolidation only in the twelfth century with the work of Peter Abelard and his generation.[9] A result of this was the partial or complete loss of many of the eleventh-century sources as they were superseded by better-informed and more sophisticated ones. Thus, the eleventh century saw the gradual calling into service of ancient authorities and the methods of inquiry and argument that they enshrined. Some

---

[6] For a translation of the commentary from London, BL MS Royal, 3. C. v, fo. 104, and for discussion, see Smalley, *The Study*, 71–2; for the original Latin, see eadem, 'La Glossa ordinaria', 576–7.

[7] Orderic Vitalis, 4, vol. 2.250–1.

[8] Near the end of Lanfranc's life (1088/9), the anti-pope Clement III eulogized him in excessive terms which included the comment that he had revived the *trivium* and the *quadrivium*: Liebermann, 'Lanfranc and the Antipope', p. 331, no. 3; the later *Chronicon Beccense* described him as 'in septem liberalibus artibus mirabiliter eruditus': col. 643. But there is no indication that his musical knowledge and skill exceeded what was basically necessary for a monastic superior: see Borghi and Tibaldi, 'Lanfranco "musicus"'.

[9] For a good general survey of developments, see Marenbon, *Early Medieval Philosophy*, esp. 80–94, and specifically as a background to Lanfranc, Gibson, *Lanfranc*, 39–62.

examples may now be given which especially bear upon Lanfranc's work. First, in logic, in the early eleventh century much attention was still given to the pseudo-Augustinian *De decem categoriis*;[10] but from the late tenth century it was gradually superseded by the so-called *Logica vetus*, the sources for which were principally the Latin translations of Aristotle's works which had been made by Boethius (c.480–524), at first especially by the *Categories* (*Praedicamenta*) and the *De interpretatione* (*Periermeneias*). Boethius also handed down commentaries on ancient writings which included Cicero's *Topica*, and his own writings on logic included his *De syllogismis categoricis* and his *De hypotheticis syllogismis*, in which he developed Aristotelian thought in a direction indicated by the Stoics.[11] Second, the eleventh century witnessed a revival of the work of the sixth-century grammarian Priscian, whose *Institutiones grammaticae* was both the subject of glosses on particular passages and of an anonymous *Glosule* in more continuous and discursive form.[12] Third, in rhetoric there was gathering interest in old and new commentaries on texts such as Cicero's *De inventione* and the *Rhetorica ad Herennium*. It is against such a background of gradual clarification and advance that Lanfranc's teaching of the arts must be considered.

So far as Lanfranc's posthumous reputation is concerned, as Orderic Vitalis claimed[13] he was regarded as having been skilled in the subjects of the *trivium*; but it was also recognized that he was pre-eminently so in dialectic. Thus, for William of Malmesbury, he revived in Normandy the study of the liberal arts but it was with dialectic that the open school that he held reverberated.[14] Sigebert of Gembloux labelled him simply as *dialecticus*, noticing that whenever opportunity presented itself in his exposition of the Pauline epistles he used the technical skills of dialectic to resolve problems.[15] In the Bec tradition, too, his intellectual achievement was recorded in terms of his having restored and renewed the art of dialectic.[16] This emphasis accords well with such testimonies as survive from his own time. Pope Nicholas II recognized him as an accomplished teacher of dialectic and rhetoric,[17] while for Abbot Williram of Ebersberg, before Lanfranc turned, in so far as time allowed, to scriptural studies he stood out as *maxime valentem in dialectica*.[18]

Lanfranc may have written two items on dialectic that are now lost. An eleventh-century library catalogue from the monastery of St Aper at Toul included a *Lantfrancus de dialectica*,[19] and an unidentified library in Saxony possessed a *Questiones Lantfranci* which, since it is listed amongst dialectical material, seems to have been

---

[10] For this work, see *Aristoteles Latinus*, 1.5: *Categoriae et Praedicamenta*, pp. lxxvii–lxxxiv, 129–75.

[11] For Boethius's work and influence, see esp. Gibson (ed.), *Boethius*.

[12] See esp. Hunt, 'Studies on Priscian'. [13] As n. 7.

[14] *GP* 1.24, 2.74, pp. 37–8, 150; cf. *GR* 3.267.2, vol. 1.492–3.

[15] Sigebert of Gembloux, *DVI* pp. 97–8, no. 156: 'Paulum apostolum exposuit et ubicumque locorum oportunitas occurrit secundum leges dialecticae proponit, assumit, concludit.'

[16] *MSN* cap. 7, p. 409: 'ipsa ars, scilicet dialectica, per eum reparata sit et renovata.' Before leaving Italy, Lanfranc 'plures ... scholas tenuerat de grammatica et rhetorica et maxime dialectica.'

[17] Southern, *Saint Anselm: A Portrait*, 32.   [18] Bartelmez, The '*Expositio*', Pref. p. 1.

[19] Becker, *Catalogus*, no. 68, item 250, p. 154.

concerned with the same subject.[20] No other details emerge, and further direct evidence about Lanfranc's teaching in the arts is provided only by a small handful of passing references in later sources, not all in terms of compliment. Thus, in rhetoric, an early twelfth-century commentary on Cicero's *De inventione* summarily dismissed as unreliable Lanfranc's appraisal of ways in which an argument might be faulted: 'non est autem fides habenda verbis illis.'[21] Lanfranc's handling of a passage from the *Ad Herennium* emerges in a similarly unfavourable light. He was reported as having commented upon a citation from an unidentified poet of a difficult speech in which Ajax at Troy claimed to wear the armour of Hector. Confused by a scribal error in the text before him by which the letter *d* was opened up as *cl*, Lanfranc interpreted the noun *dictio* (saying) as the personal name Clito; he compounded the error by reading the verb *studeamus* (we should wish) and the place-name *Pergamum* (Troy) as the names of two more soldiers, Studemus and Pergamus, while he omitted words that did not support this interpretation of the text.[22] Such crudities, if Lanfranc's, were those of a pioneer breaking fresh ground in a rapidly developing subject whose later practitioners would be slow to spare their predecessors.

Lanfranc may also be seen to have made a contribution, which has not yet been fully appraised, to commentary upon Priscian's *Institutiones*, and so to the subject of grammar. If the notes marked *L*, or *LAN*, in Harvard University Library, MS lat. 44, are attributable to Lanfranc, his work was far from inconsiderable.[23] Elsewhere, there is record of a passing comment of his that the Latin letter *v* was akin in sound to the Greek *digamma* (*F*).[24] A more substantial comment that was attributed to him concerns the status of the verb *to be*: is it different from other verbs in that it expresses the existence of its subject while they only illustrate what the subject is doing? Appealing to the principle that accidents do not exist independently but only in substances, Lanfranc argued that the verb *to be* is active in respect of substances but passive in relation to accidents.[25] In this instance, Lanfranc was getting to grips with a serious problem by taking as his starting-point a discussion by Priscian. Of Lanfranc's dialectical teaching, there are not even such crumbs of evidence outside his biblical and patristic commentaries and his discussion of the eucharist. For further light upon Lanfranc's place in the history of the arts, it is necessary to turn to their incidental use in these works.

---

[20] Ibid., no. 54, item 6, p. 138. The list is headed, 'Hi sunt libri quos bernardus proprio sumptu conscribi fecit', which is a further indication that the books in the list were chosen to represent the single subject of dialectic.

[21] Hereford Cathedral Library, MS P. I. iv, fo. 17ᵛ, cited by Gibson, *Lanfranc*, 49, n. 5.

[22] Hunt, 'Studies on Priscian', 207–8; cf. Gibson, *Lanfranc*, 49–50. The passage in question is *Ad Herennium*, 2.26.42, pp. 132–5.

[23] Gibson, *Lanfranc*, 47. For a record of a complete text, now lost, of Priscian's *Institutiones* at Christ Church, Canterbury, which was referred to as Lanfranc's, see James, *The Ancient Libraries*, 1.1, 2.289, pp. 7.53; also Gibson, *Lanfranc*, 181, n. 3.

[24] Hunt, 'Studies on Priscian', 206, n. 3; Gibson, *Lanfranc*, 47.

[25] Chartres, Bibl. mun. MS 209, fo. 86ᵛ (now destroyed); see Hunt, 'Studies on Priscian', 224; Gibson, *Lanfranc*, 47–8.

4.2 THE BIBLE AND THE CHRISTIAN FATHERS

When reviewing Lanfranc's biblical and patristic commentaries, it is convenient first to discuss the latter.[26] What survives is meagre in amount and disappointing in content. Most of Lanfranc's comments concern points of grammar. They seem to reflect a stage in his development when he was seeking to turn from the arts to sacred study and was using patristic texts as a medium for instruction in the arts while also testing the ways in which the arts might be safely and profitably used in sacred study; in this he was, perhaps, a pioneer. But about the subject-matter of his authors he had little, if anything, to say. Thus, there is substantial manuscript attestation of Lanfranc's notes upon a few passages of St Augustine's *De civitate Dei*.[27] Less well attested are some comments upon Pope Gregory the Great's *Moralia in Iob*, which Lanfranc concluded with the characteristic remark that his comments should suffice to restrain the ignorant and unskilled from incautiously corrupting Gregory's pronouncements.[28] Third, a very few notes on Cassian's *Collationes* have survived.[29] Fourth and perhaps most important, a comment by Lanfranc apparently upon St Jerome's letter 18A deals with the apparent paradox of the *ineffable* name of God. Lanfranc sought to resolve the paradox by drawing upon a passage in the Pseudo-Augustinian *De decem categoriis* where all being is classified in terms of four stages (*gradus*), the highest of which was an essence (οὐσία) which comprehends all that exists and beyond which nothing can be found or imagined;[30] the name of God can be identified with this essence that is beyond comprehension. This way of thinking seems to have impressed Lanfranc,[31] and it warns against locating him in an older world of thought before the spread of the *logica vetus* on the grounds of an indebtedness to the *De decem categoriis*.[32] For the concept of an ultimate essence as there stated looks forward to St Anselm's view of God as that than which nothing greater can be thought (*aliquid quo nihil maius cogitari possit*).[33]

During his years at Bec, Lanfranc increasingly wished to turn away from the study of the liberal arts to that of the sacred page. His attention seems to have been directed to the Psalms and to the Pauline epistles, which contemporaries designated as the work respectively of the Prophet and of the Apostle; characteristically, he concentrated upon what were generally regarded as the key texts of this subject. His method was the well-tried one of the provision of glosses—brief annotations which were interlined in an author's full text or else written in the margins. Of Lanfranc's

---

[26] See esp. Gibson, 'Lanfranc's Notes'. [27] Text and discussion in ibid. 436–41.
[28] Text and discussion in ibid. 441–6. The concluding note runs: 'Hec ideo quantum presenti volumini competere videbatur, subter annexa sunt, ne imperitorum inscientia prefatas dictiones hoc in opere inconsulte temerare presumat.'
[29] *PL* 150.443–4.
[30] Lanfranc's comment occurs in London, BL MS Sloane 1580, fo. 16ʳ; see Hunt, 'Studies on Priscian', 208, and, for a fundamental discussion, Gibson, *Lanfranc*, 41–3. For Jerome's letter, see *Epistolae*, ed. Hilberg, 84. For the discussion in the *De decem categoriis*, 3.5, see *Aristoteles Latinus*, 1.5, pp. 133–4, particularly the sentence: 'Ingenti quodam et capaci ad infinitum nomine omne quidquid est comprehendens dixit οὐσίαν, extra quam nec inveniri aliquid nec cogitari potest.'
[31] Cf. *DCSD* cap. 1, col. 409B. [32] See Lewry, 'Boethian Logic', 99–100.
[33] *Proslogion*, cap. 2, *Opera*, 1.101.

glosses on the Psalms, material that can be directly attributed to him is restricted to a few fragments, notably upon Psalms 13: 3 and 17: 30.[34] His one substantial surviving work on the Bible is his commentaries on all fourteen of the Pauline epistles (like all of his contemporaries, he did not question St Paul's authorship of the Epistle to the Hebrews).[35] These commentaries, which had a wide and enduring circulation, survive in two principal forms.[36] One of them embodies only glosses, both interlinear and marginal, by Lanfranc himself. The other includes in addition much material attributed to St Augustine and St Ambrose. The Augustinian glosses are, indeed, the work of the Christian father himself, but they have been shown mostly to be taken from a Carolingian compilation—the *Collectaneum* of Florus of Lyons.[37] The 'Ambrose' glosses are not by the Latin father but are drawn from three ancient sources of the Antiochene school of biblical exegesis which preferred a literal to an allegorical interpretation of scripture; they are derived from a Carolingian collection, already under the name of Ambrose, which drew upon 'Ambrosiaster' (an anonymous contemporary of Ambrose) for the books from Romans to 2 Corinthians, the Latin version of Theodore of Mopsuestia for Galatians to Philemon, and that of John Chrysostom for Hebrews.[38] It is not clear how far the Augustine and 'Ambrose' glosses are the work of Lanfranc, whether directly or through others working under his supervision, or whether they are entirely the work of others. In favour of Lanfranc's having taken a considerable part it may be argued, first, that a manuscript with only the Lanfranc glosses nevertheless has the title 'Glosses on the Epistle to the Romans excerpted from the sayings of the fathers by Abbot Lanfranc',[39] which indicates a tradition that he at least began this work; and second, that the patristic glosses are severely pruned to convey their meaning in a minimum of words, a procedure which has a parallel in the handling of canonical material in Lanfranc's canon-law collection.[40] However this may be, it is Lanfranc's own glosses on the Pauline epistles that are most informative about him as scholar and teacher.

While they have been studied in respect of their form and of Lanfranc's attitude to and use of the liberal arts, the substance of his commentaries has been somewhat neglected. Yet it yields much that is of importance about Lanfranc's cast of mind and about the thought that underlay his activity as monk and as archbishop. It may also be suggested that it is only in the light of Lanfranc's thought that his methods and use of the arts can fully be understood.

[34] Smalley, 'La Glossa ordinaria', 375; Gibson, *Lanfranc*, 5.3–4.

[35] For discussions and for details of manuscripts, see esp. Smalley, 'The Glossa ordinaria', 378–85, and eadem, *The Study*, 63–7; Gibson, 'Lanfranc's "Commentary"', and eadem, *Lanfranc*, 54–61.

[36] For another, and different, set of Lanfranc glosses in Berlin, Deutsche Staatsbibliothek, MS Phillipps 1650, see Smalley, 'The Glossa ordinaria', 386–9.

[37] Lanfranc took his comments on Galatians directly from Augustine's *Expositio*.

[38] The two forms of commentary are shown by the editions of Giles, who gives only the Lanfranc glosses, and of D'Achery, reproduced in *PL*, who includes the patristic material.

[39] Smalley, 'The Glossa ordinaria', 382; Gibson, 'Lanfranc's "Commentary"', 90. The MS is of early 12th-cent. date.

[40] For the abridgement of the glosses, see Gibson, 'Lanfranc's "Commentary"', 97–101. Anselm stated that the sole manuscript at Bec in his time as prior which contained Lanfranc's commentary included much of Lanfranc's own work: *Ep.* 66, vol. 3.186–7. This letter is evidence that the commentaries survive as Lanfranc's own notes, not a pupil's.

When considering Lanfranc's thinking, four points should be borne in mind. First, steeped though his mind was in the liberal arts as they were studied and taught in the early eleventh century, and although he was for long a wandering scholar who learnt and taught the arts in a secular context, he was increasingly disposed so far as he could to turn away from the arts and devote himself to the sacred page. His surviving writings reflect this deliberate choice, and they are the record of his teaching in a monastic school against the background of the monastic life. Second, in his commentaries Lanfranc was commenting upon what he saw as authoritative and, indeed, inspired texts by way of his own glosses. His prime concern was to facilitate an understanding of the texts in terms that their author intended, not to propound his own ideas or to present an ordered body of systematic teaching. His own mind was not of a speculative cast. Nevertheless, his own stamp is set upon his commentaries. The selection of passages upon which to gloss was his own. While it was in part determined by his sense of where his hearers or readers might find difficulties of a grammatical, logical, historical, or similar kind, it also reflects the subjects of doctrinal or moral instruction that Lanfranc deemed to be the most necessary for well-grounded Christians to understand. For, third, partly because Lanfranc was both teacher and monk, he was convinced that a master of study had a didactic, as well as an intellectual, responsibility. A master should teach both by word and by example. The life and the death of teachers should make for the edification of their pupils. The truest distinction of a teacher was the uprightness of his life.[41] His aim should, therefore, be the moral, as well as the mental, education of his hearers.

Fourth, Lanfranc's commentary was not directed only to a monastic house and to a monastic audience; indeed, it is not possible to find a single gloss which envisaged monks expressly or implicitly in any special way. Lanfranc always envisaged the instruction and edification of the whole body of Christian people, monastic and secular, clerical and lay. No doubt this was partly so because of the perspectives of St Paul upon whom his glosses were based, for Paul lived long before there were monks in the church. Moreover, Lanfranc's school at Bec was for external as well as internal pupils, and many would find careers in the secular rather than the monastic church. More important, however, was the growing demand in reforming circles of the church for men, both monks and non-monks, who could exercise the duties of spiritual direction and of awarding penance to all conditions of Christians with such a preparation in sound doctrine and spiritual wisdom as Lanfranc was concerned to provide.[42] Thus, in comment upon St Paul's description of the church as 'the house of God . . . which is the pillar and ground of truth', Lanfranc wrote that the church was the faithful who were the pillar of truth in that they directly upheld the truth itself, which was Christ, lest the wicked should undermine it. But also, the

---

[41] 'Vita et mors doctorum ad aedificationem subditis esse debent': 1 Cor. 3: 22, col. 167A; 'Opus evangelistae est, bene vivere et bene dicere, moribus et verbis subiectos instruere': 2 Tim. 4: 5, col. 367A; 'Ornamentum doctoris est honesta vita discipulorum': Titus 2: 10, col. 370B.

[42] See e.g. Pope Gregory VII's decree of 1080 about penances, according to which those guilty of grave sin should commit their souls to wise and religious men; they should not run for penance to those who were devoid alike of a religious life and of skill in counselling (*in quibus nec religiosa vita nec est consulendi scientia*): *Reg*. 7.14*a*, pp. 481–2.

church of God was a pillar in the great men who upheld other men; in them, too, all Christians were grounded with the grounding of truth, for they confirmed the truth of the Gospel by words and by miracles.[43]

Lanfranc's commentary envisaged both Christians in general and elite and key groups of them, whether monks or not. Thus, all Christians were to be exhorted to maintain chastity in terms of the utmost rigour.[44] The clergy were to adhere to the strictest canonical rules in this respect.[45] Again, St Paul was represented as an authority in his statement that women should keep their heads covered in church, 'for the sake of the angels': Lanfranc's comment was that by the angels Paul meant preachers who spoke from a lofty pulpit whence they might be tempted to lust by the sight of flowing feminine locks.[46] As well as envisaging the clergy, Lanfranc gave attention to St Paul's instructions on all dimensions of lay family life. While insisting upon the proper subordination of wives to their husbands, Lanfranc also held that duties were mutual. At a time when conversion to the monastic life was widely considered by lay people, Lanfranc added the prudent comment that, whatever the value of chastity, it should not induce those who were already married to forsake their wives.[47]

Lanfranc's concern for the lay order included consideration of the life and authority of secular rulers. He upheld their authority in society as the guarantors of peace and morality.[48] Nevertheless, rulers might become the recipients of sharp admonition: thus, in comment upon St Paul's outburst, 'Wherefore you are without excuse, O man who judges', Lanfranc pointed out the apostle's reproof (*increpatio*) of rulers, evidently without distinction of clerical and lay, who were guilty of the very offences that they condemned in others.[49] But Lanfranc's leading message was one of proper subordination, especially of subjects to their lords,[50] for so long as those in a position of power did not transgress the limits of humanity; in comment upon the word *plagiarii* (kidnappers) in St Paul's list of the lawless and disobedient, Lanfranc condemned trafficking in prisoners and slaves.[51]

Lanfranc's commentaries were thus far from envisaging only the internal life of the monastic order. They embraced a wide perspective of church and society, perhaps with an especial eye to those who, whether monks or secular clergy, would be the spiritual advisers and confessors of leading clergy and laity. Lanfranc's glosses

---

[43] 1 Tim. 3: 15, col. 353A.

[44] 'In alloquio iuvencularum, rectissime iuvenis de omni castitate admonetur, ut nec saltem minima titillatione moveatur': 1 Tim. 5: 2, col. 355AB.

[45] 1 Cor. 7: 2, col. 175A; 1 Tim. 3: 2, col. 352A.   [46] 1 Cor. 11: 10, col. 192B.

[47] For marital duties, see e. g. 1 Cor. 7: 14, cols. 175B–176A; Eph. 5; 21–33, cols. 302B–304B; 1 Tim. 2: 4–14, cols. 350B–351B. For Lanfranc's counsel that married men should remain with their wives, see his comment upon Paul's words *Alligatus es uxori?* 'Ne laudata castitate, uxorem aliquis vellet dimittere, hoc subiungit': 1 Cor. 7: 27, col. 178A.

[48] 1 Tim. 2: 2, col. 349B; see above, p. 38.

[49] Rom. 2: 1, col. 110B: 'Invectio in rectores. Dicit enim: Cum omnes facientes et consentientes sunt perituri, etiam et hi qui alios iudicant, si eodem peccato tenentur impliciti.'

[50] 'Blasphemaretur nomen Dei, et doctrina, si propter quod humiliari deberent, superbirent, et dominos contemnerent': 1 Tim. 6: 1–2, col. 358BC.

[51] 'Plagiarii sunt clam transferentes homines de patria in patriam, et vendentes': 1 Tim. 1: 9–10, col. 348A.

add credibility to William of Poitiers's depiction of him as the duke of Normandy's own director and as the mentor of the whole Norman church.[52]

Because Lanfranc gave similar treatment to all of the Pauline epistles, the subject-matter of his commentaries touched upon many major topics of Christian doctrine and practice. Thus, Romans and Galatians directed his attention to the theology of justification, Hebrews to that of redemption, the captivity epistles (Ephesians, Philippians, and Colossians) to the person of Christ and to the church as his body, and every epistle to matters of Christian ethics. Lanfranc wrote as a theologian glossing a sacred text, and his commentaries must be approached accordingly. Some illustrations may be given of what seem to have been his principal interests.

He was throughout much concerned with the development of the divine revelation, and so of God's demands upon men, from the Old Testament to the New. One of St Paul's first assertions in the biblical sequence of his writings is that the righteousness of God is revealed in the gospel 'from faith to faith'. Lanfranc commented that there was thus revealed how God advanced mankind from a provisional faith (*ex fide*) in the one God couched in shadows and words to a full Trinitarian faith (*in fidem*) of belief and substance in God the Three-in-One.[53] Lanfranc throughout invited his hearers and readers to explore this progression and to accept its moral consequences.

He therefore devoted much attention to Paul's teaching about justification, and especially to the contrast between justification by law and by faith. He took as his cardinal points the significance of Abraham as prefiguring justification by faith alone without the works of the law,[54] the powerlessness of the old law to provide an inheritance or a promise or a blessing,[55] and the contrast with the law of Christ which gave salvation by faith alone because it was the gift of God who alone could justify.[56]

A similar spanning of the Testaments characterized Lanfranc's glosses on passages about redemption, especially in the epistle to the Hebrews with its elaborate drawing upon Old Testament models. In his comments on the theme of God's having perfected Christ through death as the author of human salvation, Lanfranc singled out as the two reasons for its fittingness, first, Christ's destroying of the devil who had the power of death, and the resultant liberty of those whom fear of death had made subject to servitude. Those who had sought to fulfil the old law from fear of death in

---

[52] 'Potuit namque viri talis vigilans cura, cum maximam auctoritatem sapientiae pariter ac sanctitatis praerogativa comparavit, securitatem non parvam optimae sollicitudini promittere': William of Poitiers, 1.52, pp. 84–5.

[53] Rom. 1: 17, col. 108BC = Gibson, 'Lanfranc's "Commentary"', 110.

[54] e.g. Rom. 3: 31, col. 113A, 4: 1, 11–12, cols. 118AB, 119A.

[55] e.g. Rom. 8: 3, col. 130A; Gal. 3: 1–17, cols. 269A–271A; Heb. 7, cols. 390A–393A. Lanfranc gave much attention to Paul's discussion of the place of the Jews in Rom. 9–11, cols. 133–44; he commented on the restraint that Christians should show towards the Jews in view of God's ultimate plans for them: Paul 'admonet gentes ne superbiant, et ne Iudaeos despectui habeant, dicens, Quia si apostoli sancti sunt, certum est etiam quod in ipso populo multi sancti sunt; et si nondum re, spe tamen et praesentia divina': Rom. 11: 16, col. 142BC; cf. Heb. 9: 15, col. 396B.

[56] e.g. Rom. 3: 25–31, cols. 117A–118A, and esp. the lengthy comments on Gal. 2: 19–3: 29, cols. 265C–273A.

body and soul were now freed by Christ both from hell and from the unbearable yoke of the law.[57] Second, in comment upon Hebrews, Lanfranc drew attention to the Old Testament prefigurations of Christ's saving high-priesthood, especially in terms of Christ as at once the true high priest and the only sufficient sacrifice.[58]

In the authentically Pauline epistles, Lanfranc found complementary matter for comment in the imagery of Christ as the second Adam: as Adam was the father of all men according to the flesh, so Christ as Paul's *novissimus Adam* (1 Cor. 15: 45) was the father of all men according to faith. Again, for Lanfranc, Christ's saving death on the cross was critical: 'In the hour that the blood of redemption flowed from the Lord's side as he hung upon the cross, Adam's sin was forgiven to the whole human race, and peace was made between things of heaven and things of earth; for then entry into the kingdom of heaven was opened for men.'[59] As a result, a feature of Lanfranc's glosses was his insistence upon Christian hope.[60] A further feature was Lanfranc's understanding of Christ as the full revelation of the Godhead. Echoing the Nicene Creed, he proclaimed the Son as begotten of the Father before all creation, and as him by whom all things were made. It pleased the Father that in the incarnate Christ should dwell the plenitude of divinity and of all virtues, so that he who fully knows Christ knows all that should be believed about God, in what terms it should be believed, and what should be the guidelines of daily life.[61]

Lanfranc's apprehension of Paul's teaching about the solidarity of men in Adam and in Christ led him to place emphasis upon the church as the body of Christ and upon the Christian sacraments, especially baptism and the eucharist, as part of the life of that body: 'the fullness of Christ is the church, because in it and through it members are added to Christ, that is, the faithful.'[62] Quite apart from his differences with Berengar of Tours, which Lanfranc showed no sign of having had in mind when formulating his glosses, Lanfranc chose realistic language in drawing the consequences for an understanding of the church and sacraments. 'Adam', he commented, 'was the pattern of Christ. And just as Eve was formed from the side of Adam, so from the side of Christ there flowed the sacraments through which the church is saved.'[63] The day of baptism was, therefore, the day of redemption.[64] Lanfranc's language, and still more his realism, about the eucharist had their origin in Adam and Eve who, as the archetypal bridegroom and bride, were 'one flesh' (*in una carne*: Gen. 2: 24). Because Christ and the church were so related, Lanfranc found it natural to refer to the receiving of Christ's flesh (*caro*) in the eucharist: 'in the mass and in its celebrations, the church every day receives the flesh which Christ took of the Virgin.'[65] According to Paul, the eucharist was also the body (*corpus*) of

---

[57] Heb. 2: 10–18, cols. 379A–382A.   [58] Heb. 7–8, esp. 8: 4, cols. 390A–395A, esp. 394A.
[59] e.g. Rom. 5: 15–18, cols. 121C–122A; 1 Cor. 15: 45–9, cols. 212C–213B; Eph. 2: 14, col. 292BC; Col. 1: 20, 2: 13–15, cols. 322AB, 325AB.
[60] Esp. the glosses on Rom. 8, cols. 129B–134B.
[61] Eph. 1, cols. 289A–293A; Cor. 1: 15, 19, 2: 2, cols. 322AB, 323AB.
[62] Eph. 1: 23, col. 290C. For comment on Lanfranc's glosses on the eucharist, see Montclos, *Lanfranc et Bérenger*, 332–7.
[63] Rom 5: 14, col. 121B.   [64] Eph. 4: 30, col. 300BC.
[65] Eph. 5: 31–2, col. 304BC; cf. 1 Cor. 10: 16–17, col. 189B; Heb. 5: 11, col. 387B.

Christ;[66] *caro* and *corpus* were inevitable and synonymous terms to use of the eucharist. With regard to marriage, Lanfranc likewise endorsed the Pauline idea of Christ's relation to the church as being transferable to that of husband and wife; he added the characteristic caution that the use of the relationship as a figure for Christ and the church in no way derogated from its everyday relevance to the moral duties of husbands and wives.[67]

With his sense of a teacher's didactic responsibility, Lanfranc strongly insisted upon the necessity for the practice of good works here and now. Christians were committed to it because through good works there was established peace between God and man.[68] Without the testing of good works, faith was vain, for they were both the condition of eternal life and the gift of divine grace.[69] Christians could not trust that they were saved by faith alone unless they lived good lives and abstained from sin, for the truth of the gospel (*veritas evangelii*) was to observe God's moral precepts through faith.[70] Amongst good works, Lanfranc gave primacy to charity as the most excellent of the gifts of the Holy Spirit.[71] For him, good works belonged, with faith and hope, to the heart of Christian living:

> For our purpose is directed to the glory of the Lord; because now, we look through a glass and a riddle to this glory, which as yet does not appear as it is. But as in a reflection it is seen by faith, and we are being transformed by good works. For in this we are striving, so that we may be made conformable to this glory, which will lead on from the brightness (*claritas*) of faith to the brightness of hope.[72]

When viewed against the background of Lanfranc's school at Bec as a monastic school, Lanfranc's glosses should be regarded as no less an expression of the current monastic use of holy scripture than as sources for the growth of the use in biblical comment of the methods of the liberal arts.[73] From the study and teaching of the arts, Lanfranc was increasingly anxious to turn away. His glosses must be understood, not as isolated and piecemeal comments, but against their background in the continuous Vulgate text of the Pauline epistles, the teaching of which they were designed to explain and to apply. In Lanfranc's viva-voce teaching, they should be envisaged as commentary upon the sacred text by a monastic scholar more concerned to convey Paul's theological and moral meaning than to instruct his pupils in grammar, dialectic, and rhetoric. The prime importance of Lanfranc's commentaries is that they provide evidence for the formation of his own mind and for that which he deemed appropriate for hearers and readers who, whether as monks or as secular clergy, would have an impact not only within the cloister but upon the ecclesiastical and lay world outside it.

---

[66] 1 Cor. 10: 16–17, 11: 22–5, cols. 189B, 194A–195A; Heb. 13: 10–11, cols. 405A–406A.

[67] 'Quasi [Paul] diceret, quamvis ergo hoc sacramentum in Christo et ecclesia intelligam spiritualiter, verumtamen vos a morali intellectu historiae nolite recedere': Eph. 5: 33, col. 304C.

[68] Rom. 1: 7–8, col. 107B = Gibson, 'Lanfranc's "Commentary"', 109.

[69] Rom. 6: 3, cols. 123B–124A; 2 Cor. 1: 12, col. 218B.

[70] 1 Cor. 9: 27–30, col. 187A; Gal. 2: 5, col. 264B.

[71] See e.g. the glosses on Paul's praise of charity in 1 Cor. 12: 27–13: 13, cols. 198A–202B.

[72] 2 Cor. 3: 18, col. 226A.

[73] On the monastic study and use of scripture, see esp. Leclercq, *The Love of Learning*.

If Lanfranc's employment of the liberal arts was in this way ancillary to his purpose in expounding the sacred page in its depth, range, and practical import for Christian living, both individual and social, it was also necessary for his purpose. This was so not least because Paul, whose teaching Lanfranc expounded, was himself a master and exponent of secular means of exposition and persuasion. Paul's own words must be understood by way of the devices that he used, while such devices must also be brought to bear by those in later times who would deepen their own understanding. In commenting upon the first two chapters of 1 Corinthians, in particular, Lanfranc advanced his justification of Paul's own use of secular learning, and therefore of the rightfulness of its proper use by expositors of aftertime.[74] It is worth drawing together the salient points that Lanfranc made.

Of Paul's exceptional learning Lanfranc had no doubt. When Paul wrote that 'not many are wise (*sapientes*)', Lanfranc suggested that he may have implied that he was himself alone among the apostles in being versed in secular learning (*scholarium litterarum peritus*), just as he was alone in being of worldly wealth and of elevated, Roman family (1: 26). As such a man Paul served, though his glory was in the Lord (1: 30–1). Paul thus illustrated the gulf between the wisdom (*sapientia*) of this world which is to be shunned and wisdom as made subservient to Christian truth. As an end in itself, secular wisdom was to be reprobated. As a synonym of dialectic, for those who followed it simple-mindedly it made void Christ's cross and death (1: 17); when Paul came to the Corinthians he came not in the high-flown persuasiveness of logic, rhetoric, and eminent philosophers such as Aristotle (2: 1–6). Such wisdom brought no proof of Christianity; syllogistic argument might more readily disprove the truth than prove it; at best it is unprofitable, leading its practitioners to count the death of Christ as foolishness (1: 17–18). As such, it was perilous for non-believers and for weak believers (*si syllogistice convicti et crederent, non prodesset eis*) (1: 18, 20; 2: 14). The prophetic witness of the Old Testament served to confirm the vanity of the wisdom of this world (1: 19).

Yet, rightly employed, the resources of secular wisdom also served to foster and to confirm the mysteries of divine revelation which were the source of true wisdom. Lanfranc illustrated how syllogisms might establish Christian truth, and proceeded to comment that 'with regard to the virgin birth and to certain other mysterious truths (*sacramenta*), for those who . . . look with proper insight dialectic does not conceal the mysterious truths (*sacramenta*) of God but when the matter so requires, if it is held to most rightly, it demonstrates and confirms them' (1: 17).[75] Similarly, in comment upon Paul's assertion that true teachers do not speak in learned words of human knowledge (*in doctis humanae scientiae verbis*: 2: 13), Lanfranc says that, notwithstanding,

---

[74] cols. 155C–164B. Lanfranc envisaged Paul as a follower of the traditions of Greek and Latin learning; he showed no sense of Paul's indebtedness to those of Rabbinic Judaism.

[75] Cf. Lanfranc's comment on Col. 2: 4: '*In sublimitate*: Id est, in altitudine verborum, et syllogismorum, et aliorum generum disputantium; non artem disputandi vituperat, sed perversum disputantium usum': col. 323B. For Paul's use of rhetoric, see the gloss on Gal. 6: 12, col. 285A.

in Paul's writings there may be found, when the matter demands, such great subtlety in the disputation of topics and also so subtle a *captatio benevolentiae* [bid to elicit a favourable hearing] that none as great or greater are to be found in any sort of writings. Wherefore beyond doubt it is to be believed that he did not ponder the rules of secular arts in writing or in speaking, but that he spoke such things as he did, and in such a manner, through the teaching of the Holy Spirit, from whom and through whom is all profitable knowledge (*omnis utilis peritia*).

So Paul contrasted the *animalis homo* who rejects spiritual things and cannot so labour that he may understand, with the *spiritualis* who duly understands and censures whatever should be understood or censured while he himself is censured or understood by no carnal man (2: 14–17). Thus were to be set in contrast the wrong and the right use of the liberal arts which, rightly used, were an essential adjunct of sacred study.

In expounding to his pupils the text of Paul's epistles, Lanfranc therefore made good use of the arts. He drew upon the resources of grammar, rhetoric, and dialectic to show both how Paul himself had argued and how later exegetes might rightly apprehend and digest Paul's teaching. Some of the skills that Lanfranc invoked were of an elementary kind. Perhaps most frequently, he used such tags as *ordo*, *ordo est*, to introduce his establishing of the *ordo naturalis* of Paul's sometimes complex sentences—how words and phrases might be rearranged in the most straightforward or significant order for the readier comprehension of his readers or hearers. Other tags introduced often quite simple explanations of Paul's words—sometimes by way of paraphrase (*id est*, *quasi diceret*, *et est sensus*). Lanfranc was at pains to clarify points of grammar and to define difficult words. He explained and illustrated Paul's rhetorical forms and devices—*increpatio* (reproof), *ironia* (irony), the citing of a part to signify a whole (*pars pro toto*). More advanced forms of argument were pointed out—*simili* (from similarities), *a contrario* (from contraries), *a toto* (from wholes), *a parte* (from parts), *a genere* (from kinds). More advanced, still, Lanfranc not only explored the right use of syllogisms (at simplest, the form $A = D$, $B = A$, therefore $B = D$) but also of equipollent arguments which proceeded by the detection and concatenation of equivalent propositions ($A = B = C = D$, therefore $A = D$).[76] Lanfranc thus inculcated in his hearers a very wide range of skills that were shared with the liberal arts.

In so doing in his commentaries on the Pauline epistles, he was far from being a teacher of the liberal arts who used the sacred text to illustrate these subjects, nor did he use any or all of these arts as an avenue of approach to the sacred text or to the revealed truth that it embodied. The sacred text was the prime and sole vehicle of the knowledge that was proper for a spiritual man, whether in the cloister or in the world outside. In so far as the ways and means of the liberal arts were to be pressed into service, they were to be used not as antecedent and free-standing disciplines but as gifts supplied by the same Holy Spirit who was the revealer of scriptural truth

---

[76] See esp. 1 Cor. 8: 8, 9: 15, cols. 182AB, 195BC, 2 Cor. 6: 16, col. 236B, Gal. 3: 7, col. 270B. For the imprecision of Lanfranc's use of equipollent arguments, however, see Southern, *Saint Anselm: A Portrait*, 51–2.

and who provided the means of interpreting the truth that he revealed. These means were to be employed in the traditional way of faith which sought understanding (*fides quaerens intellectum*), and in no way as providing an avenue by which human understanding might approach the truth (*intellectus quaerens fidem*). The striking feature of Lanfranc's commentaries, when read in conjunction with the biblical text, is not his mastery of secular learning but the depth and range of his apprehension and communication of the doctrinal and practical content of the twelve epistles that he deemed to be Pauline.

4.3 BERENGAR AND THE EUCHARIST

The difficult subject of Lanfranc's theology of the eucharist and of his controversy about it with Berengar of Tours is best approached with his biblical commentaries in mind, especially in so far as they illustrate his view of the relation between authority and human learning.[77] But before the matters at issue are addressed, it will be well to take note of the course, extent, and importance of Lanfranc's involvement. Two considerations warn against exaggeration. First, after his death his fame as archbishop of Canterbury ensured for his anti-Berengarian tract *De corpore et sanguine Domini*[78] a circulation that it did not receive during his lifetime; it was thereafter much copied and studied with other such writings. By comparison with them, it came to be rated good but not pre-eminent. Thus, in a work completed in 1139/41, Peter the Venerable, abbot of Cluny, named as the three 'learned and catholic men of modern times' who had replied to Berengar Archbishop Lanfranc of Canterbury, Bishop Guitmund of Aversa, and Alger, sometime *magister* at Liège but now a Cluniac monk. Peter ranked their tracts as good, full, and perfect (Lanfranc), better, fuller, and more perfect (Guitmund), and best, fullest, and most perfect (Alger).[79] Second, Lanfranc's activity and writing as regards the eucharist were not, so far as evidence survives, evenly spread across his whole career at Bec, Caen, and Canterbury. As a review will show, they were largely confined to his monastic years at Bec.

While he was a monk of Bec during the 1050s and early 1060s, although no record remains of any writing before the *De corpore et sanguine Domini* which he completed after leaving Bec, he was from time to time acutely concerned with Berengar's teaching. Berengar was a charismatic figure who taught not far from the borders of the duchy of Normandy. He had a long association with the royal abbey of Saint-Martin at Tours, of which he was a canon by 1030 and of which in the 1070s

---

[77] Amongst the extensive literature on the Berengarian controversy, Montclos, *Lanfranc et Bérenger*, remains the full and essential guide to which I am greatly indebted throughout this section. Special mention may also be made of Gibson, *Lanfranc*, 63–97; of the papers collected in Ganz, Huygens, and Niewöhner (eds.), *Auctoritas und ratio*; and of Chadwick, 'Ego Berengarius'.

[78] DCSD.

[79] Peter the Venerable, *Contra Petrobrusianos*, cap. 153, pp. 87–8. The works referred to are Lanfranc, *DCSD*, Guitmund of Aversa, *De corporis et sanguinis veritate*, and Alger of Liège, *De sacramentis corporis et sanguinis Domini*. See also William of Malmesbury, *GR* 3.284.2, vol. 1.514–15; *GP* 1.67, p. 126.

he appears as *scholasticus* or master of the schools. He had a further association with the cathedral of Angers, where he was archdeacon from 1040 to 1060 and treasurer from c.1047 to c.1053. Berengar's connections with the county of Anjou, a political rival of the duchy of Normandy, must be borne in mind. It seems to have been only in the late 1040s that Berengar emerged as a centre of controversy with regard to the eucharist because he was reputed to hold that Christ's presence in the consecrated elements of bread and wine was to be understood figuratively rather than realistically. But his teachings became bitterly and extensively condemned in and beyond France.

Eucharistic controversy became the sharper because current views were linked with what were understood to have been the contrasting theologies of two ninth-century monks of the abbey of Corbie (dioc. Amiens). In his *De corpore et sanguine Domini* (c.831/3), Paschasius Radbertus presented a full and overall treatment of the eucharist in which, for reasons of ensuring human salvation, he insisted that the body of Christ as received in the sacrament was identical both with the earthly body that the incarnate Christ took from Mary and with the body now in heaven that is eternally glorified. Some ten years later another Corbie monk, Ratramnus, replied briefly in a similarly entitled work to specific questions put to him by the Emperor Charles the Bald; Ratramnus made no such outright identification of the sacramental body of Christ with his incarnate and eternal body, but wrote in terms of the eucharistic elements as sacred signs which betokened an inner reality communicated to the recipient's soul. Different though the eucharistic views of Paschasius and Ratramnus were, there was no sense of a controversy between them or of a radical incompatibility of their teachings. Such a sense developed only later, when the Paschasian view was widely accepted as normative and when Ratramnus's work, with some exaggeration of its figurative direction, became generally attributed to 'John the Scot'—Eriugena (c.810–c.877), thus compounding suspicion about its orthodoxy.[80]

From the outset of the Berengarian controversy hostility to Berengar was extremely strong in Normandy, and it remained so. The abbey of Fécamp was a centre of early resistance. The fourth part of Abbot John's *Confessio fidei*, written c.1050 under the name of Alcuin, had it in view. Some three years later his monk, Durandus of Troarn, composed his *Liber de corpore et sanguine Christi*. Norman opposition to Berengar was by no means limited to the cloister, for it was in due course the subject of forthright expression in provincial councils.[81]

The beginning of Lanfranc's involvement appears in the letter that Berengar, with whom Lanfranc may have earlier been acquainted,[82] wrote to him late in 1049 or very early in 1050.[83] Whereas various constructions have been placed upon this letter,[84] a probable interpretation is that Berengar was surprised when he

---

[80] For a discussion and appraisal of Carolingian and later works on the eucharist, see Macy, *The Theologies*, 21–35.
[81] *Die Konzilsordines*, no. 26, pp. 107–11, 568–74.
[82] See above, p. 9.   [83] See above, pp. 38–9.
[84] For a somewhat different translation and assessment, see Gibson, *Lanfranc*, 66–7.

received a report from an otherwise unknown clerk of Chartres that Lanfranc was of the opinion that the teaching about the eucharist of 'John the Scot' (Ratramnus) was heretical while that of Paschasius was to be followed. Berengar admitted that (as he said), like Lanfranc himself, he was insufficiently versed in 'divine scripture' competently to settle the matter.[85] (By 'divine scripture' Berengar probably meant not only the Bible but also early Christian writers.) He therefore proposed that he should be given the opportunity of listening to a ventilation of the problem in the presence of judges and hearers of Lanfranc's choosing. Berengar evidently had in mind a debate based on the marshalling and discussion of ancient authorities rather than on dialectical analysis and argument. In the meantime he cautioned Lanfranc that, if he held 'John the Scot' to be heretical, he must so hold Ambrose, Jerome, Augustine, and other authorities of the highest traditional standing; he implied that there was a consensus of authority in favour of his, and not Lanfranc's, position.[86]

Events so developed that Berengar's letter had a greater effect than its author intended. Lanfranc himself later described how, when Berengar's messenger brought it to Normandy, he found that Lanfranc was not in the duchy, almost certainly because of the journey that saw his joining the entourage of Pope Leo IX after his council of Rheims.[87] Berengar's teaching was denounced to the apostolic see and was debated at Rome in Leo IX's synod of April 1050, at which Lanfranc but not Berengar was present. Berengar's letter to Lanfranc was read out in public; in its author's absence, it was taken as supplying the evidence of his own words that, by extolling 'John the Scot' and by condemning Paschasius, he believed things contrary to the universal faith of the church concerning the eucharist. The synod, Lanfranc commented, deprived Berengar of the communion of holy church which he endeavoured to deprive of its own holy communion. The pope then called upon Lanfranc to clear himself of association with Berengar's opinions by declaring his own faith, drawing upon sacred authorities rather than upon arguments. This Lanfranc did to the satisfaction of all present. Leo IX prescribed that Berengar should appear in person before a further synod to be held at Vercelli in September 1050, and he ordered and urged Lanfranc to remain with him until it had taken place.[88] Lanfranc had evidently established himself at Rome as an informed, competent, and reliable upholder of the dominant Paschasian doctrine of the eucharist against Berengar's aberration.

Berengar was willing to answer for himself at Vercelli, but he was prevented by imprisonment and, as he alleged, complete despoliation of his goods at the hand of

---

[85] For Berengar's recent turning to sacred study, see the letter to him of Adelman of Liège of late 1052 in Huygens, 'Textes latins', 476–89, at p. 487. He alluded to the current incompleteness of his knowledge of *scriptura* in RCL 1.460–2, ed. Huygens, p. 48, cf. EF no. 98, p. 165.

[86] For Berengar's position at this time, cf. his account of a debate at Chartres, probably in the third quarter of 1050, to Abbot Ansfrid of the Norman abbey of Préaux: EF no. 98, pp. 164–6. For Berengar's later comment on his letter, reiterating that 'Admonebat te scriptum illud meum preproperam contra Iohannem S(cotum) te tulisse sententiam, et ut de eo mecum agere dignareris secundum scripturas', see RCL 1/259–74, vol. 1.42–3.

[87] See above, pp. 38–40.   [88] *DCSD* cap. 4, col. 413 = Huygens, 'Bérenger de Tours', pp. 375–6.

King Henry I of France.[89] Discussion at Vercelli turned on a portion of 'John the Scot' which was read out; Lanfranc was later to claim that Berengar's own opinions were considered; but Berengar himself denied, probably correctly, that they were debated or presented by clerks in his stead. Lanfranc participated in the debate, but so far as can be seen only after the bishops present and in a subordinate way. The decision of the synod was that the tract of 'John the Scot' should be condemned, and a copy of it was cut to shreds. A confession of faith was made in Paschasian terms; there does not appear to have been another express condemnation of the absent and despoiled Berengar himself.[90]

Berengar continued to maintain and to publicize his teaching,[91] and it seems to have been from this time that he began to express the extremely derogatory and bitter remarks about Leo IX and the apostolic see that Lanfranc and others were later to deplore.[92] He was quickly ransomed from his captivity at the hands of the French king; by the autumn of 1050 his travels took him to Normandy.[93] The events of his visit are obscure, but it seems that he first sought out the young Duke William, whom he endeavoured to win over to his support. But William shrewdly kept his counsel until Berengar accompanied him to Brionne, which is near Bec to which Lanfranc had evidently returned from Vercelli. At Brionne the duke assembled those whom Durandus of Troarn described as the catholic and wise men from all over the duchy. It would seem that, in considering Berengar's case, the council closely followed the lines suggested by Berengar's letter to Lanfranc of a year or so earlier.[94] Berengar was accompanied by a clerk in whose eloquence, according to Durandus, he placed his hope of victory. To the council, or perhaps apart from it to only some of the participants, Lanfranc reported on the council of Vercelli and the destruction there of the text of 'John the Scot'. There is nothing to suggest that Lanfranc expounded his own view of the eucharist against Berengar, who was later able to assert that he had never been confronted with it face to face.[95] The matter at issue may well have been limited to that proposed in Berengar's earlier letter: if 'John the Scot' was to be condemned, so must others like Ambrose, Jerome, and Augustine, for as authorities they were consonant with him. According to Durandus, the opinions of Berengar and his clerk, however stated, were publicly refuted and overcome by evident reason, so that they were reduced to silence and to a reluctant acceptance of a catholic form of words, no doubt in Paschasian terms. Lanfranc's part in the council of Brionne is hard to determine. It would seem that, on the one hand, it was important because of his eyewitness testimony to

---

[89] EF no. 98, pp. 164–6; *RCL* 1.393–411, ed. Huygens, pp. 46–7. Berengar could advance the Pseudo-Isidorian *exceptio spolii*, for which see Cowdrey, 'The Enigma', 143–5.

[90] For events at Vercelli, see *DSCD* cap. 4, col. 413 = Huygens, 'Textes latins', 376–7; *RCL* 1.393–446, ed. Huygens, 46–51.

[91] EF nos. 88, 98, pp. 152–4, 164–6.

[92] *DCSD* caps. 3, 16, 18, cols. 412, 426, 430; Bernold of Saint-Blasien, *De veritate corporis*, col. 1456 = Huygens, 'Bérenger', 381–2.

[93] Durandus, *Liber de corpore*, 9.33, cols. 1421–1; *RCL* 1.290–304, vol. 1.43–4. For a general comment on Duke William's anti-Berengarian zeal, see William of Poitiers, 1.49, pp. 80–1.

[94] Above, p. 39.   [95] *RCL* 1.1143–54, vol. 1.67–8.

Leo IX's measures at Vercelli. On the other, there is no suggestion that he took a lead in causing the duke to hold the council, at which many Norman churchmen greater than he were present and with whom the initiative probably rested.

The years between the councils of Vercelli and Brionne and the accession to the papacy in 1059 of Pope Nicholas II were eventful so far as Berengar was concerned, and there was much disputation in many regions about his eucharistic teaching. However, nothing is known of Lanfranc's involvement in any way, even at the council of Tours that the Roman legate Hildebrand held in 1054.[96] But in 1059 Berengar came to Rome for the Easter synod that Pope Nicholas held in concert with 113 bishops. It is uncertain whether Lanfranc came to Rome at or about this time and whether, if he did, he was present when the synod considered Berengar's teaching.[97] If he was present, there is no evidence that he took an active part. As for Berengar, he said repeatedly that he himself kept silent during the consideration of his views.[98] His principal opponent was Cardinal Humbert of Silva Candida, and it was he who drafted the profession to which he was required to accede. It was couched in uncompromisingly, indeed somewhat crudely, realistic terms so far as the presence of Christ's body and blood in the consecrated eucharistic elements is concerned. In view of its subsequent importance for Lanfranc,[99] it may be translated in full:

I Berengar, an unworthy deacon of the church of Saint-Maurice at Angers, acknowledging the true, catholic, and apostolic faith, anathematize every heresy, especially that of which I have hitherto been accused which seeks to assert that the bread and wine that are placed on the altar are after the consecration only a sacrament (*sacramentum*) and not the true body and blood of our Lord Jesus Christ, nor can they physically (*sensualiter*),[100] save in sacrament (*sacramento*) alone, be handled and broken by the hands of priests or crushed (*atteri*) by the teeth of the faithful. But I agree with the holy Roman and apostolic see, and with lips and heart I declare that I hold concerning the sacraments (*de sacramentis*) of the Lord's table the faith that the lord and venerable Pope Nicholas and this holy synod by evangelical and apostolic authority have delivered to be held and have affirmed to me, namely, that the bread and wine which are placed on the altar after the consecration are not only a sacrament but also the true body and blood of our Lord Jesus Christ, and that physically (*sensualiter*), not only in sacrament but in truth, they are handled by the hands of priests, broken, and crushed by the teeth of the faithful; swearing by the holy and united Trinity and by these most holy gospels. I proclaim to be deserving of eternal anathema those who go against this truth, together with their doctrines and adherents. But if I myself shall at any time presume to believe and to

---

[96] Lanfranc was aware of events, especially the council of Tours, *DCSD* cap. 4, col. 413 = Huygens, 'Bérenger', 376–7.

[97] See above, p. 42.   [98] *RCL* 1.816–96, 1127–65, pp. 59–61, 67–8.

[99] It is preserved not only in *DCSD* cap. 2, cols. 410–11 = Huygens, 'Bérenger, 372–3, but also as copied into Lanfranc's canonical collection: Cambridge, Trinity College, MS 405 (B. 16. 44), p. 210.

[100] Humbert took the adverb *sensualiter* and other phrases from the letter that Berengar wrote to Hildebrand just before the synod: EF no. 87, pp. 151–2. See Montclos, *Lanfranc et Bérenger*, 171–2; also Berengar's *Purgatoria epistola*: ibid. 534, 535, where *sensualiter* is contrasted with *intellectualiter*. The translation of *sensualiter* is difficult; as the context shows, the meaning is 'in a manner that is objective, real, complete, and capable of perception by the human senses, save that, to spare sensibilities, a veil is interposed'.

proclaim anything against these things, let me be subject to the rigour of the canons. Having read and re-read this, I have willingly subscribed.

Berengar himself lit the fire upon which, in the midst of the synod, he cast the books of his teaching.[101] But despite the last sentence of his profession, he later denied to Lanfranc that he subscribed with his own hand.[102] Pope Nicholas saw to the immediate and widespread dissemination of the profession.[103]

Upon returning to France Berengar quickly resumed his writing upon the eucharist, and he did so in a spirit of bitter resentment against the decision of the Roman synod and particularly against Humbert. He wrote a tract, conventionally known as the *Scriptum contra synodum*, which has survived only in twenty-three excerpts cited by Lanfranc in his reply, the *De corpore et sanguine Domini*.[104] When, why, and for whom Lanfranc wrote it are unclear. Nicholas II and Cardinal Humbert died in 1061; there is, however, no hint that Lanfranc wrote because they had died. Nor does he appear to have been prompted to write by any Roman agency, nor did he write on behalf of the apostolic see; in 1072 Pope Alexander II had to ask for a copy of Lanfranc's tract to be sent to him.[105] Lanfranc seems to have written on his own initiative to controvert Berengar's teaching and as a rejoinder to his derogation of apostolic authority; a note in some German manuscripts says that he was prompted by his sometime pupil at Bec or Caen, Theodoric of Paderborn.[106] Lanfranc's preface seems to suggest that, before writing, he had wished to engage in such a public debate with Berengar as had taken place at Brionne; Berengar declined.[107] Time must, perhaps, be allowed for such negotiations before Lanfranc wrote. He certainly did not complete his tract until he was abbot of Caen,[108] and he may have begun it only after moving there.[109] But he may also have begun assembling material and even the work of composition before leaving Bec.[110] All these possibilities lie open.

To Berengar, Lanfranc showed an unrelenting and uncompromising antagonism on account of his attitude towards both ancient traditional and modern apostolic authority, and also of the supposed deficiency and error of his eucharistic teaching in itself. 'Lanfranc by God's mercy a catholic to Berengar the adversary of

---

[101] *DCSD* cap. 1, col. 409 = Huygens, 'Bérenger', 371.
[102] *DCSD* cap. 2, col. 411 = Huygens, 'Bérenger', 374; *RCL* 1.12–18, p. 35.
[103] *DCSD* cap. 2, cols. 411–12 = Huygens, 'Bérenger', 374. It is important to bear in mind for how long a time both the text and the teaching of Humbert's formula remained influential. See e.g. Peter the Venerable (as n. 79).
[104] *DCSD* caps. 2–17, cols. 409–26.   [105] Lanfranc, *Letters*, no. 4, pp. 56–7.
[106] *PL* 147.334; see Montclos, *Lanfranc et Bérenger*, 196, and Huygens, 'Bérenger', 364–6; cf. *DCSD* cap. 5, col. 415: 'in hoc opusculo, quod destruendum suscepi'.
[107] See esp. the sentence 'Sed quia eligisti pravitatem, quam semel imbibisti, clandestinis disputationibus apud imperitos tueri, palam autem atque in audientia sancti concilii orthodoxam fidem non amore veritatis sed timore mortis confiteri, propterea refugis me, refugis religiosas personas, quae de verbis tuis ac meis possint ferre sententiam': *DCSD* cap. 1, cols. 407–8 = Huygens, 'Bérenger', 370;' cf. cap. 4, col. 414B.
[108] As n. 105.   [109] As argued by Montclos, *Lanfranc et Bérenger*, 196, 249.
[110] See Southern, *Saint Anselm: A Portrait*, 44, n. 7.

the catholic church': thus Lanfranc began his tract;[111] in 1072 when, as asked, he sent a copy to Pope Alexander II, the tone was similar: 'The letter which, while I was still in charge of the monastery at Caen, I sent to the schismatic Berengar I have been at pains to send to you, father, as you have commanded.'[112] Lanfranc devoted the first seventeen chapters of his tract to replying in dialogue form to the excerpts which he cited from Berengar's *Scriptum contra synodum*; in his five concluding chapters he gave an exposition of his own views and a final rebuttal of Berengar's teaching.

When Berengar saw Lanfranc's text he embarked upon an exhaustive response in his *Rescriptum contra Lanfrannum*.[113] It is a difficult and a puzzling tract. It survives only in a single manuscript, now numbered Weissenburg 101 in the Herzog August Bibliothek at Wolfenbüttel.[114] Now comprising 120 folios, it has suffered the loss of perhaps some fifty pages of writing, including its first two gatherings. For the most part, it contains a scribal copy of the first state of a reply to Lanfranc, but as well as containing many corrections or small additions which are interlined or written in the margin, a number of longer additions have been interleaved on separate pieces of parchment. No substantial part of the text or additions can be shown to be in Berengar's autograph hand. There is no indication of a date by which MS Weissenburg 101 reached its present stage of preparation. As it survives, it makes no reference to Lanfranc's transfer to Canterbury in 1070, but the only certain terminal date is Berengar's death in 1088. The manuscript should be considered as only a draft; it is not known whether a fair copy was ever made, and much less whether any such fair copy was dispatched to anyone, even Lanfranc. There is in fact, no reason to suppose that Lanfranc ever saw it. In any case, having moved to Canterbury in 1070 and having arranged for Pope Alexander II to be sent a copy of his own tract, Lanfranc shows little evidence of having been further active against Berengar, strongly though he continued to feel about 'the schismatic'.

The only evidence arising from his years at Canterbury is in two letters in which he responded to dogmatic enquiries from churchmen outside his own province. At some date between 1073 and 1078, Abbot Reynald of Saint-Cyprien at Poitiers and two other Poitevin churchmen approached Lanfranc with complaints against Berengar's strictures upon St Hilary of Poitiers's teaching about the problem of Christ's sufferings as experienced in his divine and human natures—a matter of Christology rather than of eucharistic theology. Lanfranc dissuaded his correspondents from visiting him in England, partly because so long as he was archbishop his involvement in this world's business left him no leisure for such studies as they wished to press upon him. Nevertheless he duly noted their account of the misreading of Hilary by *scismaticus ille* Berengar, vindicated Hilary as a catholic and

---

[111] *DCSD* cap. 1, col. 407 = Huygens, 'Bérenger', 170. It must be remembered that the passage of cap. 2 in the printed texts about Gregory VII—col. 411, 'Ad haec Gregorii septimi', to 'ab ea recesserant' = Huygens, 'Bérenger', 37–41—has no manuscript authority.

[112] As n. 105.   [113] *RCL*.

[114] For descriptions of the manuscript and for its history, see the introductions by Huygens and Milde to their edition of *RCL*: 1.9–31, 2.5–20. In this paragraph I am indebted to their descriptions and conclusions.

authoritative doctor, and gave a full and workmanlike exposition of the *communicatio idiomatum* in the incarnate Christ, that is, of the sharing of the attributes of Christ's divine and human natures in his single person.[115]

During Lanfranc's eleventh year in office (1080–1), he also replied to Domnall, bishop of Munster in Ireland, and others that, according to the belief of the English as of all western churches, infants who were baptized but who died before receiving holy communion might nevertheless be saved. Lanfranc broadened the discussion to cover communion in general. When receiving it, the faithful received Christ's flesh and blood both by their mouth and in their heart. When Augustine wrote of the faithful as sharing in figure in the Lord's passion, he referred to their grateful remembrance in their heart that Christ became man, suffered, and died for them. Such figurative speech does not deny but, rather, complements, by bringing home to their minds, the truth and reality of the flesh and blood that the faithful receive through the mouth. Without naming Berengar, Lanfranc referred to an error of denying that such figurative speech left room for the reality of Christ's flesh and blood, 'as it has seemed and still does not cease to seem to be so to many schismatics (*quod plerisque scismaticis visum est et adhuc non cessat videri*)'.[116] The reference to Berengar and his followers is transparent. Lanfranc's two letters show that, while archbishop, he remained deeply disquieted by Berengar's teaching, but that pressure of other business left him unable to give his mind further to it save when he received approaches that he deemed it necessary summarily to answer.

As for events at Rome under Gregory VII up to Berengar's final condemnation in the Lent synod of 1079,[117] there is virtually no evidence that Lanfranc by word or deed exerted any positive influence on either the considerable amount of polemical literature or the course of events. If the copy of the *De corpore et sanguine Domini* that Lanfranc dispatched late in 1072 in response to Alexander II's request ever reached Rome, there is nothing to suggest that it was noticed or used. The only reference to Lanfranc by name occurs in the memoir that Berengar himself wrote after his condemnation in 1079 in order to record his misfortunes. He related that, at a meeting in the Lateran at All Saintstide (1 November) 1078, he had been allowed to make an acceptable confession of faith about the eucharist: Gregory VII had then received it as sufficient and orthodox, though not necessarily as full and definitive. According to Berengar, Gregory publicly affirmed that Cardinal Peter Damiani, who was Lanfranc's inferior neither in learning nor in ecclesiastical standing, had not assented to Lanfranc's pronouncements about the sacrifice of the church. (Since Peter Damiani died in February 1072, the reference is virtually certainly not to the *De corpore et sanguine Domini* but to Lanfranc's arguments of 1050 at Rome and Vercelli.) Indeed, Gregory is said to have affirmed that Peter Damiani's

---

[115] Lanfranc, *Letters*, no. 46, pp. 142–51. The final sentences of this letter vividly illustrate Lanfranc's continuing sense of the menace of schismatics and their accomplices' and of the urgent duty of resisting them by all means.

[116] Lanfranc, *Letters*, no. 49, pp. 154–61. Lanfranc referred to Augustine, *De doctrina Christiana*, 3.55, pp. 93–4, which he had discussed in *DCSD* cap. 17, col. 429.

[117] *Reg.* 6.17a, pp. 425–7.

judgement was to be preferred to Lanfranc's, commenting that Peter was the better versed in divinity according to the Lord's own command to search the scriptures (John 5: 39). Berengar claimed the support of many persons of weight at Rome.[118] His testimony is partisan in his own cause, but Lanfranc seems indeed at this time to have been of only marginal importance in debates at Rome; there is no reason to see an influence upon the oath that Berengar was compelled to take in 1079, with its inclusion of the adverb *substantialiter* to safeguard the reality of Christ's body and blood in the consecrated elements. Indeed, Lanfranc's letter of 1080–1 to the Irish bishops contains a strong hint that he soon heard of the proceedings of 1079 and deemed them insufficient. His complaint that the 'schismatics' still did not cease to hold to their false view of the eucharist suggests that he deemed Gregory's condemnation to have been ineffectual;[119] in Lanfranc's eyes, the Lent synod of 1079 had merely scotched a snake that needed to be killed.

While it would be wrong to understate Lanfranc's contribution between 1050 and 1079 to the opposition to Berengar, especially in the light of the posthumous circulation of his *De corpore et sanguine Domini*, it must be said that his perceptible involvement was episodic rather than sustained. In 1079 Pope Gregory VII's condemnation of Berengar's teaching owed little directly to Lanfranc in its circumstances and formulation. Lanfranc may not have given to Gregory's statement of eucharistic orthodoxy in 1079 the full approval that he had given to Cardinal Humbert's in 1059.

As for the doctrinal subject-matter of Lanfranc's exchanges with Berengar, it would exceed the scope of the present study to attempt a full exposition and appraisal. But attention may be given to some principal respects in which it discloses Lanfranc's own way of thinking and cast of mind. Of great significance is the strong ecclesiological conviction that Lanfranc held and expressed. It led him to form and to retain a strong admiration for Cardinal Humbert, who formulated the profession that Berengar was made to take at Pope Nicholas II's Roman synod in 1059. Lanfranc censured Berengar for his error in describing Humbert as a Burgundian when he was in fact a Lotharingian, and for his consequent denigration of him. He praised Humbert not only for his stand in the eucharistic debate, but also for his distinction as a cardinal-bishop and for his salutary prominence in the affairs of the Roman church;[120] Humbert spoke not only for himself but also for the pope, for the synod, and for the whole church.[121]

Especial authority attached to the synod of 1059 because it was an assembly of Pope Nicholas II, supreme pontiff of all Christians (*totius christiani nominis summo pontifice*), and of 113 bishops assembled at Rome.[122] Comparable authority attached to Leo IX's Roman synod of 1050, with its large attendance of bishops.[123] It was a natural step for Lanfranc to regard these synods in the light of the four great

---

[118] Huygens, 'Bérenger', 388–403, at pp. 388–92.   [119] As n. 116.
[120] *DCSD* cap. 2, cols. 409D–410A; 16, col. 426AB.
[121] Ibid., cap. 2, cols. 410A, 412A = Huygens, 'Bérenger', 374.
[122] Ibid., cap. 1, col. 409B = Huygens, 'Bérenger', 371; 3, col. 412D = Huygens, 'Bérenger', 374.
[123] Ibid., cap. 4, col. 413A = Huygens, 'Bérenger', 375.

councils of the early church—Nicaea (325), Constantinople (381), Ephesus (431), and Chalcedon (451)—which Pope Gregory the Great had said that he venerated as he did the four gospels of the Lord. Lanfranc appealed especially to Ephesus, a council at which the true doctrine of eucharistic consecration had been proclaimed.[124] With the authority of councils went that of the writings of the fathers whom the church venerated and of the holy scriptures.[125] Like his contemporaries, Lanfranc regarded as *auctoritates* excerpts from all these sources without regard to time; he allowed no place for a development of Christian doctrine. Whatever the church proclaimed about the body of Christ was universally acknowledged to be the truth—by Greeks and Armenians no less than by Latins; and it was always the truth, at all times in the Christian dispensation. No one member of the church should deviate from the whole body deployed in space and time.[126]

The offence of Berengar was to have so deviated; hence Lanfranc's arraignment of him as an adversary of the catholic church.[127] Not only was he a perjurer in respect of the oath that he took when he accepted Humbert's formula at the Roman synod of 1059,[128] but by reason of compounding his eucharistic error by contumacy towards the Roman church and the doctors of the past he was the worst of heretics.[129] He and his followers were a mere sect in which he was leading his followers to perdition.[130] The one, essential remedy was that he should repent and return to the catholic church in loyalty and in teaching.[131]

Lanfranc's insistence upon the completeness and fixity of Christian doctrine at all times and places, and upon the duty of accepting the teachings of holy scripture and of the councils and fathers of the church, led him to adopt a strong, conservative position about the relation between authority and reason in determining Christian truth. In adopting it, he distanced himself radically from Berengar: he declared that, even if reason and authority were lacking to him as proofs of his faith, he would rather be a simple and unlettered catholic than, like Berengar, a polished and courtly heretic. Time and again, Lanfranc wrote of the eucharistic presence as a mystery of faith which it was healthful to believe but which could not usefully be searched out; the righteous man who lives by faith should seek neither to probe it by arguments nor to grasp it by reason.[132] Lanfranc nevertheless claimed that he could in fact defend his case about the eucharist both by divine authorities and by evident reasons.[133] This was the proper order when the truth was in itself beyond comprehension and beyond expression.[134] In dogmatic inquiries, the order was always first

---

[124] DCSD cap. 17, col. 428BC; see Gregory I, *Reg.* 1.24, vol. 1.32, and *Concilium Ephesinum: Epistola tertia Cyrilli ad Nestorium* and Anathematism 11, in *COD* 54–5, 61.

[125] DCSD cap. 1, col. 408AB = Huygens, 'Bérenger', 330–1; 17, col. 429AB.

[126] Ibid., cap. 4, col. 414A; 8, col. 419A; 17, col. 429AB; 19, col. 435D; 22, cols. 440D–441D; 23, cols. 441D–442C.

[127] Ibid., cap. 1, cols. 407A, 408C = Huygens, 'Bérenger', 370, 371–2,; cf. cap. 21, col. 439D.

[128] Ibid., cap. 4, col. 414CD; cf. cap. 5, cols. 414D–415D.

[129] Ibid., cap. 9, col. 420C; 16, col. 426BCD.

[130] Ibid., cap. 1, col. 409B = Huygens, 'Bérenger', 371; 2, cols. 440A–441D.

[131] Ibid., cap. 1, cols. 407A–408A = Huygens, 'Bérenger', 370; 4, col. 414BC.

[132] Ibid., cap. 7, col. 416D; 10, col. 421D; 17, col. 427AC; 18, col. 430BC; 21, cols. 439C–440B.

[133] Ibid., cap. 4, col. 414BC.   [134] Ibid., cap. 4, col. 414BC; 8, col. 419AB.

authorities and only secondarily reasons.[135] Lanfranc therefore wrote of the use of dialectic in the terms which he used in his biblical commentaries.[136] Where possible it was to be avoided or played down:

> God is my witness as is my conscience that when considering subjects of divinity I would wish neither to raise questions of dialectic nor to reply to them when they are raised. Even when the matter under discussion is such that it is patient of being more precisely explained by the rules of this art, so far as I can I conceal art by equipollences of propositions,[137] lest I should seem to trust more in art than in truth and in the authority of the holy fathers.[138]

As in his commentary on 1 Corinthians, Lanfranc conceded that dialectic, under due safeguards, had its proper use: it might serve to clarify what was accepted by faith upon proper authority and to underscore or elucidate its meaning; it might expose and banish error which obscured or contradicted Christian truth; recourse to it might be expedient in order to show that believers, too, could use reason effectively in matters of divinity.[139] But to range reason above the appropriate authorities, and thereby to subject the teaching of the church to the test of dialectic, was to subvert the faith and to number oneself amongst the enemies of the cross of Christ. Such, in Lanfranc's eyes, was Berengar's offence; in simplest terms, 'having abandoned sacred authorities, you have taken refuge in dialectic'.[140]

As Lanfranc presented his case against Berengar, it was the priority that Berengar accorded to dialectic which led him into his cardinal error about the eucharist: that, after consecration, the bread and wine remained altogether bread and wine; they were not in their reality and essence changed into the flesh and blood of Christ. According to Berengar, the elements remained as a sign of a Christ whose body was now in heaven and could not be divided upon earthly altars. The eucharistic elements remained only a *sacramentum* or sign; they were other than the *res sacramenti* or reality of Christ's body in heaven.[141]

Lanfranc was at pains to discredit Berengar's prior reliance upon dialectic by fixing upon his assertion that, as a matter of logic, 'not every affirmation will be able to stand, a part having been undermined (*non constare poterit affirmatio omnis, parte subruta*)'.[142] Lanfranc selected two statements by Berengar for criticism in the light of it: 'The bread and wine are only sacraments'; 'The bread and the wine are only the body and blood of Christ'. Each was an affirmation. If, therefore, part (bread and wine) were taken away by consecration, according to Berengar the sacrament, or else the body and blood, would also be taken away; the bread and the wine must persist after consecration. But, as Lanfranc pointed out, Berengar had cast his major premiss in the form of a particular negative: *non . . . affirmatio omnis*, not of

---

[135] Ibid., cap. 4, col. 414B; 7, cols. 416D–417A, 418BC; 19–21, cols. 434–40.
[136] See above, pp. 56–9; cf. *DCSD* cap. 21, col. 439BC.
[137] See above, p. 58. In effect, this implied a restriction to the citation or paraphrase of ancient authorities without venturing upon hazardous commentary.
[138] *DCSD* cap. 7, cols. 416D–417B.   [139] Ibid., col. 417AB.
[140] Ibid., col. 416D; cf. caps. 8, 21, cols. 418D, 439C: 'Hoc colligitis secundum humanam scientiam, non secundum divinam.'
[141] Ibid., cap. 4, col. 414B; 7–8, cols. 416–19; 20, col. 436A; 22, col. 440BC.
[142] For Lanfranc's discussion of this phrase, see ibid., caps. 7–8, cols. 416–19.

a universal negative: *affirmatio nulla*. Therefore even as a matter of logic his syllogism failed as a support for his argument. A particular negative allowed for exceptions. In the case of the eucharist, there might be such an exception, allowing for divine action to bring it about that Christ's body and blood became really and essentially present while bread and wine in some sense remained. By thus seizing upon the particular negative, Lanfranc came near to making only a debating point, albeit a successful one. But it served his purpose of discrediting Berengar in his alleged prior reliance on dialectic and of clearing the ground for him to place authority before dialectic.

Lanfranc's own teaching about the eucharist had as its heart and centre the conviction that from New Testament and patristic times the universal and express certainty of the church was that, at the consecration, the bread and wine were transformed: their external appearance remained, but in themselves they became the real, not only the figurative, flesh and blood that Christ took of the Blessed Virgin, offered in sacrifice upon the cross, and took to heaven in his ascension. Save that he avoided the adverb *sensualiter* (which Humbert had taken from Berengar's own writings), Lanfranc's position in no way differed in respect of its realism from that expressed by Humbert in his formula of 1059.[143] To cite Lanfranc's own words:

The sacrament of Christ's body, so far as concerns that which the Lord himself immolated on the cross, is his flesh which, covered by the outward form of bread (*forma panis opertam*), we receive in the sacrament, and his blood which we drink under the appearance and taste of wine (*sub vini specie ac sapore*).[144]

Lanfranc argued that such an extreme realist understanding of the conversion of the eucharistic elements was confirmed by the long record of divine corroborations through which, during the celebration of mass, doubters were assured or spiritual men rewarded by the miraculous withdrawal of the corruptible veils so that their eyes saw in its patent reality the flesh and blood of Christ.[145] Old Testament miracles, too, offered an *a fortiori* reassurance that such a real conversion was possible to God: if by God's word Moses's rod could be turned into a serpent or water from the Nile be made blood, how much more conceivable was the change effected in the Christian eucharist.[146]

The realism of Lanfranc's view appears the starker on account of the limitations of the vocabulary and concepts at his disposal when he sought in terms of current philosophy to express the eucharistic consecration and its effects. His most frequent recourse was to speak of the change as taking place in essence (*essentialiter*). The relation of appearance to reality after consecration was stated in terms of the

---

[143] See above, pp. 63–4. Lanfranc evidently avoided the adverb *sensualiter* to convey the reality of Christ's presence in the consecrated bread and wine in order to avoid confusion with his teaching that in the sacrament the flesh and blood of Christ are invisible, intelligible, and spiritual, i.e. that they are recognized by the faithful mind of the devout believer: see *DCSD* cap. 14, col. 424A.

[144] Ibid., col. 423D; cf. caps. 5, 13, 19, cols. 415A, 423C, 435C.

[145] Ibid., cap. 17, col. 427AB; 19, col. 435CD.

[146] Ibid., cap. 9, col. 420AB; 18, col. 431A–C.

Aristotelian distinction between principal and secondary essences (*principales et secundae essentiae*). By employing them, he set in contrast the interior nature (*interior essentia*) and the external appearance (*visibilis species*) of the consecrated elements, that is, what the senses could perceive and what the mind could know. Such a contrast rested upon no developed metaphysical view; it was evidence of the incomprehensible mystery that the righteous man must accept but cannot explain.[147] More seldom, Lanfranc introduced into his discussion the word substance (*substantia*).[148] He did not use the adverb *substantialiter*. He used the noun much as he used *essentia* to express the inner reality of objects. Although in his biblical commentaries he showed acquaintance with the contrast of substance and accidents (but with little awareness of the Aristotelian definition of the contrast),[149] he did not refer to it in connection with the eucharist. *Substantia*, like *essentia*, was appropriate in order to convey the reality of the eucharistic change. But beyond their signification as nouns, what they and cognate words expressed was utterly inadequate to convey the mystery:

We therefore believe that the earthly substances (*terrenas substantias*) which on the Lord's table are divinely consecrated through the ministry[150] of priests are incomprehensibly, inexpressibly, and wonderfully by the working of divine power converted into the essence (*converti in essentiam*) of the Lord's body, the appearances (*speciebus*) of the things themselves being preserved along with certain other qualities lest those who saw them raw and bloody should shudder, and so that those who believe should receive more ample rewards of faith; while the body of Christ itself remains in heaven at the right hand of the Father, immortal, inviolate, whole, uncorrupted, intact.[151]

This passage illustrates how Lanfranc usually reserved the word body (*corpus*) for the glorified body of Christ which is in heaven; when speaking of Christ's presence in the eucharistic bread he normally used the word flesh (*caro*). *Corpus* might nevertheless be used of the eucharist (as in the phrase *Hoc est corpus meum*), because a thing that is signified may lend its name to that which signifies it; moreover, a thing may properly be described in terms of that of which it consists, as when scripture describes man as *terra* (Gen. 3: 19).[152] Lanfranc's distinction between body and flesh enabled him to claim that it might truly be said both that devout communicants receive the very body taken by Christ of the Virgin and that they do not receive the very body. They receive it as regards its essence and the properties and power of its true nature (*ad essentiam veraeque naturae proprietatem atque virtutem*); they do not if attention be directed to the appearance of bread and wine and to the other things that remain.[153]

---

[147] Ibid., cap. 5, col. 415BC; 7, cols. 417D, 418A; 9, col. 420D; 17, col. 427A; 20, col. 436D.
[148] Ibid., cap. 8, col. 419AB; 18, col. 430BC; 22, col. 440B.
[149] Commenting on Gal. 4: 12, Lanfranc contrasted the necessary identity of all men *in substantiali essentia* with their possible, acquired identity *in accidentali essentia* in respect of holiness; see also his comment on Heb. 3: 14, where faith as *substantia* underlies good works as their foundation: col. 383A.
[150] Correcting the reading in *PL* from *mysterium* to *ministerium*.
[151] *DCSD* cap. 18, col. 430A–C; cf. cap. 8, col. 410A.
[152] Ibid., cap. 6, cols. 415D–416A; 10, col. 424B–D; 14, cols. 423–5; 17, col. 427BC; 20, cols. 438A–439B.
[153] Ibid., cap. 18, col. 430CD; cf. cap. 14, col. 424A–D.

Lanfranc's gravamen against Berengar was that, proceeding according to the false constraint of dialectic, he not only demystified but also oversimplified the manner of Christ's presence in the eucharist: for Berengar, his presence was either real or figurative. Since 'not every affirmation will be able to stand, a part having been undermined', if the reality, or essence, of bread and wine were taken away by consecration, it could not be claimed that there was present flesh (or body) and blood. Therefore the reality of bread and wine must persist; they could only signify, and not essentially be, flesh and blood. For Lanfranc, however, Christ's presence in the bread and wine was both real and figurative; communion was both corporal and spiritual. When at Canterbury, Lanfranc explained this duality in simple terms to the Irish bishops.[154] In his riposte to Berengar, he moved on from his affirmation of the reality of Christ's flesh and blood under the appearances of the consecrated bread and wine to consider them as also figuratively a *sacramentum* pointing to a *res sacramenti* which was the wholeness of Christ's body as glorified in heaven.

In so developing his thought, Lanfranc probably owed a larger debt to his adversary than he was prepared to declare. Berengar's salutary and enduring contribution to eucharistic theology was to revive Augustine of Hippo's definition of a sacrament as a sacred sign (*sacrum signum*)—something material and visible which was invested in the mind with a religious and spiritual significance.[155] When Lanfranc addressed Berengar's use of the definition, he somewhat brusquely asserted that he, too, set store by it, although he acknowledged no debt to Berengar.[156] But one suspects that it was to be found among the roses that Lanfranc admitted Berengar to have interspersed amongst the thorns of his *Scriptum contra synodum*.[157] For Lanfranc, the consecrated elements in which Christ's flesh and blood were in reality present and which the communicant received as such were also in two senses signs. In the action of the mass, the breaking of the host and the pouring of the chalice into the communicants' mouths signified sacramentally Christ's immolation of his body on the cross and the flowing of blood from his side. By imitation, though not by repetition, in every eucharist there was a sacrificial immolation of Christ's body and blood.[158] And further, because in this manner there was a memorial of Christ's passion, faithful communicants through its signification fed upon Christ spiritually in their hearts as well as physically through their mouths. Christians on earth could feed by faith upon the whole Christ who was in heaven, and in their lives they could bear the fruit of their meditation upon him as now glorified.

Lanfranc brought together the three leading themes of his eucharistic doctrine—the real presence of Christ's flesh and blood in the consecrated elements, their figurative immolation in the eucharistic sacrifice, and the fruitful spiritual communion of the well-disposed communicant—in the following words:

In himself, Christ was immolated once and for all; . . . for as true God and true man he hung only once upon the cross, offering himself to the Father as a living sacrifice . . . for the

---

[154] See above, p. 66.   [155] See Montclos, *Lanfranc et Bérenger*, 133, 140, 452–3.
[156] *DCSD* cap. 12, col. 422B–D; cf. cap. 13, col. 423C; 20, col. 437C.
[157] Ibid., cap. 1, col. 409C = Huygens, 'Bérenger', 372.
[158] Ibid., cap. 12, col. 423A; 14, col. 424AB; 19, col. 435C.

living and the dead, for all, that is, whom the depth of divine counsel judged should be redeemed.... But in the sacrament that the church often repeats as a memorial of this thing, the flesh of Christ is each day immolated, divided, and eaten, and his blood is drunk from the chalice by the mouths of the faithful. Both are true, both are as taken from the Virgin. The flesh is taken through itself, and the blood through itself, not without a certain quality of mystery. However, in another manner of speaking, the whole Christ is said and believed to be eaten—namely, when the life eternal who is himself is longed for with spiritual desire, when the remembrance of his commandments is held in the mind as sweeter than honey and the honeycomb, when brotherly charity, whose sign this sacrament bears, is cherished for the love of Christ, when it is sweetly and healthfully treasured in the memory that for the salvation of men he was bruised by insults, hung from a cross, pierced by nails, and wounded by a lance. Both manners of eating are necessary, both are fruitful. The one needs the other if it is to work anything that is good.[159]

For those, therefore, who received unworthily, communion was real but to damnation. For those who received worthily, there was a communion both of body and of heart and mind, so that they had a part in the Christ who died in sacrifice on the cross and who now reigns for ever in heaven.

The spiritual, even the devotional, depth and the pastoral dimension of Lanfranc's eucharistic theology as of his biblical commentaries are apparent. He recognized no such qualities in Berengar's mind and writings. In this it must be said that he did not give a fair representation of his adversary. Berengar's letters, such as the pastoral letter to King Philip I of France in which he urged him to frequent and devout communion, and the deeply moving poem *Iuste iudex* which is probably attributable to him, suggest more attractive sides to Berengar that Lanfranc did not have the generosity to recognize.[160] Nor did Lanfranc give a fair picture of Berengar's intellectual power and range, which are apparent despite the obscurity and repetitiveness of the *Rescriptum contra Lanfrannum*.[161] In this work Berengar was able to mount a formidable challenge to Lanfranc on his own ground and according to his own presuppositions: in the long second book he presented a sustained case that the authority of Ambrose, of which Lanfranc had made much, could be claimed in his own defence and that it might the better be so claimed when Lanfranc's use of dialectic was brought to bear. In the third book Berengar applied the same manner of argument to other patristic authorities.

There was an element of *ad hominem* argument here. For at root, Lanfranc was correct in arguing that Berengar approached authorities by way of dialectic and not vice versa. Even so, there were limitations to Lanfranc's vision. As a traditional monastic theologian, he saw in Berengar's use of dialectic only the vain and pernicious pursuing of this world's wisdom which he roundly condemned in his commentaries on the Pauline epistles.[162] But Berengar, archdeacon and *scholasticus*, was

---

[159] Ibid., cap. 15, cols. 425–6; cf. cap. 17, cols. 429A–430A. For the value that Lanfranc set upon the cross as an aid to devotion while celebrating mass, see Lanfranc, *Letters*, no. 20, pp. 100–3.
[160] Letter: EF no. 82, pp. 132–6; poem: Martène and Durand, *Thesaurus*, 4.115–16. Cf. William of Malmesbury's appraisal of Berengar, citing Hildebert of le Mans: *GR* 3.284, 3–9, vol. 1.514–19.
[161] Cf. the comments of Huygens: *RCL* 1.30–1; and Chadwick, 'Ego Berengarius', 417–18, 441, 444–5.
[162] See above, p. 57.

beginning to grasp the potentialities of dialectic as a tool of a human reason that might constructively be brought to bear over the whole range of Christian truth in order the more effectively to comprehend it.[163] However tentatively and even clumsily, he may be regarded as taking early steps towards the use of reason to promote understanding by the early scholasticism of the twelfth century. This was a development that Lanfranc did little to anticipate or to prepare for.

Against the background of this contrast of approaches and lack of sympathy, it can scarcely be denied that Lanfranc gave a less than fair account of Berengar's teaching about the eucharist. Not only did he not acknowledge the value of Berengar's revived understanding of a sacrament as a sacred sign, but he did not acknowledge that Berengar repeatedly asserted in formulas that Lanfranc himself might have written that the bread and wine are by consecration converted into the true body and blood of Christ, basing such assertions not on his own opinion but upon ancient authorities.[164] Yet, from his own uncompromisingly realist standpoint, Lanfranc was justified in condemning Berengar as he did. It was for reasons of dialectic that Berengar also affirmed that the reality of bread and wine must persist in the consecrated elements. Therefore he could not but regard the reality of body and blood after consecration as existing not by identity but by analogy. Berengar could not satisfactorily rebut Lanfranc's retort that:

What you claim to be the true body of Christ is in sacred writings called appearance, likeness, figure, sign, mystery, sacrament. But these words must refer to something else. And no things that are referred to something else can be those things to which they are referred. Therefore there is no body of Christ.[165]

Such argument by analogy as Berengar used did not admit of such a true change of essence or substance as Lanfranc maintained that the church's authorities always and rightly taught.

With their different appraisals of the role of dialectic in establishing and securing Christian teaching, Lanfranc and Berengar were arguing at cross purposes. Lanfranc was taking his stand upon what he regarded as the firm and given authority of the past; Berengar was feeling his way, however tentatively, towards the inquiring scholasticism of the future. There can be no easy conclusion about which was right and which was wrong. They became locked in a debate at a time when the intellectual tools for its satisfactory conduct were not yet available.

---

[163] Thus, Berengar wrote in commentary upon Augustine, *De ordine*, 2.15.38, 2.16.44, pp. 128, 131, 'Circa dialecticam quantum oportet satagenti de videndo luce clarius deo et anima spondere in eodem libro minime dubitavit, nec sequendus in eo es ulli cordato homini, ut malit auctoritatibus circa aliqua cedere quam ratione, si optio sibi detur, preire': RCL 1.1799–1824, vol. 1.85–6; see also 1.2255, vol. 1.98.

[164] '... ego interim dico panem et vinum per consecrationem converti in altari in verum Christi corpus et sanguinem non mea, non tua, sed evangelica apostolicaque simul autenticarum scripturarum, quibus contraire fas non sit, est sententia...': RCL 1.749–53, vol. 1.57.

[165] *DCSD* cap. 20, col. 436A.

5
Retrospect

In 1070, when Lanfranc left his abbacy at Caen to become archbishop of Canterbury, he was probably about 60 years old—by medieval standards an advanced age. In Lombardy, and then in Normandy, he had had a long and varied experience of lay, monastic, and general church life, and not least of the aspirations and concerns of the early reform papacy and of secular rulers who, for whatever reason, had sympathy with them. At each stage of his life he had demonstrated his ability to adapt himself with integrity and effectiveness to the demands that he encountered. He gave little evidence of originality or initative, but when the time called for this he could put the past behind him to meet fresh demands and to identify himself with fresh situations. He was a man of the present moment, without nostalgia for the phases of his own past though with respect for its abiding loyalties, and without any compelling vision for the future save in so far as current circumstances and commitments pointed a way to attainable improvement.

Lanfranc had migrated from Lombardy to France almost forty years before. It may well be that the most lasting effects upon him of his early years in Italy were the result, not of his own family and activities, but of the prevailing political events and climate of the region. If Lanfranc was too young to remember Pope Benedict VIII's and the Emperor Henry II's synod at Pavia in 1022, with its programme of collaboration in church government and of practical reform, he is likely to have learnt of it; his presence in 1049 at Mainz when Pope Leo IX and the Emperor Henry III of Germany similarly held a synod together may have renewed in his mind the benefits of such collaboration. So, too, in the Norman duchy may Duke William's part in provincial councils. Lanfranc's view of the relations of *sacerdotium* and *regnum* may thus have had its origin in the Lombardy of his childhood. No less important may have been the memory of civic unrest and of military campaigns in forming in Lanfranc's mind a sense of the value of public order enforced by firm and effective government. Whether Lanfranc gained the proficiency in the study and practice of secular law that later sources claimed for him must be regarded as far from certain; even if he did, the secular law of the Lombardy in which he grew up was as yet at an early stage of its medieval development, and he quickly put it behind him so that it left little trace in his later life. His childhood was nevertheless spent in a milieu in which the skills of law and government were actively pursued. What is certain is that Lanfranc left Lombardy after much study of the liberal arts, of which he was already a recognized teacher.

Having settled at Bec, he was a monk there for some twenty years: for most of them he was the prior, or second-in-command, of the new abbey. This seems to have been the main formative experience of his life. By dint of an initially painful process of adjustment, at Bec he learnt and settled down to a living of the cenobitic life according to the Rule of St Benedict; for Lanfranc, Bec was indeed Benedict's *dominici scola servitii*—a 'school of the Lord's service'. For him as for most monks, life in an ordered community of obedience and mutual support provided a necessary and a sufficient way to Christian perfection. In terms of material wealth, endowment, and patronage, Bec was not well provided. Lanfranc had, therefore, to continue to teach the liberal arts, in part to provide revenue for his house. He did so by teaching not only monks but also external pupils. This brought him fame as a teacher far and wide, and not least with the reform papacy. His pupils included many who would be prominent in the monastic order and beyond; many who had been instructed by him at Bec, whether in the monastic life or in the liberal arts, retained a bond with him which persisted after he became archbishop of Canterbury. But Lanfranc's development as a monk led him increasingly to wish to turn from secular to sacred studies. His surviving writings from his years at Bec and Caen deserve careful appraisal in the light of this wish. His commentaries on the twelve Pauline epistles are, in the final form that he gave them, far from being adjuncts to the study of the liberal arts. When read with the Vulgate text which they follow, they provide a remarkably comprehensive theological exposition, both doctrinal and practical, of the whole scope of Christian belief. Lanfranc envisaged not only the life of monks in the cloister but also that of clergy and laity in their various callings. The commentaries help to show how he furnished his mind not only in terms of the cloister but also of the Christian world at large. Similarly, for all its polemic, his anti-Berengarian tract *De corpore et sanguine Domini* offers abundant evidence of his understanding of the place of the eucharist in the devotion of the church at large and of individual Christians, monks, clergy, and laity. In his biblical and in his eucharistic writings alike, Lanfranc set high value upon authority and obedience to authority. His mind was in no way speculative or innovatory. But the depth of religious conviction and feeling should not be mistaken or overlooked. The religion of the commentaries and of the tract was at the heart of the pastoral care that Lanfranc brought to bear at Canterbury.

As prior of Bec, Lanfranc had prolonged experience of administration and of practical affairs, since Abbot Herluin left such matters largely in his hands. An especial concern was the siting and construction of monastic buildings and offices, and the provision of finance for their inception and maintenance. His experience was greatly augmented during the seven years when he was abbot of Saint-Étienne at Caen, and so at last in a position of ruling authority, the new foundation associated him the more closely with its ducal founder, and also lay within the diocese of the duke's half-brother Odo of Bayeux, who after the conquest of England was earl of Kent.

A cardinal feature of Lanfranc's monastic years at Bec and Caen was his close and sympathetic relationship with the reform popes of the time, especially Leo IX, Nicholas II, and Alexander II, all of whom held him in high regard. From his Pavian boyhood, he is likely to have retained memories of the first positive, if not very effective, stirrings of reform under Benedict VIII. His year-long association with Leo IX in 1049–50, during which he had every opportunity of observing the reform papacy in resolute action, confirmed him in his approval of the popes of his monastic years. Especially noteworthy is his praise for Cardinal Humbert of Silva Candida, whom he applauded not only for his anti-Berengarian stance but also for his wisdom and zeal as a general mentor of the papacy. Lanfranc may have visited Rome again under Nicholas II in 1059; in any case, Nicholas's letter to him makes clear the pope's warm commendation, while the copying of Nicholas's encyclical *Vigilantia universalis* into Lanfranc's canonical collection testifies to Lanfranc's approval of the most characteristic and full manifesto of the early reform popes. Under Alexander II, Lanfranc certainly travelled to Rome from Caen in 1067. It is not too much to claim Lanfranc as having been in mind and in action a man of the reform papacy, and as having been recognized as such by successive popes from Leo IX to Alexander II.

Such was the man who, in 1070, William, duke of Normandy and by then for four years also king of England, chose for the see of Canterbury and for the chief ecclesiastical office in a land with which he had no known earlier contact.

6

The Move to Canterbury

In a letter probably of early in 1073, in which he begged of Pope Alexander II that he might be released from his archiepiscopal office in England and return to the monastic life,[1] Lanfranc eloquently testified to his long and stubborn resistance in 1070 to accepting a promotion which had been for him a source of distresses (*calamitates*) which the pope had brought upon him. Like his advancement to be abbot of Caen, his choice to be archbishop had been made by the king-duke William. As in 1067 Lanfranc resisted election to the see of Rouen,[2] so now he resisted many endeavours to induce him to accept that of Canterbury. It is clear that two persons were mainly instrumental in overcoming his resistance. The first was Herluin, his sometime abbot at Bec, to whom he acknowledged a lasting obedience; King William used him to assist in persuading Lanfranc. Tradition at Bec had it that, a few days before royal agents came there, Herluin had a vision of Lanfranc as a great and fruitful apple tree in Bec's orchard which William wished to transplant to a garden of his own. Because he was lord, he had his way. But he could not cause all the roots of the tree to be dug up; many suckers therefore sprouted in Normandy to provide more great trees, so that both the abbot and the king benefited when the abbot, although unwilling, reinforced the king's command that Lanfranc, who was obedient to the abbot as to God himself, should cross to England and pass on to its people the precepts of true religion (*ob religionis sacre institutionem tradendam Anglis*).[3]

Lanfranc provides evidence that a probably still greater part in overcoming his resistance was played by Pope Alexander II.[3] He reminded the pope that King William had been unable to prevail upon him until Alexander's legates, Bishop Ermenfrid of Sion and the Roman clerk Hubert,[4] came from Rome and at a meeting of the Norman bishops, abbots, and leading laity ordered him by authority of the apostolic see to accept the church of Canterbury. He crossed to England where, on the feast of the Assumption (15 August) 1070, the king constituted him archbishop; on the feast of the Decollation of St John the Baptist (29 August) he received consecration at Canterbury.[5] At every stage, nothing was spared to mark and to record the authority and solemnity of the process. In Normandy, he agreed to accept Canterbury in a comprehensive assembly held by legates of the apostolic see. It was made clear that he became archbishop under constraint by king and pope

---

[1] Lanfranc, *Letters*, no. 1, pp. 30–5. The probable date range is 25 Dec. 1072 to 21 Apr. 1073.
[2] See above, p. 37.   [3] *VH* caps. 78–84, pp. 99–100/200–1; *VL* cap. 6, pp. 685–6.   [4] As n. 1.
[5] For the legates and their activities in Normandy and England, see Cowdrey, 'Bishop Ermenfrid of Sion'.

acting in concert.⁶ When he came to Canterbury, Lanfranc was met and accompanied to the city by the monks of both the cathedral monastery (Christ Church) and the abbey of St Augustine.⁷ His formal appointment and his consecration alike took place on solemn days; his formal election in England—'he was elected by the senior monks of the church of Canterbury with the bishops and princes, clergy and people of England in the king's court'⁸—was as impressive as had been his acceptance of the see in a Norman gathering. It was claimed at Canterbury that, according to ancient custom, all the bishops of the English kingdom took part in or consented to his consecration.⁹ In fact, the northern province of York was not represented. The metropolitan see was vacant since the death on 11 September 1069 of Archbishop Aldred, and Bishop Ethelwine of Durham had been outlawed.[10] Eight bishops of the southern province joined in Lanfranc's consecration: William of London, Walchelin of Winchester, Remigius of Dorchester, Siward of Rochester, Herfast of Elmham, Stigand of Selsey, Herman of Sherborne, and Giso of Wells. The three absentees, Leofric of Exeter, Walter of Hereford, and Wulfstan of Worcester, were said all humbly to have sent acceptable excuses for absence.[11] It was an impressive demonstration of unanimity and support by ecclesiastical and lay sections of society alike.

It would be outside the scope of this study of Lanfranc to attempt a full survey of the circumstances and state of the English church, secular and monastic, of which he thus assumed the leadership.[12] But two matters, which are perhaps closely interrelated, call for especial discussion as illustrating Lanfranc's approach and actions: the career and character of his predecessor at Canterbury, Archbishop Stigand; and the standpoint taken with regard to the English church by the apostolic see under Pope Alexander II.

A royal clerk by background, Stigand first became a bishop in 1043 when he received the somewhat impoverished East Anglian see of Elmham. Upon translation to Winchester in 1047, he resigned it to his brother Ethelmar. When in 1052 he received the see of Canterbury he retained Winchester, so that he was open to a charge of pluralism. But since the see of Rochester was subject to Canterbury and since his brother was bishop of Elmham, he disposed of extensive ecclesiastical authority and wealth; and under King Edward the Confessor he seems to have been a great deal at court. As a secular clerk he was also able to amass great personal wealth; for example, in Domesday Book he is recorded as having had property extending over ten shires.[13] It does not seem possible to pin upon him any blatant simony, and he could be generous to churches and monasteries. But he had an air of excessive affluence

---

⁶ 'compellente rege Willelmo et iubente papa Alexandro': *AL* p. 84; see also the résumé of Lanfranc's succession in Lanfranc, *Letters*, no. 3/i, pp. 38–41, and cf. *VH* cap. 78, pp. 99/200, and *VL* cap. 10, p. 695.

⁷ *AL* 84.   ⁸ Ibid.

⁹ 'Ad quem consecrandum omnes episcopi regni Anglorum, servato antique more, venerunt': ibid.; cf. Lanfranc, *Letters*, no. 3/i, pp. 38–41; Hugh the Chanter, 4–5.

[10] Symeon of Durham, 3.17, pp. 192–5.   [11] As n. 9.

[12] For a full discussion, see Barlow, *The English Church 1000–1066*.

[13] For Stigand's wealth and for a good general account of him, see Smith, 'Archbishop Stigand'.

and worldliness. Of especial seriousness for his reputation was the irregularity of his acquisition of the *pallium*—the stole of lamb's wool which signified a metropolitan's participation in the pastoral office of the vicar of St Peter and for which an archbishop was normally expected to visit the apostolic see. At the outset, Stigand had merely appropriated the *pallium* of his predecessor Robert of Jumièges, who was still alive; in 1058 a *pallium* of his own was sent to him by the short-reigning anti-pope Benedict X. Doubt might therefore be felt about Stigand as an exemplar of the pastoral office; as Eadmer later put it, a man might not wish to receive his ministrations lest he seem to put on a curse in place of a blessing (*ne maledictionem videretur induere pro benedictione*).[14]

There was, therefore, always an ambivalence of attitude towards Stigand's ministrations which seems to have become more pronounced during the last years before the Norman Conquest. In 1058 Bishops Ethelric of Selsey and Siward of Rochester were consecrated by him, though that may have been before the *pallium* from Benedict X arrived.[15] In 1060 Giso of Wells and Walter of Hereford, both by origin Lotharingians, travelled to Rome for consecration by Pope Nicholas, to whom, no doubt, they explained their reasons.[16] Nevertheless, in 1062 at the king's Easter court, two papal legates, including Bishop Ermenfrid of Sion, were willing for Stigand as well as Archbishop Aldred of York to support them in their choice of Wulfstan to be bishop of Worcester.[17] But it was to Aldred that Wulfstan turned for consecration.[18] Under the English kings, Stigand consecrated no more bishops but only abbots: Ethelsig of St Augustine's at Canterbury (1061), Baldwin of Bury St Edmunds (1065), and Thurstan of Ely (1066).[19] In 1062, while still earl, Harold Godwinson apparently did not allow Stigand to consecrate the church that he founded at Waltham Cross.[20] In view of this, despite a conflict of evidence about who crowned Harold on 6 January 1066, it is likely that Aldred did so rather then Stigand.[21]

After his conquest of England in 1066, which had been well prepared by seeking papal favour, William I took no risks where the establishing of his regality was concerned. At Christmas 1066 Aldred of York, not Stigand, performed his coronation in Westminster Abbey, though there is a possibility that Stigand assisted him.[22]

---

[14] *Hist. nov.*, 1, p. 9, cf. Mal. 2: 2.

[15] *ASC* DE *a.* 1058, p. 134. Benedict X was elected and inthroned on 5 Apr. For consecrations between 1052 and 1058, see Stubbs, *Registrum sacrum*, 36–7.

[16] John of Worcester, *a.* 1061, vol. 2.586–9; *CS* no. 77, vol. 1/1.548–9.

[17] *VW* 1.10–11, pp. 17–18; John of Worcester, *a.* 1062, vol. 2.590–1.

[18] *VW* 1.11, p. 19; John of Worcester, *a.* 1062, pp. 590–2, according to which Wulfstan nevertheless made a canonical profession to Stigand.

[19] Ethelsig: *ASC* E, *a.* 1061, pp. 135–6; Baldwin: Hermann, *De miraculis*, cap. 28, p. 66; Thurstan: *Liber Eliensis*, 2.98, 118, pp. 168, 201 (according to which Stigand consecrated Thurstan at King Harold's command).

[20] *The Waltham Chronicle*, cap. 16, pp. 32–5.

[21] According to the Worcester Chronicle, Harold was crowned by Aldred of York; *a.* 1066, vol. 2.600–1. Stigand is named as the officiating archbishop by William of Poitiers, 2.1, pp. 100–1; BT Pl. 31; and *The Waltham Chronicle*, cap. 28, pp. 44–5.

[22] *ASC* D *a.* 1066, p. 145; William of Poitiers, 2.30, pp. 150–1. The *Carmen de Hastingae proelio* said that two unnamed metropolitans who were equal in rank (*honore pari*) supported the king as he entered the abbey church: lines 803–4, pp. 46–7.

Aldred also crowned Queen Matilda at Pentecost 1068;[23] the text of the *Laudes regiae* which was composed for the occasion referred to Aldred as though he were head of the entire clerical order of society.[24] Yet, in less exalted connections, Stigand seems for more than three years to have been accorded a greater and more active prominence than he had enjoyed for some time before 1066. In 1067 he was allowed to consecrate Remigius, monk of Fécamp, as bishop of Dorchester.[25] At the royal court of 1068, during which Aldred crowned the queen, two royal charters were witnessed by Stigand who attested before Aldred.[26] Perhaps somewhat earlier a royal writ addressed to Stigand and to Count Eustace of Boulogne referred to a grant of land to Westminster Abbey.[27] So late as 1069 Stigand with due precedence witnessed two further royal charters.[28] Given Stigand's vast wealth and connections, William of Poitiers was probably right to say that, despite the king's suspicion of him, he could not but suffer him and hold him in honour on account of his high authority among the English.[29]

It was probably the death on 11 September 1069 of Archbishop Aldred, whom the Normans seem to have held in high regard,[30] that persuaded the king to set in motion the train of events that led to Stigand's deposition and replacement by Lanfranc. The politically troubled state of the kingdom must have added urgency to the proceedings.[31] At Easter 1070 two Roman clerks, the cardinal-priests John and Peter, assisted by Bishop Ermenfrid of Sion, held a legatine council at Winchester which was followed at Pentecost by a further legatine council held by Ermenfrid.[32] According to the Worcester Chronicle, Stigand was deposed at Winchester for three reasons: (i) he had wrongfully held the see of Winchester after his promotion to Canterbury; (ii) while his predecessor at Canterbury, Robert of Jumièges, was still alive he had taken not only his see but also his *pallium*; and (iii) he had also received a *pallium* of his own from Benedict X, whom the Roman church excommunicated because he had simoniacally invaded the apostolic see. Stigand's brother Ethelmar was also deposed from Elmham.[33] Stigand's power in the church was thus totally ended.

Having succeeded him as archbishop, Lanfranc adopted an attitude to him and his ministrations that was no less rigorous and dismissive than that which he had adopted towards Berengar of Tours. There was an implicit dissociation from the king's toleration and use of Stigand since 1066. The evidence for Lanfranc's stance is the written professions of obedience which he exacted from three recently consecrated bishops—Wulfstan of Worcester, Remigius of Dorchester, and Herfast of Elmham.[34] Their phraseology differed according to the various circumstances of

---

[23] *ASC* D a. 1067(1068), p. 148.
[24] 'Aldrado Eboracensi archiepiscopo et omni clero sibi commisso salus et vita': Cowdrey, 'The Anglo-Norman *Laudes regiae*', 71–1, with discussion on 52–5.
[25] *Canterbury Professions*, ed. Richter, no. 32, p. 27.
[26] *Regesta WI*, nos. 181, 286, pp. 594–601, 863–5.   [27] Ibid., no. 291, p. 882.
[28] Ibid., nos. 138, 254, pp. 463–5, 767–9.   [29] William of Poitiers, 2.34, 38, pp. 160–1, 166–7.
[30] e.g. William of Poitiers, 2.30, 49, pp. 150–1, 186–7.   [31] *ASC* DE aa. 1068–9, pp. 149–50.
[32] *CS* nos. 86–7, vol. 1/2.565–81.   [33] John of Worcester, a. 1070, vol. 3.12–13.
[34] *Canterbury Professions*, nos. 31–3, pp. 26–8. No. 32, at least, cannot be dated before Lanfranc and

their promotion, but they were unanimous in their arraignment of Stigand. Lanfranc did not expressly take up the charge of pluralism that the papal legates had made at Winchester. But he dwelt upon Stigand's moral turpitude in his progress from Elmham to Winchester and Canterbury, accusing him of ambition, guile, plotting, and violence. As at Winchester, much was made of his contempt of apostolic authority in seizing the *pallium* of Robert of Jumièges. No mention was made of the *pallium* from Benedict X.[35] But after hearing of his invasion of the see and misappropriation of Robert's *pallium*, Stigand was often summoned to Rome—the phrase is not without irony in view of Lanfranc's own later disregard of such summonses—and at last condemned and excommunicated. For nineteen years he persisted in his obduracy. Each of the five popes of this period—Leo IX, Victor II, Stephen IX, Nicholas II, and Alexander II—excommunicated him for his contumacy and sent legates to England who forbade anyone to show him reverence or to be ordained by him. Remigius was made to state that, when at Rome in 1071 with Lanfranc, he recognized upon Pope Alexander's authority that Stigand had not been been Lanfranc's predecessor, neither was Lanfranc his successor. Stigand's pontificate was as though it had never been. But there is no evidence whatever to corroborate the claim that five successive popes had condemned Stigand, whose recorded actions under Kings Edward the Confessor, Harold, and William also do not bear it out.[36] It must be regarded as almost certainly an invention. Moreover, Lanfranc did not win lasting support for his contention that Stigand's archiepiscopate must be deemed never to have existed. Canterbury tradition continued to list him among the archbishops,[37] and after Lanfranc's death Bishop Wulfstan, whose profession was strong in its condemnation of Stigand, could write to Anselm, by now archbishop, of 'Stigandus, vestrae excellentiae praedecessor'.[38] Lanfranc carried his animus against Stigand beyond the bounds of fact and of acceptability. As he did with Berengar, he exaggerated Stigand's moral shortcomings; he also exaggerated the frequency and the character of papal sanctions against him.

Remigius visited Rome in 1071. The consecration of each bishop was of special importance for Lanfranc. Wulfstan's consecrator was Archbishop Aldred of York; Remigius's was Stigand. Herfast's is unknown, though it is a fair guess that, like Walchelin of Winchester, he was consecrated by Bishop Ermenfrid of Sion in 1070; at Elmham he succeeded Stigand's brother.

[35] It is not difficult to understand why Lanfranc saw the seizure of his predecessor's *pallium* as the graver offence. (i) The conferring of the *pallium* signified a participation in the pope's pastoral office which called for it to be directly and individually conferred. (ii) Its conferment was customarily accompanied by a papal letter, using hallowed language from the Roman *Liber diurnus*, which inculcated the duty of vigilance in the cure of souls by one who acted not as a mercenary but as answerable to Christ as the shepherd of shepherds, and who inwardly and outwardly exhibited the virtues which would render him irreprehensible and an example to his subjects. Lanfranc's own reception of the *pallium* no doubt impressed such thoughts upon his mind and increased his condemnation of Stigand. See the fuller discussion of the *pallium* in Cowdrey, 'Archbishop Thomas I of York'.

[36] See further the comments of Barlow, *The English Church, 1000–1066*, 304–10.

[37] e.g. Stigand is included in the list of papal conferrings of the *pallium* which is appended to the A version of the *ASC*: *The Anglo-Saxon Chronicle, MS A*, p. 94. The list states that Pope Victor II (1055–7) sent a *pallium* to Stigand by Godric, dean of Christ Church. This statement cannot be dismissed out of hand, for Stigand at last himself consecrated bishops in 1058: see above, p. 80.

[38] Anselm, *Ep.* 171, vol. 4.53.

Nevertheless, the standpoint that, especially under Alexander II, the papacy adopted towards the English church deserves consideration as part of the background to Lanfranc's move to Canterbury. The history of episcopal consecrations in Stigand's time, and especially Pope Nicholas II's consecrations at Rome, makes plain papal unease. Duke William of Normandy's successful bid to secure papal support for his invasion of England in 1066 is likely to have been based upon a depiction of King Harold as a perjurer and of Archbishop Stigand as his accomplice.[39] Especial significance attaches to surviving fragments of a letter that Alexander II sent to King William at a date after the conquest.[40] They are as follows:

> Your prudence knows that the kingdom of the English from the time that the name of Christ has been celebrated there has been under the hand and protection of the prince of the apostles, until certain men, made members of an evil head (*membra mali capitis effecti*), burning with the pride of Satan their father, have cast away the covenant of God (*pactum Dei abiecerunt*) and have turned the people of the English from the path of truth. *And a little after*: For, as you know well, so long as the English were faithful, from regard to devotion and in recognition of duty they used to render to the apostolic see an annual payment, part of which was brought to the Roman pontiff and part to the church of Saint Mary which is called the *schola Anglorum* for the use of the brothers.

Alexander first referred to the special bond of duty and responsibility between England and the papacy because of its conversion by missionaries sent by Pope Gregory the Great in 597. From the papacy's side this implied apostolic protection, and from the English side devotion and dutifulness. But there had supervened a state of national apostasy. Alexander, whose early years as pope had been marked by the Cadalan schism (1061–4), wrote of virtual apostasy in England. The 'evil head' of whom 'certain men' had been made members may probably be understood as Stigand, against whom a vituperative campaign had been waged in Rome as part of the justification of the Norman invasion; those who adhered to him did so as sons of Satan.[41] By thus focusing upon English apostasy, Alexander implicitly arraigned Stigand no less severely that did the three Canterbury professions, even though the accusations were differently conceived and formulated. Indeed, the severity of the professions, which represented what Lanfranc wished to hear, may have owed much to Alexander's appraisal of English affairs.

Alexander's concern was one factor in causing the flurry of legatine activity for some years after 1066 in the Anglo-Norman lands. Of especial significance was the journey to England in 1070 of the cardinal-priests John and Peter and the legatine councils of Winchester at Easter and Windsor at Pentecost.[42] The letter of summons

---

[39] Orderic Vitalis, 3, vol. 2.142–3.

[40] *Ep.* 139, *PL* 146.1413. The fragments are preserved in Deusdedit, *Coll. can.* 3.269, p. 378. It is usually dated 1071, but any date between the Norman conquest and Alexander's death on 21 Apr. 1073 is possible.

[41] The phrase *membra mali capitis* is unusual and difficult. It can be taken as referring to the members of Satan and as anticipating the following clause; if so Stigand is doubtless subsumed in the 'certain men'. But there seems to be a progression of thought from Satan's agent to Satan himself; *malum caput* would be a weak designation for Satan and more appropriate for Stigand. Alexander could refer to his Milanese fellow-citizens as *mea membra*, i.e. as members of himself as a human head: *Ep.* 1, *PL* 146.1280–1.

[42] *CS* nos. 86–7, vol. 1/2.565–81. The cardinal-priests left for Rome after Easter, and the Worcester

to Winchester which the two legates sent to Bishop Wulfstan of Worcester survives. It begins as does Pope Alexander's by referring to the special concern of the Roman church for English affairs which resulted from England's conversion upon Pope Gregory I's initiative: it must inquire into English religious observance and by its visitation renew its pristine standard (*conversationis vestrae mores . . . inquirere et Christianam religionem qua vos primitus instruxit diligentia suae visitationis reparare*). Therefore the legates convened their council to grub out whatever evils flourished in the vineyard of the Lord of hosts and to plant whatever should promote the welfare of men in both body and soul. Two points especially deserve notice. First, by placing their work against the background of the Gregorian mission of 597, the legates implied a concern with the whole English church and people.[43] Second, they claimed a general responsibility for the spiritual, moral, and physical welfare of all Englishmen as the prime motive in all the measures that they might take.

At the two councils, the legates and their agents were energetic in implementing their responsibilities. At Winchester, Stigand and his brother Ethelmar of Elmham were deposed, along with three unnamed abbots. Bishop Leofwine of Lichfield was summoned to appear and answer for his marriage; he was condemned for contumacy in his absence. The case of Ethelwine of Durham may have been discussed. At Windsor, Ethelric of Selsey was deposed along with more abbots. At the time of this council, the king filled a number of bishoprics—York by Thomas, Winchester by Walchelin, Selsey by Stigand, and Elmham by Herfast. In anticipation of an appointment to Canterbury, considerable steps were taken towards renewing the upper echelons of the church.

Not least important, if the surviving lists of sixteen canons of a council of Winchester and of thirteen of a council of Windsor are correctly attributed to the legatine assemblies of 1070, a remarkably comprehensive renewal of the English church was adumbrated.[44] It agrees well with the purposes that the legates set out in their summons to Bishop Wulfstan of Worcester. Moral reform was called for. There was legislation about the life and behaviour of clerks (Wind. canon 3). Clerical chastity was enjoined on pain of forfeiture of office (Winch. canon 15), probably with the requirement earlier made in Normandy and England that all in major orders (priest, deacon, and subdeacon) should abandon their wives.[45] Bishops and priests were to invite laymen to penance (Wind. canon 7). Due reverence must be shown to clerks and monks (Wind. canon 13), and no one might invade the church's goods (Wind. canon 11). Other evils, too, were to be rooted out. Perhaps with an eye

---

Chronicle referred to Ermenfrid as holding the synod at Windsor: John of Worcester, *a.* 1070, vol. 3.12–15. But Alexander wrote to Lanfranc of business done 'suppositis legatorum nostrorum', suggesting that at Windsor as at Winchester the Worcester Chronicle exaggerated the role of Ermenfrid and that the ultimate authority at Windsor was the two cardinal-priests acting through deputies of whom Ermenfrid was one: Lanfranc, *Letters*, no. 7, pp. 62–3.

[43] Cf. the Worcester Chronicle's comment that, had there currently been an archbishop of York, he would have been present and participating: John of Worcester, *a.* 1070, vol. 3.12–13.

[44] For the canons and for fuller discussion, see *CS* 1/2, nos. 86/IX, 87/III, pp. 566–8, 574–8, 580–1.

[45] See Brooke, 'Gregorian Reform in Action', 83–4 with n. 32.

to Archbishop Stigand, no one was to hold two bishoprics at once (Winch. canon 1). Simony was prohibited (Winch. canon 2, Wind. canons 1, 2). The determination of penances for crimes was reserved to bishops (Winch. canon 11). No clerk was to bear secular arms (Wind. canon 11), while fugitive monks were debarred from military service and clerical assemblies (Winch. canon 12). Careful attention was to be given to implanting what was good. To this end, bishops were to have free course in their dioceses with regard to both clergy and laity (Wind. canon 6). They were to have settled sees (Wind. canon 9).[46] They were to hold synods twice a year (Winch. canon 13,[47] Wind. canon 4), and they were to appoint in their churches archdeacons and other ministers of holy order (Wind. canon 5).[48] To support the ecclesiastical structure, tithes were to be paid by all (Winch. canon 14, Wind. canon 10). No one was to conspire against the king (Wind. canon 9). If Windsor laid weight on the structure of the church, Winchester passed a number of canons on the details of liturgical observance which were the common concern of contemporary councils. The proper celebration of mass was a repeated concern (canons 5,6,8,10,16). Baptisms were normally to be reserved for Easter and Pentecost (canon 7), and ordinations were likewise to be performed at the proper times (canon 4). The dead were not to be buried inside churches (canon 9). Stranger clerks were not to be received without letters of commendation (canon 3). Both councils legislated about apostate clerks and monks (Winch. canon 12, Wind. canon 8). The canons are thus remarkable alike for their range and for their comprehensiveness as a programme for the whole English church.

Lanfranc is certain to have been fully informed about these councils, held only some four months before his succession to the see of Canterbury, by Ermenfrid of Sion when, with the legate Hubert, he urged Lanfranc to accept. After long disuse, councils of a kind familiar on the continent had been revived in England. They were councils for the whole English church, and they took place under the aegis of a papacy with whose aims and methods Lanfranc sympathized and of a pope whom he admired. As the commission of the legates in 1070 shows, there was an intention to renew the morality and social order of the whole English people. Councils were to be a means of uprooting what was evil and of planting what was good. This intensity of moral purpose was reinforced by measures, such as the regular holding of diocesan synods and the appointment everywhere of appropriate diocesan officials, especially archdeacons, to secure the effective discharge of the church's pastoral office. Down to the humblest of churches, proper liturgical and pastoral provision was to be secured. Before Lanfranc came to Canterbury, the councils of 1070 seem already to have sketched the outlines of much of his duty as archbishop. There was promise of his being able to fulfil his duty in close understanding with a papacy that acknowledged a special responsibility towards the English church and people;

---

[46] Cf. the transfer of sees at the council of London (1075): below, p. 125.
[47] The reading *bis* should be noticed and probably accepted.
[48] The last phrase foreshadows the introduction of rural deans and rural chapters: see Scammell, 'The Rural Chapter'.

indeed, to the whole of Britain. Lanfranc would come to renew the task which Pope Gregory the Great had committed in 597 to St Augustine.

Such was the ecclesiastical background to Lanfranc's becoming archbishop. The Worcester Chronicle, in particular, indicates another aspect—that of the king's aspirations regarding control of the church. There is no question of the king's not giving his full support to the legates and their councils. But as king of England, he saw to it that, as he was accustomed as duke of Normandy, the councils took place by his command and in his presence. The deposition, promotion, and consecration of bishops and abbots was a matter for the king himself, often acting apart from the councils, as when it was by his command that Bishop Ermenfrid ordained Bishop Walchelin of Winchester; William sometimes had scant regard for canonical order and justice, condemning many without legal cause and imprisoning them on mere suspicion. The king was determined to use the bishoprics and abbeys of England as of Normandy as a support for his own power and regime.[49] When Lanfranc became archbishop, it was apparent that, in England as in Normandy, William intended to be the master of his own household. Though genuinely concerned for the well-being of the church on lines adumbrated by the councils of 1070, he regarded bishops and abbots as his men no less than as members of the clerical order. Whatever his own indebtedness to the pope, he would look for their deference to the political necessities of a king who needed to secure his position in his kingdom.

[49] John of Worcester, *a.* 1070, vol. 3.10–15.

7

The Primacy of Canterbury

The author of the *Vita Lanfranci* stated Lanfranc's priorities in terms that are significant because they epitomize his immediate duties as they seemed to his later admirers: 'Not forgetful of wherefore he had come, Lanfranc directed his entire concern to the correction of men's morals (*mores*) and to setting in order the state of the church. And first he was at pains to renew (*renovare*) the mother church of the kingdom—that of Canterbury.'[1] An ultimate pastoral motive thus lay behind Lanfranc's thoroughgoing reform and development of the structure and organization of the church. It should be noticed that this was in accordance with the precedent set by Pope Alexander II's legates in their councils of 1070.[2] But Lanfranc was in a position to take the further step of re-establishing the church of Canterbury as the mother church of the kingdom of the English. The *Vita Lanfranci* went on to notice that he did so, first, by giving attention to the cathedral church and see of Canterbury itself in ways which will be discussed in the next chapter, and second, by claiming for Canterbury a primacy which carried authority over the English church as constituted by the provinces of Canterbury and York and also more widely over the whole of the British Isles.

Lanfranc's claim to primacy has so large and prior a place in the sources and so dominated the first two years of his archiepiscopate that it is expedient to discuss it first. In particular, it is the initial and the most important topic of Lanfranc's letter collection, the opening thirteen items of which, representing more than a third of its length, may be described as dealing with matters of papacy and primacy, whether directly or by implication.[3] The letters include the so-called *Scriptum Lanfranci de primatu*, an assembly of material probably made under Lanfranc's own supervision which covered events up to the council of Winchester at Eastertide 1072 and which appears to have been compiled before the council of London in 1075.[4] The compilation and other material from the letter collection were drawn heavily upon by the *Vita Lanfranci* and by William of Malmesbury.[5] The prominence that they gave to the matter of the primacy was reflected in other chronicle sources which for the most part shared the Canterbury point of view.[6] This was also naturally shared by the written professions of obedience that Lanfranc required from other archbishops and bishops.[7] The case of the church of York is represented only in the late,

---

[1] *VL* cap. 9, p. 692.   [2] See above, pp. 83–5.
[3] Lanfranc, *Letters*, nos. 1–13, pp. 30–83.   [4] Ibid., nos. 3–4, pp. 38–57.
[5] *VL* caps. 10–12, pp. 695–707; William of Malmesbury, *GP* 1.25–7, 42, pp. 39–43, 66–8; see also *GR* 3.298–302, vol. 1.530–9.
[6] Esp. Eadmer, *Hist. nov.*, 1, pp. 10–12.   [7] *Canterbury Professions*, nos. 31–47, pp. 26–33.

brief, and garbled account of the origins of the primacy dispute by Hugh the Chanter, who spoke for the chapter of his cathedral.[8] The surviving evidence for the primacy issue is, therefore, presented largely from a Canterbury point of view.

Nevertheless, the need for Lanfranc to establish the primacy of his see of Canterbury as a necessary means to his discharging in and beyond the English kingdom the pastoral office that he deemed to be committed to him is immediately apparent from a contrast between the structures of the church in the Norman duchy and in the English kingdom. In the Normandy with which he was familiar there was a single church province, that of Rouen, which was almost coterminous with the secular duchy. The province of Rouen comprised the diocese of Rouen and six suffragan dioceses, all of them of comparable and manageable size with settled borders and with episcopal successions which, for all the vicissitudes of history, could be traced back in fact or legend to dates well before the coming of St Augustine to Canterbury in 597. In the English kingdom there were two provinces, those of Canterbury and York. In theory they were equal to and independent of each other. But, in 1070, Canterbury consisted of fourteen dioceses while York had only one subject diocese, that of Durham; this was not sufficient for it to function as an independent province. Moreover, unlike the Norman dioceses, those in England were of widely differing sizes, those of Dorchester and York being extremely large. As Lanfranc was quickly to experience, there were serious matters of dispute about boundaries and areas of jurisdiction. If Lanfranc was effectively to undertake the pastoral task of correcting men's morals and the structural task of setting in order the state of the church that was its necessary condition, he must renew the church of Canterbury as a centre of authority that was powerful enough to cover the whole English church. It was no less to be desired that in England as in Normandy there should be a matching unity of church and secular authorities. King William claimed to be *rex Anglorum*; as in Normandy, a structured and ordered English church was to be both the subject and the means of his dominion. To provide the services that the king required and to reap the benefits of his lordship, the English church must mirror the unity of the kingdom. The church of Canterbury must therefore be the mother church of the whole kingdom; for it effectively to be so, its primacy was a necessary means. It is not surprising that, with William's eventually forthcoming support, Lanfranc from the start asserted the primacy of the see of Canterbury in the whole of the English church and kingdom.

If the disorganized state of the English church in 1070 created a pressing need for Lanfranc at once to claim an effective primacy for Canterbury, the closeness, cordiality, and detail of his dealings with Pope Alexander II gave grounds for an expectation that the apostolic see might readily confirm the primacy that Lanfranc sought. The regard and confidence between pope and archbishop were mutual. Thus, after Eastertide 1072 Lanfranc wrote to Alexander of his appreciation of the pope's unique condescension to him on his recent visit to Rome, when Alexander had granted all the reasonable requests of those for whom Lanfranc stood as

---

[8] Hugh the Chanter, 4–11.

The Primacy of Canterbury

advocate; a host of such favours pleasantly recalled Alexander's name to Lanfranc's mind whenever he did anything that was good.[9] Lanfranc later wrote to Alexander of a more prolonged stay at the Lateran that Alexander wished him to arrange and that Lanfranc longed to make if his affairs in England allowed.[10] Collaboration extended to specific matters. It should be remembered that, in 1070, papal legates had already done much to map out the pattern of necessary reforms.[11] Before Lanfranc left for Rome in 1071, he wrote to Alexander as supreme ruler of the whole church of Christ (*universae Christi aecclesiae summo rectori*) for papal direction about two bishops—the aged Herman of Ramsbury who wished to become a monk and Leofwine of Lichfield who, having shown himself contumacious to the legates of 1070 about his carnal incontinence, now wished to return to his former monastery; Lanfranc sought Alexander's urgent guidance about both bishops and would not take steps to fill the see of Lichfield in advance of instructions from Rome.[12] While Lanfranc was at Rome later in the year, Eadmer reported that he successfully interceded with Alexander for the restoration to office of Archbishop Thomas of York and Bishop Remigius of Dorchester, who were respectively accused of being the son of a priest and of simony: 'You are father of that country [England]', Alexander is reported to have said, 'and so it is your concern to determine what is suitable.'[13]

Lanfranc's return to England in October 1071 prompted a letter from Alexander to the king in which he praised William's piety and rule and exhorted him to promote virtue and religion in his kingdom, caring especially for the churches that were within it. To these ends he was to follow the advice and counsel of Lanfranc as archbishop of Canterbury. Alexander referred to two further cases that he remitted to Lanfranc for settlement—that of Bishop Ethelric of Selsey/Chichester, who had been deposed by legatine authority but after insufficient examination, and a border dispute between Archbishop Thomas of York and Bishop Remigius of Dorchester about the boundary between their dioceses.[14] Alexander went on to inform the king that he had given Lanfranc an authority that made him virtually a standing papal legate:

In considering and determining cases we have so given him a delegation of our own and of apostolic authority (*ita sibi nostrae et apostolicae auctoritatis vicem dedimus*) that whatever he shall determine with respect to them in accordance with righteousness shall thereafter be held as firm and binding as if it was settled in our own presence.[15]

---

[9] Lanfranc, *Letters*, no. 4, pp. 54–7.   [10] Ibid., no. 1, pp. 32–5, cf. no. 7, pp. 60–3.
[11] See above, pp. 83–5. It is, indeed, possible that the 11th-century idea of Canterbury's primacy had its genesis, not with Lanfranc, but in reflection on Pope Gregory I's mission of St Augustine in the Rome of Alexander II after the events of 1066. But the evidence does not warrant more than the pointing out of such a possibility.
[12] Lanfranc, *Letters*, no. 2, pp. 34–9.
[13] Eadmer, *Hist. nov.*, 1, p. 11; see also *Canterbury Professions*, no. 32, p. 27. William of Malmesbury, *GP* 1.42, pp. 65–6, partly follows Eadmer.
[14] This dispute did not in itself raise issues about the primacy. For its origins, see *CS* nos. 74, 78, vol. 1/2.538–43, 550–2.
[15] Lanfranc, *Letters*, no. 7, pp. 60–3.

In form, this was a concession to Lanfranc personally, and it was not explicitly made with respect to the whole kingdom, although there was no barrier to its being so understood. When taken in the light of other dealings between Lanfranc and Alexander, it is likely to have established a presumption that, when the historical and practical case for Canterbury's primacy was fully made to the pope, he would look favourably on it and underwrite it.

The issue of Canterbury's authority first arose very soon after Lanfranc's consecration. On Whitsunday (23 May) the king had already nominated to be archbishop of York a clerk of Bayeux and royal chaplain named Thomas; he was a well-educated man who had been Lanfranc's pupil, and he had a reputation for being mild and honourable.[16] He lost little time in coming to Canterbury for consecration by Lanfranc.[17] But when Lanfranc, safeguarding (as it was claimed) the custom of his predecessors, asked Thomas for a written profession of obedience with the addition of an oath, Thomas demanded written evidence for such a custom and arguments to justify it. Lanfranc is said to have produced his evidence in the presence of the bishops who were assembled to consecrate Thomas, but Thomas rejected it and departed without consecration. The king was displeased and deemed that Lanfranc's demands upon Thomas were excessive and unreasonable. Lanfranc requested an audience of the king in his court, and he persuaded William and those present of the justice of his case. Thomas was told forthwith to return to Canterbury ('the mother church of the whole kingdom') and to write a profession that he could duly read before the consecrating bishops; at this stage there is silence about an oath.[18] In the profession, Thomas was to promise to obey absolutely and unconditionally Lanfranc's instructions in all matters belonging to the observance (*cultus*) of the Christian religion. But he should not render such obedience to Lanfranc's successors until he received sufficient proof either before the king or in a council of bishops that his own predecessors had and should have so promised to primates of the church of Canterbury. On these terms Thomas was consecrated. The memorandum concluded by asserting that Lanfranc soon afterwards exacted similar professions from all bishops of the English kingdom who in Stigand's time had been consecrated either by other archbishops or by the pope.[19]

The elements of strength and weakness in Lanfranc's position in 1070 as he pressed it upon Thomas of York and as it is witnessed by other evidence call for appraisal. It must first be said that it is altogether unclear what evidence Lanfranc's memorandum can have drawn upon when stating that, safeguarding the custom of

---

[16] For Thomas's character and nomination, see esp. Lanfranc, *Letters*, no. 3/1, pp. 40–1; Hugh the Chanter, 2–3; John of Worcester, a. 1070, vol. 3.12–13; Orderic Vitalis, 4, 8.1, vols. 2.238–9, 4.118–19.

[17] The principal source for the events of 1070 is the first part of the memorandum on the primacy in Lanfranc's letter collection: Lanfranc, *Letters*, no. 3/1, pp. 38–43; see also Hugh the Chanter, 2–9.

[18] It should be noticed that the memorandum spoke of Lanfranc's initially requiring of Thomas a customary written profession *cum adiectione iusiurandi*. It is unclear whether the addition was deemed customary or whether it was made by Lanfranc.

[19] This is the sole evidence for a general requirement of professions at this juncture. Copies survive only of the professions to Lanfranc of Bishops Wulfstan of Worcester, Remigius of Dorchester, and Herfast of Elmham: *Canterbury Professions*, nos. 31–3, pp. 26–8.

his predecessors, Lanfranc required of Thomas a written profession of obedience with the addition of an oath.[20] There is no clear evidence for the recent requirement of such written professions,[21] let alone for the taking of an oath; nor is there documentary witness from any juncture of the Anglo-Saxon past for claims by archbishops of Canterbury to such obedience on the part of archbishops of York as Lanfranc was asking of Thomas. Just how Lanfranc formed and justified his claims is nowhere made clear. However, there is a strong probability that, in view of his practical need to exercise the authority and power of primacy, he was influenced by the place assigned to primates in the Pseudo-Isidorian Decrees. In particular, a letter attributed to the first-century pope Anacletus set forth as a model for the church a graded hierarchy in which, following the structure of Roman secular government, primates occupied a place midway between the apostolic see and metropolitans:

And although particular metropolitan cities may have their own provinces and should have their own metropolitan bishops, just as aforetime they used to have metropolitan secular judges, yet . . . they have been commanded both then and now to have primates, to whom, after the apostolic see, the highest matters of business may come, so that in the same way relief may be given and restitution may justly be made to those for whom it shall be necessary, and so that those who are unjustly oppressed may be justly restored and supported, and, saving the authority of the apostolic see, the cases of bishops and judgements in the highest matters of business may be settled most justly.[22]

Indirect evidence that in Norman England such rulings of early fathers and popes were made the standard for bishops' loyalties and duties to the see of Canterbury is provided by the liturgical formula for their liturgical profession before consecration which, by the early twelfth century, was distinctive of English pontificals:

Question: Will you with veneration receive, teach, and uphold the traditions of the orthodox fathers and the decrees of the holy and apostolic see?
Answer: I will.
Question: Will you in all matters show fidelity and subjection to the holy church of Canterbury?
Answer: I will.
Here let a profession be required.[23]

Sources from Lanfranc's own time, and especially the written professions of the bishops whom he ordained, repeatedly insisted upon the theme that bishops who looked for due obedience in their subjects should equally pay it to their

---

[20] Lanfranc, *Letters*, no. 3/1, pp. 40–1.
[21] Remigius of Dorchester's profession of 1070 to Lanfranc alluded to his earlier profession to Stigand and his successors: *Canterbury Professions*, no. 32, p. 27; but it does not emerge whether the profession was written or only verbal.
[22] Ps.-Anacletus, *Epistola secunda*, cap. 26, ed. Hinschius, pp. 79–80. In 1079 this chapter was cited verbatim in Pope Gregory VII's confirmation of the primacy of the see of Lyons: *Reg.* 6.35, pp. 450–2; for further discussion, see Cowdrey, *Pope Gregory VII*, 389–90, 602–4.
[23] Cited by Richter, *Canterbury Professions*, p. lvi; he refers to the early 12th-century pontificals, Cambridge, Trinity College, MS B XI 10, Cambridge, University Library, MS Ee 11. 3, and London, British Library, MS Cotton Tiberius B viii. For the limited changes made by Lanfranc on his arrival in England, see ibid., p. lx.

superiors;[24] he thus presupposed a hierarchical order of rule and subjection comparable with that of Pseudo-Isidore. It seems likely that, from an early stage of his archiepiscopate and perhaps from its beginning, Lanfranc was confident that, in general terms, he had a strong legal and moral case for the primacy of Canterbury. Its weakness lay in the lack of documentary evidence that referred in fact or name to Canterbury's primacy or to past archbishops of York as having made, or as having a duty to make, any recognition of a primacy.

Lanfranc therefore had a case to prove; he could not be altogether sure of King William's support in establishing and implementing it as he wished. In one respect, the events of 1070 had shown the king to be remarkably deferential to the ecclesiastical position of his archbishop. Up to the coming of the papal legates in 1070, William had shown Archbishop Stigand a conspicuous degree of recognition, even allowing him to consecrate the Norman monk Remigius to the see of Dorchester.[25] But Lanfranc's view, and indeed that of the apostolic see, as reflected in Remigius's profession to Lanfranc, was that all Stigand's acts were to be set aside and his tenure of the see of Canterbury was to be treated as though it had never been. The prevailing of Lanfranc's view over that of the king was a tacit censure of William's initial church policy which showed that, in some connections, so masterful a king might defer to his ecclesiastical mentors. It was an earnest of future co-operation. But there were also indications that William's compliance might have its limits. William had clearly been unprepared for Lanfranc's demanding a written profession of Thomas of York; he had at first been displeased with Lanfranc, who had to dispel his anger.[26] More serious and enduring, Lanfranc initially wanted a written profession from Thomas with the addition of an oath. Time was to show that Lanfranc would have to abandon the requirement of an oath 'for love of the king'.[27] The phrase was never explained, but almost certainly the king was unwilling for one ecclesiastical tenant-in-chief of the crown to swear obedience to another such tenant-in-chief, even one so trusted as Lanfranc. However this may be, the Canterbury memorandum of the events of 1070 is eloquently silent about an oath in its record of Thomas's profession and consecration.[28] The king, it may be inferred, was not prepared to let Lanfranc have everything his way.

And, in respect of the oath, that was a serious matter. It has been pointed out that the sanction of a profession, even when favourably worded, was not a strong one. Canonically, the breach of a profession constituted a lie (*mendacium*) which was punishable only by excommunication; the breach of an oath was technically perjury (*periurium*), and it carried the graver penalty of deposition.[29] This suggests the reason why Lanfranc was concerned to bind the archbishops of York by oath. But

---

[24] See Richter, *Canterbury Professions*, pp. lxv–lxviii. Besides the text of the professions of Lanfranc's time: ibid., nos. 31–47, pp. 26–33, see Lanfranc's letter of reproof to Bishop Herfast of Elmham: Lanfranc, *Letters*, no. 47, pp. 152–3, with its Pseudo-Isidorian citations, especially from the eleventh council of Toledo, cap. 3 = Hinschius, 408, and Lanfranc's concluding assertion of Canterbury's jurisdiction: 'through God's mercy it is established that this whole island that men call Britain is the one jurisdiction of our one church.'
[25] See above, p. 81.   [26] Lanfranc, *Letters*, no. 3/1, pp. 40–1.   [27] See below, p. 99.
[28] Lanfranc, *Letters*, no. 3/1, pp. 40–3.   [29] See Richter, *Canterbury Professions*, pp. xix–xxi.

such a consideration was not likely to weigh greatly with a king who was anxious to claim a monopoly of loyalty in his new kingdom from all his tenants-in-chief.

In any case, from Lanfranc's point of view Thomas's profession of 1070 was far from favourably worded. It secured his obedience only to Lanfranc, and he was not to promise obedience to Lanfranc's successors without further consideration before the king or in an episcopal council. It is small wonder that the text of the profession did not survive at Canterbury, or that this was the only profession to which the York writer Hugh the Chanter did refer.[30] It left open for future settlement the question of whether earlier archbishops had made, or should have made, professions to their contemporaries of Canterbury in the capacity of primate. It is eloquent of how little assured gain Lanfranc secured in 1070 that the episcopal professions of 1070 gave him no wider title than *sanctae Cantuariensis aecclesiae metropolitanus*, or *eiusdem sanctae metropolitanae sedis antistes*.[31] And the issue of whether Thomas was to regard him as more was referred, not to the pope and his legates, but to the king and bishops of England. So, too, it was at a well-attended meeting of the king's court, led by the king and Lanfranc, and held at the royal manor of Petherton (Somerset), that Bishop Wulfstan of Worcester was able to ward off a bid by Archbishop Thomas of York to secure certain Worcester lands that Archbishop Aldred of York had retained but that since his death had been in the king's hands, and by implication to claim that the see of Worcester was rightly subject to that of York.[32]

Accordingly, such letters as passed in 1071 between England and the apostolic see made no mention of matters touching the primacy. But it was raised at Rome when, in October, Lanfranc and Thomas journeyed to Rome together to fulfil their duty of collecting their *pallia*.[33] Their party also included Bishop Remigius of Dorchester and Abbot Baldwin of Bury St Edmunds.[34] While each archbishop was received at Rome with appropriate honour, Lanfranc was singled out for especial recognition. Not only did he himself take from the altar of St Peter's the customary *pallium*, but he also received from the hand of Pope Alexander the rare gift of a second *pallium* which the pope had himself worn liturgically. Alexander accorded him the further honour of rising to greet him—not, the pope declared, in his archiepiscopal capacity but by reason of the learning to which he was himself indebted. According to

---

[30] Hugh the Chanter, 6–7.

[31] *Canterbury Professions*, nos. 31–3, pp. 26–8. Thereafter, Thomas of York's second profession (1072) did not expressly refer to the primacy of Canterbury: no. 34, p. 28. The earliest profession to do so was that of Osbern of Exeter (before 27 May 1072): no. 35, pp. 28–8. Thereafter, reference was normal, the exceptions in Lanfranc's time were Donatus of Dublin (1085), William of Elmham (1086), and Robert of Chester (1086): nos. 42–3, 45, pp. 31–2.

[32] John of Worcester, *a*. 1070, vol. 3.12–13, 16–17; *VW* 2.1, pp. 24–6, cf. *Abridgement*, cap. 13, p. 79; *Chron. mon. de Evesham*, 89–90. The account in *VW* must be treated with reserve; Wulfstan's recourse to prayer is similar to the monk Osbern's description of Lanfranc at Penenden Heath: *Mirac.*, cap. 18, pp. 143–4, and the roles of Lanfranc and Odo of Bayeux correspond.

[33] The main source is Lanfranc's memorandum: *Letters*, nos. 3/2, 4, pp. 42–5, 50–1, 54–7; of the chronicles which refer to the journey, see esp. Eadmer, *Hist. nov.*, 1, pp. 10–12; William of Malmesbury, *GP* 1.42, pp. 65–6, *GR* 3.203, vol. 1.536–9, *VW* 2.2, pp. 24–5.

[34] For Baldwin's consecration by Stigand, see above, p. 80.

Eadmer, Alexander deputed to Lanfranc the consideration of charges against Thomas of York that he was the son of a priest and against Remigius that his advancement to his see had been tainted by simony; in the pope's presence, Lanfranc returned to them their pastoral staffs.

But it was also in the pope's presence that Thomas advanced his claim (*calumniam movit*) against the primacy of Canterbury and also that the bishops of Dorchester/Lincoln, Worcester, and Lichfield were rightly subject to his and not Lanfranc's metropolitan authority.[35] He claimed that the churches of Canterbury and York were equal in honour to each other, basing his case upon Pope Gregory the Great's disposition that the two English archbishops should in no way be subject to each other and that precedence should be determined by date of consecration.[36] Suppressing his anger, Lanfranc rejoined that Pope Gregory's disposition was not promulgated about the churches of Canterbury and York but about those of London and York. After further long discussion of the two issues that Thomas had raised, Pope Alexander remitted their consideration to England and for settlement by the testimony and judgement of the bishops and abbots of the whole kingdom.[37] Ironically, this was very much the procedure that Thomas was himself said to have canvassed in England in the previous year.[38] Alexander II wrote to the English king a letter which, while being prudently silent about the two issues that Thomas had broached at Rome, was warm in its commendation of Lanfranc.[39]

In England the matters at issue between Lanfranc and Thomas were considered at gatherings in the royal chapel at Winchester Castle after Easter (8 April) 1072 and at the royal court that assembled at Windsor for the festival of Pentecost (27 May).[40] Although as a papal legate the Roman subdeacon Hubert subscribed the record of both meetings, his role was inconspicuous. The Winchester meeting was stated to have taken place 'by command of Pope Alexander and with the king's agreement', and perhaps with the pope's direction in mind reference was made to the presence

---

[35] Thomas's preparedness to seek counsel and judgement at Rome finds a measure of confirmation in Hugh the Chanter's statement that, with reference to his first profession, he refused to promise subjection to Lanfranc's successors 'nisi iudicante summo pontifice': pp. 6–7.

[36] For Gregory's letter, see *Reg. Greg. I*, 9.39, vol. 2.934–5, whence Bede, *Eccl. Hist.*, 1.29, pp. 104–7.

[37] Lanfranc, *Letters*, no. 4, pp. 50–1; the text does not survive.

[38] Ibid., no. 3/1, pp. 40–3.   [39] Ibid., no. 7, pp. 60–2.

[40] The principal source for the events of 1072 is Lanfranc's memorandum on the primacy; it deals with events up to the immediate sequel to the council of Winchester but does not include the council of Windsor: Lanfranc, *Letters*, nos. 3/2–4, pp. 44–57. It comprises the following parts: (1) no. 3/2, pp. 44–5: an introductory account of the Easter meeting of the king's court; (2) no. 3/3, pp. 44–5: Archbishop Thomas's second profession to Lanfranc as made at the Easter court; (3) no. 3/4, pp. 44–9: a record of the council of Winchester; (4) no. 4, pp. 48–57: Lanfranc's letter to Pope Alexander II written very soon after the council of Winchester to give a full account of it and to request a papal privilege. Item 3 closely follows the text on a single sheet, Canterbury, Dean and Chapter Library, Chartae Antiquae A 2; the text as lightly revised at Windsor is preserved on another single sheet, Canterbury, Dean and Chapter Library, Chartae Antiquae A 1, and in a number of copies. Besides the edition in Lanfranc, *Letters*, there are discussions and texts of the two versions in *Facsimiles of English Royal Writs*, ed. Bishop and Chaplais, pl. 29; *CS* no. 91, vol. 1/2.591–6, 601–4; *Regesta WI*, nos. 67–8, pp. 307–14. William of Malmesbury's account of the exchange at Winchester between the two archbishops with Lanfranc's arguments in direct speech is of little evidential value since Lanfranc's arguments are largely drawn from Eadmer's account of much later events: *GP* 1.40–1, pp. 62–5.

of bishops and abbots. But both meetings were royal occasions involving the king's court; at Eastertide the *generale concilium* held at the same time was regarded as being separate from the dispute about the primacy and the three dioceses.[41] Lanfranc accordingly wrote to Pope Alexander of how at Winchester there came together in the king's court (*ad regalem curiam*) an assembly of bishops, abbots, and laity of suitable integrity. They were urged by Lanfranc upon Alexander's authority as committed to him[42] and then by the king in his own power to hear the matters at issue faithfully and impartially and to bring them to a sure and right conclusion (*ad certum rectumque finem*).

Lanfranc set out to Alexander the arguments that were advanced in support of Canterbury's case.[43] Modern historians have found them to be weak. First, there was adduced the *Ecclesiastical History* of Bede, whom Lanfranc tendentiously described to Alexander as a priest of the church of York. Passages from it were read out which were claimed to show that, during the almost 140 years between the coming of St Augustine in 597 and Bede's *ultima senectus* (the *History* covers events to 731), archbishops of Canterbury exercised primacy (*primatum gessisse*) over the church of York and over the island of Britain and Ireland; they ordained bishops and held councils wherever they wished, including at York itself. The force of this argument is weakened when it is remembered that the word *primatus* does not occur in evidence of this period, nor, apart from the episode of Paulinus, was the see of York itself of metropolitan status until Bishop Egbert received a *pallium* in 735. Second, it was argued that, after this juncture, records of councils took a similar view of Canterbury's primacy and jurisdiction, while episcopal professions of obedience to Canterbury survived from those whom its archbishops had ordained to the three disputed sees.[44] The unanimous testimony of those who had been present at Winchester confirmed the continuing force of these conventions. Third, the evidence of annals told in the same direction, notably the story of a Northumbrian king who had simoniacally sold the church of York to a certain bishop and who, when he ignored an archbishop of Canterbury's summons to a council, was excommunicated by him with widespread approval. This case, of which Lanfranc gave Alexander no circumstantial details, is otherwise unknown.

Fourth, Lanfranc told the pope that:

As the final strength and foundation of the entire case (*ultimum quasi robur totiusque causae firmamentum*), there were produced privileges and writings (*privilegia atque scripta*) of your

[41] *AL* p. 85. For canons probably of this council, see *CS* no. 91/5, vol. 1/2.596–7, 605–7.
[42] See above, p. 89.
[43] It should be noticed that, in Lanfranc's letter to Alexander, the four arguments that follow are said to have been presented impersonally and not expressly by Lanfranc himself—a fact which is obscured in Dr Gibson's translation by her repeated importation of the first person plural. Similarly, in the record of the Winchester assembly, Lanfranc himself is expressly stated to have intervened only at a late stage, when the issue arose of Thomas of York's profession and oath. It is not excluded that Lanfranc presented the entire Canterbury case himself but wished not to vaunt his victory; it is also possible that, to preserve his authority and detachment as archbishop and papal representative, he caused Canterbury's substantive case to be presented by a spokesman. That he was in agreement is not, of course, in doubt.
[44] Pre-conquest professions survive for Worcester and Lichfield, and for Leicester which became part of the see of Dorchester: *Canterbury Professions*, nos. 3, 9–11, 15, 17, 20–1, pp. 3–4, 9–11, 13–16, 18–19.

predecessors Gregory, Boniface, Honorius, Vitalian, Sergius, again Gregory, Leo, and again the latest Leo [Leo IX] which were issued or sent to prelates of the church of Canterbury and to kings of the English at one time or another for various purposes (*aliis atque aliis temporibus variis de causis*).

Lanfranc added that other documents of other popes, originals and copies, had perished in the Canterbury fire of 1067. The clinching argument in the Canterbury case thus seems to concern less the content of the papal writings concerned, which was summarily described as referring to diverse times and subjects, than to the names and titles of the prelates and kings that popes, beginning with Pope Gregory the Great, habitually and frequently used in items surviving and lost by fire: prelates of the church of Canterbury and kings of the English. Consistent reference to the archbishops and church of Canterbury established that Pope Gregory the Great's initial plan for a southern province centred upon London had no practical relevance;[45] reference to kings of the English even before there was a politically united kingdom showed that popes who envisaged a church owing overall subjection to the see of Canterbury envisaged as its counterpart a single and overall kingdom. In the context of the meeting of the royal court at Winchester in 1072, the Canterbury case if thus presented had the merit of simplicity and ready comprehensibility by laity as well as clergy; the king himself may have been impressed by an age-long juxtaposition of a single primacy and a united kingdom.[46] Turning to the Canterbury list of papal documents, Pope Gregory the Great may have provided an excellent starting-point. He addressed a letter to King Ethelbert of Kent as *rex Anglorum*.[47] Moreover, the Canterbury case referred to papal *scripta* as well as privileges; a scrutiny of Bede can hardly have overlooked the reference at the beginning of Gregory's *Responsiones* to Augustine to him as *episcopus Cantuariorum ecclesiae* and in the body of them to his having committed to Augustine all the bishops of Britain (*Brittaniarum ... omnes episcopos*) so that he might teach the uninstructed, strengthen the weak by persuasion, and correct the perverse by authority.[48] Gregory the Great could thus be claimed as having started a usage which was established at the outset of the Anglo-Saxon period and which clinched Canterbury's case.[49]

[45] For this plan, see *Reg. Greg. I*, 11.39, vol. 2.934–5 = Bede, *Eccles. Hist.*, 1.29, pp. 105–7.

[46] Hugh the Chanter represented Lanfranc as arguing to the king in 1072 that 'it was, moreover, expedient for preserving the oneness and stability of the kingdom that all Britain should be subject to one man as primate' as a safeguard against external attack and internal treachery and division: pp. 4–5. It would be hazardous to accept these as Lanfranc's actual words, but they may be based upon a memory of his arguments and in any case they illustrate current ideas about the unity of church and kingdom.

[47] *Reg. Greg. I*, 11.37, vol. 2.929–32 = Bede, *Eccles. Hist.*, 1.32, pp. 110–15; it is perhaps more likely that this letter was cited in 1072 than *Reg.* 11.39, partly on grounds of subject-matter but also because the latter letter uses no relevant titles in established form.

[48] Bede, *Eccles. Hist.*, 1.27, pp. 78–103, at pp. 78–9, 88–9. In his introductory paragraph, Bede described Augustine as having been ordained as *archiepiscopus genti Anglorum*; by him the *gens Anglorum* had received the faith of Christ from him as their papally constituted archbishop. The *Responsiones* occur in Pseudo-Isidore: Hinschius, 738–43, and in the *Collectio Lanfranci*, fos. 99ᵛ–100ʳ; the passage about the bishops of Britain is marked as for attention: Philpott, 'Archbishop Lanfranc', 100.

[49] The letter of Pope Leo III that may have been adduced in 1072 used the word *primatus* in relation to Canterbury: 'Sed primatum illum sicuti Doroverni constitutus est, primam sedem et concedimus et censentes promulgamus.... Et ideo canonice oportet illum primatum existere et vocari, et per ordinem

The question next arises of the relationship between Lanfranc's list of popes and the nine forged or falsified papal privileges which were later associated with Canterbury's case against York.⁵⁰ The similarity between the lists of popes invoked is sufficiently close for it to be virtually certain that, at very least, the list of popes of 1072 served as a model for that of the forgeries. But there are several reasons for doubting whether the forgeries themselves were presented in 1072, even on the unlikely supposition that they were already in existence. First, while the number of papal names which are common to the list of 1072 and the nine forgeries is more than sufficient to indicate that the latter took account of the former, they are not identical: the forgeries have no items of Gregory the Great or Leo IX, but they add privileges of Popes Formosus and John XII. Second, if Lanfranc is correctly interpreted as telling Pope Alexander that names and titles provided important evidence, none of the forgeries was strictly speaking addressed to kings of the English, in the sense of single rulers of the whole people.⁵¹ Third, the repeated express reference in the forgeries to the primacy of Canterbury is not easy to reconcile with Lanfranc's statement that the papal documents were issued *variis de causis*. Fourth, if the forgeries were immediately dismissed as forgeries when in 1123 they were presented at Rome,⁵² why were they not so identified earlier, especially if (as Lanfranc's letter to Alexander suggests) he sent at least some papal documents to Rome in 1072?⁵³ Fifth, if the forgeries were in existence, it is strange that no further attempt to use them was made in several contingencies in subsequent decades when they could have been useful.⁵⁴

Such difficulties make it impossible today to propose such a simple solution to the problem of the date and circumstance of the forgeries as Heinrich Böhmer proposed at the beginning of the last century: their date, Böhmer proposed, was between the Winchester and the Windsor assemblies of 1072, and the hand that constructed or falsified them was Lanfranc's. Having failed to make his case for Canterbury's primacy at Winchester, Lanfranc secretly and alone worked far into the night to fabricate the evidence that enabled him to prevail at Windsor.⁵⁵ Most

sicut a praedecessoribus nostris constituitur, archiepiscopalem sedem ita venerare et honorare in omnibus': *CED* 3.523–5, at p. 524. It has been rightly noted that, in their context, these words had no juridical force in respect to York but nevertheless derived significance from the fact that, at the time of writing (798), there was an archbishop of York: see Southern, 'The Canterbury Forgeries', 216. The forgeries themselves include a different item of Leo III: Böhmer, *Die Fälschungen*, no. 8, pp. 155–6.

⁵⁰ The privileges were edited by Böhmer, *Die Fälschungen*, nos. 2–10, pp. 147–61 = JL 2007, 2021, 2095, 2132–3, 2243, 2510, 3506, 3687. They first appear together in their entirety as entered c.1121/3 into British Library, MS Cotton Cleopatra. E. i, fos. 41ʳ–47ᵛ, although nos. 2–9 had been copied, not in chronological order and by different hands, in the Christ Church, Canterbury, manuscript British Library, MS Cotton Tiberius A. ii. All nine items appear in chronological order as in MS Cotton Cleopatra. E. i in Eadmer, *Hist. nov.*, 5, pp. 261–76, in the context of events in 1120, and in William of Malmesbury, *GP* 1.31–9, pp. 47–62, in the context of the Winchester assembly of 1072, before which he implausibly states that they were read in their entirety.

⁵¹ Böhmer, *Die Fälschungen*, no. 5, p. 151, is jointly addressed to three kings as *reges Anglorum*, but such an indication of political division would not have suited Lanfranc's case.

⁵² Hugh the Chanter, 192–5. ⁵³ Lanfranc, *Letters*, no. 4, pp. 54–5.

⁵⁴ See Southern, 'The Canterbury Forgeries', 206–10.

⁵⁵ Böhmer, *Die Fälschungen*, pp. 24–31, 44–5, 103–16, 128–38. A similar case was argued by Dueball, *Die Suprematstreit*, 24–35. While accepting Böhmer's date, Z. N. Brooke argued that the Canterbury

scholars would not now give the forgeries an eleventh-century date, and virtually none would regard Lanfranc as their fabricator, even if he was aware of them.[56] If, as suggested above, the Canterbury case in 1072 turned upon titles and designations, the documents used were already to hand and were not identical with the forgeries.[57] They were documents that were believed to be genuine. The discomfiture of Archbishop Thomas of York before the king's court at Winchester gives added support to this view. According to Lanfranc, Thomas rested his case primarily upon Pope Gregory I's letter in which he declared the churches of London and York to be equals, with neither being subject to the other.[58] If Canterbury had already produced a catena of papal documents, beginning with Gregory I, which spoke of archbishops of Canterbury and of the kingdom of the English, it is not surprising that the letter upon which Thomas depended was said by the assembly to be irrelevant: Lanfranc was not bishop of London nor was the right of the church of London at issue. Nor is it surprising that, confronted by a matter of terminology that he could readily grasp, the king paternally rebuked Thomas for coming with so feeble a case.[59] In the full session of the Easter court, matters proceeded so far as for it to be ordered that a written document should be prepared to record the settlement of the whole matter. Moreover, before the king and his court Thomas made a second profession of obedience to Lanfranc, which has survived.[60]

Thomas's profession offered Lanfranc much that he wanted, but by no means all. It opened with an acknowledgement of a Christian's duty to be subject to Christian laws and on no account to go against the precepts of the holy fathers; to do so led to common and individual perdition. And the higher a man's order, the greater was his duty to obey divine commands. There may have been here an implicit acknowledgement of the Pseudo-Isidorian principle of church hierarchy.[61] Therefore (*propterea*) Thomas, now metropolitan ruler (*antistes*) of the church of York, made

---

monks may have made the forgeries, perhaps without Lanfranc's knowledge: *The English Church*, 116–26.

[56] Against Böhmer, Macdonald argued for 1120 as the date of the forgeries and was inclined to rest responsibility upon Eadmer: *Lanfranc*, 271–7, 296A–T. Southern postponed the date to 1120/3: 'The Canterbury Forgeries', and later to the 1120s: *Saint Anselm: A Portrait*, 352–9. Against his powerful argument, which would largely exculpate Lanfranc, it has been noticed that some manuscript evidence suggests an earlier date which cannot be precisely determined; especially important is the copying of a number of them by a plurality of apparently earlier hands into Athelstan's Gospel-book: see above, n. 50; for this and other unresolved difficulties in Southern's argument, see Gibson, *Lanfranc*, 234, n. 2. Following upon Levison's discussion of forgery in eleventh-century Canterbury, especially at St Augustine's: *England and the Continent*, 201–6, some scholars have argued for the existence of the forgeries by 1070: Gibson, *Lanfranc*, 231–7, or even before the Norman Conquest: Kelly, 'Some Forgeries'. But for wellfounded criticism of these arguments, see Hugh the Chanter, p. xxxvii, n. 1. Uncertainty remains about the origin of the forgeries, but in the present state of inquiry there is little to suggest that Lanfranc may have been directly involved and much to remove them from consideration in the events of his lifetime. It should be added that, towards the end of her life, Dr Gibson inclined to a date between 1089/93 and 1109: 'Normans and Angevins', 49–53.

[57] The question arises as to what happened to such originals and copies of papal privileges from Canterbury archives when the forgeries were made. The probable answer, as Southern suggests, is that they were discarded or destroyed by the forger or forgers: 'The Canterbury Forgeries', 211.

[58] Bede, *Eccles. Hist.*, 1.29, pp. 104–7 = *Reg. Greg. I*, 11.39, vol. 2.934–5.
[59] Lanfranc, *Letters*, no. 4, pp. 52–5.   [60] Ibid., no. 3/2–4, pp. 44–7.   [61] See above, p. 91.

an absolute profession of canonical obedience to Lanfranc, archbishop of Canterbury, and to his successors. From Lanfranc's point of view, so far, so good. But there were three grave weaknesses. First, Thomas professed obedience only on his own behalf, making no reference to his own successors. Second, a final sentence of his profession was potentially weakening to the Canterbury case. Thomas added that 'Concerning this matter, while I was still about to be ordained by you, I was uncertain (*dubius fui*), and so I promised that I would be obedient to you, indeed, without condition, but to your successors conditionally'. Thomas said only that he had been uncertain (*dubius*), not that he had been wrong; it was open for him or his successors to retract and say that his former thoughts had, after all, been his best ones. Third and most serious, as in 1070 Lanfranc had wished at Winchester to underpin Thomas's profession by an oath to himself; but again, 'for love of the king', he waived the oath, and so was denied the stronger sanction that an oath provided.[62] There can be little doubt that, once again, the king would not allow one subject to take such an oath to another. The best that Lanfranc could do was to limit the prohibition to the present case, so that future archbishops of Canterbury might be able to require an oath as well as a profession from Thomas's successors.[63] The church of Canterbury was thus left in need of a stronger guarantee of its rights than it received.

In the full assembly, matters were taken only so far as Thomas's profession; much remained to be done to settle the detail of relations between Canterbury and York and to reduce it to writing. Lanfranc's letter to Pope Alexander makes it sufficiently clear that, as was common practice in medieval councils, this was done in the days after most who attended had departed, and the result was regarded as decisions of the council.[64] No less important, the letter indicates that an endeavour was made to settle the dispute between Canterbury and York according to widely recognized norms for dealing with such matters; modern German historians describe them as *Spielregeln*—'rules of the game'.[65] They may be summarily stated as including the following norms. A ruler—king, pope, or bishop—or his agents stood as arbiter. His prime concern was less the determination of absolute justice than to restore fractured human loyalties and relationships. In hallowed terms, the object was to establish peace (*pax*) and concord (*concordia*). Their basis was not the entire victory of one party over another; even if one party were essentially in the right, peace and concord could ensue only if the other party were given something tangible to take away in recognition of some element of proper claim on his side. The upshot should be a visible and duly expressed friendship, even cordiality, between the hitherto antagonistic parties.

---

[62] See above, pp. 92–3. Dr Gibson's footnote suggesting that Lanfranc waived the oath from love for Thomas is to be discounted in the light of statements that he did so from love for the king: Lanfranc, *Letters*, 55, n. 10.

[63] In fact, they became able to do so only from the mid-13th century: see Richter, *Canterbury Professions*, pp. lxxviii–lxxix. For the York view of the oath, see Hugh the Chanter, 8–9.

[64] See Southern, 'The Canterbury Forgeries', 200.

[65] See esp. Althoff, *Die Spielregeln*, 1–125, and further discussion, especially with reference to conflicts in Bohemia, in Cowdrey, *Pope Gregory VII*, 448–51, 576–8.

Accordingly, Lanfranc represented Thomas, after his debating debacle and profession in full session, as turning to pleading: *Versus itaque ad preces est.* He besought the king to ask Lanfranc to banish from his mind all rancour for his own ill-conceived stand, to cherish peace and to create concord (*quatinus . . . pacem diligerem, concordiam facerem*). And he asked that Lanfranc should grant him from concern for charity some things that were his (Thomas's) by right. Lanfranc states that he willingly and thankfully agreed. Thus with the common support (*astipulatio*) of all a written record of the consequent agreement was to be prepared and circulated.

Such, in the days immediately after the full session of the council of Winchester, was the background to the first text of the agreement.[66] Canterbury's primacy was asserted in strong terms: the church of York should be subject to that of Canterbury, and in all matters concerning the Christian religion it should obey the decisions of the archbishop of Canterbury as primate of the whole of Britain.[67] The matter of the three disputed dioceses was not highlighted, but they were effectively reserved to Canterbury. The metropolitan (*sic*) of Canterbury confirmed to the archbishop of York and his successors in perpetuity jurisdiction over the bishop of Durham and over the whole region from the borders of the see of Lichfield and the River Humber to (here in all probability was the charitable quid pro quo of which Lanfranc wrote to the pope) the farthest limits of Scotland. The duty of the archbishop of York to attend Lanfranc's councils was affirmed and the claim of future archbishops of Canterbury to require an oath as well as a written profession of obedience from future archbishops of Canterbury was reserved. Provision was made for future consecrations of archbishops of Canterbury and York. Consistently with its having been prepared in the aftermath of the council of Winchester, the first version of the agreement bears the signa, besides those of the king and queen, the legate Hubert,[68] and the two archbishops, of only four bishops and no abbots.

In this state and at this time, the document was probably not circulated. Lanfranc's words in his letter to the pope once again call for careful reading: copies distributed to the principal churches of England would bear (*ferant*) witness to what conclusion this matter will be brought. (The subjunctive mood of the first verb and the future perfect tense of the second should be noticed.) The matter was brought to its conclusion at the council of Windsor at Pentecost. The agreement was renewed and thereafter widely circulated with no substantial change to its provisions, though a brief explanatory note about the two councils of Winchester and Windsor was added. But Pope Alexander had directed that the matters which he referred to the English kingdom should be settled by the testimony and judgement of its bishops and abbots. Besides the signa of the king and queen, the Windsor document was attested by the papal legate Hubert, the two archbishops, thirteen

---

[66] i.e. to that exemplified in Canterbury, D. & C. Library, Cart. Antiq. A 2; see above, n. 40.

[67] In the Canterbury professions such a phrase occurs for the first time in that of Osbern of Exeter, who was consecrated between the councils of Winchester and Windsor: *Canterbury Professions*, ed. Richter, no. 35, pp. 28–9.

[68] That of Hubert may have been added after an interval of time: see *Regesta WI*, 308.

bishops, and twelve abbots.[69] The matter was brought to its conclusion at Windsor by fulfilling the pope's direction.[70]

That the agreement of Easter and Pentecost 1072 was successful in restoring human relationships between Lanfranc and Thomas according to current norms is well illustrated by the latter's effusiveness to Lanfranc in a letter written within the next few months.[71] Yet for all that had been agreed at Winchester and given expression in Thomas's profession and in the document of peace and concord that followed, Lanfranc remained deeply disquieted by what had not been secured to the church of Canterbury: there was no certainty that future archbishops of York would acknowledge the primacy of Canterbury; the making of a profession of obedience was not reinforced, as Lanfranc wished, by the archbishop of York's taking an oath. A papal privilege for the church of Canterbury was imperatively necessary to secure its rights in perpetuity. Lanfranc's haste in turning to the apostolic see betrays his anxiety.

Without waiting for the fully authenticated document of agreement as produced at Windsor, Lanfranc sent it, in its Winchester form,[72] to Pope Alexander II together with other items which probably included some at least of the papal privileges which had been cited at Winchester; from these evidences, Lanfranc told the pope, 'you may clearly know from the custom (*ex more*) of your predecessors what you should grant to me and to the church of Christ [Christ Church, Canterbury] which I have undertaken to rule'. The very length and immediacy of Lanfranc's letter—it is the longest in the letter-collection—are eloquent of his anxiety. He continued in terms that verge upon importunity and even indiscretion:

I ask that this shall take place duly and without delay (*honeste et sine dilatione*) by the granting of a privilege of the apostolic see, so that from this as well [as from earlier favours] it may clearly be shown how much you love me. And concerning me, judge indeed as concerning a loyal follower and servant of blessed Peter and of yourself, and of the holy Roman church.[73]

Lanfranc also wrote briefly but no less urgently to the Roman archdeacon Hildebrand, who was a key figure in the papal household. Lanfranc asked him to read his whole dossier with becoming diligence, 'so that your charity may most surely grasp what the apostolic see should by confirming grant and by granting confirm to me and to my church through a privilege'.[74]

No answer from Alexander survives; Hildebrand replied courteously, if tersely. He much regretted that the wish conveyed by Lanfranc's messengers for a privilege to be sent in Lanfranc's absence from Rome could not properly be satisfied. There seemed to be no recent precedent, and it seemed necessary that Lanfranc should

---

[69] i.e. the text of Canterbury, D. & C. Library, Cart. Antiq. A 1.

[70] It is important to notice that the words *et abbates* at the end of the text of the agreement in Lanfranc, *Letters*, no. 3/4, p. 46, do not appear in Canterbury, D. & C. Library, Cart. Antiq. 1 and 2.

[71] Lanfranc, *Letters*, no. 12, pp. 78–81. Such effusiveness in expressing a close relationship between churchmen is not unparalleled: cf. the meeting between Abbot Herluin of Bec and Archbishop Lanfranc as described in *VH* caps. 91–4, pp. 101–2/202–3; *VL* cap. 7, pp. 688–9.

[72] i.e. as in Canterbury, D. & C. Library, Cart. Antiq. A 2.

[73] Lanfranc, *Letters*, no. 4, pp. 48–57, esp. pp. 54–5.   [74] Ibid., no. 5, pp. 56–9.

come to the threshold of the apostles where this and other business could be the better resolved by face-to-face discussion.[75] Hildebrand did not further explain. But he seems unlikely to have seen an objection in principle to Lanfranc's primatial claims, for very soon after becoming pope in April 1073 he countenanced them by implication in a letter charging him to root out grave moral offences amongst the Irish and throughout 'the island of the English'.[76] Possibly Roman prerogatives seemed to be at stake in the quid pro quo offered to Thomas of York in an agreement brokered by the English king that the archbishop should exercise jurisdiction through a vast and ecclesiastically unmapped area from the Humber to the far limits of Scotland. Possibly, too, the pope and his archdeacon wished to be sure that Lanfranc was not trying to secure by a privilege new or uncertain rights that should be tested. And they may well have felt that the pressing and prescriptive tone of Lanfranc's requests were presumptuous in one supplicating for a privilege from the apostolic see.

Lanfranc did not travel to Rome either in 1072 or ever again, and he did not secure the papal privilege that he urgently desired. In 1072 pressure of business may have been the sole reason:[77] having upheld the rights of the church of Canterbury in its relation to York, he had no less pressingly to uphold them in Kent by the process that led, probably in the summer of 1072, to the meeting on Penenden Heath.[78] But it is likely that the result of Hildebrand's letter was to draw Lanfranc more closely to the king. The clinching guarantees that Lanfranc sought had not been forthcoming: 'for love of the king', he had, at least for the present, abandoned his claim that an oath should reinforce the archbishop of York's profession; but the apostolic see had withheld a privilege pending a visit by Lanfranc to Rome which he could not immediately make. It was therefore from the king and his court that Lanfranc had secured what he gained by the constitution of 1072, and the gains were great and tangible. For this and for other reasons, the king should be looked to and supported for his benefits such as they were. As Lanfranc expressed it at the end of his last letter to Pope Alexander: 'While he lives we have peace of a sort; but after his death we expect that we shall have neither peace nor anything good.'[79]

The benefit that Lanfranc received as regards the primacy was similarly restricted. It was to his advantage that Thomas of York lived until 1100, and for the rest of Lanfranc's life he seems to have honoured the spirit and the letter of the constitution of 1072.[80] There is a York story that some years later (it would probably have been in 1086/7), when the king was about to cross to Normandy, both archbishops followed him to the Isle of Wight; the writing and sealing of the constitution of 1072 was denounced to the king as a forgery, and the king promised on his return to England to settle the matter justly and canonically (*iuste et canonice*) between the two archbishops. But the story lacks credibility.[81] Under Pope Paschal II

---

[75] Lanfranc, *Letters*, no. 6, pp. 58–9.   [76] Ibid., no. 8, pp. 64–7.
[77] For Lanfranc's expressed wish to visit Rome when political circumstances in England allowed, see ibid., no. 1, pp. 34–5.
[78] See below, pp. 109–11.   [79] Lanfranc, *Letters*, no. 1, pp. 34–5.
[80] For their good official and personal relations, see ibid., nos. 12–13, 23, 26, pp. 78–83, 104–7, 110–11.
[81] Hugh the Chanter, 8–11. There is just sufficient circumstantial detail to preclude rejecting the story out of hand. But there is no confirmation in other sources and some details are not credible, esp. that the

The Primacy of Canterbury

(1099–1118), the primacy of Canterbury came near to finding papal confirmation to Archbishop Anselm and his successors in such terms as Lanfranc had desired.[82] But the precise nature of the primacy remained unestablished. When the resolute Thurstan succeeded to the see of York in 1114 and five years later received consecration from Pope Calixtus II (1119–24), Lanfranc's plans for Canterbury's primacy upon his own terms were at an end. A difference between the two archbishops about constitutional principle degenerated into a squabble about personal dignity and precedence.

Yet there was soon compensation for Canterbury. Early in 1126 Pope Honorius II (1124–30) granted to William of Corbeil, archbishop of Canterbury (1123–36), a personal legateship for life in England and in Scotland, enjoining general attendance at synodal assemblies that he convened.[83] Thereafter a legateship was granted to archbishops up to Thomas Cranmer in the sixteenth century. The legateship of William of Corbeil was foreshadowed in Pope Alexander II's grant to Lanfranc of standing authority to act on his behalf,[84] and also by Archbishop Anselm's claim that as archbishop he was the pope's permanent legate in England.[85] The see of York was not expressly mentioned in Pope Honorius II's grant of a legateship to William of Corbeil; but as renewed in future years it eventually ensued that if the archbishop of Canterbury had little hold upon York by reason of primacy, he secured an effective superiority as papal legate. The leadership of Canterbury in the English church was irreversibly assured. If this did not entirely happen as Lanfranc envisaged, it was before all else the result of his personal stature as archbishop and the energy, resolution, and wisdom of his administration in the English church and polity. When he succeeded to the see, despite Stigand's wealth and influence Canterbury was overshadowed by the York of the able and assertive Archbishop Aldred; Lanfranc quickly and, as it transpired, enduringly consolidated Canterbury's pre-eminence.

---

king did not know about the writing and sealing of the document at Windsor, when he had himself sponsored and attested it.

[82] Anselm, *Epp.* nos. 222, 283, 303, 307, vol. 4.124–5, 200, 224–5, 229–30; for comment, see Southern, *Saint Anselm*, 136–8; id., *Saint Anselm: A Portrait*, 341–2.
[83] *CS* no. 131, vol. 1/2.741–3. For William's legatine councils, see *CS* nos. 132, 134, vol. 1/2.743–9, 750–4.
[84] See above, p. 89.
[85] Southern, *Saint Anselm*, 130–2; id., *Saint Anselm: A Portrait*, 335–6.

8

The Church of Canterbury

If the endeavour to assert the primacy of Canterbury was one aspect of Lanfranc's renewal of the mother church of the kingdom, a second and complementary concern was with the primatial see itself. This concern comprehended all aspects of its material, economic, and religious life.[1]

8.1 THE BUILDINGS OF THE CATHEDRAL AND CATHEDRAL MONASTERY

When Lanfranc arrived in Canterbury in 1070 a programme of building there was an urgent necessity. On 6 December 1067 the Anglo-Saxon cathedral had been very severely damaged by fire, along with the baptistery adjacent to its south-eastern corner. In the baptistery had been stored the cathedral's most precious muniments, including papal privileges given to past archbishops; these records suffered grave damage.[2] Fortunately the old cathedral had at its west end an apse and an altar that were similar to those at its east, as well as an oratory of the Virgin. The west end was not destroyed, and it was also possible to improvise over St Dunstan's tomb in the crypt below the choir a modest building in which masses and offices could be maintained.[3] The monastic buildings also suffered grave destruction, but the refectory and dormitory escaped, together with part of the cloister adjacent to them.[4] A continuity of monastic life was thus possible.

With his experience of building at Bec and Caen, where major churches were still in process of construction, Lanfranc lost no time in taking in hand the building of a new cathedral. The work is said to have taken seven years and so to have been complete, at least in major respects, by 1077, when it was consecrated on Palm Sunday (9 April).[5] This was also the year of the consecration of the monastic churches at Bec and Caen in Normandy. Lanfranc had immediately decided that the rebuilding

---

[1] Discussion of Lanfranc and the monastic life at Christ Church is reserved for a later chapter: see below, pp. 149–60.
[2] Lanfranc, *Letters*, no. 4, pp. 52–3; Eadmer, *Life of St Bregwine*, in Scholz, 'Eadmer's Life', cap. 11, pp. 142–5; Eadmer, *Life of St Ouen*, in Wilmart, *Opuscula*, 366.
[3] Eadmer, *Mirac.*, caps. 12, 14, pp. 231, 232.
[4] Osbern, *Mirac.*, cap. 16, p. 142; whence Eadmer, *Mirac.*, cap. 12, p. 231.
[5] Eadmer stated that Lanfranc almost completely restored the church within seven years: *Hist. nov.*, 1, p. 13; Goscelin of Saint-Bertin implausibly dated the completion of Lanfranc's entire building programme to five years after the destruction: *Vita s. Edithae*, Pref. p. 38. For the date of the consecration, see *Annales Anglosaxonici*, a. 1073 (*recte* 1077), p. 4, with Gibson's comments: *Lanfranc*, 172, 218.

should be a complete one. As a first step he carefully and with appropriate solemnity assembled the relics of all the saints of the cathedral at the west end of the cathedral in the oratory of the Virgin. When, in order to extend the cathedral, it became necessary to demolish the west end, the relics were again solemnly transferred from the oratory to the refectory within the monastic buildings.[6]

There is later confirmation that, for his rebuilding, Lanfranc had Caen stone shipped from Normandy;[7] he may have employed Norman masons. In any case, his cathedral is likely to have been in the style of contemporary Norman Romanesque churches like those at Bec and Caen, though not a close imitation of any of them. Very little of it remains; knowledge of it depends particularly on the monk Gervase of Canterbury's recollection of it as written after another major destruction by fire in 1174 and upon a few visual representations.[8] Gervase began his description with the great tower which, as he put it, stood like the centre of a circle at the middle of the circumference. Externally it was topped by a golden cherub; according to the Canterbury monk Osbern, Lanfranc himself told him to publicize the anecdote of a pirate guilty of much cruelty and many homicides who delighted to be called Barabbas. Having escaped from the custody of royal officers he fled towards Canterbury for sanctuary. But as soon as he could see the cherub on the pinnacle of the church he could progress no further; it was as though a heavenly cherub were blocking his path. Such was the penalty of impenitence, and he perforce returned to his captivity and to secular punishment.[9] Such was one moral that Lanfranc's cathedral was intended visually to convey.

Internally, Gervase next described the nave, or *aula*, to the west of the tower. Its roof was supported on either side by eight columns, and it culminated at the west end in two towers with gilded pinnacles; unlike at Saint-Étienne at Caen, the interior of the towers formed an integral part of the nave rather than a distinct westwork. In the middle of the nave hung a *corona* or circular chandelier; its north aisle included an oratory and altar of the Virgin. Across the nave there was a

---

[6] Osbern, *Mirac.*, cap. 19, pp. 148–9; whence Eadmer, *Mirac.*, cap. 16, p. 236. See also Eadmer, *Life of St Bregwine*, in: Scholz, 'Eadmer's Life', cap. 11, pp. 144–5. Eadmer later described how as a boy he had witnessed the solemnity of Lanfranc's transfer of Dunstan's body from its original tomb: *Epistola Eadmeri ad Glastonienses*, in *Reliquiae Dunstanianae*, no. 35, pp. 413–14.

[7] *VL* cap. 9, p. 693. Considerable amounts of Caen stone from Lanfranc's rebuilding survive *in situ*.

[8] Gervase, *Tractatus*, esp. pp. 9–11; especially as concerns the transepts and adjacent chapels, Gervase apparently does not sufficiently distinguish between Lanfranc's original plan and the results of the rebuilding under Anselm. Further details may be gleaned from Lanfranc, *Decr.* As regards visual evidence, the tower, transept, and nave are shown from the north in the Waterworks Drawing of *c*.1160: Cambridge, Trinity College, MS R 17 1, fos. 284^v–285^r, reproduced in Woodman, *The Architectural History*, 28. Before the destruction in 1834 of the north-west tower, J. C. Buckler made drawings: London, Society of Antiquaries, Red Portfolio. Modern discussions of Lanfranc's church and monastic buildings start with the still useful books by R. Willis. Recent discussions include Woodman, 26–45; Gem, 'The Significance'; Strik, 'Remains of the Lanfranc Building'; Fernie, 'Anselm's Crypt'; Klukas, 'The Architectural Implications'; and Crook, *The Architectural Setting*, esp. 178–81. All must, however, be read in the light of the excavations of 1993: see Blockley (ed.), *Canterbury Cathedral Nave*, esp. 15–16, 23–30, 111–27, 146, 212. For plans and diagrams, see Fig. 20, between pp. 24–5; Figs. 45–6, pp. 113–14; Figs. 48–9, pp. 116–17; Fig. 53, p. 122. For Buckler's drawings, see Figs. 50–2, pp. 118–20.

[9] Osbern, *Mirac.*, cap. 22, pp. 154–5.

pulpitum or screen over which Lanfranc set images of the cross, two cherubs, and St Mary and St John. Before it was an altar dedicated to the Holy Cross which was the principal nave altar. According to Osbern, Lanfranc balanced his anecdote of the impenitent pirate Barabbas with that of a man whom Bishop Odo of Bayeux had condemned to the permanent wearing of fetters because he had killed one of the bishop's stags. The man became of exemplary piety and the sound of his chains became a public symbol of penitence until, after two years, his chains fell off as he prayed prostrate before the altar of the Holy Cross.[10] There was evidently complete public access to the nave, which was probably entered by a door opening to the south.

To the north and south of the central tower were transepts of broadly symmetrical design. Recently discovered archaeological evidence suggests that four chapels, two opening from the east wall of each of the transepts, which flanked the choir were of considerable though differing size and that, like the choir, they terminated in apses. They were profoundly affected when, only some twenty years after Lanfranc's work, the choir of the cathedral was rebuilt and enlarged by Archbishop Anselm and Prior Ernulf (c.1096–1107). Gervase's memory that the chapels of the north transept were dedicated to St Blaise (lower) and St Benedict (upper), and those of the south transept to St Michael (lower) and All Saints (upper), may recall the dedications of Lanfranc's day. The rebuilding completely swept away Lanfranc's presbytery and sanctuary. The presbytery was of the width of the central tower. It was approached by steps under the tower which allowed entry to a crypt beneath, which must have been too small for access other than by the monks. It is virtually certain that the monks' choir was at the east end of the nave, from which a screen enclosed it.[11] It was in order to provide a larger and more suitable choir for the monks that Lanfranc's east end was so soon demolished. The high altar is likely to have been situated in the eastern apse, where Lanfranc probably already located the archbishop's throne behind the altar.[12] The matutinal altar stood in the presbytery to the west of the high altar; both altars would have been readily visible from the monks' choir. There is virtually no certain evidence for Lanfranc's final location of the relics and shrines of the Canterbury saints, though the chapels of the transepts are likely to have received some of them; for Dunstan and Elphege, there is no clue whatever.[13] It is, however, certain that to the east of the tower Lanfranc's

---

[10] Ibid., cap. 22, pp. 153–5.

[11] The location of the monks' choir under the tower, with possibly extensions to the east or into the transepts, has been canvassed.

[12] Gem argues that the archbishop's throne probably remained at the west end of the nave as in the Anglo-Saxon cathedral and that Anselm removed it to the eastern apse: 'The Significance', 3. This is possible, but it is not easy to envisage that Lanfranc's west end, with no apse and with the extension of the nave, provided a suitable setting for the throne.

[13] Eadmer wrote of the saints with regard to their ultimate resting-place in Lanfranc's cathedral that 'Post aliquot annos in aecclesiam iam fundatam illati sunt, et in aquilonali parte super voltum singuli sub singulis ligneis locellis, ubi cotidie mysterium sacrificii salutaris celebratur, positi sunt': *Life of St Bregwine*, in Scholz, 'Eadmer's Life', cap. 11, p. 145. This has been interpreted as meaning that they were placed high in the north transept, though it might refer to the north side of the choir. Comparison with the story of the monk Lambert that follows suggests that there may be some confusion with the arrangements of Anselm's church: cap. 14, p. 146. Eadmer does not in this Life refer expressly to the remains of Dunstan and Elphege.

cathedral was richly decorated and equipped, and that the liturgical vestments in use were sumptuous. Not without good reason did Goscelin of Saint-Bertin address Lanfranc as 'noster ille Beseleel'.[14]

Lanfranc's *obit* commemorated the comprehensiveness with which he also carried through the complete replacement of the monastic buildings to the north of the cathedral.[15] He lost no time in replacing what had been destroyed in the fire of 1067, and in due course he attended to the replacement of what had survived by structures large enough to accommodate the enlarged monastic community that he built up.[16] His cloister was situated to the north of the nave of the cathedral, with a cellarer's range on its west side. To the north of the cloister was his very large new dormitory, of which a substantial part survives in a ruined state. His chapter house was to the east near the transept of the cathedral, and beyond it was a refectory. To these principal works were added all necessary offices. Lanfranc surrounded the whole monastic area with a strong and high wall, thus creating what was in England a new kind of monastic precinct which became a model for other religious houses in England. Immediately to the west of the cathedral he built an archiepiscopal palace (*curia*) set in a three-acre precinct. It was a T-shaped construction with a great hall as a principal feature. Its building entailed the destruction of twenty-seven dwellings.[17]

At a time and in circumstances that are uncertain, Lanfranc signalled a new stage in the cathedral's history by adding to its dedication to Christ the Saviour a dedication to the Holy Trinity. Especially in a monastic context and within the city, the cathedral continued to be called Christ Church. But the new dedication augmented its standing in the world at large, not least with regard to its rights and property.[18]

8.2 LANFRANC'S CHARITABLE FOUNDATIONS AT CANTERBURY

In addition to his building work in the cathedral and monastic offices of Christ Church, Lanfranc was remembered for his foundation, construction, and endowment near the city of three charitable institutions. Not far outside the north gate, on either side of the present Northgate Street, were the closely related hospital of St John the Baptist and priory of St Gregory the Great; on a hill to the west of the city, this hospital was complemented by the leper hospital of St Nicholas.[19] These were

---

[14] Eadmer, *Hist. nov.*, 1, p. 13; William of Malmesbury, *GP* 1.43, pp. 69–70. For *coronae* and other illuminations, see Lanfranc, *MC* caps. 20, 65, 66, pp. 28–9, 88–9, 90–1; for later inventories, see Wickham Legg and Hope, *Inventories*, 9–17, 32, 53, 57. For Goscelin's comment, see *Vita s. Edithae, Praef.* p. 34, cf. Exod. 31: 1–11.

[15] Gibson, *Lanfranc*, 228.

[16] Eadmer, *Hist. nov.*, 1, pp. 12–13; William of Malmesbury, *GP* 1.43, p. 69.

[17] Rady et al., 'The Archbishop's Palace', esp. pp. 2–6. Domesday recorded the loss of twenty-seven dwellings (*mansurae*) 'in nova hospitatione archiepiscopi': *DB Kent*, fo. 3ᵛ, no. 2.16.

[18] Thus, in Domesday, the name of Holy Trinity was used rather than Christ Church: *DB Kent*, fos. 1ᴿ, nos. D 17, 19; 2ʳ, nos. C 6, 8; 2ᵛ–3ʳ, no. 2.2.

[19] For these foundations, see esp. Eadmer, *Hist. nov.*, 1, pp. 15–16, whence William of Malmesbury, *GP* 1.44, p. 71; *Annales Anglosaxonici*, a. 1085, p. 4; Gervase of Canterbury, *Actus pont.*, pp. 368–9;

works of Lanfranc's latter years, after the completion of the rebuilding of Christ Church and with the stricter monastic life that is expressed in Lanfranc's monastic constitutions. A main motive was the concern to perform and to encourage works of charity which will find repeated illustration in future chapters of this book. But while Christ Church did not cease to be the cathedral of the city and diocese to which, with Lanfranc's encouragement, the laity had recourse,[20] the very fact of a stricter monastic observance inevitably in some respects set limits upon the availability of the cathedral and its clergy and resources. Some illustrations are the preoccupation of the monks with a demanding and strictly articulated monastic round; the reservation of the east end of the cathedral, with its chapels, altars, and relics, for monastic purposes; the enclosure of the monastic precinct by a high wall; and the tendency to concentrate almsgiving, generous though it might be, upon appropriate ritual occasions.[21] Much was diminished for the laity that needed to be made good outside the cathedral precincts.

The prime purpose of the hospital of St John was to provide, with the oversight of competent wardens, residence, food, and clothing for infirm and aged men and women. Surviving remains of Lanfranc's buildings and archaeological excavation have made clear the scale of the dormitories and associated reredorters which provided for the separate accommodation of men and women; there was also an adjoining chapel. The spiritual needs of the hospital were served by the clerks of St Gregory's priory, established probably in 1084/5. Lanfranc's *obit* laid emphasis upon the wider function of St Gregory's as a burial church, in which decent burial was provided without charge for those unable to afford it; here, Lanfranc supplied a pastoral need for the city which was no doubt accentuated by the monastic order of the cathedral. To facilitate such external ministrations, Lanfranc provided for the priory to be served by regular canons rather than by monks. It is unlikely that the canons as yet lived according to the Rule of St Augustine, which was probably introduced under Archbishop William of Corbeil.[22] The text of Lanfranc's foundation charter as given in the cartulary of St Gregory's is almost certainly a later composition, the details of which represent its later functioning as an Augustinian house; they cannot safely be used as evidence for Lanfranc's arrangements, although they testify to the role that St Gregory's came to have in the city.[23] According to the priory's tradition, in 1085, and so very soon after its inception, Lanfranc translated from Lyminge the relics of the two saints, Mildrith and Eadburga, who

Lanfranc's *obit* in Gibson, *Lanfranc*, 228. For a discussion with maps and plans, see Tatton-Brown, 'The Beginnings'.

[20] See e.g. Lanfranc's anecdotes referred to above, pp. 105, 106.
[21] Lanfranc, *MC* caps. 32, 113, pp. 48–51, 192–3, provide examples of caritative acts.
[22] For early evidence of William's reorganization, see *Cartulary of the Priory of St Gregory*, no. 14, p. 10.
[23] For the foundation charter, see *Cartulary of the Priory of St Gregory*, no. 1, pp. 1–3. Cogent reasons for questioning its authenticity are given in Tatton-Brown, 'The Beginnings', 42. The rent of twelve burgesses and thirty-two dwellings 'which the clerks of the town hold in their gild' and of a mill, all of which the archbishop held in Domesday Book but which in the *Domesday monachorum* the clerks of St Gregory held for the benefit of their church, may have been assigned to the canons during his last years: *DB Kent* fo. 3, no. 2.1; *The Domesday Monachorum*, 82.

were Lyminge's co-founders.[24] The twin foundations of St John and St Gregory were complemented by the house for lepers at Harbledown. Taken together, the three institutions represent a strong endeavour on Lanfranc's part to ensure that the more stringent organization of a monastic cathedral did not lead to the neglect of charitable and pastoral care of the city. Instead, the church of Canterbury was so strengthened in its monastic and non-monastic aspects that it was suitably distinguished as a primatial see and equipped to support the archbishop in his primatial role.[25]

8.3 THE SECURING OF CHRIST CHURCH'S LANDS AND PRIVILEGES

The maintenance of the round of religious observance, ecclesiastical governance, and (not least important) almsgiving for which it was Lanfranc's purpose to provide required a firm legal and economic base. Thus, hardly less critical than the vindication of Canterbury's primacy was the securing of Canterbury's lands and privileges. The urgency was the greater on account of depredations and losses of estates and resources under the pre-Conquest archbishops Eadsige (1038–50) and Stigand (1052–70),[26] which were aggravated after 1066 by the virtual replacement of the Anglo-Saxon uppermost strata of society by predatory Norman invaders. Lanfranc's strenuous and in no small degree successful attempts, in the contemporary term to 'deraign' (*dirationare*)—that is, to vindicate or maintain—the rights and possessions of his church and see were and are above all associated with a meeting of the shire court of Kent at the customary place on Penenden Heath, near Maidstone. The extensive documentation of the meeting testifies to its critical importance.[27] Yet there remains uncertainty about every aspect of the occasion.

This is so partly because no record or minute of the court survives which is near to it in time or demonstrable origin.[28] The most substantial evidence is a report or memorandum recording what were later seen as the results of the pleading which survives in two versions. Version I has its earliest attestation in a late eleventh- or early twelfth-century Christ Church manuscript which belonged to Rochester cathedral priory, where a copy was made soon afterwards. An incomplete text survives on a thirteenth-century roll from Christ Church. It is important because it opens with a full dating clause; in this respect as in some others it resembles in form

---

[24] See Rollason, *The Mildrith Legend*, 23–4, 59–60, 65–8, 80.

[25] Cf. Lanfranc's statement that, in compiling his monastic constitutions, he sought both to follow the customs of monasteries 'que nostro tempore maioris auctoritatis sunt in ordine monachorum' and to make certain additions and changes which were appropriate 'propter primatem sedem': *MC* cap. 1, pp. 2–3.

[26] Brooks, *The Early History*, 300–3 (Eadsige), 307–9 (Stigand). Stigand accumulated a vast personal lordship while neglecting the estates of his church.

[27] The sources are assembled and discussed in *English Lawsuits*, no. 5, vol. 1.7–15; *Regesta WI*, no. 69, pp. 315–26. I use Bates's designation of the versions as in *Regesta WI*.

[28] For full discussion of the sources, see Bates, 'The Land Pleas', and his editorial notes in *Regesta WI*.

the constitution on the primacy of 1072. A fragment of a fourteenth-century cartulary includes a much-amplified list of the lands that Lanfranc deraigned at Penenden. Version II occurs only in two fifteenth-century manuscripts, although it was certainly used by the chronicler Gervase of Canterbury and perhaps known to Eadmer.[29] Although the two versions are closely related, there are considerable differences. Version I opens with a long narrative account of the assembly at Penenden and of Lanfranc's resolution in winning back lands seized by Odo of Bayeux and his men; this is lacking from Version II. For the rest, among many small differences Version I tends to fix upon the procedures of the court, whereas Version II is more concerned with its determination of Canterbury's rights, about which it is more precise. Version II may depend upon Version I though not vice versa; or it could be that both Versions draw upon a common source. In either case, they seem to reflect the definition of Canterbury's liberty at different stages of its development at about the end of the eleventh century.[30] It is the more striking that both versions end with an assertion that, by recording the upshot of the proceedings at Penenden, they are establishing a virtual Magna Carta of Canterbury's liberties as vindicated there:

This has been written down here in order both that it may for ever be profitable for future memory and that the future successors of this Church of Christ at Canterbury may themselves know what and how much they should hold from God in the privileges (*dignitatibus*) of this church and should require by eternal right from the kings and princes of this kingdom. (Version I)

These things have been committed to memory in order that in future times they may prove to be of help and that the successors of the Canterbury church may know what and how much it was entitled to hold from God in the privileges (*dignitatibus*) of this church and to require by eternal right from the kings and princes of this kingdom.   (Version II)

Partly because the report of the meeting on Penenden Heath was thus the subject of development and modification, there is uncertainty about the date of meeting; each year from 1070 to 1077 has found its supporters.[31] However, the thirteenth-century fragment of Version I opens with a full dating clause that points to a date between 25 March and 28 August 1072, while both texts of Version II, though late, give the date 1072.[32] References in the sources to the presence of Ethelric as bishop 'of Chichester', to which city the see of Selsey was transferred in 1075, and to Ernost as 'bishop of Rochester', a see which he held only for a few months in 1075/6, are not decisive as indications of date since both may result from looseness of reference by later copyists: Selsey may have been replaced by the current name of the see, and Ernost may have been present but in a pre-episcopal capacity. A further consideration that makes a date in 1072, or possibly early in 1073, probable is that Lanfranc

---

[29] Bates, 'The Land Pleas', 5–6.
[30] For a detailed discussion, which is here summarized, see ibid. 6–12.
[31] For the much-discussed problem of date, see esp. Le Patourel, 'The Date', and Bates, 'The Land Pleas', 12–13.
[32] Version I (b), *Regesta WI*, 322; Version II, ibid. 325. *AL* assigns Penenden Heath to Lanfranc's third year, i.e. that beginning 29 Aug. 1072: 85–6.

cannot easily be envisaged as writing to Pope Alexander II (died 21 April 1073) so unhopefully as he wrote in his last letter to him if he had, with the king's strong support, already secured for his see the benefits that, as will emerge in the following paragraphs, he secured at Penenden Heath; Lanfranc pleaded to be allowed to resign his see against a background of unrelieved tribulations and setbacks and of only modest advantage from William's rule.[33] Penenden Heath is probably to be dated to mid- or late 1072.

It is widely held that the first, and perhaps the principal, business of the court was Lanfranc's complaint that Bishop Odo of Bayeux (as earl of Kent) and his men had since the Norman conquest encroached upon the lands and rights of the see of Canterbury. Such a view was already adopted in the medieval historical sources,[34] and it found strong expression in the opening section of Version I of the report of the Penenden trial.[35] In the latter it was noticed that Odo's coming to England and his accumulation of power in Kent had by some years preceded Lanfranc's arrival. When Lanfranc appreciated the scale of Odo's depredations he appealed to the king, who referred the matter for settlement to the shire court. Lanfranc successfully deraigned certain named lands against Odo and his men and against Hugh of Montfort, and also certain customs properly belonging to his see.

While it cannot be doubted that Lanfranc's confrontation with Odo was a feature of the Penenden assembly, there are strong reasons for questioning whether it was of predominating importance. First, all the chronicle sources were written after, and with knowledge of, the vicissitudes of Odo's fortunes in the 1080s: his imprisonment by the king in 1082, and his rebellion and warfare against William Rufus after the Conqueror's death in 1087. The opening paragraph of Version I of the report may also reflect these events and later animus against Odo. For the paragraph can easily be read as a separate account of the Penenden assembly which was at some later date prefixed to that as in Version II.[36] An arresting feature of Version II is that, as it stands, it merely notes Odo's presence and does not single out his depredations as a key issue, saying that

in this plea Lanfranc asserted that there rightfully belonged to his church a number of lands which the princes and magnates of the kingdom who were present and their men were themselves holding, and at length through God's remembrance (*per Dei memoriam*) he deraigned and claimed for himself and his church the lands and all customs associated with them.

The account of Penenden in the *Acta Lanfranci* likewise made no reference by name to Odo;[37] it appears to have followed a report like Version II which focused upon other business. It is well to avoid too large a preoccupation with Odo of Bayeux.

---

[33] Lanfranc, *Letters*, no. 1, pp. 30–5.
[34] See esp. Osbern, *Mirac.*, cap. 18, pp. 143–4; Eadmer, *Mirac.*, cap. 17, pp. 288–9, and *Hist. nov.*, 1, p. 17; William of Malmesbury, *GP* 1.43, p. 70; *VL* cap. 9, p. 693; Gervase of Canterbury, *Act. pont.*, 369.
[35] *Regesta WI*, 319–20.
[36] e.g. if Version I or its antecedent account were drafted as a whole, it is surprising that the list of those present should not have come earlier; the last sentence of the first paragraph reads like the conclusion of an originally separate document.
[37] *AL* 85–6.

Second, not only had many of Canterbury's lost estates passed from the possession of the see before 1066, so that Odo and his men were not directly responsible for their seizure,[38] but at least up to 1082 Lanfranc's relations with Odo seem often to have been positive and co-operative. There is an almost total lack of evidence about how each regarded the other, but there should be no presumption of hostility or endemic antagonism. In Normandy before 1066 Lanfranc may well have seen some things to imitate and even to admire in Odo as his diocesan bishop.[39] In England the two men can scarcely have afforded completely to fall out—Lanfranc in view of Odo's status and power as the king's half-brother and as earl of Kent; Odo because of Lanfranc's rapid ecclesiastical mastery of the diocese that corresponded to his English earldom. At least, royal *acta* disclose them as acting in each other's interest,[40] while Domesday also shows that they had worked together.[41] Penenden Heath does not appear to have been for long traumatic to their relationship; as often in medieval litigation, personal relationships were not lastingly compromised.

Third, when it came to detail, in Version I of the report Lanfranc deraigned only a very few named possessions: from the men of Odo, four estates plus numerous other, unnamed portions of land (*multas alias minutas terras*); from Hugh of Montfort, two estates; and from Ralph of Courbépine, one further pasturage.[42] A fourteenth-century copy extended the list to comprise twenty-eight properties that Lanfranc recovered.[43] But the extended list, evidently intended to fill out Lanfranc's success at Penenden, is closely related to a list in a Canterbury *obit* of King William I which comprises possessions restored by the king to Christ Church.[44] The implication is that Canterbury's estates were recovered by a series of pleas over a number of years, with Penenden as a limited if critical beginning. That the process was thus cumulative finds confirmation in a survey, probably assignable to the late 1070s, listing estates in which Christ Church had an interest.[45] Only a few of their localities appear in the report on Penenden, while much unsettled business remained for settlement in the hundred courts. That lawsuits were not infrequent is indicated by an anecdote of Eadmer. With the king's leave, Odo of Bayeux once embarked upon a suit that was well prepared and presented. Lanfranc was said not usually to become involved in such cases, which were evidently of common occurrence. But this time there was imminent danger of failure. Fortified by a vision of St Dunstan, Lanfranc intervened to such good effect that for the rest of his life the

---

[38] See above, pp. 79–80. [39] See below, pp. 193–4.
[40] e.g. *Regesta WI*, nos. 70–2, 74, 85, 87, pp. 328–9, 332–3, 351, 354–5. [41] *DB Kent*, fo. 2, no. C 8.
[42] *Regesta WI*, 320. [43] Version I (a), *Regesta WI*, 321–2.
[44] Edited in Le Patourel, 'The Reports of the Trial', 24–6; English trans. in Du Boulay, *The Lordship of Canterbury*, 42. The statement that William restored to Christ Church 'omnes fere terras antiquis et modernis temporibus a iure ipsius aecclesiae ablatas' demonstrates a recognition that some of the losses were long-standing.
[45] Discussed and edited by Douglas, 'Odo, Lanfranc, and the Domesday Survey', with text on pp. 51–2; English trans. in Du Boulay, *The Lordship of Canterbury*, 38–9. The list provides further evidence of Canterbury's losses to Earl Godwin before the Norman conquest. For a tradition that Abbot Ethelwig of Evesham (1058–77) was called upon by Lanfranc to help with the recovery of Christ Church lands, see *Chron. mon. de Evesham*, 90.

case was never reopened against him.[46] In the light of such evidence, the recovery and defence of Canterbury's property was a gradual and piecemeal process that was by no means ended at Penenden.

When Lanfranc's achievement at Penenden in safeguarding Canterbury's lands is thus viewed, it remains considerable. The accounts of the trial also present him as vindicating Canterbury's jurisdictional rights. The two versions of the report cover the same ground, but with differences of order and detail. First in Version I but last in Version II, Lanfranc deraigned a renewal of Canterbury's liberties and customs in the composite formula of English law,[47] with the rider that as the king held his lands free and quit in his demesne, so the archbishop of Canterbury held his lands in his demesne. The court further determined that the king had no customs in the lands of the church of Canterbury save three of which the financial consequences were indicated: if the archbishop's man dug up the king's highway; if he obstructed it by felling a tree; or if anyone committed upon it bloodshed, murder, or other offence. Similarly, it was shown that the archbishop rightly had many customs in all the lands of the king and the earl of Kent—that is, of Odo of Bayeux. Examples given were that from Septuagesima until Low Sunday anyone who shed blood paid a fine to the archbishop; all the year round the archbishop had a claim to part or all of the fine for the offence called *cildwite*.[48] In all these lands he also had whatever pertained to the cure and salvation of souls.

So far as the particular rulings attributed to the court are concerned, and especially those which concern the king's highway, it seems likely that they in fact concern matters that were ventilated over a number of years both before and after the Domesday survey, and so well beyond Lanfranc's lifetime.[49] He may have initiated claims which the Domesday commissioners disallowed or, at least, left unresolved;[50] the versions of the Penenden trial as they survive embody claims of inflated privileges as they were being advanced in the 1090s. But even when such dubious

---

[46] Eadmer, *Hist. nov.*, 1, pp. 17–18. Eadmer presented the incident as a counterpart to Penenden as it came to be viewed by his time. Odo began the plea with the king's leave, bringing to it all who were most versed in the laws and customs of the English kingdom. Lanfranc 'ita processit ut quae super eum pridie dicta fuerunt sic devinceret et inania esse monstraret, ut donec vitae praesenti superfuit nullus exurgeret qui inde contra eum os aperiret'.

[47] 'Et renovatas ibi diratiocinavit soca, saca, toll, team, flymenafyrmthe, grithbrece, foresteal, haimfare, infangennetheof, cum omnes aliis consuetudinibus paribus istis vel minoribus istis, in terris et aquis, in silvis, in viis, et in pratis, et in omnibus aliis rebus infra civitatis et extra, infra burgum et extra, et in omnibus aliis locis': Version I, *Regesta WI*, 320, 323; cf. Version II, ibid. 326. For writs of Cnut regarding Christ Church, Canterbury, containing similar formulas, see Harmer, *Anglo-Saxon Writs*, nos. 26, 28, pp. 181–3; with comment on pp. 168–73, and of Edward the Confessor, ibid., nos. 31–4 with comment on pp. 166–8, 172–1; all are of highly suspect authenticity, and esp. in the case of no. 33 falsification or forgery at the time of the Penenden plea may be suspected. For a writ of William I in favour of St Augustine's, Canterbury, which may pre-date Penenden and which confirms its rights similarly, see *Regesta WI*, no. 80, pp. 341–2.

[48] A fine paid to a lord by one who gets his bondwoman with child; but Domesday associated a similar fine with adultery: *DB Kent*, fo. 1ʳ, no. D 19; cf. *The Domesday Monachorum*, 98.

[49] See Cooper, 'Extraordinary Privilege'. Cooper, however, seems to go too far in impugning the accounts of the Penenden trial as historical evidence and as guides to the significance of the trial: see esp. pp. 1167, 1187–8.

[50] See e.g. *DB Kent*, fo. 2ʳ, no. C 9, where the archbishop's claim is noted.

passages in the accounts of Penenden are set aside, the parts which are not open to such challenge make it clear that Lanfranc secured a wide-ranging definition in the afforced shire court of Kent of the rights and customs of his church which was critical in itself and which future times might seek to amplify and to particularize.

Three points stand out from the report of it, especially from Version I. First, for the benefit of Canterbury as for other persons and places in his kingdom, the king was determined to uphold the processes and the findings of Old English law. A royal writ, almost certainly of earlier date, succinctly set out his essential concerns: men should be worthy of the laws of which they were worthy in the day of King Edward the Confessor; there should be continuity of inheritance from generation to generation; and the king would suffer no one to do any wrong to another contrary to the king's will.[51] Later royal writs of the Conqueror drove home the law of the Confessor's time as the norm alike for personal and corporate rights and for legal pleading.[52] The reason for the Conqueror's insistence upon Old English law and the witness of those who knew it is apparent: they provided a strong counterweight in a turbulent society to a new and predatory upper class of princes and magnates. Rights like those of Canterbury as declared and vouched for by them were made more secure by local and prescriptive warranty.

Second, the forum for the defence of such rights was not, like the question of the primacy, a matter for the royal court at which the leading persons had no knowledge of the Confessor's law but in the shire court as it was accustomed to meet at Penenden. The written outcome was not a final constitution such as was settled about the primacy at Winchester and Windsor but a unilateral, Christ Church memorandum of pleading which was a 'living document' open to accommodate changing needs and rulings of later generations.[53] It recorded proceedings that set under scrutiny not only matters between Archbishop Lanfranc and Odo of Bayeux but also between archbishop and king. Nevertheless, according to the record, at every stage the meeting at Penenden had the warmest support and approval of the king. Upon Lanfranc's request it was the king who commanded the whole shire to sit without delay and the men of the shire to be convened, especially the English who were expert in ancient laws and customs. As a neutral figure who was not *parti pris*, as both William and Odo as earl were, Bishop Geoffrey of Coutances presided *in loco regis*. It was by the king's order that Bishop Ethelric of Chichester, deposed in 1070 but 'a man of great old age and most wise in the laws of the land', was brought in a carriage to testify to what those laws were. Most important, when the king heard of the upshot of the court he warmly applauded it, confirming it with the consent of all his princes, clearly now in the royal court, and ordering that it should henceforth be inviolably observed. The rights of Canterbury were thus built into the law of the

---

[51] Writ to the citizens of London: *Regesta WI*, no. 180, p. 583.

[52] See esp. the series of royal writs relating to the abbey of Ely: *Regesta WI*, nos. 117–26, pp. 410–37, and particularly no. 123, pp. 431–2. Cf. the terms in which Bishop Wulfstan of Worcester was said to have defended the lands and liberty of his church against Archbishop Thomas of York: John of Worcester, a. 1070, vol. 3.16–17.

[53] See Bates, 'The Land Pleas', esp. 4–5, 8–11.

land with the strongest sanction of the king and his court. Not without reason did the monks of Christ Church later commemorate on the anniversary of King William's death the recovery of their lands.[54]

Yet, thirdly, not only were the privileges of Canterbury as set out in the record thus assured by the shire and by the king in his court; the last sentence of the report asserted their inviolability to all human intervention. For future archbishops should know what and how much they should hold from God; the privileges of their church came directly from God and not mediately through any man. And so by eternal right they had just demands that they must require of both the kings and princes of the kingdom.[55] This was not an assertion of a generalized liberty of the church as the papacy of Gregory VII conceived it. But it was a claim that the liberties of the church as rooted in the ancient custom of the land were severally and collectively immune from human will and violation.

The importance of Penenden did not arise from its being a victory of Lanfranc over Odo about the lands of Canterbury; in the interest of their future relations Lanfranc had reason to avoid making it appear so. Rather, it lay in its seminal vindication of the rights and customs of Canterbury under the law against all manner of challenge. They were secured under the strong authority of the king in the shire court and confirmed in the royal court. The support of the king was in contrast with Lanfranc's concurrent failure to secure papal confirmation of Canterbury's primacy, which had received such security as it gained from a royal constitution. It was an object-lesson for Lanfranc that the firmest foundation for the church of Canterbury as a force for the Christianization of the British Isles lay within the Anglo-Norman state.[56]

8.4 THE ADMINISTRATION OF CANTERBURY'S LANDS AND INCOME

There is ample evidence to show that Lanfranc was both assiduous and to a large degree successful in recovering lands and rights of his see that had been lost both before and after the Norman conquest. There is less evidence to make clear the character and result of his administration of the resources that were possessed by his church. But it is clear that his concern was with the stewardship of what it already rightly had, rather than with a programme of fresh acquisitions. As was generally the case with older English churches, most of Canterbury's medieval landed wealth had come to it by the time of the Domesday survey. Further, the distinction

---

[54] See Lanfranc's *obit* in Gibson, *Lanfranc*, 228.

[55] See above, p. 110. As the concluding sentence of a 'living document' it may have been coloured by Archbishop Anselm's conflicts with William Rufus and Henry I, but it remains a significant comment on how at Penenden the dealings of both William I and Odo of Bayeux were set firmly under the law with Lanfranc as a major influence.

[56] Cf. Eadmer's comment on Lanfranc's astuteness (*sagacitas*) with the king in securing the recovery of church lands: *Hist. nov.*, 1, pp. 12, 23.

of Domesday between the land of the archbishop of Canterbury and the land of the archbishop's monks, that is, of the community of Christ Church, had been established for centuries before the conquest and was not an innovation by Lanfranc.[57] Lanfranc was able to provide what Domesday described as the land of the archbishop's knights, and thus to meet his *servitium debitum* of sixty knights without retaining them in his household, by assigning them holdings in the land of the archbishop; he thus enfeoffed the whole number of those for whom he was answerable to the king.[58]

The wealth represented by the lands of the archbishop was very great. While Domesday provides only an approximate and incomplete indication of the wealth of the English bishops, it has been calculated to suggest an annual revenue of some £1,170 for the archbishop of Canterbury, thus making him the richest landholder in the country apart from the king himself; among the other bishops, Winchester came second with £920 and Lincoln a distant third with £660.[59] Lanfranc had already shown his business acumen as prior of Bec.[60] During his early years at Canterbury his employment as his household vicegerent (*rei familiaris suae procuratorem*) of the monk Gundulf, whom he brought from Caen in 1070, provided him with an accomplished right-hand man in his affairs.[61] He was also concerned himself to attend faithfully to his rights and duties by assiduous itinerary of his manors in Kent and Sussex, where he built churches and houses for their better administration.[62] As he told Bishop Stigand of Chichester about those rights which arose from Canterbury lands that were situated in that bishop's diocese: 'For just as we desire by skilful vigilance to preserve inviolate the things that our predecessors possessed from of old until our own times, so by no usurpation (which heaven forbid!) would we deny to others whatever things are owing to them.'[63]

There are indications that, in so pursuing his rights, Lanfranc met with a qualified success. Too much cannot be claimed. If, as is probable, an assessment list of Kentish lands which survives in a thirteenth-century copy gives their values as at a few years before the Domesday survey,[64] comparison with assessments in Domesday and the *Domesday monachorum* as in King Edward's time and as at the time of the respective surveys is sometimes possible. Such comparison suggests that losses in value in the earlier part of the Conqueror's reign were, on the whole, held but not recouped by the end of the eleventh century.[65] Such a conclusion is consistent with the gradual and piecemeal recovery by Lanfranc of the lands and rights of his see. When ecclesiastical dues and renders were concerned, Lanfranc seems to have been

---

[57] See Kissan, 'Lanfranc's Alleged Division', where the division as alleged by Gervase of Canterbury is denied.

[58] *DB Kent*, fo. 4^{r-v}, no. 2.28–43; cf. the list *De militibus archiepiscopi* in *The Domesday monachorum*, 105.

[59] Brett, *The English Church*, 68–70, 103. [60] See above, pp. 12, 15–16, 24.

[61] *The Life of Gundulf*, cap. 10, p. 32. [62] Eadmer, *Hist. nov.* 1, p. 16.

[63] Lanfranc, *Letters*, no. 30, pp. 118–19.

[64] In London, Lambeth Palace Library, MS 1212, p. 340; see Hoyt, 'A Pre-Domesday Kentish Accessions List', pp. 199–202 and Plate XIV.

[65] See Hoyt's tables and conclusions: pp. 198–9.

more successful in securing what he believed to be just and favourable arrangements. Thus, a charter of Archbishop Anselm noted that, after inquiry, Lanfranc had divided offerings at the main altar of Christ Church in equal parts between himself and the monks.[66] Lanfranc also radically revised the list of customary payments owed to the archbishop at Eastertide by the priests and churches of Kent. The opening item of the *Domesday monachorum* is a list of payments expressed entirely in cash from each of some eighty-seven named localities. It was said that Lanfranc settled and instituted (*ordinavit et instituit*) this arrangement to replace that in force before his time. The obsolete obligations of the opening fifteen localities were given.[67] They included substantial renders in kind (honey, sheep, lambs, wethers, loaves) as well as payments in cash; in some instances, to small cash payments at Eastertide were added large payments at Pentecost.[68] It is apparent that Lanfranc was responsible for a major revision of customs due to the archbishopric at Easter and Pentecost, a feature of which, at Easter, was the commutation of most renders in kind.[69] The figures that survive do not provide a basis for comparison of the income derived. But Lanfranc's arrangement undoubtedly provided the archbishop with an annual assured sum of money that was at his immediate disposal for the discharge of his archiepiscopal office as he envisaged it. A comparable determination to receive in full all payments that were rightly owing to him is manifest in Lanfranc's letter to Bishop Stigand of Chichester, whom he prohibited from making any exactions from clergy of Lanfranc's manors in the diocese of Chichester except only his ancient right to receive chrism money at Eastertide.[70]

There are only occasional pieces of evidence by which to judge Lanfranc's skill or success in managing the income of his office. In a time of depressed financial values following the negligence of his predecessors and the disturbances of the Norman conquest, he seems to have made no major changes or innovations. But he was evidently closely attentive to the defining, securing, and enforcing of his rights. He was also aware of the advantages of commuting renders in kind to cash payments. The scale and reputation of Lanfranc's building and charitable endeavours are testimony to the overall competence of his financial management.

8.5 THE SEE OF ROCHESTER

Although by comparison with most dioceses of the English church that of Canterbury was small and manageable, the demands of the primacy and of Lanfranc's

---

[66] Anselm, *Epp.* no. 474, vol. 5.422; Anselm assigned to the monks the whole income from the altar. He also restored to the monks the manor of Stisted (Essex), which he recognized to be rightfully theirs: cf. Whitelock, *Anglo-Saxon Wills*, 26–8.

[67] *The Domesday monachorum*, 77–9.

[68] The first eleven places in the two lists correspond. In the later list the two Boughtons are then separated and Romney is then inserted before Ruckinge.

[69] An exception was made for the annual payments in kind and cash by St Augustine's Abbey: *The Domesday monachorum*, 78.

[70] Lanfranc, *Letters*, no. 30, pp. 116–19.

place in the Anglo-Norman kingdom made necessary a substantial amount of episcopal help in the routine of diocesan ministrations. Before 1066 such assistance seems often to have been provided by a clerk in episcopal orders who resided at the ancient church of St Martin, which was outside the city wall to the east. Thus, in 1049 John of Worcester recorded the death of *Siuuardus Edsii Dorubernensis archiepiscopi corepiscopus*, while the Anglo-Saxon Chronicle also noted in 1061 the death of Godwine, bishop of St Martin's.[71] These persons belonged to a category of rural bishops (*chorepiscopi*) which had proliferated in the west by the ninth century but which then became the subject of the severest criticism, especially in the Pseudo-Isidorian decrees.[72] It is therefore entirely credible that Lanfranc should have been resolute in immediately discontinuing the arrangement.[73]

Instead, upon the death in 1075 of Bishop Siward of Rochester, Lanfranc began to use the Norman bishops of that see as his episcopal assistants; for their support he endowed and reordered their see in a manner that imitated his renewal of the see of Canterbury itself. His first choice as bishop was Ernost, a monk of Bec and Caen in whose abilities he seems to have placed high trust.[74] But Ernost died after only a few months in office; to succeed him Lanfranc chose Gundulf, who had been his prior at Caen and who had been his right-hand man in matters spiritual and temporal at Canterbury since 1070; Gundulf remained at Rochester as an exemplary bishop until his death in 1108.[75] According to his biographer, Lanfranc henceforth rarely performed in his diocese dedications of churches, ordinations of clerks, or confirmations of children, but delegated them to a willing Gundulf.

As a diocese, Rochester was exceptional in its direct and detailed subjection to the archbishop of Canterbury. The archbishop himself nominated a new bishop whose appointment was then subject to confirmation by the king. Not only did the archbishop ordain him but he also invested him with his see; the bishop's quota of knight service to the king was rendered mediately through the archbishop.[77] Such being the relationship between archbishop and bishop, the Norman revival of the see of Rochester was generally noticed as having been overseen by Lanfranc himself with Gundulf's willing assistance.[78] A major innovation was the introduction of a

---

[71] John of Worcester, *a*. 1049, vol. 2.552–3; *ASC* D, *a*. 1049, p. 115; *ASC* DE *a*. 1061, p. 135.

[72] For the prohibition of two bishops in one city by the council of Nicaea (325), see can. 8, *COD* p. 10, cited in Hinschius, 259. For other Pseudo-Isidorian material, see the letters attributed to Popes Damasus, Leo I, and John III in Hinschius, 509–15, 628, 715–18, and canon 7 of the second council of Seville, 439. For fuller discussion, see Gottlob, *Der abendländische Chorepiskopat*, esp. 117–29.

[73] *VL* cap. 13, p. 708; Gervase of Canterbury, *Act. pont.*, 361.

[74] Eadmer, *Hist. nov.*, *Praef.*, 2; *AL* 86. For Lanfranc's regard for Ernost, see Lanfranc, *Letters*, no. 61, pp. 176–9.

[75] *AL* 86; *VL* cap. 13, p. 709; *The Life of Gundulf*, caps. 8–9, pp. 30–1.

[76] *The Life of Gundulf*, cap. 30, p. 52. As Lanfranc's intention to consecrate the church that he built on his extra-diocesan estate at Harrow (Middlesex; dioc. London) illustrates, Lanfranc himself consecrated churches within and outside his diocese: Eadmer, *HN* 1, p. 45, and *VA* 2.6, pp. 67–8; Anselm, *Epp*. no. 170, vol. 4.51–2.

[77] Eadmer, *Hist. nov.*, *Praef.*, 2; William of Malmesbury, *GP* 1.71, pp. 136–7.

[78] See esp. *The Life of Gundulf*, caps. 17–18, 26, 38, pp. 40–2, 49, 61; Eadmer, *Hist. nov.*, 1, p. 15; William of Malmesbury, *GP* 1.44, 71, pp. 72, 136–7; Lanfranc's *obit* in Gibson, *Lanfranc*, 228; *The Textus Roffensis*, fos. 171ʳ–172ʳ.

large and observant monastic chapter in the cathedral of St Andrew. Although Bishop Siward had been a monk, under him the chapter had consisted of four or five secular canons who lived in ruinous buildings according to a poor quality of common life and religious observance. Gundulf built up a monastic community of some forty monks whose life he sought to share, as Lanfranc sought to share that of Christ Church, Canterbury. Lanfranc largely supplied the money for a complete rebuilding of the cathedral and for the provision of the necessary monastic buildings. By activity that began as early as Penenden Heath,[79] he sought to recover and to augment the endowments of the see. With Lanfranc's consent, Gundulf imitated the arrangement at Canterbury by dividing the estates of the bishop from those of the monks. Lanfranc thus raised the standard of church life in both the dioceses of Kent and provided for his own support in the discharge of the wide range of his duties.

[79] *The Textus Roffensis*, fos. 168ʳ–170ᵛ.

9

The Ordering of the English Church

Lanfranc's assertion of the primacy of the church of Canterbury and his endeavours to renew its buildings, rights, and resources were seen by his biographer as having been directed towards his overriding purpose of correcting men's morals and setting in order the state of the English church.[1] During his nineteen years of energetic rule, his indefatigability towards this end is manifest; it found well-merited commemoration in the words of his Canterbury *obit* that he was 'a most faithful custodian and a most sure consolidator of the catholic faith (*catholice fidei fidelissimus observator et firmissimus roborator*)'.[2] Yet for the most part it is not easy to discern in precise terms how Lanfranc set about the ordering of the English church. Largely this is owing to the scarcity of evidence; for example, only a very few *acta* survive of Lanfranc and his episcopal contemporaries. It would be anachronistic to look in his time for settled institutions, offices, or ecclesiastical structures; in England as in the western church at large, these were largely formed in the twelfth and later centuries. Just as royal government as exemplified by the king-duke William was a personal rather than an institutional matter, so archiepiscopal rule was personal. Lanfranc gave memorable expression to the fatherly quality of episcopal rule, which he said made it similar to that of a good abbot: 'for bishops, if they bestow fatherly care upon their subjects in the place of Christ, can not inappropriately be called abbots, that is, fathers, for the name suits their actions.'[3] Nowhere is this perspective upon an archbishop's activities more apparent than in the councils and synods that punctuated Lanfranc's years at Canterbury.[4] In macrocosm they called upon the archbishop, and *mutatis mutandis* other bishops who arranged such occasions, to act as a good abbot would act at the daily chapter of his monks, with its programme of ordered prayer, homily, reading, business, and discipline. Lanfranc's renewal and use of councils and synods was an attempt to place them at the centre of church life, rather as the chapter was a high point of the monastic day.

9.1 LANFRANC'S PRIMATIAL COUNCILS

A considerable effort of the imagination is required in order to envisage both the ideal and the reality of church councils and synods as they took place in Lanfranc's day. The

---

[1] See above, p. 87. [2] Gibson, *Lanfranc*, 227. [3] *MC* cap. 1, pp. 4–5.
[4] In 11th-century usage, the terms council and synod were virtually synonymous and inter-

best avenue of approach is by way of the *ordines* for their conduct which begin so long ago as the Visigothic church of the early seventh century.⁵ They were far from being simply business or administrative occasions. For the most part their agenda was spread over four days, though it might be limited to three days or extended to a longer period. As envisaged in the *ordines*, the underlying purpose was throughout religious and the procedures from beginning to end may be broadly described as liturgical. The keynote, expressing the characteristic early medieval aspiration for unity, peace, and concord after the model of the apostolic church, was set by the prayer to the Holy Spirit with which proceedings across the centuries were normally opened:

... join us to yourself by the gift of your grace alone, in order that we may be one in you and that we may in nothing turn aside from the truth (*ut simus in te unum et in nullo deviemus a vero*); thus, being gathered together in your name, we may in all things so hold fast to righteousness (*iustitiam*) tempered by mercy that both here our judgement may in nothing differ from you and in future we may for our well-doing receive eternal rewards.⁶

Proceedings were set in a context of processions, litanies, homilies, absolutions, and benedictions. Much attention was devoted to securing the profession of a right faith, with close reference to the pronouncements of the council of Nicaea and other statements of Christian antiquity. The order and discipline of the early church were likewise held up as the standard for pastoral and judicial dealings, with readings from popes, fathers, and councils. As thus envisaged, councils and synods were means to the regular renewal of the Christian life set in a context of worship and devotion and firmly rooted in the standards and pronouncements of early and therefore normative Christianity. While they were thus at their heart and centre gatherings of clergy according to their various orders, the presence and participation of the laity were envisaged at appropriate parts of the proceedings.

So far as surviving *ordines* are concerned, those of special relevance for seeking to understand Lanfranc's councils are associated with two junctures in their history. First, in Carolingian times a version of an *ordo* which was compiled in the last years of Visigothic Spain began to receive a very wide circulation, not least because it was prefaced to the canonical collection known as the *Collectio Hispanica Gallica*, whence in a lightly modified form it figured at the beginning of the Pseudo-Isidorian Decrees.⁷ Thus, on the one hand, a full order for the holding of a council was made generally available, and on the other, influential canon-law collections were accompanied by a paradigm which showed how the rulings of ancient fathers and councils might be applied to the current problems of the church. Second, in Ottonian Germany the Romano-Germanic Pontifical in the decades after its compilation *c*.960 disseminated two *ordines* for church councils. One was an order for a

---

changeable, though the former tended more often to be used of major assemblies and the latter of lesser ones.

⁵ Surviving *ordines* up to the twelfth century are edited in *Die Konzilsordines*. For a historical discussion, see Klöckener, *Die Liturgie der Diözesansynode*, esp. 25–103. The earliest *ordo* to survive is associated with the fourth council of Toledo (633): *Die Konzilsordines*, Ordo 1, pp. 1, 12–13, 125–41.

⁶ See e.g. Ordines 2.3, 14.16, 18.7, *Die Konzilsordines*, 198, 423, 498.

⁷ Ordo 2, *Die Konzilsordines*, 12–21, 142–86; see Hinschius, 17, 22–4.

general council which, with its origin in Carolingian times, is headed *Ordo Romanus qualiter concilium agatur*.[8] The title refers, not to its having been drawn up or directed at Rome, but to its being based upon Roman models, after the manner of Carolingian liturgical reform. The other text was an order for a diocesan council (*concilium provinciale*) which is not much older than the Romano-Germanic Pontifical itself.[9] The liturgical observances of the council were especially full, and the *ordo* is the first expressly to refer to the celebration of mass during a council. The pastoral functions and duties of the clergy were emphasized,[10] and prominence was given to the judicial aspect of the synod. If the prefacing of the Pseudo-Isidorian Decrees by an *ordo* of a synod associated councils with canon law, the *ordines* of the Romano-Germanic Pontifical stood as reminders that councils were part of the liturgical concern of archbishops and of bishops.

From the earliest days of their history, conciliar *ordines* thus provide a reminder that councils should not be viewed as being solely juridical or administrative in their purpose; rather, they were conceived to be powerful occasions of liturgical observance and religious renewal as these things were understood in the early middle ages. The *ordines* provided a well-known and accepted framework for assemblies of several days' duration which was widely disseminated by inclusion in books of canon law and in pontificals. Yet because, until the time of Pope Innocent III (1198–1216), their contents were not prescribed by superior authority, they were adaptable to meet the needs of different persons and circumstances. In particular, in the tenth and eleventh centuries they left more room than they stated for the presence and authority of lay rulers—emperors, kings, and also such provincial rulers as the dukes of Normandy. Indeed, the line between church councils and meetings of the courts of lay rulers was in no way sharply drawn; councils and courts could on occasion merge and aspects of the one could be ascribed to the other. Conciliar *ordines* were themselves 'living texts' which were open to local adaptation and selection in the light of experienced needs. There could be interchanges of programme between regional and local councils. There was a fruitful blend of age-long prescription and ready adaptability. As with all such documents, it is a matter for question how far the provisions of conciliar *ordines* were followed in practice, whether in the church at large or on particular occasions. But there can be no mistaking the opportunity that they offered for a zealous reforming archbishop or bishop to promote the renewal of the Christian life according to the standards set by the popes, bishops, and councils of the early church, especially as they were to be found in such canonical sources as the Pseudo-Isidorian Decrees.

During the two decades before the Norman conquest of England, the Norman church as Lanfranc knew it provides a contrast with the church in England as regards the holding of church councils. In Normandy, both before and after 1066, there was a series of provincial councils in the sense of councils held by the

---

[8] *Ordo* 7, *Die Konzilsordines*, 44–53, 296–315 = *PRG* no. 79, vol. 1.269–74.
[9] *Ordo* 14, *Die Konzilsordines*, 71–5, 413–37 = *PRG* no. 80, vol. 1.275–91.
[10] Thus, it included a recitation of the *Admonitio synodalis* attributed to Pope Leo IV (847–55) (JE 2659): *Ordo* 14.51, *Die Konzilsordines*, 430–4.

archbishop of Rouen which his episcopal suffragans attended. The principal councils were those held at Caen (1047), Brionne (1050), Caen (1061), Lisieux (1064), Rouen (1070, 1072, 1074, 1078, 1079), and Lillebonne (1080). They were regularly held in the presence or under the direction of Duke William; occasionally a papal legate was present.[11] There survives, evidently from the time of Archbishop John (1069–79), a draft *ordo* dealing with the opening stage of a provincial council for Normandy.[12]

Until 1070 there is no history of the holding of comparable councils in eleventh-century England; their regular convening, which had been a feature of the periods of Northumbrian and Mercian supremacy, came to an end after c.850.[13] References to gatherings that could be described as synodal were not, indeed, entirely lacking. An early eleventh-century memorandum on bishops' behaviour headed 'Incipit de synodo' opened with three chapters on the unity and true concord that befitted bishops in synod (*on sinoþe*) after the manner of continental *ordines*; but it quickly turned to general admonitions.[14] There is no body of evidence to suggest the holding of even occasional bishops' synods. As at the levels of hundred and shire, so at the centre of government gatherings of a kind peculiar to the Old English state transacted ecclesiastical as well as secular business under the king or his agents, with close attention to ecclesiastical discipline and to the correction of clerical and lay morals. In so acting with his witan or counsellors, a king like Cnut voiced his concern 'for the praise of God and for his own royal dignity', as well as that his subjects 'should ever love and honour one God and unanimously hold one Christian faith'. He issued both an ecclesiastical and a secular ordinance (I and II Cnut) which illustrate an awareness of the distinction between the two kinds of law but also the singleness of the royal authority that lay behind them.[15]

Such is the pre-Conquest background to the statement in the record of Lanfranc's council of London in 1075 that 'for many years past in the English kingdom the practice of councils had faded (*multis retro annis in Anglico regno usus conciliorum obsoleverat*)'.[16] The retrospect of Lanfranc's pontificate known as the *Acta Lanfranci* testifies to the revival of the practice of councils throughout it. It records the following occasions: 1072, Winchester, *generale concilium*; 1075, London, *generale concilium*; 1076, Winchester, *concilium*; 1077/8, London, *concilium*; 1080, Gloucester, *concilium*; 1085, Gloucester, *concilium*.[17] There can be little doubt that, as the record

---

[11] Norman provincial councils are discussed and listed by Foreville, 'The Synod of the Province of Rouen.' For comparative studies of Norman and English councils, see Schnith, 'Die englischen Reichskonzilien' and 'Wesen und Wandlungen'.

[12] *Ordo* 26, *Die Konzilsordines*, 107–11, 568–74. For its record of Archbishop Maurilius's condemnation of Berengar of Tours, see above, p. 60.

[13] See Vollrath, *Die Synoden Englands*, esp. 382–90; Barlow, *The English Church, 1000–1066*, 137–46, 237–8.

[14] *CS* no. 54, vol. 1/1.406–13, esp. caps. 3–5; there are similarities between the devotions prescribed in cap. 1 and those set out in *Ordo* 14.8, *Die Konzilsordines*, 421. See also *CS* no. 53, vol. 1/1.402–7.

[15] *CS* no. 64, vol. 1/1.468–506. The laws were drafted by Archbishop Wulfstan of York (1002–23) and agreed at Winchester at Christmastide 1020/2.

[16] *CS* no. 92, vol. 1/2.612 = Lanfranc, *Letters*, no. 11, pp. 74–5; *VL* cap. 10, p. 695.

[17] *AL* 85–7; the omission of Windsor 1072 should be noticed as suggesting that the Pentecost assembly had no features or continuation that were recognized as being more than a meeting of the king's council. Lanfranc's councils are discussed and the relevant documents edited in *CS* nos. 91–3, 97–8, vol. 1/2.591–620, 629–34.

of the council of London in 1075 implies, it was intended to be a new beginning in respect of its conciliar procedure and of its being a model for regular imitation. It was not the first council to be held under the Norman regime. In 1070, before Lanfranc became archbishop, there had been the two legatine councils of the English church at Winchester and Windsor, with their high aspirations and impressive record of canons.[18] But, exemplary though they were for Lanfranc, he no doubt wished a primatial council of his own to be seen as the true new beginning. In 1072, probably after the royal court had considered the question of the primacy, he held a *generale concilium* which was a distinct assembly and which discharged the characteristically conciliar business of deposing Abbot Wulfric of the New Minster at Winchester and of prescribing many proper Christian observances (*multaque de cristianae religionis cultu servanda instituit*).[19] Important though such a council may have been, it was held in the shadow of the meetings of the royal court at Petherton in 1071 and at Winchester and Windsor in 1072 which had considered major ecclesiastical business;[20] Lanfranc may have wished his paradigm council to stand alone and so to command authority.

Several considerations mark the council of London as in this way special. Its proceedings found a place in Lanfranc's letter collection as the concluding and culminating item of the opening section which concerned the primacy of Canterbury.[21] According to the *Acta Lanfranci*, at the request of many Lanfranc set down in writing how the council was conducted (*generale concilium Londonie celebravit, cuius gestionem rogatu multorum litteris commendavit*);[22] the report circulated both in chronicle sources and as a separate item.[23] The council was dated by the ninth year of King William, who was however on a military campaign across the sea; it was a council of the whole English region. It met by order and under the presidency of Lanfranc, 'archbishop of the holy church of Canterbury and primate of the whole British island'. Its first canon settled the order of precedence of the English bishops, having made inquiry of aged men who were deemed to know the truth. As archbishop of York, Thomas came second to Lanfranc. For the rest, the order of subscriptions at Windsor in 1072, by seniority of consecration, was followed, with the important exception that Walchelin of Winchester was interpolated after Thomas of York and William of London amongst bishops of especially privileged sees.[24] Twenty-one abbots also subscribed, in no discernible order save that Abbots Scotland of St Augustine's at Canterbury and Riwallon of the New Minster at

[18] See above, pp. 83–5.
[19] *AL* 85. For a list of fourteen canons which may belong to this council, see *CS* no. 91/V, vol. 1/2.596–7, 605–7.
[20] See above, pp. 93–101.   [21] Lanfranc, *Letters*, no. 11, pp. 72–9.   [22] *AL* 86.
[23] From Lanfranc's letter collection, the record appears in William of Malmesbury, *GP* 1.42, pp. 66–8, and *VL* cap. 12, pp. 705–7. For its circulation as a separate item, see *CS* no. 97, vol. 1/2.609–10; the manuscript concerned preserves the subscriptions.
[24] For the Windsor and London subscriptions, see *CS* nos. 91 and 92, vol. 1/2.603–4, 613–16. In 1072 Bishops Odo of Bayeux and Geoffrey of Coutances subscribed between the English bishops and abbots, while in 1075 Geoffrey subscribed after William of London and Walchelin of Winchester; Odo of Bayeux was not present. In 1072 Riwallon of the New Minster subscribed last among the abbots. In 1075 the final subscription was that of Anschitill, archdeacon of Canterbury.

Winchester came first and second. The procedural matter was also settled that only bishops and abbots should have a right to speak; others might do so only with the metropolitan's leave (canon 5). As befitted the record of a council convened to renew the life of the English kingdom according to salutary ancient law and authority, the nine canons were drawn up with exemplary clarity and care, in most cases citing as appropriate monastic sources like the Rule of St Benedict, and the *Dialogues* of Pope Gregory the Great or the Pseudo-Isidorian Decrees. The effect was one of Canterbury's primacy being firmly and duly exercised in order to correct morals and to settle the state of the church.[25]

The little that is known of the proceedings of Lanfranc's primatial councils serves to confirm this. The evidence is mainly derived from the canons certainly or putatively enacted by certain of the councils—Winchester (1072), London (1075), and Winchester (1076),[26] from the *Acta Lanfranci*, and from a small number of brief chronicle references. Some pointers may be found to the respective authority and role of Archbishop Lanfranc and King William. In England as in Normandy,[27] William was usually present and strongly asserted his will and purpose. Councils were often associated in time and place with royal crown-wearings at the Christian festivals of Christmas, Easter, and Pentecost.[28] Even when the king was overseas, as was the case with the paradigm council of London (1075), the canonically warranted transfer of three sees from villages to towns—Sherborne to Salisbury, Selsey to Chichester, and Lichfield to Chester—was effected 'by royal bounty and by synodal authority'; consideration of other such transfers must await the king's own hearing.[29] Nevertheless, there was a distinction between royal courts and church councils, especially apparent at Gloucester (1085), when the five-day royal court was followed by a three-day church synod.[30] It is significant that the *Acta Lanfranci* could attribute every conciliar matter to which it referred, except the consecration of Bishop William of Durham, to Lanfranc's authority and action. Masterful as the king's will and presence were, there can be no doubt that the church councils of his reign were councils as generally understood in the eleventh century.

An incident recounted in William of Malmesbury's *De antiquitate Glastoniensis ecclesiae*, as it appears at the council of Gloucester (1080), offers a rare insight of the interaction of king and archbishop at a church council.[31] It concerned a claim by the abbots of Muchelney and Athelney that they were free from the jurisdiction of Bishop Giso of Wells and justiciable before only the abbot of Glastonbury in that

---

[25] For further discussion of the council, see Brooke, 'Archbishop Lanfranc'.

[26] For the canons, see *CS* (as n. 17).

[27] Cf. the account and canons of the council of Lillebonne (1080): Orderic Vitalis, 5.5, vol. 3.24–35.

[28] For the time and place of William I's crown-wearings, see Biddle, 'Seasonal Festivals', esp. 52–3, 54–7, 64–5.

[29] Especially in the year of the rebellion of the earls (see below, pp. 188–92), the location of episcopal sees was of strategic importance to William: see Brooke, as n. 25.

[30] *ASC* E, *a.* 1085, p. 161; *AL* 86.

[31] *CS* no. 97/II, vol. 1/2.630–2 = *De antiquitate*, cap. 76, in: *The Early History of Glastonbury*, 154–7, 209; see also John of Glastonbury, *Cronica*, cap. 84, in: *The Chronicle of Glastonbury Abbey*, 156–7. William of Malmesbury's *De antiquitate* survives, in a much-interpolated version, in a 13th-century MS, but the style and detail of the account of the council support its substantial authenticity.

clergy from living with women;[39] and the papal legates of 1070 issued a canon in similar terms (council of Winchester, canon 15).[40] It should be noticed, however, that according to Lanfranc's canon, as a temporary dispensation priests should not be compelled to put away their wives; this would have been consistent with their also being urged to do so. And examples can be found of earlier popes of the highest standing who temporarily suspended the strict imposition of current law upon clergy for pastoral reasons. Pope Gregory I ruled that subdeacons of Sicilian churches who had received their order in ignorance of the Roman requirement of chastity might keep their wives, although those ordained in future must be made by their bishops to accept it.[41] At his Lateran council of 1060, Pope Nicholas II enacted a canon recognizing that the dire necessity of the time (*temporis nimia necessitas*) to find enough suitable clergy warranted a relaxation of the strict law against simony, so that clerks who had unknowingly received their orders from simoniacal bishops might notwithstanding be allowed to minister.[42] Neither case presents an exact parallel with Lanfranc's canon, and he cannot be shown to have been aware of them. But such precedents may have satisfied him that in a country where bishops had been lax in publicizing the obligation of chastity and where there was a pressing pastoral need for parochial ministrations, a dispensation on the lines of Gregory I or Nicholas II might be appropriate. There are no grounds for doubting his continuing commitment to requiring the chastity of the clergy as the law of the church.[43]

The evidence for Lanfranc's councils is often fragmentary and fragmented, yet they stand out as a principal means whereby he made effective his primatial authority over the whole English church. He held them in close association with a king who oversaw them closely as part of his masterful control of the church as of the kingdom. But the king was also genuinely concerned according to his lights for the well-being and reform of the church. Lanfranc's own authority in and over them was safeguarded. Their character as liturgical occasions should not be overlooked. They were ordered assemblies of bishops and abbots in which their corporate observances and commitment to unity and concord did something to offset their habitual preoccupation with the rights and interests of their own churches. They were well reminded of the authority of the fathers, writings, and law of the ancient church which were a standard of authenticity. All aspects of the moral life and Christian observance of clergy and laity alike were to be reviewed according to this standard. And what the bishops saw in Lanfranc's assemblies and heard in his directives was to be mirrored in their own dioceses and monasteries.

---

[39] Council of Lillebonne: Orderic Vitalis, 5.5, vol. 3.26–7: King William's active concern should be noted. On other Norman conciliar rulings, see *CS* no. 93, vol. 1/2.616–17. For Anselm's strict adherence in c.1079 to current papal legislation, see Anselm, *Epp.* no. 65, vol. 3.182–3.

[40] See above, p. 84.   [41] *Reg. Greg. I*, 1.42, vol. 1.54–5.

[42] cap. 2, *MGH Const.* 1, p. 550, no. 386; caps. 1–4 of this council were copied into the *Collectio Lanfranci*, fo. 105[r–v].

[43] Cf. Lanfranc's firm comments on chastity in *Letters*, nos. 41, 43, 51, pp. 134–5, 138–9, 162–3. His stipulation in his monastic constitutions that a priest-*conversus* might not celebrate mass within a year of his conversion unless he were of proven chastity and had the abbot's special permission implies a low view of the standards of the secular clergy: *MC* cap. 104, pp. 162–3.

9.2 THE DIOCESES AND DIOCESAN SYNODS

At the level of the sixteen dioceses in the English kingdom, it is perhaps surprising that there is no evidence in Lanfranc's time of any proposal to create new dioceses, for some dioceses, notably Dorchester/Lincoln and York, were extremely large and unwieldy. Moreover, only limited action was taken to satisfy the canonical rule that bishops should have their sees in *civitates*. Probably in 1072, a royal writ addressed to the sheriffs of the counties concerned and witnessed by Lanfranc transferred the see of Dorchester-on-Thames to the *civitas* of Lincoln. The king was said to have made the transfer by authority of Pope Alexander II and his legates, as well as of Lanfranc and the other bishops of the realm.[44] The motive was not stated, but strategic considerations may have been decisive: Lincoln's commanding situation above the River Witham and near the junction of the Fosse Way and Ermine Street made it critical for protecting communications with the north of England. In 1075 three more transfers were made at the council of London; again, the king's involvement was stated, while consideration of other moves was postponed until the king could be consulted.[45] No further transfers are known to have been initiated during Lanfranc's lifetime. Reasons why so little was done under Lanfranc about the number and location of episcopal sees do not emerge. It may be surmised that the canonical need for papal sanction was a hindrance, since neither William I nor Lanfranc was anxious to take business to Pope Gregory VII; the creation of new sees also had implications for the balance of lay and ecclesiastical among the king's tenants-in-chief. It is probable, despite the paucity of evidence, that the most important development in the dioceses that Lanfranc encouraged was the holding of regular and organized synods that mirrored his provincial councils and communicated throughout the kingdom the standards of Christian observance and conduct that he was concerned to promote.

It is extremely difficult to know how widespread was the holding of diocesan synods in the decades before the Norman conquest. The evidence is most unequivocal in the north. The Northumbrian Priests' Law of the first quarter of the century provided that if a priest stayed away from a synod he should compensate for it.[46] Archbishop Aldred of York is recorded as holding a synod there not long before the conquest.[47] Synods may have been more customary in the north than in the south, where much of the business later associated with them was transacted in the shire and hundred courts, with separate treatment of ecclesiastical matters but still with much confusion of spiritual and secular persons and matters. It is more than unlikely that episcopal synods were a general feature of church life under Edward the Confessor. The requirement of the papal legates of 1070 that they be made so tends to confirm this; it was also an indication of what the new archbishop when appointed should endeavour to do.[48] In Normandy, by contrast, episcopal synods

---

[44] *Regesta WI*, no. 177, pp. 587–9.
[45] See above, p. 125.
[46] cap. 44, *CS* no. 63, vol. 1/1.460.
[47] Folcard, *Vita s. Johannis*, Prol., 241.
[48] See above, p. 85.

were already established as a regular practice of the energetic group of bishops there. For example, Pope Alexander II's privilege of 1068 for Lanfranc's abbey of Saint-Étienne at Caen assumed that there were synods in the diocese of Bayeux.[49] In 1061 Bishop John of Avranches stipulated that the abbot of Mont Saint-Michel should attend his synods twice a year.[50] The bishops and abbots who crossed the channel after 1066 to rule English churches were well used to the holding of twice-yearly synods as the papal legates of 1070 prescribed. They are likely to have expected that such synods would quickly be made regular in England, both as a means of episcopal government of its dioceses and for the very considerable financial advantages that the holding of synods conferred.

Lanfranc's letters yield brief but decisive evidence that the holding of diocesan synods became an established practice both in the diocese of Canterbury and in other dioceses. Of especial importance is a letter of Lanfranc to Bishop Stigand of Chichester about the position of the clergy of Lanfranc's vills in that diocese.[51] Lanfranc recalled that, contrary to past custom, he had allowed the clerks to attend Stigand's synods and to obey their rulings about Christian observance (*ea quae ad christianae religionis noticiam prodesse possunt*); if they were accused of faults, old custom was to be followed by sending them for examination by Lanfranc. But Stigand's archdeacons had been collecting fines for such faults. Lanfranc therefore forbade any of his priests who were based outside Kent to go to the synod of Stigand or any other bishop; all that they might receive from Stigand was their chrism, or baptismal oil, and then at the customary rate. It appears that, since Stigand's succession in 1070, there had been a substantial modification of earlier arrangements which involved the institution of synods. The new arrangement gave rise to conflicts of interest which Lanfranc was quick to remedy, in relation to the synods of Chichester and of other dioceses. Synods were becoming the norm. In another letter, Lanfranc took it for granted that Bishop Herfast of Thetford was holding synods.[52] A few passing references in other sources tend to confirm the meeting of synods in Lanfranc's day. Thus, Symeon of Durham presents Bishop Walcher and Earl Waltheof as sitting together *in synodo presbyterorum*; Waltheof 'humbly and obediently carried out Walcher's orders as necessary to correct the state of Christianity in his county';[53] this sounds like a synod on the Norman model. The Battle Abbey Chronicle later referred to the diocesan synod of Chichester in Lanfranc's day.[54] Such references are few, but their incidental character suggests that, under Lanfranc, synods became part of the established order.[55]

There survives in a number of English manuscripts an *ordo* for a three-day episcopal synod, based upon the four-day model of the Romano-Germanic

---

[49] See above, p. 27.   [50] For the agreement, see *PL* 147.265–8, at col. 267.
[51] Lanfranc, *Letters*, no. 30, pp. 116–19.
[52] Ibid., no. 43, pp. 138–9. In letter 45, pp. 140–3, Lanfranc's reference to guidance that Bishop Walcher of Durham hoped to have received by St Martin's day (11 Nov.) may refer to the bishop's autumn synod.
[53] *Hist. regum*, 200.   [54] *The Chronicle of Battle Abbey*, 194–7.
[55] It should be noted that the record of Bishop Wulfstan's synod at Worcester (1092) can no longer be claimed as authentic evidence for an eleventh-century synod: *CS* no. 100, vol. 1/2.635–9; see Barrow, 'How the Twelfth-Century Monks', esp. 60–9.

Pontifical; the earliest copy of the *ordo* is to be dated only a few years after Lanfranc's death.[56] Though it cannot be proved to stem from his lifetime, a number of considerations favour its doing so. (1) The first chapter of the *ordo* affirms the Nicene canon that provincial councils shall be held twice a year.[57] The model cited the Nicene canon much later;[58] the English *ordo* may be concerned to implement the revival of councils as required by the papal legates in 1070.[59] (2) The model *ordo* cites along with the Nicene canon on councils a canon on clerical chastity.[60] The English *ordo* omits the latter. This may take account of Lanfranc's relaxation of rules about clerical marriage at the council of Winchester (1076); it would be less readily explicable in an *ordo* dating from after Archbishop Anselm's stricter legislation.[61] (3) Like its model, the English *ordo* placed great weight upon the judicial aspect of the council: at the beginning, there were laid upon a prominently placed stool the relics, gospel book (*plenarium*), and stole that were the instruments of oath-taking and justice; those present were exhorted to uphold justice and equity; times were set for the presentation of complaints; judges were required to fast.[62] (4) The unusual, three-day duration of the council according to the English *ordo* may be compared with the three-day synod that the archbishop and bishops of England held at Gloucester at Christmastide 1085.[63] The coincidence suggests that the English *ordo*, or something similar, may have been well established and normative in England by this date, and that it may have been adapted for primatial as well as for episcopal gatherings.

Provision was made for a numerous lay attendance. On the first day, laity of suitable character and marital status entered in due order. On the second day, after the opening procession, prayer, and gospel reading, all laity were to withdraw during the pleas of the clergy. They were thereafter readmitted and in their hearing the Nicene creed was recited. Then judges, who must be fasting, 'decided the laws and judgements (*iudices . . . leges et iudicia discernant*)', and whoever of the laity had a plea laid it before them. On the third day there was further consideration of questions and pleas; the bishop preached in admonishment of the clergy and instruction of the people before pronouncing the remission of sins.[64]

It seems clear that, in line with the instruction of the legates of 1070, episcopal synods became a regular feature of the church in the English kingdom as they were in the Norman duchy. It is also likely that the English *ordo* gives a fair impression of how synods were intended to be held in Lanfranc's day, even if it is impossible to know how far the model presented by the *ordo* was followed in practice.

---

[56] *Die Konzilsordines*, no. 18, pp. 87–90, 489–504; cf. no. 14, pp. 419–37.
[57] Council of Nicaea (325), can. 5, *COD* 8.
[58] *Die Konzilsordines*, no. 14, cap. 18, p. 424. [59] See above, p. 85.
[60] As n. 58, citing council of Nicaea, can. 3, *COD* 7.
[61] See above, pp. 127–8; for Anselm's strict legislation at his council at Westminster in 1102, see caps. 5–8, *CS* no. 113/III, vol. 1/2.675.
[62] *Die Konzilsordines*, no. 18, esp. caps. 2, 5, 9, 15–17, 21, pp. 496–504.
[63] See above, p. 125.
[64] *Die Konzilsordines*, no. 18, caps. 3, 11–17, 21–2, pp. 497, 501–3, cf. no. 14, caps. 35–8, 46, 57, pp. 428, 430, 435.

9.3 THE SEPARATION OF ECCLESIASTICAL JURISDICTION

The introduction into Norman England of primatial, and perhaps still more important, diocesan synods provides a context for seeking to understand the writ of King William I which is commonly referred to as his ordinance on church courts.[65] Such a description is unfortunate. The writ makes no reference to church courts, a term which is in any case anachronistic when used of the Conqueror's reign. Nor is any secular unit of government expressly referred to except the hundred. Its subject is the separation, at least in part, of ecclesiastical from secular jurisdiction. The king's concern seems to be with how councils and synods on the continental model to be seen in the *ordines* could, at least in the lower levels of church and society, be naturalized in England, and with how a balance might be established between them and the continuing Old English institutions of hundred and shire. In the simplest terms, it was a pragmatic attempt to have the best of both worlds.

The writ cannot be dated more precisely than between 1072 and 1085.[66] It is a thoroughgoingly royal document expressing the king's sovereign will: *Mando et regia auctoritate precipio . . .; Hoc etiam defendo et mea auctoritate interdico . . .* It exhibits a concern to clarify the position of spiritual courts and to confirm the king-duke's jurisdiction in appropriate matters over the clergy which, probably with his English experience in mind, William was also to show at the council of Lillebonne in 1080.[67] Issues of deep concern for the king were involved. The addressees of surviving versions of the writ were also primarily lay. One version was addressed by name to the sheriffs of the shires, Essex, Hertford, and Middlesex, which comprised the diocese of London, and to the king's faithful subjects (*fideles*) in them; the address seems to envisage the shire communities. A second version was addressed 'to earls, sheriffs, and all, French and English, who hold lands in' the diocese of Lincoln. Again, the seven shire communities involved may have been in mind as prime recipients of the writ. It was declared to be for the direction of all the king's *fideles* in England. This desire for general publicity and the fact that the London and the Lincoln texts were both followed by a word-for-word Old English translation point to an intention that they should be publicly read in the shire courts. The writ should probably be regarded as having been primarily addressed, not to the dioceses, but to shires and their officials as falling within the dioceses.

Royal command though it was, the writ was carefully prepared 'by common council and by counsel of the archbishops and bishops and abbots and all the princes of my realm'; this sounds like discussion in a full meeting of the king's court

---

[65] *CS* no. 94, vol. 1/2.620–4 = *Regesta WI*, no. 128, pp. 440–2; for discussion, see esp. Morris, 'William I and the Church Courts'. The writ may also be compared with the German canonist Bishop Burchard of Worms's expectation that bishops itinerating in their dioceses would hold local assemblies of clergy and laity which would deal expeditiously with spiritual and moral matters: Burchard, *Decretum*, 1.90–4, cols. 572–9.

[66] It appears to postdate the earliest form of the report on Penenden Heath, according to which the archbishop seems to be guaranteed the profits of what belongs to the cure and salvation of souls rather than the jurisdiction itself: see above, p. 113.

[67] Foreville, 'The Synod of the Province of Rouen', 26–7.

at which Archbishops Lanfranc of Canterbury and Thomas of York were present and consenting. The king's reason for addressing the problem of jurisdiction was expressed in words that are reminiscent of that given at the council of London in 1075 for the revival of councils:[68] the king recognized that up to his time the episcopal laws (*episcopales leges*) were not well ordered or according to the precepts of the holy canons (*non bene nec secundum sanctorum canonum precepta*); they should be set right (*emendandas*). It would be hazardous and anachronistic to attempt to define the terms used with precision. But 'episcopal laws' probably meant such regulations about Christian faith, practice, and morals as appeared in the ecclesiastical codes of the Old English kings—what would later be called the *iura Christianitatis*; the 'precepts of the holy canons' were the rulings of the popes, fathers, and councils of the early church such as were preserved in the Pseudo-Isidorian Decrees.

To promote a proper canonical separation of jurisdictions, the king issued commands first in the form of injunctions and second, to reinforce his injunctions, in the form of prohibitions. His injunctions were couched in general terms and addressed to his *fideles* at large. No bishop or archdeacon was henceforth to hold pleas regarding the *episcopales leges* in the hundred, nor was anything involving the rule of souls to be subject to the judgement of laymen. Anyone accused of a matter or offence (*causa vel culpa*—both civil and criminal matters were envisaged) should come to the place which the bishop appointed; there he should do right to God and his bishop not according to the hundred but according to the canons and episcopal laws (*secundum canones et episcopales leges*; by canons should probably be understood the rulings of ancient authorities; by episcopal laws modern rulings now duly made by bishops, especially in their councils and synods). Given the juridical concerns of episcopal synods, it is probable that matters regarding the *episcopales leges* would normally, though not necessarily exclusively, be directed to them. The king next specifically addressed the problem of the man who, 'inflated by pride', sought to evade the novel requirement that he come to his bishop. He was to receive the threefold summons that was the general rule of ecclesiastical discipline;[69] if contumacious he would be excommunicated and subject to coercion by royal or shrieval power and justice; if his contumacy was overcome, he should pay a fine for the summons that he had ignored.[70] The king finally added some prohibitions which were more directly addressed to his sheriffs and agents and which strengthened his commands. No sheriff, provost, or servant of the king—indeed, no layman might intrude himself into legal matters that were the bishop's preserve. No layman might bring another to judgement apart from the justice of the bishop. And judgement might be transferred to no place save an episcopal see or a place that the bishop appointed. All this reads very much like a determined attempt to promote and

---

[68] See above, p. 123.
[69] See e.g. its citation in the letters of Pope Gregory VII, such as *Reg.* 5.8, p. 359.
[70] This procedure was also prescribed in can. 5 of the council of Winchester (1076): *CS* no. 93, vol. 1/2.619–20, the penalty for disobedience to a summons was expressed in traditional English terms (*overseuuenesse seu laxelit*). This canon does not provide clear evidence for the date or priority of the royal writ, which it may anticipate, accompany, or repeat and elucidate.

safeguard the operation of the episcopal synods that were being introduced by compelling royal officials and the laity in general to accept them.

If this were so, the concentration of the writ upon the hundred becomes comprehensible. It was probably from the hundred much more than from the shire that bishops and archdeacons might expect to find most of their jurisdiction in spiritual and moral matters and with it most of their aggregate financial benefit. More important still, the meeting of the Kentish shire court on Penenden Heath graphically illustrates, and must have brought home to Lanfranc himself, the importance of the bishops' retaining their place in the shire courts on account of the protection that they offered to ecclesiastical possessions and rights. As the report of the Penenden meeting shows, from the church's point of view the witness of the shire and an appeal to ancient law was, and continued to be, a palladium of rights and even of liberty. For the king, such protection was necessary in order to restrain a predatory aristocracy and to promote domestic peace and order.[71] In Norman England, the church needed the protection that was provided by the participation of its bishops in both new synods and old shire courts; the two complemented each other, and lines of institutional and legal competence were not finely or precisely drawn. In harmony with growing eleventh-century demands for the freedom of the church, the growth of synods placed spiritual and moral matters in the hands of bishops and archdeacons, subject to the increasing effectiveness of canon law. But the church's secular interests, and its own stake in the promotion of public order and justice, also required its presence in the shire, with the benefit of appeal to the old law of the Confessor's day and to the witness of local men who knew what should be the case by ancient right in matters under challenge or dispute.

It thus comes as no surprise that, in a royal writ addressed to Lanfranc and two counts and to the magnates of all England, William should fully restore to St Augustine's abbey at Canterbury eight prebends at Newington (Kent) as the county of Kent had borne witness before Archbishop Lanfranc, the king's steward Eudo, and others, so that the abbey should hold them on the best terms enjoyed by the abbot's forbears.[72] Nor does it surprise that, according to the *Leges Henrici primi*, in the early twelfth century bishops as well as laity attended the shire court where the order of business was (1) *christianitatis iura*, (2) pleas of the crown, and (3) the causes of individuals.[73] The Conqueror's writ about ecclesiastical jurisdiction was a beginning of the grafting in of new laws and institutions into an ancient and beneficially working system. Its purpose was to supplement it but not to weaken or to subvert it.

9.4 ARCHDEACONS

It is not surprising that while Lanfranc was archbishop archdeacons began to have a new prominence in the English dioceses as officers of the bishop: the separation of ecclesiastical jurisdiction as prescribed in the Conqueror's writ and the holding of

---

[71] See above, p. 115. [72] *Regesta WI*, no. 88, pp. 356–7. It cannot be precisely dated.
[73] *Leges Henrici Primi*, cap. 7.1–3, pp. 98–101.

primatial and diocesan synods both served to invest them with new and indispensable functions.[74]

There were archdeacons in England before the Norman conquest, but they were few and far between. In the ninth century several were referred to by name at Canterbury; they seem to have been the senior deacon of the archbishop's household.[75] In the last years of Anglo-Saxon England an archdeacon may have performed personal and administrative services to bishops of at least the major sees as they itinerated through their diocese. Even before 1066 the archdeacon of Bishop Wulfstan of Worcester may have gone ahead of him to announce and prepare his coming.[76] In the Winton Domesday, Aluric the archdeacon held a tenement at Winchester during the Confessor's reign.[77] When the Conqueror's diploma of 1068 for the London church of St Martin-le-Grand freed it from the exactions of bishops, archdeacons, deacons, and officials, it is hard to think that, if authentic, this provision does not testify to the archdeacon as a familiar figure.[78] In the north, the Northumbrian Priests' Law briefly refers to archdeacons as having certain disciplinary powers over priests.[79] The evidence remains very meagre. In Normandy before 1066 it is not abundant, though it becomes more plentiful thereafter.[80] References to archdeacons occur in the canons of councils from the 1040s,[81] and the archdeacon played a conspicuous part in the *ordo* for a provincial council which survives from the time of Archbishop John of Rouen (1068–79).[82] By 1066 there were archdeacons in each of the Norman dioceses. Lanfranc's letters give evidence of aspects of their work in Normandy and so, presumably, of his expectations of them in the England that he knew. In a letter to the archdeacons of Bayeux, probably written after Bishop Odo's imprisonment in 1082, Lanfranc advised them so far as he could about their treatment of a priest who had committed a justifiable homicide; he stressed an archdeacon's duty of examining carefully the whole way of life of a clerk with whom he dealt.[83] In an earlier letter to Archbishop John of Rouen he referred to an archdeacon's distinctive role in the prescribed ceremonies of ordination, thus providing evidence for an archdeacon's liturgical part in pontifical services.[84] Norman usage evidently provided models for the archdeacon's duties in England. When the papal legates in 1070 provided that bishops should both hold twice-yearly councils and establish in their churches archdeacons and other ministers of sacred order, they were seeking to remedy related and recognized deficiencies in the Old English church.[85]

---

[74] For references in the *ordines* to the place of archdeacons and deacons at synods, see *Die Konzilsordines*, Index of words, s.v. *archidiaconus*, 621.

[75] See Brooks, *The Early History*, 161–2.   [76] *VW* 3.10, pp. 51–2.

[77] The Survey of *c*.1110, no. 176, in: Biddle (ed.), *Winchester*, 58.

[78] *Regesta WI*, no. 181, pp. 594–601.   [79] caps. 6–7, *CS* no. 63, vol. 1/1.454.

[80] For a list of early archdeacons in Normandy, see Spear, 'L'Administration épiscopale', 85; for the diocese of Rouen, see id., 'Les Archidiacres'.

[81] Rouen (*c*.1045), can. 11, Mansi, 19.751; Rouen (1074), can. 1, Mansi, 20.397.

[82] *Die Konzilsordines*, no. 26, pp. 568–74.

[83] Lanfranc, *Letters*, no. 51, pp. 162–5; see also the archdeacon's duties according to the canons of Lillebonne (1080): Orderic Vitalis, 5.5, vol. 3.28–9.

[84] Lanfranc, *Letters*, no. 14, pp. 86–7.   [85] See above, p. 85.

Undoubtedly, the charge to appoint archdeacons was speedily and generally obeyed after Lanfranc took office at Canterbury. At the highest level, the last of the subscribers to the record of the paradigm council of London in 1075 was *Anschitillus sanctae Dorobernensis ecclesiae archidiaconus*;[86] it is the first credible reference to an archdeacon of Canterbury since the ninth century, and it is reminiscent of the *archidiaconus ecclesiae metropolitanae* of some of the conciliar *ordines*.[87] In Lanfranc's letters, his complaint to Bishop Stigand of Chichester about exactions from the clerks of Canterbury lands took it for granted that Stigand had archdeacons.[88] Similarly, the king's writ about ecclesiastical jurisdiction referred to the bishop or the archdeacon as if the latter were generally to be encountered.[89] When, perhaps c.1080, Archbishop Thomas of York surveyed rights of jurisdiction in and around that city and briefly listed certain matters as belonging to the bishop and archdeacon,[90] the influence of the king's writ is to be suspected. In any case, such incidental references to archdeacons establish that, by Lanfranc's death, they had been appointed in most, if not all, of the English dioceses.[91]

In Lanfranc's day the office of archdeacon remained at an early stage of its development. It related to the person and household of the bishop, providing him with help when present and with representation when absent rather than as yet being an institution of the diocese. The existence of territorial archdeaconries cannot be proved in Lanfranc's time; although Remigius of Lincoln's appointment before 1092 of seven archdeacons with responsibilities related to the seven shires of his unwieldy diocese was a major step on the way which could have been taken in Lanfranc's time.[92] Lanfranc's importance is that, following the direction of the papal legates of 1070, he energetically oversaw the general appointment in England of archdeacons on the continental model. In concert with a willing king, he assigned to them a lasting place in the jurisdictional arrangements of church and kingdom. By holding and encouraging provincial and diocesan synods he greatly enlarged their role in church life, both in synods themselves and in implementing at large the oversight of the clergy and laity that they facilitated and called for.

9.5 PARISHES AND DEANERIES

It is generally recognized that the development in England of a system of territorial parishes in which a church served by a single priest provided the essential

---

[86] See above, p. 124 n. 24.   [87] As n. 74.   [88] See above, p. 130.   [89] See above, p. 133.
[90] Liebermann, 'Drei nordhumbrische Urkunden', 278–83; see esp. cap. 9, p. 280.
[91] See Brooke, 'The Archdeacon'; full details of what is known about archdeacons are being assembled in successive volumes of Le Neve, *Fasti*, compiled by Greenway. In brief summary, the impression is one of archdeacons to whom references before 1070 were scarce becoming widely attested under Lanfranc in contexts that can best be related to bishops' households and to councils. More continuous lists of archdeacons as established officials in the diocese at large who acquired territorial jurisdictions begin soon after, rather than during, Lanfranc's archiepiscopate. The two stages were closely connected but should be clearly distinguished.
[92] Henry of Huntingdon, 8: *De contemptu mundi*, cap. 4, pp. 590–3.

ministrations, especially baptism, and pastoral oversight of those who lived within recognized boundaries was a very long one. The Norman conquest occurred when it was well advanced but far from complete. Despite the light shed by the Domesday survey, the state of the evidence leaves far from clear the effects of the conquest and of Lanfranc's archiepiscopate in particular.[93]

So far as Domesday Book is concerned, the churches to which it refers have usefully been classified as 'superior' and 'ordinary'. The term 'superior' covers a range of churches, many ancient but some of recent foundation, of a minster or collegiate character. They represent an order of pastoral care, widely established by the mid-eighth century, in which minster parishes (*parochiae*) covering large territorial areas depended upon central churches staffed by a number of priests which were baptismal churches; these churches were supplemented by outlying chapels, served by priests from the centre, at which Sunday mass and occasional ministrations were provided. But especially in the last hundred years or so before the Norman conquest, landholders were establishing proprietary churches on their own lands which were served by a single priest who fulfilled an inclusive parochial ministry, including baptism. Such single-priest arrangements may have been encouraged by the long-term influence of Carolingian manuals and tracts on pastoral care.[94] They account for the number of 'ordinary' churches that are encountered in Domesday. So far as the early Norman church in England is concerned, it is now acknowledged that the old minsters had not fallen into a state of terminal decay but that they retained a vitality and adaptability that yielded place only gradually and incompletely to the system of territorial parishes of later medieval and modern times. However, Norman lords were also widespread founders and endowers of churches on their lands, thus augmenting the number of 'ordinary' churches and preparing the way for them to become as widespread as the scholars' epithet 'ordinary' implies. The long-term effect of the Norman conquest was to expedite this development within the constitutionally structured church that eventually but only gradually resulted from it.

Lanfranc's policy towards and impact upon the parishes are difficult to determine, not least for lack of evidence. In the diocese of Canterbury, his *obit* declared him to have built many fine churches (*multas et honestas ecclesias*) upon his archiepiscopal manors; this probably means that they were built of stone and well appointed.[95] That he thereby set an example that other lords followed is suggested by the consecration of churches on his behalf by Bishop Gundulf of Rochester.[96] But if he thus actively furthered the spread of 'ordinary' churches, his foundation of St Gregory's at Canterbury, with its complement of *clerici* who probably followed a Rule, suggests that, where appropriate, he looked favourably upon collegiate churches.[97] There was certainly no radical move away from 'superior' to 'ordinary' churches, however many of the latter may have been built. The *Domesday monachorum* provides evidence from after his lifetime for the existence of twelve

[93] For a general survey, see Blair, 'Secular Minster Churches' and 'Local Churches'.
[94] e.g. the *Admonitio synodalis*: see above, p. 122 n. 10.
[95] Gibson, *Lanfranc*, 228.   [96] See above, p. 118.   [97] Lanfranc's *obit*, as n. 95.

churches of an old minster type, together with their dependencies.[98] But Lanfranc's commutation of renders in kind into money payments may have facilitated the direct exaction of ecclesiastical dues from local churches.[99] The assessment of archiepiscopal customs payable at Easter, which are clearly related to chrism money, in terms of priests and churches (*de presbiteris et aecclesiis*) tells in a like direction.[100] Perhaps the best conclusion that can be formulated is that, within his diocese, Lanfranc's intention was to make such arrangements as he found or introduced work well in their own terms; but the effect in the long term was to assist the transition from old minsters to territorial parishes which often were closely related to secular manors and vills.

Lanfranc's conciliar legislation does not add materially to an understanding of his intentions for the ordering of the church at its lower levels; it was concerned with the state of clerical morality and competence, and with the protection of clerks in society, without regard to changes in structural or administrative arrangements.[101] Thus, although the papal legates of 1070 had enjoined the appointment by bishops of archdeacons 'and other ministers of sacred order',[102] it is not possible to determine how far steps were taken in Lanfranc's day towards the emergence of the rural deans and the rural chapters that became a notable feature of church life in the twelfth century.[103] It should be recalled that, in England before the establishment of territorial archdeaconries, archdeacons themselves were often closely associated with emergent rural chapters, thereby increasing their importance for local church life. Lanfranc's own influence is probably to be looked for in the multiplication of archdeacons and in the encouragement of diocesan synods which met according to continental models and to which the attendance of clergy was obligatory for oversight, edification, and social contact.

9.6 CANON LAW

Archdeacons and synods as they emerged in the time of Lanfranc carried with them a need for great attention to be paid to canon law as providing a true model and guide for all aspects of the Christian life. It looked back to the precepts of the early popes, councils, and fathers which it was Lanfranc's concern to renew. It was highly congenial to him in view of the sanction of ancient and true authority that he sought in all matters of Christian teaching and practice. It was the more so because, for Lanfranc and for eleventh-century churchmen in general, there was no such distinction between canon law and theology as was to develop in the age of scholasticism and as has been subsequently current. Alike in sanction and in substance, the appeal to the authority of ancient tradition that characterized Lanfranc's tract on the eucharist determined his use of canonical collections. These were in any case concerned with a wide spectrum of matters of doctrine, morality, and pastoral care

---

[98] *The Domesday monachorum*, pp. 78–9.   [99] Ibid. 70.   [100] Ibid. 77–8.
[101] See above, pp. 126–8.   [102] See above, p. 85.
[103] See esp. Scammell, 'The Rural Chapter' and Brett, *The English Church*, 211–15.

as well as with ecclesiastical structure and the rights and duties of grades of clergy and laity in the church.

Attention must necessarily be concentrated upon the codex which recent generations of scholars have called the *Collectio Lanfranci*, now Trinity College, Cambridge, MS B 16 34.[104] Throughout the middle ages it belonged to Christ Church, Canterbury. An inscription on the penultimate folio records its provenance and ownership:

Hunc librum dato precio emptum ego Lanfrancus archiepiscopus de Beccensi cenobio in Anglicam terram deferri feci et ecclesiae Christi dedi. Si quis eum de iure praefatae ecclesiae abstulerit, anathema sit.

This book, bought for a sum of money, I Archbishop Lanfranc have caused to be brought from the monastery of Bec to England and I have given it to Christ Church. If anyone shall remove it from the possession of this church, let him be anathema.

The inscription reads as though dictated by Lanfranc himself. The codex comprises 204 folios and its dimensions are 312×226 mm.; it is thus readily portable and convenient to use.

Its contents are for the most part a somewhat abbreviated and rearranged version of the Pseudo-Isidorian Decrees.[105] Most texts of Pseudo-Isidore are in three parts: papal decretals from Clement to Melchiades (311–14); councils from Nicaea (325) to Seville II (619); and papal decretals from Silvester I (314–35) to Gregory II (715–31). The *Collectio Lanfranci* reduces this material to two parts: the first comprises papal decretals consecutively from Clement to Gregory II, with much abbreviation and omission which reduces their bulk by between a third and a half; the second consists of councils with very much less curtailment, Most of the Greek councils are unusual in that they follow the text of the Dionysio-Hadriana collection, not that of the Hadriana. Especially in the decretals, subdivisions are introduced which seem to be new in the *Collectio Lanfranci* and to be intended for convenience of reference. A similarly practical purpose seems to have guided the abbreviation or omission of items. There is no evidence of an intention to change the doctrinal or ecclesiological content of Pseudo-Isidore, and certainly not its view of papal authority. Although material relating to doctrinal and pastoral subjects is reduced, it is far from being eliminated. The purpose of the compiler seems to have been to cut away what was repetitive or otiose in order simply to produce a shorter and more manageable

---

[104] Modern study of the *Collectio Lanfranci* begins with Z. N. Brooke, *The English Church*, esp. 57–83. His conclusions were reconsidered and in some respects revised by Philpott, 'Archbishop Lanfranc', which includes a full description of the material contained in the collection; I am deeply indebted to this thesis in the present section. See also Brett, 'The *Collectio Lanfranci*' and, for details of the MSS and full bibliography, Kéry, *Canonical Collections*, 239–43.

[105] The following additions were made. I: at the end of the decretals. (1) Pope Nicholas II's encyclical *Vigilantia universalis* (1059), Schieffer, *Die Entstehung*, 212–24. (2) Pope Nicholas II's decrees at his Lateran council, 1060, *MGH Const.*, 1.550–1, no. 386, caps. 1–4. (3) Berengar's oath of 1059, Lanfranc, *DCSD* cap. 2, col. 411 = Huygens, 'Bérenger de Tours', 372–3. (4) Pope Nicholas II's letter to Lanfranc (1059/61), Southern, *Saint Anselm: A Portrait*, 32–3. II: at the end of the councils. (1) Pope Alexander II's letter to Lanfranc (1061/70), *Ep.* 70, *PL* 146.1353. (2) Lanfranc's note of the gift of the volume to Christ Church, Canterbury, above, p. 000. (3–5) Three letters of the anti-pope Clement III to Lanfranc (1085–9), Liebermann, 'Lanfranc and the Antipope', 330–2.6–8. Three forged items on monastic matters, Böhmer, *Die Fälschungen*, 161–4.

codex for consultation and perhaps for copying or transporting. The two parts of the *Collectio Lanfranci* are written by different hands. Three twelfth-century texts of Norman provenance which seem to be ultimately derived from the Bec/Canterbury copy contain only the councils.[106] The decretals and the councils therefore may not have been bound together until they were sent to England or, indeed, until after their arrival there; although the copying into both parts of mid-eleventh-century papal letters and the layout of the final folio of the decretals creates a likelihood that they were together while still at Bec.

However this may be, there is reason to think that books of canon law were in considerable use in mid-eleventh-century Normandy as elsewhere. Especially interesting evidence is provided by the *ordo* for the opening of a provincial council from the time of Archbishop John of Rouen. According to it, the archdeacon, solemnly vested in a dalmatic, was instructed by the archbishop to read from the book of canons (*codex canonum*) chapters relating to the holding of councils: three conciliar canons were prescribed to be read. In due course the archdeacon recited another conciliar canon, given at length, about the conduct that was appropriate during councils.[107] Such citations at councils, especially provincial, were customary since Carolingian times.[108] They must have called for the availability of books, whether of complete collections like Pseudo-Isidore or of abridgements like the *Collectio Lanfranci* or of parts of it such as the conciliar canons. Conversely, the *Collectio Lanfranci*, or at least the conciliar half of it, may have drawn upon models that have perished because they did not come into such hands as those of Lanfranc.

It follows that Lanfranc's part, if any, in the compilation of the so-called *Collectio Lanfranci* is altogether uncertain. All that is certain is that, at some time after he became archbishop of Canterbury, Lanfranc bought the manuscript (or manuscripts of the two parts) from his former monastery of Bec and presented it to Christ Church, Canterbury.[109] It may or may not have been compiled at Bec; if it was, the extent of Lanfranc's work upon it by way of selection or supervision is unknown. That he did not take it with him from Bec to Caen and that he eventually bought it from Bec tell against his having any such claim to it as might have arisen from its being in a substantial way his work. It would be hazardous to draw conclusions from its intrinsic characteristics about Lanfranc's own mind and interests.

But once brought to England, the circulation which it achieved and the uses to which he put it marked a new and decisive stage in the currency in England of the canon law of the western church. In the eleventh and early twelfth centuries Canterbury was the centre for the dissemination of its text, by direct copying of Lanfranc's manuscript or derivatively, to many cathedrals and monasteries in England; besides the Canterbury exemplar, nine full copies survive from the sees of Durham,

---

[106] For the Norman MSS, see Brooke, *The English Church*, 231.

[107] *Die Konzilsordines*, no. 26, caps. 1, 8, 13, pp. 570–4.

[108] See esp. *Die Konzilsordines*, nos. 1, cap. 4, p. 140; 2, caps. 5, 7, pp. 178–80; 20, cap. 7, pp. 512–13; 21, cap. 28, p. 537. Similar directions do not occur in the *ordines* of the Romano-Germanic Pontifical: nos. 7, pp. 296–315; and 14, pp. 413–37; as with the latter, they are absent from the English *ordo*: no. 18, pp. 489–504.

[109] See the record of Lanfranc's gift: above, p. 139.

Hereford, Salisbury, Worcester, and Lincoln, and from the abbey of Gloucester.[110] This suggests that every diocese and some major monasteries were expected to possess a copy. Until the arrival of Gratian's *Decretum* (c.1140) the *Collectio Lanfranci* was the principal code of canon law in England.[111]

Of its importance for Lanfranc as archbishop there can be no doubt. An initial note of caution must first be sounded. The Canterbury text of the *Collectio* has in its margins more than 200 instances of the symbol ·A· (or ·a·), which has been understood to be an abbreviation of *Attende* ('for attention'); other manuscripts of the *Collectio* have similar symbols. The symbols have been supposed to be added under Lanfranc's direction in order to mark passages that were required for convenient reference. Comparison with letters of Lanfranc that cite canonical authority has been held to bear this out.[112] While there is a substantial correlation between such citations and marked passages in the *Collectio*, recent study suggests that though significant, it is far from complete; Lanfranc also cites or has in mind unmarked authorities. Moreover, his references to the decrees and canons is frequently in general terms (*sicut canones iubent; ex multis Romanorum presulum decretis diversisque sacrorum canonum auctoritatibus*), so that a determination of his sources cannot be made.[113] Without a much fuller investigation of the marginalia they are only a limited guide to how and by whom the manuscripts of the *Collectio* were used, although they certainly testify to its great importance.

So far as Lanfranc's rule in the English church and kingdom are concerned, four principal ways may be discerned in which canon law, and especially its exemplification in the *Collectio Lanfranci*, guided his mind. First, it seems to have been a subject for study by means of which he informed himself of the authentic, because ancient and traditional, guidelines for all aspects of the Christian life—church order, clerical rights and duties, doctrine, morals, liturgy, in so far as canonical sources bore upon them. At the outset of his archiepiscopate, when the reigning pope—Alexander II—was friendly and congenial, Lanfranc consulted him in detail about numerous specific issues. In one case at least, that of Bishop Ethelric of Chichester, Alexander instructed Lanfranc to settle the matter at home as canonical tradition directed (*iuxta censuram canonicae traditionis*); he further gave Lanfranc virtually the authority of an apostolic vicar to settle cases in a manner that called for familiarity with the spirit and the letter of the canons.[114] Alexander's creation of a need to know the canons became all the more pressing when he was succeeded by Gregory VII, with whom Lanfranc's dealings were cool and distant, while there was diminished contact between England and Rome. Both as archbishop and as

---

[110] See Brooke, *The English Church*, 73–83, 231; cf. Webber, *Scribes and Scholars*, 47–8. Its circulation in Lanfranc's lifetime may have been only to Durham amd perhaps Salisbury: Lanfranc, *MC* p. xxxi; Gullick, 'The English-Owned Manuscripts'.

[111] Brooke, *The English Church*, 84–105; Brett, 'The *Collectio Lanfranci*'.

[112] See esp. Brooke, *The English Church*, 68–70. He had in mind Lanfranc's letters to Bishop Herfast of Elmham: nos. 24, 47, pp. 106–9, 150–3.

[113] See Philpott, 'Archbishop Lanfranc', 94–9.

[114] Lanfranc, *Letters*, nos. 2, pp. 34–9, and 7, pp. 60–3.

primate, Lanfranc must be well schooled in canon law, and it was a necessary subject for his deep study in order that he might himself make the right decisions.

Second, this need for canonical formation if he was to act with informed authority in guiding other bishops is apparent in his letters. When Bishop Herfast of Elmham sent to him a clerk charged with a grave offence, he replied according to the evidence of holy authors (*sanctarum scripturarum testimonio*), citing passages as written in the holy canons (*in sacris canonibus*) by Popes Eusebius, Leo the Great, Silverius, and Gregory the Great.[115] Replying in 1076 to inquiries of Hugh, bishop-elect of London, Lanfranc deferred ruling about the penance to be imposed on the captors of a prisoner who had died in their hands until he knew more of the circumstances; then he would decide in the light of the canons (*canonica auctoritate*). A clerk accused of apostasy must either leave the diocese of London or produce a commendatory letter from his former bishop 'as the canons require'.[116] In the light of the canons and decrees of the holy fathers, Lanfranc instructed Bishop Walcher of Durham that a monk, even if unprofessed, who had publicly worn the religious habit might not thereafter return to secular life.[117] The confidence to which Lanfranc advanced in giving such rulings is to be noted.

Third, canon law was of the greatest significance for Lanfranc in authenticating and guiding the multifarious business of councils and synods, and especially of his own primatial assemblies. This is clearly shown in the record of the council of London (1075). With the declared intention of renewing things that had been laid down in ancient canons, the record cited specific or general authority for all but one of the canons.[118] The development by Lanfranc and King William of ecclesiastical jurisdiction throughout the country, with the intention that spiritual matters should be decided *secundum canones et episcopales leges*,[119] generated a need for canon law to be actively disseminated throughout the realm. It was especially needful for the conduct of episcopal synods and for the discharge of their duties by bishops and archdeacons who conformed to Lanfranc's intentions for their offices.

Fourth, therefore, Lanfranc expected bishops, in particular, to follow him in familiarizing themselves with the spirit and the letter of canon law. His letter to Hugh, bishop-elect of London, opens with an indication that Lanfranc carefully counselled new bishops about their conduct and pattern of life;[120] it is likely that the duty of studying the holy writings of the early fathers and councils was impressed upon them. A call for amendment of life that Lanfranc addressed to Bishop Herfast of Elmham made much of this duty, when Herfast had in some way questioned Lanfranc's primatial and metropolitan authority:

Put behind you the dice—not to mention greater things—and worldly pastimes in which you are said to waste time all day long; read divine writings and above all pay attention to the decrees of Roman pontiffs and to the sacred canons. There indeed you will discover what you

---

[115] Lanfranc, *Letters*, no. 24, pp. 106–9. The comments of Brooke, *The English Church*, 68–9, should be compared with Philpott, 'Archbishop Lanfranc', 94–9.
[116] Lanfranc, *Letters*, no. 40, pp. 132–3; cf. can. 4 of the council of London (1075): no. 11, pp. 76–7.
[117] Lanfranc, *Letters*, no. 45, pp. 142–3.   [118] Ibid., no. 11, pp. 72–9 = *CS* no. 92, vol. 1/2.612–14.
[119] See above, pp. 132–4.   [120] Lanfranc, *Letters*, no. 40, pp. 132–3.

do not know; when you have thoroughly read them, you will consider trivial the way upon which you are counting to flee from ecclesiastical discipline.

Lanfranc launched into a catena of four papal and conciliar excerpts which inculcated, explained, and defended with penal sanctions the dutiful obedience of bishops to their metropolitans:

There are a host more of such passages about the excellence and power of primates and metropolitans, both in these writings and in other genuine books of orthodox fathers. If you were to read them attentively and having read them to commit them to memory, you would harbour nothing unsuitable against your mother church [of Canterbury], and what you are said to have said you would not have said; rather, you would have rebuked it with salutary rerproach when said by others.[121]

There can be no mistaking Lanfranc's purpose of using canon law to build up amongst the bishops an *esprit de corps* of informed obedience to his own primatial leadership.

9.7 CONCLUSION

The effects of Lanfranc's reordering of the church were profound and lasting. They were so because they were the result not of any personal vision or novel programme but of an intention to renew the authentic Christian faith and life of the early centuries of the church as they were to be learnt in holy scripture, the decrees and formulations of popes and fathers, and the canons of councils that had won general acceptance. With the support of King William, Lanfranc sought to revive the spiritual authority and jurisdiction of the church at every level. The holding of councils and synods, primatial and episcopal, was a means to this end, and the quickening of church life in the localities and parishes was to consolidate it. The rapid appearance of archdeacons who played a prominent role testifies to a purpose of intensifying pastoral and judicial oversight. The introduction and dissemination by Lanfranc of a version of the Pseudo-Isidorian decrees effectively introduced canon law to the country as a normative and educative medium for reform and guidance. Yet, still in co-operation with the king, Lanfranc retained and valued much of the setting of the church in the strong order of law and society that the Norman kings inherited from their Old English predecessors. The records of Penenden Heath make clear both the fact and the benefit to the church of this involvement. The new canon law and the old law of Edward the Confessor were both to be accommodated. It was a powerful and potentially fruitful balance of *sacerdotium* and *regnum* in which conflicts arose, especially in later Norman and Angevin times. But far more important were the ways in which the order established by Lanfranc and William provided a matrix for the structured church of succeeding centuries, the growth of both canon and secular law, the formation of spiritual and lay courts, and (to a larger degree than Lanfranc probably envisaged) the inclusion of the English church within the papal monarchy of western Christendom during the rest of the middle ages.

[121] Ibid., no. 47, pp. 150–3.

10

The Wider Primacy

From the beginning of his archiepiscopate, Lanfranc insisted that the primacy of his church of Canterbury extended beyond the two English provinces of Canterbury and York to include the whole of the British Isles. His insistence upon the obedience of Bishop Herfast of Elmham to him as metropolitan culminated in a declaration that, by the mercy of God, the whole island that men called Britain was agreed to be the single jurisdiction (*parrochia*) of his own one church of Canterbury.[1] In 1072 Lanfranc had drawn upon Bede to claim before Pope Alexander II that his early predecessors had exercised a primacy over the church of York and over the whole island called Britain including Ireland, dispensing pastoral care to all and holding ordinations and councils wherever they thought fit.[2] Thereafter the most usual formulation of Lanfranc's title in episcopal professions of obedience to him upon ordination was 'primate of the Britains and archbishop of the holy church of Canterbury (*Britanniarum primas et sanctae Dorobernensis ecclesiae archiepiscopus*)'.[3] Such were the limits within which Lanfranc considered himself bound to work, but his impact was in practice different with regard to the three regions of Ireland, Scotland, and Wales. This was largely the result of the differing power and initiatives of the secular rulers concerned.[4]

10.1 IRELAND

During his fourth year as archbishop Lanfranc was presented with an opportunity of acting with regard to Ireland when he was asked to consecrate Patrick as bishop of Dublin; he did so in 1074 at London, receiving a profession of obedience to himself as primate.[5] His authority in so doing was reinforced by a letter from Pope

---

[1] Lanfranc, *Letters*, no. 47, pp. 152–3. [2] Ibid., no. 4, pp. 50–1.
[3] *Canterbury Professions*, nos. 35–47, pp. 28–33; there are minor verbal variations of this formula.
[4] The interpretation of Lanfranc's wider primatial claims in this chapter may be compared with that of Flanagan, *Irish Society*, esp. 15–19, 23–5, 28–9, 41–6, according to which Lanfranc sought and to a degree founded a Canterbury patriarchate over the British Isles which mirrored claims to hegemony advanced by pre-Conquest kings and which was intended to buttress the primatial claims of Canterbury over York. But Lanfranc did not envisage a patriarchate in any strict canonical sense; his inspiration seems to have been less any royal aspirations of the Saxon or Norman kings than the purposes in England of the papal legates of 1070; his actions seem to have been initiated in response to events in Ireland, Scotland, and Wales rather than directed by an overall programme of how to implement the primacy as he envisaged it. See also the reconsideration of relations between the English and Irish churches during the Norman period in Philpott, 'Some Interactions'.
[5] *AL* 86; *Canterbury Professions*, no. 36, p. 29; *Annals of St Mary's Abbey*, a. 1074, pp. 249–50.

Gregory VII who, despite the refusal of the apostolic see in 1072 to grant him a privilege, was moved by consideration of his pastoral duty tacitly to confirm Lanfranc's primatial office: he admonished him to extirpate grave moral offences wherever they occured (*usquequaque*), and especially instanced the custom of the Irish (*Scotti*) who abandoned and even sold their wives; such evils should also be uprooted elsewhere in the 'island of the English (*in Anglorum insula*)'.[6]

According to Patrick's profession, Patrick had been elected to rule Dublin, 'the metropolis of Ireland'. He did not claim to be personally metropolitan; in view of the absence of such a term from his successor's profession to Lanfranc in 1085 and of Anselm's later strong rebuttals of the bishop of Dublin's claim to metropolitan privileges, it is probable that Patrick's profession reflected self-assertion in Ireland by the see of Dublin and not any countenancing by Lanfranc of Dublin as a metropolitan see subject to Canterbury on the model of York.[7] This is borne out by the terms in which the clergy and people of Dublin notified Lanfranc of Patrick's election and asked for his consecration.[8]

When Patrick returned home he carried letters from Lanfranc to two Irish kings. The first was to Guthric, king of Dublin, informing him that 'according to the custom of our predecessors' he had consecrated Patrick.[9] But the high-king of Ireland, who increased his power in Ireland up to his death in 1086, was the king of Munster, Toirdhealbhach Ó Briain; to him Lanfranc wrote somewhat more fully.[10] Lanfranc had evidently sought from Patrick a briefing of his own about the state of Irish church and society, for to Gregory VII's alleged abuses of marriage he added unions within the prohibited degrees. To Toirdhealbhach he also listed ecclesiastical irregularities: bishops were consecrated by only one bishop; some bishops were, or were similar to, *chorepiscopi*;[11] infants were baptized without chrismation; bishops were ordaining clerks simoniacally. Both kings received advice that illustrates Lanfranc's notion of good kingship: they should perform works that were worthy of the Christian faith; it was praiseworthy to treat good men with godly humility, to visit stern severity upon the wicked, and to show the strictest equity to all; they were obediently to follow the guidance of godly bishops and to correct all manner of wrongs according to evangelical and apostolic authority and to the

---

[6] Lanfranc, *Letters*, no. 8, pp. 64–7. That the *Scotti* are Irish is certain because (i) Gregory's letter in Lanfranc's letter-collection introduces two letters to Irish kings: nos. 9–10, pp. 66–73; (ii) in two letters, Anselm attributed to those *in Hibernia* such offences and irregularities as were in question in 1074: Anselm, *Epp.* nos. 427, 429, vol. 5.373–5, cf. Lanfranc, *Letters*, nos. 8–10, pp. 66–73.

[7] *Canterbury Professions*, no. 42, p. 71; Anselm, *Epp.* nos. 277–8, vol. 4.191–2.

[8] *Ep.* 36, *PL* 150.534–5.

[9] Lanfranc, *Letters*, no. 9, pp. 66–9. Patrick had been a monk at Worcester: Gwynn, *The Letters of Bishop Patrick*, 7, 9–10.

[10] Lanfranc, *Letters*, no. 10, pp. 70–2.

[11] Lanfranc's phrase 'quod in villis vel civitatibus plures ordinanter' is best read as referring to there being more than one bishop in a single diocese as at Canterbury when Lanfranc arrived there, rather than to there being many bishops in villages or small towns. If so, there is no tacit contradiction with canon 3 of the council of London (1075): Lanfranc, *Letters*, no. 11, pp. 76–7 = *CS* no. 92, vol. 1/2.613. Lanfranc may have learnt from Patrick that there were too few urban centres in Ireland for the Pseudo-Isidorian rule about *civitates* to be implemented.

canons. Lanfranc called upon Toirdhealbhach to convene an assembly of bishops and religious men; in their presence he and his right-minded advisers were to correct, as guided by canon law, such abuses as Lanfranc had instanced. Lanfranc clearly envisaged a council such as those current in Normandy and Norman England which would similarly issue reforming canons. His initiative was probably a first step towards such Irish councils as those of Cashel (1101) and Rath Breasail (1111).[12] In general, the similarity between Lanfranc's counsel to the kings of the periphery of Christendom and that of the contemporary papacy is striking.[13]

An indication that in Toirdhealbhach's realms some such episcopal collaboration as Lanfranc had pressed upon him took place is provided by a letter of 1080/1 from Lanfranc to Domnall Ua h-Énna, bishop of Munster, and to others unnamed who had sought his instruction.[14] They had posed a further problem about infant baptism: could baptized infants be saved, even though they died before receiving holy communion? Although journeying far from his books Lanfranc deployed much learning in dispelling Irish misconceptions about what the English and continental churches believed. He broadened the discussion into an exposition of eucharistic doctrine that seems to mirror his own continuing misgivings about the currency of Berengarian ideas.

In 1085 Lanfranc consecrated at Canterbury an Irish monk, Donatus (Donngus), to the see of Dublin. According to the *Actus Lanfranci*, this was requested by the king, clergy, and people of Ireland, to whom Lanfranc again sent letters of exhortation, which have not survived.[15] It emerges from two letters sent to Ireland by Anselm in 1101/3 that, probably at about the time of Donatus's consecration, Lanfranc was responsible for sending monks from Canterbury, evidently to settle in Dublin at Christ Church cathedral; Lanfranc sent to the church a gift of books, vestments, and other church ornaments. There is nothing to suggest that Donatus in any way acted contrary to Lanfranc's intention; however, Anselm wrote on account of rumours that his successor Bishop Samuel (1096–1121) had expelled the monks and misappropriated the gift.[16] So far as Lanfranc is concerned, his consecration to the see of Dublin of English-trained monk-bishops and his concern to export Canterbury monks to the significantly dedicated cathedral of Christ Church, Dublin, represent a step towards the opening of the Irish church to contemporary Latin monasticism which was to progress widely there in the twelfth century. In this as in general, whatever Lanfranc may have intended, his actions helped towards the emergence of the Irish church during the twelfth century as an independent province.

---

[12] For relevant developments, see Watt, *Church and Society*, 5–9, and the papers collected in Gwynn, *The Irish Church*.

[13] Cf. Cowdrey, *Pope Gregory VII*, 423–5, 456–8, 632–3.

[14] Lanfranc, *Letters*, no. 49, pp. 152–61; *AL* p. 86.

[15] *AL* 86–7; for Donatus's profession to Lanfranc, see *Canterbury Professions*, no. 42, p. 31. See also *Annals of St Mary's*, a. 1085, p. 250, where King Toirdhealbhach is also named, with the bishops of Ireland, as electing Donatus.

[16] Anselm, *Epp.* nos. 277–8, vol. 4.291–2.

10.2 SCOTLAND

Lanfranc claimed and exercised a similar primacy with regard to Scotland; the death in 1072 of the powerful Adalbert, archbishop of Hamburg–Bremen, and the preoccupation of his successor, Liemar, with German affairs left no obstacle for the outlying regions of Scotland to look to Canterbury. The settlement of the primacy in 1072 at Winchester and Windsor granted to the archbishops of York in perpetuity, but subject to the overriding authority of Canterbury, jurisdiction over all lands from the Humber northwards to the farthest limits of Scotland.[17] It should be recalled that, in 1072, the king led a naval and land force to Scotland, where he was said to have caused the strong king, Malcolm III Canmore (1058–93), to do homage and give hostages.[18] Whatever hopes may have been entertained in 1072, no regular effect was given to English jurisdiction over Scottish sees. However, probably in 1072 or 1073, a particular instance confirmed the terms of the settlement of the primacy.[19] There came to Archbishop Thomas of York a clerk named Ralph who was sent by Earl Paul of the Orkneys with a request that, 'according to the manner of his predecessors' he might be consecrated bishop by the archbishop of York. Since Thomas did not have in his province the canonically requisite co-consecrators, he had perforce to apply to Lanfranc. He did so with an obsequious expression of humility, depicting Lanfranc as 'supreme shepherd of the whole of Britain', describing himself as Lanfranc's *fidelis* with its overtones of loyalty and service, and attributing to Lanfranc a quasi-papal role of justly opening and closing on St Peter's behalf the gates of heaven to the just and to the unjust. He renounced any aspiration to subject to York the English bishops of Dorchester/Lincoln or Worcester. Lanfranc acceded to Thomas's request upon this understanding, and ordered Bishops Wulfstan of Worcester and Peter of Chester to travel to York and assist with the consecration. Thus the settlement of the primacy in 1072 was implemented and confirmed in a particular instance,

For the rest of his archiepiscopate Lanfranc had no further recorded dealings, whether direct or indirect, with a Scottish king or ruler or with any Scottish episcopal see. But considerable lasting importance attaches to his having been the mentor and spiritual adviser of Margaret, the queen of Malcolm Canmore, who was the daughter of Edmund the Atheling and thus of the Old English royal line; for her holiness of life she was eventually canonized.[20] In a letter of unknown date he acceded to Margaret's request that he should be her spiritual father. According to her petition he also sent a Canterbury monk, Goldwin, to Margaret and to her husband in order, if they saw fit, to assist with a work that they had begun.[21] Lanfranc appears to refer to the foundation of the monastic priory of Holy Trinity, Dunfermline (Fife), again named after the cathedral monastery of Canterbury,

---

[17] See above, p. 100. [18] *ASC* DE, a. 1072, pp. 154–5.
[19] Lanfranc, *Letters*, nos. 12–13, pp. 78–83; *VL* cap. 13, pp. 707–8. *AL* 86, dates the consecration to 1077, but see the note in Lanfranc, *Letters*, 78.
[20] For Scottish affairs, see esp. Barrow, *The Kingdom of the Scots*, pp. 167, 189, 193–6, 211.
[21] Lanfranc, *Letters*, no. 50, pp. 160–3.

which achieved the status of an abbey c.1128.[22] Margaret was credited with many other reforming endeavours, and with the encouraging of church councils.[23]

Thus, through his dealings with Margaret, Lanfranc had some influence by sponsoring monasticism in introducing at Dunfermline as in Dublin the Latin monasticism of the eleventh century and, through the family succession of the Canmores, he fostered in Scotland as in Ireland the institutions of the western church of the central middle ages.

10.3 WALES

In view of the relation of the Welsh church to the see of Canterbury from the time of Anselm up to the disestablishment of 1920, it is at first sight surprising that no concern with it on Lanfranc's part is recorded. It is the more surprising since, although King William I was not so directly concerned with Wales as his two sons would be, in 1081 he led an expedition across South Wales with the ostensible object of creating some kind of political stability there after the death of Caradog ap Gruffudd, ruler of Morgannwg.[24] Part of the explanation may lie in the archaic and disorganized state of the Welsh church; no name has survived of a Welsh bishop of Lanfranc's time. Lanfranc himself may have been influenced by Bede's stories of the recalcitrance of the British.[25] Perhaps the setting up of the marcher earldoms of Chester and Shrewsbury, the beginnings of Norman campaigning and settlement in Wales, and the Conqueror's expedition of 1081 provoked hostility among the Welsh to ecclesiastical as well as political inroads by the Normans. Possibly most important, it is clear that Lanfranc's primatial acts with regard to Ireland and Scotland were never, so far as they are known, taken upon his own initiative; they were all in response to approaches by native rulers or churches. No such approaches came from Wales or were likely to come, given the fragmented and locally orientated state of church and lay society alike. In such circumstances, Lanfranc's intervention is scarcely to have been expected.

---

[22] For the queen's foundation of an unnamed monastery which was probably Holy Trinity, see Turgot, *Vita s. Margaretae*, cap. 4, pp. 238–9.
[23] Ibid., cap. 8, pp. 243–5.
[24] *ASC* E, *a.* 1081, p. 160. For the political and ecclesiastical state of Wales, see Davies, *Conquest, Coexistence and Change*, 27–34, 172–80. I have benefited from an exchange of ideas with Dr Huw Pryce.
[25] e.g. Bede, *Eccles. Hist.* 1.14–15, 22; 2.2, 20; 5.23; pp. 46–53, 66–9, 134–43, 202–5, 560–1.

11

The Monastic Order

Although Lanfranc had not embarked upon the monastic life as a boy but as a young man with considerable worldly experience and success to his credit, when he became archbishop of Canterbury in 1070 he had some two-and-a-half decades of monastic life behind him. As monk and then prior of Bec and as abbot of Saint-Étienne at Caen, he had, not without an initial struggle, come to identify himself fully with cenobitic monasticism according to the Rule of St Benedict as it was to be found in the Norman monasteries of his time and especially in the Bec of Abbot Herluin. Thus, early in 1073, he pleaded with Pope Alexander II to be allowed to return to the cenobitic life, 'which I love before all things.'[1] Conversely, when constrained to continue as archbishop, he commented to the prior and monks of Christ Church, Canterbury, upon what good bishops and good abbots had in common: bishops, if they bestow fatherly care upon their subjects on Christ's behalf, may not incongruously be called abbots, that is, fathers, so long as the name is matched by their deeds.[2] Accordingly Lanfranc urged Bishop Peter of Chester, a sometime royal clerk, to behave towards the monks of Coventry as befitted a true bishop; to care for their souls with pastoral discernment, and to set them a healthful example of good customs and of holy actions in words and deeds.[3] Lanfranc's episcopal model, for himself as a monk and for others who shared his pastoral care, was that of a monk-bishop who, according to his circumstances, combined the qualities of the cloister with those requisite for his wider responsibility.

11.1 CHRIST CHURCH, CANTERBURY

The churchmen from Normandy who assumed control of English churches after the Norman conquest found that, in the wake of the tenth-century reform led by the monk-bishops Dunstan of Canterbury, Ethelwold of Winchester, and Oswald of Worcester, four cathedrals, Canterbury, Winchester, Worcester, and Sherborne, had monastic chapters.[4] Thus, when Lanfranc arrived at Canterbury in the late summer of 1070 there was in his cathedral, ruinous though it was after the fire of 1067, a small community of monks who followed the customs of the *Regularis concordia* which was the principal document of the tenth-century reform.[5] The royal

---

[1] Lanfranc, *Letters*, no. 1, pp. 32–3.   [2] See above, p. 78.
[3] Lanfranc, *Letters*, no. 27, pp. 112–13.
[4] For the Norman monastic cathedrals, see Knowles, *The Monastic Order*, 129–34.
[5] The presence of a monastic community at Christ Church in Lanfranc's early years is attested by Eadmer's *Epistola ad Glastonburienses*, in: *Reliquiae Dunstanianae*, 413–14. The following of the *Regularis*

clerk Walchelin had been appointed bishop of Winchester in the spring of 1070 and had doubted the desirability of a chapter of monks in a cathedral which served as the centre of a secular diocese. He therefore planned to replace the monks of the Old Minster at Winchester by canons, but met with Lanfranc's strong opposition. According to Eadmer, Walchelin joined with other bishops, with the support of the king, in challenging the position of the monks at Canterbury itself.[6] Little credence can be placed in Eadmer's account of Lanfranc's appealing to Pope Alexander II in defence of the monks of Canterbury and receiving from him a letter of support.[7] But there is no reason to doubt that Lanfranc was from the start a strong defender of the monastic chapter at Canterbury or that he persuaded the king of its desirability, thus overcoming a further early point of difficulty with the king.[8]

At Canterbury, Lanfranc as archbishop was ex officio abbot of the cathedral monastery of Christ Church. Pressure of external business and frequent absence in practice left much responsibility in the hands of his second-in-command. It appears that for some years Lanfranc depended upon the English *decanus* Godric, a monk of good reputation whose association with Christ Church went back to the days of Archbishop Elphege (1006–12),[9] but c.1076 he was succeeded by Henry, who like Lanfranc was Italian by birth and a sometime monk of Bec and who had the title of prior.[10] Lanfranc prudently proceeded gradually with the reforming of monastic life at Christ Church in his early years, seeking to abate abuses and propagate virtues piecemeal rather than prematurely attempting more radical change.[11]

An important step towards change was Lanfranc's bringing to England for service in his household and church a small group of monks from Bec and Caen, for whom references in the letters of Anselm are the principal evidence. In 1070 Anselm concluded his letter of congratulation to Lanfranc upon his succession at Canterbury by referring to the monks of Bec who were with him in England;[12] their presence there from the outset suggests that Lanfranc may have gone to England in awareness of the monastic character of Christ Church and with an intention of

---

concordia is suggested by Eadmer's reference to the Easter liturgical drama: *Mirac.*, cap. 13, p. 231; cf. *Regularis concordia*, cap. 79, pp. 124–6. While prior of Bec, Anselm asked Lanfranc to send him a copy of the *Regularis concordia*: *Epp.* no. 39, vol. 3.151. For a monastic school at Christ Church, see Osbern, *Mirac.*, cap. 15, pp. 140–2; Eadmer, *Mirac.*, cap. 12, pp. 229–31.

[6] *Hist. nov.*, 1, pp. 18–21; whence William of Malmesbury, *GP* 1.44, pp. 71–2. William did not expressly mention a challenge to Christ Church, Canterbury, as well as to Winchester, but he wrote of a general assault upon cathedral monasteries that Lanfranc frustrated. However by the papal *scripta* that Lanfranc received he clearly means *Accepimus a quibusdam*, which he saw in Eadmer.

[7] Eadmer is the sole source for Alexander II's alleged letter *Accepimus a quibusdam*: *Hist. nov.*, 1, pp. 19–21 = Alexander II, *Ep.* 142, *PL* 150.1415–16. It is unlikely to be genuine or to date from the early 1070s. Its authenticity was questioned by Clover, 'Alexander II's Letter'; for further discussion, see Cowdrey, 'Lanfranc, the Papacy, and the See of Canterbury', 489–93.

[8] Cf. King William's early resistance to Lanfranc's primatial claims: above, p. 90. For a different estimate of Lanfranc's early attitude to the monastic chapter at Christ Church, see Southern, *Saint Anselm: A Portrait*, 308–10, where *Accepimus a quibusdam* is treated as genuine.

[9] For Godric, see Osbern, *Mirac.*, cap. 11, pp. 137–8; id., *Translatio*, cap. 6, cols. 389–90.

[10] Henry is first mentioned as prior in Anselm, *Epp.* no. 58, vol. 3.172–3, probably to be dated in 1076; he appears to have been well established in office.

[11] William of Malmesbury, *GP* 1.44, pp. 70–1; Eadmer, *Mirac.*, cap. 16, pp. 227–8.

[12] Anselm, *Epp.* no. 1, vol. 3.98.

preserving it. As prior and (from 1078) abbot of Bec, Anselm retained an interest in and care for the monks of Bec who had become Lanfranc's subjects. Besides Gundulf, later bishop of Rochester, and Henry, the first prior of Christ Church, Anselm referred to the Bec monks Ernost, Gilbert Crispin, Guy, another Henry, Herluin, Maurice, and Osbern, who were at Canterbury for a longer or shorter time. From Caen there were Vitalis, Roger, and Samuel, and from outside Normandy the able scholar and later prior of Christ Church and bishop of Rochester, Ernulf of Saint-Simphorien at Beauvais. Another figure who came from Bec to Canterbury was the evidently valued medical doctor, Albert.[13] There was also traffic in the opposite direction. Lanfranc seems to have sent to Bec for correction by Prior Anselm the able but recalcitrant English monk Osbern, the future hagiographer of St Dunstan and St Elphege, with beneficial results; a monk named Salwio may have been similarly dispatched to Bec, and Holvard, Osbern's kinsman, also spent time there.[14] From Normandy, Lanfranc was concerned to obtain manuscripts for Christ Church as well as men. His purchase for it from Bec of the text of his canon-law collection has already been discussed.[15] Another apparent deficiency in the books available at Canterbury was with regard to the great Latin doctors.[16] Lanfranc at an early date sought from Normandy a copy of Pope Gregory the Great's *Moralia in Iob* and works of Ambrose and Jerome. Later, Anselm obeyed his request to send him his own commentaries on the Pauline epistles.[17] Lanfranc was evidently concerned from the start to furnish his monks at Christ Church, English and Norman, with such reading-matter as had shaped his own mind and outlook.

The years 1076 and 1077 seem to have been critical for Lanfranc's revival of stricter monastic life at Christ Church. This is strongly suggested by reports of an incident concerning a young English monk of the community, Egelward, which seems to have quickly attracted notoriety;[18] it certainly left a deep imprint upon the historical record of Lanfranc's time.[19] The basic elements of the incident are that while Egelward was assisting as deacon at a mass which Lanfranc was publicly celebrating, and at the point where, after the Lord's prayer, the deacon hands the paten to the celebrant, Egelward was violently seized internally by a demon and uttered loud cries. In fear he grasped Lanfranc for protection.[20] He was carried off by knights

[13] Besides references to Albert in Anselm's letters, he appears as a doctor at Christ Church in Osbern, *Mirac.*, cap. 19, pp. 147–8. (Osbern noted that he had seen Albert at Rome as a cardinal-clerk; this suggests that Osbern may have accompanied Anselm to Rome in 1098 or 1103.)

[14] For the monks referred to as at Canterbury and for Albert, see the references in Anselm, *Op.* vol. 6, s.vv.

[15] See above, pp. 139–43.

[16] For book production at Canterbury before 1066, see Brooks, *The Early History*, 266–78.

[17] Anselm, *Epp.* nos. 23, 25–6, 66, vol. 3.130, 133, 134, 186–7. For Anselm's wish to receive books from Canterbury, see *Epp.* nos. 39, 42, 43, vol. 3.131, 154, 155–6.

[18] If the last sentence of Lanfranc, *Letters*, no. 15, pp. 90–1, refers to the Egelward incident, news of it quickly reached Archbishop John of Rouen.

[19] For accounts, see Osbern, *Mirac.*, cap. 19, pp. 144–51; Eadmer, *Mirac.*, cap. 16, pp. 234–8; *The Life of Gundulf*, cap. 11, pp. 33–4; *VL* cap. 14, pp. 709–11.

[20] That Egelward seized Lanfranc from fear and to seek fatherly protection is clearly stated by Osbern and implied by Eadmer; their evidence is to be preferred to the remoter account in *VL*, where the monk made a violent assault upon the archbishop.

who were present while Lanfranc concluded the service. Over a period of some days while he was confined in the infirmary there was much concern for his care, both in the monastic chapter and privately in pastoral and penitential dealings. Only after grave difficulties and violent scenes was Egelward delivered from demonic possession. This eventually happened through the miraculous power of St Dunstan; Egelward thereafter lived a holy life and died an exemplary death.

These dramatic events can be fairly securely dated to the year 1076. The sources show that Henry was well established as prior, while Gundulf had not yet become bishop of Rochester (he was consecrated on 19 March 1077).[21] Moreover, during the course of events the relics of St Dunstan were transferred from the oratory of St Mary to the monks' refectory for temporary safe-keeping; Lanfranc's rebuilding programme was advancing towards the consecration of the church on 9 April 1077.[22] A date for the incident some months before may be presumed; moreover, the state of the building marked the approach of a time when a proper regulation of the monastic life might be introduced.

As regards the two fullest accounts of the Egelward incident, Eadmer knew that of Osbern. Both writers were mainly concerned with the miraculous part played by St Dunstan; Lanfranc's part was of secondary concern to them both, although Osbern gave much greater attention to Lanfranc than did Eadmer. This was because, apart from the role of St Dunstan, they concentrated upon different, indeed contrasting, aspects of the incident. Osbern wrote mainly upon its inner, personal, and secret aspect. The morals for monks to draw were that confession of sins should be complete, that the making of a complete confession rendered powerless the devil and all malign spirits, and that, in public or private penance as appropriate, all should be disclosed to the fatherly wisdom and judgement of the abbot. This provided Osbern with an opportunity to present in some detail Lanfranc's mastery of spiritual and pastoral guidance.[23] Eadmer, however, dealt with this aspect of the incident, and so with Lanfranc's part, quite briefly. His focus was upon the all too public and external aspects of what happened—not upon the secret sins of monks within the community but with their public lifestyle which, up to this point, had been more that of lay nobles than that of monks. He instanced their sumptuous apparel and ornaments, and the horses, dogs, and hawks with which they were wont to range abroad. (He made no reference to the more personal and sexual sins at which Osbern more than hinted.) To this endemic worldliness the Egelward incident administered a salutary shock (*percussio*):

---

[21] According to *VL*, Gundulf was already bishop, but this contradicts the clear evidence of the other sources.

[22] See above, pp. 104–5.

[23] The *VL* also presents the incident as showing the strength of confession and absolution to deprive the devil of the memory of a sin which has been fully confessed and of the power to accuse a man; it makes no mention of Dunstan and describes the story as an anecdote of Archbishop Anselm. The Life of Gundulf also omits reference to Dunstan. There is no direct or indirect allusion to Lanfranc; the story turns on the profound impact of the incident upon Gundulf, who was led to reconsider his entire faith and practice, especially with regard to penitence.

By this scourge, by the mercy of Christ and with the help and sagacity of the good father Archbishop Lanfranc, the monks were impelled to the point of renouncing all these abuses. Turning to the true manner of religion for monks, they counted them all as dung. As for us who know for a certainty how things happened at this time, we profess that there would never have occurred so sudden and salutary a change of affairs if we had not seen before our own eyes this cruel and ferocious ordeal (*examinatio*) which terrified everyone.

A certain reserve is necessary in considering Eadmer's presentation of the Egelward incident, for he invoked the propaganda version of recent church history in England that was the common theme of Anglo-Norman historians: an age of reform and observance extending from St Dunstan to St Elphege was followed by an age of stagnation and decay up to the coming of the Normans, who were responsible for the infusion of new life and vigour into English churches and monasteries.[24] Yet Eadmer credibly suggests that *c*.1076 Lanfranc undertook to introduce a much stricter monastic regime at Christ Church with the new prior, Henry, as a key figure; in view of the impact made by the Egelward incident, Lanfranc may well have made it a pretext for thorough reform.

Lanfranc's relations with the monastic community at Christ Church and with its individual members undoubtedly were and remained as close as the Egelward incident suggests. Nothing whatever is known of his dealings with the *decanus* Godric whom he retained in office. His relations with Prior Henry are not altogether easy to understand. Henry had caused disquiet with Anselm and the community at Bec by a journey to Italy, including Rome, in order to secure the freedom of his sister from unjust servitude and to visit his family; Anselm sought to dissuade him from a journey made against the counsels of many and then expressed surprise and regret that neither on his outward nor his return journey did he pass through Bec.[25] It is scarcely likely that he travelled from Canterbury to Rome without Lanfranc's leave and financial support. It may have been his caring disposition, which he showed to English as well as French confrères, that commended him to Lanfranc for the office of prior.[26] But at least in his early years in office, his relations with Lanfranc were not without difficulties which were of some duration. Two letters from Anselm to Henry counselled him to obedience and patience in face of a loss of Lanfranc's favour and of painful calumnies against him which raised the question of his leaving Canterbury and returning to Bec. It is wholly unclear what difficulties were involved, but against a background of the concern of the abbot and community at Bec, a reconciliation between Lanfranc and Henry was evidently effected at Canterbury.[27] The two men settled down to a working relationship that shows no further evidence of personal tensions.[28]

---

[24] See esp. Eadmer, *Hist. nov.*, 1, pp. 3–5, 12–13; William of Malmesbury, *GP* 1.18, 23, 44, pp. 27–8, 35–6, 70–1, and *GR* 3.345–6, vol. 1.456–61; Orderic Vitalis, 4, vol. 2.246–9.

[25] Anselm, *Epp.* 17, 24, vol. 3.122–4, 131. The letters appear to relate to the same journey.

[26] Besides Henry's part in the Egelward incident, see Anselm, *Epp.* 33, 40, vol. 3.141, 151–2, where the English monk Holvard is described to Henry as *vester Holvardus*. (Holvard was a kinsman of the English monk Osbern: Anselm, *Epp.* 69, 74, vol. 3.189, 196.)

[27] Anselm, *Epp.* nos. 63, 73, vol. 3.178–80, 194–5.

[28] See e.g. Lanfranc's letter to Henry commending his monastic constitutions: Lanfranc, *MC* cap. 1, pp. 2–5. Henry became abbot of Battle (1096–1102). On him, see further *MC* pp. xviii, xxviii.

Lanfranc was posthumously remembered for his great skill in the spiritual and moral direction of individual souls (*regimen animarum*)—for Pope Gregory the Great the art of arts.[29] So far as the monks of Christ Church are concerned, his skill is apparent in the Egelward incident as related by Osbern.[30] Egelward had received especial advice from Lanfranc that he keep himself chaste and bodily pure lest he be vulnerable to an evil spirit while serving at the altar; when a demon seized him during mass it was to Lanfranc that he looked for protection. As soon as mass was over, Lanfranc went alone to him; after exorcism he absolved him from his fault and secured temporary quiet. Having been disciplined in chapter, Egelward again broke out, threatening to reveal the secret deeds of each member in turn. He turned upon a young monk upon whom Lanfranc set great hopes as the especial partner of his own offences. Lanfranc at once took the young man from chapter, received a life confession, and by absolution rendered him immune from all malignant attacks. Thereafter it was Lanfranc who carefully set the stage for Dunstan's healing of Egelward. Whatever may be made of the details, Osbern's account illustrates Lanfranc's reputation as one who, after the manner of a good abbot, knew and cared for individual monks. Lanfranc was also remembered for his material generosity towards individual monks and needy members of their families; a story tells of his allowing a pension of as much as thirty shillings a year, paid quarterly, to a monk's widowed mother.[31]

Under Lanfranc's rule, the Christ Church community grew strongly in numbers; a fair estimate would be that it reached upwards of sixty.[32] It was provided with a church, monastic buildings, and an income which were appropriate for one of the greatest monastic houses of the land. Its confidence was increased by a belief that Lanfranc had recalled to proper subjection to the church of Canterbury the northern archbishop and all the bishops of the kingdom.[33] Alike from the point of view of Lanfranc as its archbishop and abbot and from that of its own identity and standing, Christ Church needed a body of legislation which embodied what was most authoritative in the Benedictine practice of the time.

11.2 LANFRANC'S MONASTIC CONSTITUTIONS

Such a body of legislation Lanfranc provided in his monastic constitutions.[34] It was a necessary instrument of the monastic life of the Benedictine kind. The bedrock of this life was the Rule of St Benedict, which all monasteries followed in the matters

---

[29] William of Malmesbury, *GP* 1.44, pp. 70–1.

[30] As above, n. 19. It may perhaps be added with regard to Lanfranc's repeated reference to the abbot (see *MC* 228–9, s.v. *abbas*) in constitutions intended for a priory that the term 'cathedral priory' was not yet current; such priories were not seen by Lanfranc and his contemporaries as being generically distinct from other monasteries or as having a structure of their own.

[31] Eadmer, *Hist. nov.*, 1, pp. 13–14; *VL* cap. 15, p. 712. Since Lanfranc took great care to bestow his alms in secret, Eadmer's story may well relate to him and his own mother.

[32] Knowles, *The Monastic Order*, 126; Knowles and Hadcock, *Medieval Religious Houses*, 61.

[33] See Lanfranc's *obit*: Gibson, *Lanfranc*, 228.   [34] Lanfranc, *MC*.

with which it dealt. But no monastery could be ordered and governed in terms only of the Rule. It required to be complemented by acknowledged regulations which met the needs of each particular house or association of houses. There was thus a proliferation of monastic constitutions that normally, in black-monk houses, covered two areas: first, that of the details of the liturgical year in respect of worship and observances; and second, matters concerning the duties of monastic office-holders, the administration and discipline of the community, and the contingencies of the lives of individual monks, from entering upon the religious life until death and burial. Lanfranc's constitutions covered these two areas. They were compiled and introduced by his authority. The prefatory letter that he addressed to his beloved brothers Prior Henry and the rest of the monks came from him as bishop (*antistes*) of the holy church of Canterbury. The customs of his and their monastic life that he sent them were his compilation. Like all such customs, they could be added to or subtracted from if good reason or proper authority were alleged. But as they were currently laid down they must be followed by each and all: whatever has been appointed by superiors (*a pastoribus*) must be observed by subjects; it can in no wise be transgressed without fault by those whose whole life is subject to obedience.[35] Such was the sanction of Lanfranc's monastic constitutions.

The date at which he compiled and imposed them is uncertain. An early date has been canvassed in view of a later St Albans tradition that, when in 1077 Lanfranc's nephew Paul went to be its abbot, he took with him the customs and statutes of Lanfranc 'which the lord pope had deservedly approved'; if such papal approval had been given, it was presumably during Lanfranc's visit to Rome in 1071 upon which, according to the St Albans source, Paul accompanied him. But such a papal approval of a body of monastic constitutions would be unparalleled and hard to understand, and the same St Albans source later referred to Archbishop Anselm as approving the constitutions that Lanfranc had sent to Paul.[36] Everything points to a date in the middle, rather than at the beginning, of Lanfranc's years at Canterbury. The prefatory letter is addressed to Prior Henry; the constitutions would have been difficult to implement before the rebuilding had reached the point represented by the consecration of the church in 1077; the other problems that Lanfranc encountered in the convent between c.1074 and 1077, such as his unsettling difference with Prior Henry and the Egelward incident, are more likely to have given Lanfranc an incentive to establish his authority by compiling the constitutions than to have arisen against their background. On the other hand, time must be allowed for their dissemination during Lanfranc's lifetime to other houses, including St Albans. A date before 1080 is likely for their completion and dispatch to the prior and monks of Christ Church.[37]

In his prefatory letter, Lanfranc wrote that he had compiled his constitutions 'from those of the monasteries which in our time are of greater authority in the monastic order'. He reveals no indebtedness to the *Regularis concordia*, which was

---

[35] Lanfranc, *MC* cap. 1, pp. 2–5.   [36] *Gesta abbatum monasterii sancti Albani*, 1.46–7, 52, 61.
[37] The case for such a date is presented by Sheerin, 'Some Observations'; Brooke suggests completion in or soon after 1077: *MC* pp. xxxiv–xxxv.

the principal document of the tenth-century monastic reform in England that was associated with Archbishop Dunstan. The customs of Bec, which he probably contributed to establishing and which he seems to have followed at Caen, were a significant but not a major source.[38] He drew more largely upon the two current customaries of Cluny—the *Liber tramitis*, which dates from the time of the Cluniac Abbot Odilo (994–1048), and above all, on that which goes by the name of the monk Bernard and which in its first recension dates from the mid-1060s. Lanfranc was doubtless attracted by Cluny's prestige in the monastic order under Abbot Hugh (1049–1109), and perhaps also by the coincidence that both Christ Church and Cluny had to provide for the frequent absence of the abbot—Christ Church because of archiepiscopal duties and Cluny because of the round of visitation of dependent houses and general involvement in ecclesiastical affairs. The king and queen, who were devotees of Cluny, may have been an influence.[39]

There is very little self-disclosure in Lanfranc's constitutions save indirectly through the matters to which he gave particular and detailed attention. But his letters attest his keen interest in and memory of correct liturgical and ritual detail.[40] In his prefatory letter, he referred to the especial solemnity with which certain feasts should be observed in the cathedral monastery of a primatial see. This was no doubt the reason why Lanfranc followed the Cluniac *Liber tramitis* in first dealing with the liturgical year, rather than Bernard, who began with offices, administration, and discipline. Adapting and developing Bernard, he listed feast-days according to their degree of solemnity. Five were in the first rank: Christmas, Easter, Pentecost, the Assumption, and the *festivitas loci*.[41] Seventeen feast-days were categorized as to be celebrated *magnifice* although less so than the five foregoing; they included the feasts of Pope Gregory the Great,[42] St Augustine 'archbishop of the English',[43] St Benedict, St Elphege the martyr, and the dedication of the church.[44] There is also a third list of sixteen feasts, to which others might be added, which were less solemnly celebrated; it mainly consisted of New Testament saints, certain martyrs, St Augustine the doctor of the church, and the invention and exaltation of the holy cross.[45] It is an appropriate principal *sanctorale* for a cathedral monastery.

Such liturgical dispositions were readily compatible with the discipline of the monastic order; in other respects, the dual function of a cathedral monastery as at once a city and diocesan and also a monastic institution was potentially more

---

[38] For the customs of Bec and for Lanfranc's use of them as a source, see *Consuetudines Beccenses*, pp. xxx–xxxiii, xxxvii–xli; but see Brooke's note of caution: *MC* p. xl. For the sources in general, see ibid., pp. xxxix–xlii, 226–7.

[39] For the numerous contacts of the Anglo-Norman lands with Cluny that may have brought Cluniac customs to Lanfranc's notice, see Cowdrey, 'William I's Relations with Cluny'.

[40] Lanfranc, *Letters*, no. 14, pp. 84–7.

[41] Lanfranc, *MC* caps. 62–5, pp. 82–9. Lanfranc's ranking of feasts may be compared with Bernard, 1.49–50, pp. 242–5.

[42] Lanfranc concluded his provision for this feast with the personal observation that 'we reckon the feast of blessed Gregory amongst the more exalted because he is the apostle of our people, that is, of the English': Lanfranc, *MC* cap. 66, pp. 92–3.

[43] The implicit primatial claim should be noted.   [44] Lanfranc, *MC* caps. 66–72, pp. 88–97.

[45] Ibid., caps. 73–5, pp. 96–101.

difficult to sustain without harm to monastic discipline. Lanfranc seems therefore to have been at pains to do everything possible to ensure that both collectively and individually abbot, prior, and monks held fast to the spirit and the letter of the monastic life as lived in the most exemplary houses. Hence Lanfranc's insistence in his prefatory letter that the constitutions currently laid down by superiors must be fully observed by those whose whole life is subject to obedience.[46] And hence the almost entire concern of the constitutions with the monastic life as it was to be found in any observant Benedictine house.

Lanfranc sought to safeguard the integrity of this life by formulating strict regulations which were clearly expressed and rigorously enforced. Thus, he set out the treatment of light faults, grave faults, and fugitives in ascending order of seriousness, using material from Bernard's chapters on the instruction of novices and on returned fugitives, but clearly defining the procedures and setting out the punishments, including the severe corporal punishments, appropriate for each when dealt with in chapter or otherwise.[47] The strictness of the conducting of the daily chapter was to be a constant reminder of the standards of the monastic life. Lanfranc returned to this subject in a section on accusation and punishment in the chapter of faults.[48] Lanfranc insisted that an accusation should refer only to the order or office that a monk held within the monastic community; there must be no reference to a title held in the world. Lanfranc surprisingly specifically instanced a monk of Christ Church, Edward, who should not be referred to by his sometime designations of 'archdeacon' or 'of London'.[49] Within the monastery all external connections must be set aside.

Lanfranc's determination to exclude undue contacts with the outside world is further manifest in his characteristically elaborate regulations for the roundsmen (*circatores*), whose task was to seek out the carelessnesses and negligences of the monks and their breaches of appointed discipline, reporting them to the chapter. They were to pay due attention to the church where crypts and alcoves provided places for laxity. While they themselves might not leave the monastic buildings, they must look out through the doors lest any monks were wandering outside or gossiping.[50] Lanfranc was no less stringent and detailed in his rules for monks who were travelling outside the monastery, with regard both to their fulfilling their duty of saying the divine office and to their avoiding the inquisitiveness, gossip, and idle words to which worldly contacts exposed them.[51] Lanfranc's lengthy treatment of such matters shows his purpose of safeguarding monastic separation from the secular order, even in a cathedral monastery.

His treatment of the life and commitment of individual monks suggests a similar concern. As regards novitiate and profession, although Lanfranc drew upon

[46] As n. 35.   [47] Lanfranc, *MC* caps. 99–101, pp. 146–55; cf. Bernard, 1.18, 58, pp. 176–7, 252–5.
[48] Lanfranc, *MC* cap. 106, pp. 164–7; cf. Bernard, 1.74.47, p. 275.
[49] For Edward, who was made sacristan of Christ Church soon after his profession, then wished to return to the world, but finally died an exemplary monastic death, see Osbern, *Mirac.*, cap. 23, pp. 155–6; Eadmer, *Mirac.*, cap. 20, pp. 241–5.
[50] Lanfranc, *MC* cap. 85, pp. 116–19; cf. Bernard, 1.4, p. 144.
[51] Lanfranc, *MC* cap. 97, pp. 144–5; cf. Bernard, 1.2, 75.8, pp. 140, 268.

Bernard he proceeded somewhat differently. Bernard discussed the admission of adult *conversi* and child oblates at different stages of his customary, treating the latter at great length.[52] Lanfranc dealt with them together.[53] He considered the adult *conversus* first, strongly developing by comparison with Bernard the abbot's initial admonition about the *dura et aspera*—the things hard and disagreeable—that according to St Benedict a monk must pass through in his journey to God.[54] Adult commitment to strict community life in full awareness of the cost was essential in Lanfranc's eyes. Accordingly, his treatment of child oblation was brief; it concluded with an insistence that, when a child became of age to make his profession, he should perform everything that Lanfranc had prescribed for an adult *conversus*. For every monk however recruited, commitment to the monastic community must be deliberate and complete. At the end of a monk's life, Lanfranc's long provision for his terminal sickness and burial reinforces this expectation; there is nothing novel about the provisions, but as formulated by him they give an impression of the care of the whole community for an individual member that was especially characteristic of him.[55]

An important feature of Lanfranc's constitutions is that, in legislation envisaging a cathedral monastery of which an archbishop was ex officio abbot, he invariably referred to the superior as abbot, not as archbishop or bishop. In his prefatory letter, he concluded with the observation that this should not excite surprise: he was describing a monks' way of life (*ordo monachorum*), and monks were more often ruled by an abbot than by a bishop; although if in Christ's place bishops bestowed a fatherly care upon their diocesan subjects, they might not unreasonably be called abbots, that is, fathers.[56] A reading of the constitutions suggests that the choice of the word abbot also had a twofold significance within the community. On the one hand, when Lanfranc as archbishop had often to be elsewhere or else preoccupied by other business, it was a standing reminder to the prior and monks that authority in the monastery always rested with him. Saving the reverence due to the abbot in all things, the prior was more worthy of honour than the other ministers of God's household.[57] Thus, for example, in chapter graver faults properly belonged to the abbot for correction; but if he were away from the neighbourhood and not expected soon to return, they might be corrected by the prior with the community's consent.[58] The whole ordering of the monastery depended on the abbot's will; if in his absence change were called for, upon his return he should be informed and his will should prevail.[59] On the other hand, the references to the abbot should perhaps also be seen as Lanfranc's reminder to himself and to future archbishops of their responsibilities as abbot, which were the same as if it were their sole office. Lanfranc

---

[52] Bernard, 1.15, pp. 164–7 (adult novices), 1.27, pp. 200–10 (child oblates).

[53] Lanfranc, *MC* caps. 102–4, pp. 154–63 (adult novices), cap. 105, pp. 162–5 (child oblates). Lanfranc deals elsewhere with some matters regarding children that Bernard includes in his chapter.

[54] See *RSB* 58.8, vol. 2.628–9. Bernard's reference is in 1.15, pp. 164–5.

[55] Lanfranc, *MC* caps. 111–14, pp. 176–95.   [56] Ibid., cap. 1, pp. 4–5.

[57] Ibid., cap. 83, pp. 112–13.   [58] Ibid., cap. 100, pp. 152–3.

[59] Ibid., cap. 82, pp. 110–11. Lanfranc's attendance at royal crown-wearings must often have entailed his absence from Canterbury at Christmas, Holy Week and Easter, and Pentecost.

drove this home with regard to the Maundy foot-washing upon which he characteristically set especial store: if numbers allowed the abbot to wash the feet of all the monks he should do so, in the light of St Benedict's declaration that the abbot acts in the monastery on behalf of Christ; in Lanfranc's eyes this was never more truly so than in the service of foot-washing.[60]

There can be no doubt that Lanfranc compiled his monastic constitutions with his own community of Christ Church, Canterbury, in view. They were not intended as a document to be adopted by, still less to be imposed upon, the generality of other monastic houses; it was in principle for each house to adopt such customs as were appropriate for its circumstances,[61] and in any case by eleventh-century conventions no authority such as the archbishop of Canterbury could exercise general legislative authority over the monastic order.[62] There seem to be no passages of the constitutions that positively envisage the circumstances of houses other than Christ Church. Lanfranc's provision for the election of the abbot by the community alone has been claimed as an exception, in view of the king's decisive voice in the appointment of the archbishop of Canterbury.[63] But this would apply to most episcopal and major abbatial elections; Lanfranc's formulation is sufficiently explained if, as suggested above, his purpose was to describe only what pertained to the inner integrity of the monastic community: he set down only the monastic aspect of an abbatial election.

Nevertheless, Lanfranc avoided, perhaps deliberately, topographical references that tied his constitutions closely to Canterbury. In his rulings for the Palm Sunday procession with the Blessed Sacrament outside the walls of the monastery, Lanfranc provided a minimum of detail about its destination, referring to a station 'at the gates of the city (*ad portas civitatis*)'.[64] Likewise, the Rogationtide procession was to an unspecified church of the vicinity.[65] Lanfranc may from the start have wished his constitutions to be available for use by other monasteries; his concern for the cathedral priory at Rochester and for the St Albans of his nephew Paul springs to mind. His formulating of the constitutions in terms of the abbot rather than of the bishop, 'because the life of monks is oftener regulated by abbots than by bishops',[66] and his general purpose of envisaging Christ Church as a well-constituted monastic community made his constitutions in practice readily adaptable to other monasteries. This was further assisted by their clear formulation and efficient ordering.

They were undoubtedly widely adopted or drawn upon. There is a considerable survival of manuscripts, the most important being the late eleventh-century copy

---

[60] Lanfranc, *MC* cap. 39, pp. 52–5, 58–9; cf. *RSB* 2.2, vol. 1.440–3, 63, 16, vol. 2.646–7.
[61] As Lanfranc wrote in his prefatory letter: *MC* cap. 1, pp. 2–5.
[62] Knowles, *The Monastic Order*, 123–4; Lanfranc, *MC* pp. xxxii–xxxiii (Brooke).
[63] Lanfranc, *MC* cap. 82, pp. 108–9; cf. Sheerin, 'Some Observations', 25–6.
[64] Lanfranc, *MC* cap. 25, pp. 38–9; For comment on its possible adaptation at Winchester, see Biddle (ed.), *Winchester*, 268–9.
[65] Lanfranc, *MC* cap. 55, pp. 76–7. Bernard, whom Lanfranc was using, was precise about the course of the procession to the church of Cluny's patron saints, St Peter and St Paul, within the abbey: 2.22, p. 328.
[66] Prefatory letter, Lanfranc, *MC* cap. 1, pp. 4–5.

belonging to Durham cathedral monastery.[67] Among such monasteries, Worcester, Rochester, and Winchester certainly or probably followed them; the list of other houses includes St Albans, Crowland, St Augustine's at Canterbury, Evesham, Battle, Eynsham, and Westminster.[68]

In assessing Lanfranc's constitutions, it must be remembered that like all such compilations they record rules the manner and extent of whose application are uncertain. In all likelihood, at Christ Church and so under Lanfranc's direct supervision the liturgical and administrative rules will have been strictly applied. As regards the penal rules, and especially those involving corporal punishment, often publicly in chapter, it can only be said on the one hand that Lanfranc is shown to have countenanced the severity that generally marked such ordinances, but that on the other, the Egelward incident as recorded by Osbern suggests that he was capable of applying sanctions with a measure of mercy and pastoral care. But they were part of the *dura et aspera* upon which he dwelt as being inseparable from the monastic life.[69] Lanfranc's constitutions have the strength that they served the needs of the Christ Church community well during half a century and more of expansion and consolidation. Their weakness was that, in the long process of time, not all the archbishop-abbots would share the opportunities and the dedication of Lanfranc to serve the monastic round. Even a monk like Anselm was unable to avoid prolonged absences; archbishops who were regular canons or secular clergy were in any case not dedicated to the Benedictine life. And in the long run, the integrity of the monastic life that Lanfranc sought to safeguard was inevitably challenged by the exigences of a community that also served as a cathedral chapter, while the cathedral chapter was also compromised in respect of its role in the diocese.

11.3 OTHER CATHEDRAL AND EPISCOPAL MONASTERIES

Of the cathedrals other than Canterbury which in 1066 had monastic chapters, Worcester had as its bishop the monk, Wulfstan II, who had been consecrated in 1062 and who lived until 1095; no change in the constitution of the cathedral was thinkable during his lifetime.[70] Bishop Herman of Sherborne and Ramsbury (1058–78) had kept his see at the abbey, but when after the council of London (1075) he transferred his see to Salisbury the cathedral at Old Sarum had a secular chapter. The reasons do not emerge from the evidence, but it may well be that the Conqueror's strategic considerations determined the choice of a site that did not provide the space or the amenities, especially water, for a monastic community.[71] Neither at Worcester nor at Salisbury does Lanfranc's reaction become apparent.

[67] For the manuscript tradition, see Lanfranc, *MC* pp. xliii–xlix.

[68] For the adoption of Lanfranc's constitutions by other monasteries, or for evidence of their influence, see Knowles, *The Monastic Order*, 123–4; Barlow, *The English Church, 1066–1154*, 189; Lanfranc, *MC* pp. xxxi–xxxvi (Brooke).

[69] Cf. Knowles's comments: Lanfranc, *MC* p. xxvi.

[70] For a general discussion of monastic cathedrals, see Knowles, *The Monastic Order*, 129–34.

[71] The pre-Conquest history of the see of Sherborne and Ramsbury is summarized by Barlow, *The English Church, 1000–1066*, 222–4.

However, twelfth-century writers attributed to him a decisive role in frustrating Bishop Walchelin of Winchester's intention at the outset of his episcopate of expelling the monks from his cathedral and replacing them by a large body of canons.[72] Walchelin was later said to have been the leader of a group of Norman bishops who wished to remove monks from all cathedrals, who gained the king's support, and who expected Lanfranc to concur; but Lanfranc straightway and decisively came to the monks' defence. There appears to be considerable exaggeration in the accounts of Walchelin's initial hostility to them, for example in the statements that before approaching Lanfranc he had some forty canons ready and vested to take over the cathedral. Two letters of Pope Alexander II, one addressed to Lanfranc and the other to the Winchester monks, in support of the latter are probably, in so far as they relate to Winchester, later forgeries.[73] There is no doubt that, after whatever initial hesitations, Walchelin came greatly to value his monastic chapter, following a monastic manner of life, favouring and fostering the cathedral monastery, and thereby winning eulogies both from William of Malmesbury and from the Winchester annalist. Probably after Lanfranc's decisive intervention, Winchester thus retained its monastic chapter.

During Lanfranc's episcopate such chapters were introduced at two other cathedrals. It was with Lanfranc's strongest prompting and support that, after Gundulf became bishop of Rochester in 1077, he replaced the handful of laxly living clerks by a community of monks on the Christ Church model. Lanfranc supplied the money for a rebuilding of the church and for the construction of monastic buildings. Under Gundulf the community rose to number some sixty monks.[74] At Durham, a chapter of Benedictine monks was introduced, or in the Durham view reconstituted, in 1083 by Bishop William of Saint-Calais (1080–96).[75] According to the principal source, Symeon of Durham, who was strongly propagandist in William's favour, in 1082 William took counsel with the king and queen and with Lanfranc about such an introduction in order to replace the clerks whom Bishop Walcher (1071–80) had made to observe a stricter regime than they had hitherto followed as lax monks.[76] Further fortified by the encouragement of Pope Gregory VII, in 1083 Bishop William brought twenty-three monks from Wearmouth and Jarrow to

---

[72] Eadmer, *Hist. nov.*, 1, pp. 18–19; William of Malmesbury, *GP* 1.44, 2.77, pp. 71–2, 172; *Ann. de Wintonia*, a. 1098, pp. 39–40. The last source quotes at length from William of Malmesbury.

[73] Alexander II, *Epp.* 143–4, *PL* 146.1416–17; for further consideration of their authenticity, see Cowdrey, 'Lanfranc, the Papacy, and the Church of Canterbury', 489, 493–5. They may have a similar origin to Alexander's supposed letter *Accepimus de quibusdam*, although their MS attestation is entirely different: see above, p. 150.

[74] *The Life of Gundulf*, cap. 17, p. 75, with excerpts from the unpublished *Vita beati Ythamari*, p. 75, nn. 9–10, and from the *Textus Roffensis*, cap. 2, p. 77; Eadmer, *Hist. nov.*, 1, p. 15; William of Malmesbury, *GP* 1.71, pp. 126–7; Lanfranc's *obit*, in Gibson, *Lanfranc*, 228.

[75] Symeon of Durham, *Libellus*, 4.1–3, pp. 224–35; William of Malmesbury, *GP* 3.133, pp. 272–3. Among recent discussions, see esp. Rollason, 'Symeon of Durham'; Aird, 'An Absent Friend' and *St Cuthbert and the Normans*, esp. 100–41; Bates, 'The Forged Charters'.

[76] Symeon of Durham, *Libellus*, 3.18, pp. 194–7; William of Malmesbury, *GP* 3.132, p. 272. For Walcher's supposed plans to introduce monks at Durham, see Symeon of Durham, *Libellus*, 3.22, pp. 210–11.

establish a monastic priory at the cathedral. Symeon's account has been challenged on several counts, notably of exaggerating the laxity of those who were replaced, of overstating the virtues of Bishop William, and of obscuring a probable political reason for the replacement of the clerks in their close connections with the family of Bamburgh who in 1080 had been responsible for the murder of Bishop Walcher.[77] Nevertheless, Lanfranc's part in introducing Benedictine monks was probably important even though it cannot be precisely documented. He was well aware of Durham's peculiarities and importance under Bishop Walcher in relation to both the ecclesiastical and the military problems of the north: an undatable letter to Walcher shows him to have been concerned by a number of points put to him, particularly about the commitment to the monastic life of a priest who was brought up in a monastery but not professed as a monk—a problem that seems to reflect anomalies in the cathedral community;[78] after the quelling of the rebellion of 1075, Lanfranc was again in touch with Walcher, praising his part in securing peace and urging him to garrison and supply his castle against an expected inroad of the Danes.[79] Lanfranc may have been made aware of and have accepted Bishop William's view that an ancient monastic church was being reconstituted at Durham; Lanfranc's monastic constitutions were among the books that William gave to his monks,[80] and twelfth-century forgers deemed the recollection of Lanfranc's concern for Durham to be strong enough to be much built upon.[81]

The monastic cathedrals so far considered have been cases where monk-bishops sought to renew or to introduce monasticism in the present cathedrals of their diocese. Other Norman bishops wished to take possession of a monastery in their diocese so that it became an episcopal monastery; securing control of the wealth of the monastery concerned was a powerful incentive. In Lanfranc's lifetime the most successful steps to this end were taken in the Somerset bishopric, that from 1060 until his death in 1088 was held by Giso with his cathedral at Wells.[82] If there is any truth in William of Malmesbury's statement that King William I frustrated any transfer of the bishop's seat to the abbey of Bath, Giso must have wished to make such a move.[83] The death in 1087 of Abbot Elfsige of Bath and the succession of King William II in the same year gave Giso's successor, John de Villula (1088–1122),

---

[77] For Walcher's death, see Symeon of Durham, *Libellus*, 3.23–4, pp. 212–21; John of Worcester, *a*. 1080, vol. 3.32–7.

[78] Lanfranc, *Letters*, no. 45, pp. 140–3.   [79] Ibid., no. 36, pp. 126–7.

[80] See above, pp. 159–60. But William's use of Prior Turgot as his deputy in the diocese during his prolonged absences rather as Lanfranc used Bishop Gundulf of Rochester was a departure from Lanfranc's view in his constitutions of the role of a monastic chapter; Symeon of Durham, *Libellus*, 4.8, pp. 244–7; William of Malmesbury, *GP* 3.133, p. 273.

[81] See e.g. *Regesta WI*, nos. 109–11, pp. 390–401.

[82] For the Somerset bishopric, see esp. *Ecclesiastical Documents*, 15–22; William of Malmesbury, *GP* 2.90, pp. 194–6 and *GR* 4.340, vol. 2.588–91. For Bishop John of Tours, or de Villula, see Smith, 'John of Tours'; for the bishopric, see *English Episcopal Acta*, 10, esp. pp. xxi–xli.

[83] *GP* 2.90, p. 194, where John de Villula is said to have failed to secure a transfer of the see to Bath in the lifetime of the elder King William; for reasons of chronology, the reference, if correct, must be to Bishop Giso. It is plausible that William I should have resisted change at Bath during the lifetime of Abbot Elfsige, who was a member of the important peace-association of Bishop Wulfstan of Worcester, six abbots, and the dean of Worcester: Thorpe, *Diplomatarium*, 615–17.

whom Lanfranc consecrated, an opportunity to buy from the new king the abbey of Bath and extensive possessions in the city. In 1090 John transferred his see to Bath; the abbey became a cathedral monastery.[84] Lanfranc's active concurrence in the preparatory stages of the transfer is apparent from his attestation of King William II's charter of 1088 concerning the gift of Bath Abbey to John, 'in order that he might establish there an episcopal seat'. Lanfranc confirmed with the unusual formula, 'Lanfranco archipraesule machinante'.[85]

It may be that Bishop Peter of Lichfield (1072–85), who in 1075 transferred his see to Chester, thereafter sought to advance his control over the abbey of Coventry. A letter of sharp rebuke from Lanfranc, sent in the king's name and his own, referred not only to harassment and depredation of Coventry but also to forcibly entering and robbing the abbey and to billeting himself and his *familia* upon the monks for eight days. This sounds like a bid to use a rich and well-situated monastery as a centre of episcopal power. Lanfranc reminded Peter of a bishop's duty towards monks of pastoral care and edifying example; his plans were not to be advanced by such high-handedness as Peter had shown. But his successor, Robert I (1086–1117), in 1102 transferred his see to Coventry which became a cathedral priory, thus fulfilling an intention which may have been forming in Lanfranc's day.[86]

Lanfranc's propagation of and provision for monastic cathedrals represents a major feature of his impact upon the English church. After his death such cathedrals were also established at Norwich and Ely, and when the see of Carlisle was set up it was given a chapter of Augustinian canons. Under the Conqueror and his sons more than half of the English dioceses came to have cathedrals with monastic chapters. They remained a feature of the English church until the dissolution. It would be wrong to represent them as exerting a major spiritual influence; Lanfranc's blueprint for Christ Church, Canterbury, expressed in his constitutions, as an internally sufficient and functioning Benedictine community could scarcely be entirely followed amid the realities of diocesan life. The cathedral monasteries shared the vicissitudes of the Benedictine life of the later middle ages, and there were tensions and distractions in their diocesan environment. Alike in their strengths and in their weaknesses, they were an enduring legacy of Lanfranc's archiepiscopate.

11.4 THREE ABBEYS

Lanfranc's dealings with three abbeys, besides those already discussed, are sufficiently documented and of sufficient importance to warrant further discussion.

---

[84] For most of the twelfth century the usual title of the bishops was 'bishop of Bath', though following the establishment of a see at Glastonbury in 1197 the title 'Bath and Glastonbury' was used from 1213 to 1219. 'Bath and Wells' was used from 1245.

[85] *Monasticon Anglicanum*, 2.266, no. 9.

[86] Lanfranc, *Letters*, no. 27, pp. 110–13. For the background, see *English Episcopal Acta*, 14, esp. pp. xxix–xxxvi. After 1102 Chester ceased until the 16th century to be a bishopric; from 1228 both Coventry and Lichfield were recognized as bishop's sees; as in Bath and Wells a monastic and a secular cathedral were paired.

11.4.1 St Albans

In 1077 Lanfranc was responsible for the appointment as abbot of St Albans of his nephew Paul, who was in office until his death in 1093.[87] Of at least half Norman parentage, Paul was held in such affection by Lanfranc that the archbishop was later rumoured to have been his natural father; this was probably an unwarranted inference from Lanfranc's bounty to St Albans. Paul had been a monk at Caen. At St Albans he gained a reputation for introducing a strict and salutary monastic discipline which, like Lanfranc at Christ Church, he prudently introduced by stages; he had a copy of Lanfranc's constitutions to which was added a brief appendix. He was a great builder, at once embarking upon a new church and eventually reconstructing most of the monastic offices. He established a scriptorium and did much to restore the abbey's possessions; he also founded a number of monastic cells. The later *Gesta abbatum monasterii sancti Albani*, which is the principal source for Paul's work, added a list of his 'negligences', which included the loss of some properties, the contemptuous destruction of the tombs of former abbots, whom he called *rudes et idiotae*, a refusal to transfer to his new church the bones of the founder, King Offa of Mercia, and bestowing abbey property on his own unworthy relatives; nevertheless, the *Gesta* concluded that the benefits of Paul's rule far outweighed the damages.

The *Gesta* made clear Lanfranc's enduring care for St Albans and its abbot. He was Paul's 'best friend and continual helper'. He contributed with great generosity to the cost of rebuilding—it was said, as much as 1,000 marks. Besides his monastic constitutions, he gave books for the scriptorium. Together with the king he advised about the restoration of the abbey's properties, and according to the *Gesta*, he counselled the establishment of cells at Wallingford and Tynemouth—both of them places with strategic significance.[88] Lanfranc's oversight of St Albans is the major example of his care for an abbey which did not become a cathedral monastery; it prepared the way for the renown of St Albans as a monastic and literary centre in succeeding centuries.

11.4.2 Bury St Edmunds

For the whole of Lanfranc's archiepiscopate the abbot of Bury St Edmunds was Baldwin (1060–97), who was physician to Kings Edward the Confessor, William I, and William II.[89] On at least one occasion Lanfranc, at William I's insistence, placed himself under Baldwin's medical care,[90] and he had other medical and business

---

[87] For Lanfranc and Paul, see esp. *Gesta abbatum mon. s. Albani*, 1.51–65; also William of Malmesbury, *GP* 1.44, 4.179, pp. 72, 317; Eadmer, *Hist. nov.*, 1, p. 15; *VL* cap. 13, p. 709; Lanfranc's *obit*: Gibson, *Lanfranc*, 228. For the letter of counsel that Paul invited from Anselm upon his appointment to St Albans, see Anselm, *Epp.* no. 80, vol. 3.203–4. As regards Lanfranc's sponsorship of his nephew, it must be remembered that, far from being seen as an abuse, the patronage of kinsmen was regarded in the middle ages as a duty and responsibility of a great and powerful man.

[88] For the problems that surrounded the acquisition of Tynemouth, see Symeon of Durham, *Libellus*, 4.4, pp. 234–7.

[89] For an overall study of Baldwin, see Gransden, 'Baldwin'.

[90] Lanfranc, *Letters*, no. 44, pp. 140–1.

dealings with him.[91] Baldwin was much at the kings' court. His abbatiate was much troubled by bishops of the East Anglian see who wished to assert jurisdiction over the abbey of Bury and who had designs to make it the seat of their bishopric.[92] When the king's chancellor Herfast was appointed to the see in 1070, the see was located at Elmham, but in 1072 he transferred it to Thetford where it remained until his death in 1084. But the threat to Bury was not finally lifted until 1094/5, when Bishop Herbert Losinga (1091–1119) settled the see at Norwich, where a monastic chapter was established. Baldwin enjoyed much support from William I and from Lanfranc, but in neither case without some qualification. The king seems at times to have wavered somewhat between favouring Herfast and Baldwin; probably after Herfast's death, he is reported to have wished Baldwin to become bishop with his see at Bury.[93] As in the case of Bath, William may have sought for strategic reasons to establish a centre of power with a bishop who controlled the resources of a wealthy monastery. While generally supporting Baldwin, Lanfranc was much concerned to keep a monastery which was free from episcopal jurisdiction within his own primatial authority.

Baldwin initially sought and secured papal approval for the independence of his abbey from episcopal claims upon it. In the autumn of 1071 he accompanied Archbishops Lanfranc and Thomas of York to Rome.[94] He secured from Pope Alexander II a privilege which took Bury under apostolic care and protection, confirmed its rights and possessions, and prohibited its being made an episcopal see, although primatial rights over it were confirmed (*salva primatis episcopi canonica reverentia*).[95] After Herfast's transfer of his see to Thetford, it appears that, from the point of view of the monks of Bury, Lanfranc had acted with less than appropriate firmness. This came to the notice of Pope Gregory VII, who on 20 November 1073 wrote to Lanfranc reproving him for allowing Herfast to act contrary to Alexander II's privilege and reminding him of papal rights and duties towards monasteries commended to the protection of the apostolic see. On Gregory's behalf, Lanfranc was to restrain Herfast and to implement the terms of Alexander's decree; Gregory was careful to keep his directions to Lanfranc within the bounds of the authority to act on the pope's behalf which Alexander II had conferred upon him.[96] Lanfranc was also to warn King William against giving any support to Herfast's designs upon Bury. If Herfast persisted with them, by apostolic authority, that is, according to his authority as defined by Alexander, Lanfranc was to order both Herfast and Abbot Baldwin to go to Rome for their dispute to be settled by the apostolic see.[97]

---

[91] Ibid., nos. 22, 41, pp. 104–5, 136–7.
[92] The main source is Hermann, *De miraculis*, caps. 25–9, pp. 60–7. Hermann was Herfast's archdeacon and secretary, and may be the subject of Lanfranc's severe censure: *Letters*, no. 47, pp. 152–3. But after Herfast's death he entered Bury as a monk; his *De miraculis* is written as a strong partisan of the abbey.
[93] Hermann, *De miraculis*, cap. 26, p. 67; Galbraith, 'The East Anglian See', 227.
[94] See above, p. 93.
[95] Alexander II, *Ep.* 81, *PL* 146.1363–4; the privilege has similarities with that which Lanfranc had secured for Saint-Étienne at Caen: see above, p. 27. William of Malmesbury particularly noticed the safeguarding of the primacy: *GP* 2.74, p. 156. Eadmer alleged that Lanfranc was so aggrieved at Alexander's privilege that he confiscated it from Baldwin and consented to return it only at the end of his life: *Hist. nov.*, 3, pp. 172–3; but there is no confirmation of this.
[96] See above, p. 89.   [97] *Reg.* 1.31, pp. 51–2.

The chronology of events in the rest of the 1070s is uncertain. However, Lanfranc's immediate response may be represented by two letters about Herfast's dealings with Bury. One, couched in very severe terms, dealt with two issues. The first concerned the particular case of Berard, a clerk and servant of Abbot Baldwin. Herfast had publicly and contumaciously rejected a letter from Lanfranc about his affairs; Herfast must answer to Lanfranc for this according to proper canonical authority and meantime suspend any sanctions of his own against Berard. The second was an injunction by Lanfranc that Herfast lay no claim against the property of Bury that could not indisputably be warranted by proofs of his predecessors. Lanfranc rebuked Herfast for his idle and trivial manner of life and exhorted him at length to the study of divinity, the decrees of Roman pontiffs, and above all the holy canons. But the main thrust of his exhortation was to due deference to the metropolitan and primatial authority of the church of Canterbury.[98] Lanfranc's reaction to a further attempt by Herfast to press claims over Bury was couched in more brotherly terms. The king had reserved for his own hearing or for Lanfranc's a lawsuit between Herfast and Abbot Baldwin about some of the latter's clerks. But the king had gone overseas with the lawsuit still unheard. So Lanfranc took action himself: Herfast was to release the clerks from excommunication and from detention without condition; Lanfranc was about to come to East Anglia and would himself bring their protracted case to a settlement, saving the fealty of the king.[99]

Bury's rights had effectively become a matter of royal justice with Lanfranc acting on behalf of the king. Thus, Hermann related how, at the king's command, Lanfranc was sent to Bury in order to discuss Herfast's claim and to consider it in the light of local testimony; at a meeting drawn from nine shires, Bury's liberty was vindicated.[100] After a time of quiet, Herfast returned to the attack. At Easter 1081 his claim was considered by an assembly comprising the two archbishops and many others. A decision in Bury's favour was embodied in a royal charter, the authenticity of which has been much disputed, though it now seems probable, and in a royal writ the authenticity of which is virtually certain. Neither Herfast nor his successor was to have any rights over the church and vill of Bury or to claim Bury as an episcopal church.[101] The matter was thus so settled that no further claim was advanced by a bishop of East Anglia until the succession of Herbert Losinga.

The case of Bury St Edmunds well illustrates the change that could come over the position of an established monastery in the time of King William I and Archbishop Lanfranc. In 1070 Abbot Baldwin, when in Rome with Lanfranc, sought protection for his abbey in a privilege of the apostolic see of which the pope would be the guarantor. Such protection gradually receded from the picture in favour of protection by English law and courts and by a royal justice. Lanfranc's visit to Bury as such and

---

[98] Lanfranc, *Letters*, no. 47, pp. 150–3.
[99] Ibid., no. 42, pp. 136–9. When neither Bury nor primatial rights were involved, Lanfranc's relations with Herfast could be even more amicable: ibid., no. 43, pp. 138–9.
[100] Hermann, *De miraculis*, cap. 27, pp. 64–5.
[101] Ibid., caps. 28–9, pp. 65–7; *Regesta WI*, 39–40, pp. 201–10, where the authenticity of no. 39 is fully discussed.

his defending Bury against Herfast by the testimony of nine shires suggest that the lesson of Penenden Heath had impressed itself upon him: the liberties of churches could be defended against arbitrary intervention and predatory seizure by the duly procured testimony of local men.[102] This implied no derogation of canon law, for Lanfranc was not behindhand in asserting his metropolitan and primatial rights on Pseudo-Isidorian lines. Customary and canon law must be made to work together. Nevertheless, in 1081 it was by royal diploma and writ, not by papal privilege, that, with Lanfranc's corroboration, Bury received the culminating guarantee of its liberties in this period. Subject to the safeguarding of the rights of the church of Canterbury, Lanfranc showed himself to be an active furtherer of this process, especially as against the claims of Herfast as diocesan.

11.4.3 St Augustine's at Canterbury

When Lanfranc arrived at Canterbury in 1070, the ruinous cathedral monastery of Christ Church, with its small community of monks, was somewhat overshadowed by the monastery of St Augustine which lay just outside the city wall to its east.[103] It traced its foundation to the mission of St Augustine, who with the sanction of Pope Gregory the Great established it to complement the cathedral by providing a burial-place for the archbishops and for the Kentish kings. Dedicated initially to St Peter and St Paul, it later received an additional dedication to St Augustine as the apostle of the English. St Augustine's was the burial church for archbishops and for the royal dynasty until the mid-eighth century; in the eleventh century it enjoyed the prestige of having the remains of the apostolic figure Augustine and of his early successors.

In Lanfranc's time the prestige of St Augustine's is marked by its abbot's attestation of both ecclesiastical and royal documents as first amongst his order.[104] Once the Danish incursions had ceased, St Augustine's experienced a time of growth, especially in its buildings, liturgy, and documentation, which lasted through and beyond the eleventh century and which was little troubled by the Norman conquest of 1066. As early landmark occurred in 1030, when Abbot Elfstan (1023/7–1045/6) brought the body of St Mildrith (died *c.*700), a princess who became abbess of Minster-in-Thanet, from her burial-place at Minster to St Augustine's.[105] The reigns of the next four abbots, Wulfric II (1045–61), Ethelsig (1061–67/70), Scotland (1070–87), and Guy (1087–93), for all their vicissitudes, witnessed a complete rebuilding of the abbey church which led in 1091 to a spectacular and epoch-making dedication ceremony.[106] The long building process testifies to the wealth of

---

[102] See above, pp. 109–15.
[103] For the history of St Augustine's and of Minster-in-Thanet, see esp. *Anglo-Saxon Charters*, 4, pp. xiii–xxxvii.
[104] See *CS* nos. 91/III, 92, vol. 1/2.603–4, 614–15; *Regesta WI*, nos. 39, 68, pp. 208, 314.
[105] Of the by now extensive literature about Mildrith, the items of greatest importance for the study of Lanfranc are: Rollason, *The Mildrith Legend*; Colker, 'A Hagiographic Polemic'; Sharpe, 'Goscelin's St Augustine'.
[106] The principal written source for the history of the rebuilding is Goscelin of Saint-Bertin's

St Augustine's, which was mainly derived from its extensive estates in East Kent and which was not seriously affected by the Norman conquest, in part because of the favour of Bishop Odo of Bayeux. Added prestige had come (or was later claimed to have come) from Pope Leo IX's fulsome favour towards Abbot Wulfric at the council of Rheims (1049) and from Pope Alexander's grant to Abbot Ethelsig of the right to wear the pontifical mitre and sandals.[107] At least up to the mid-eleventh century there is little evidence of serious rivalry between the monastic communities of Christ Church and St Augustine's or of tensions between the latter and the archbishops. Indeed, a close relationship with Stigand may have been a reason for the unexplained flight, perhaps in 1070, of Abbot Ethelsig, the monk of the Old Minster at Winchester whom Stigand had 'chosen' to be abbot and whom he had consecrated at Windsor.[108] Given the position, history, and wealth of St Augustine's, Lanfranc had perforce to determine and to pursue a policy towards it.

In the state of the evidence, some of which may be coloured by events after his death, it is difficult to establish and to appraise the steps that he took. He seems to have been determined to claim the loyalty and to control the succession of abbots. In 1070 Scotland, a Norman monk from Mont Saint-Michel, was chosen before Lanfranc arrived—perhaps at the Pentecost council at Windsor.[109] But Lanfranc consecrated him in London after his return from Rome; probably at this juncture Scotland made a written profession of obedience 'to the church of Canterbury and its vicars'.[110] The *Actus Lanfranci* recorded in graphic detail the events that followed Scotland's death in 1087.[111] At Canterbury Lanfranc examined and consecrated as abbot Guy (Wido) (1087–93), who may have been, though this cannot be demonstrated, a monk of Christ Church. Guy made a written profession in the same terms as Scotland.[112] Only after the consecration did Lanfranc, allegedly accompanied by Odo of Bayeux,[113] conduct Guy to St Augustine's and call upon the monks to obey him as their abbot. This they unanimously refused to do; Lanfranc ordered all who would not receive him forthwith to leave the abbey. Most of the monks left, and Lanfranc installed Guy in what must have been a nearly empty church. He committed the prior, Edwin, with some others to monastic custody at Canterbury, and the ringleaders of the resistance to imprisonment in the castle. When Lanfranc learnt that the monks who had left had settled below the castle near the church of St Mildrith, he presented them with the alternative of immediate return with

---

Historia translationis, written by 1099; on its significance, see Sharpe, 'The Setting of St Augustine's Translation'.

[107] See the judicious discussion by Kelly in *Anglo-Saxon Charters*, 4, pp. xxi–xxii.

[108] For Ethelsig's promotion and consecration by Stigand, see *ASC* E, *a*. 1061, pp. 135–6; for Stigand's great munificence to St Augustine's, see Gervase of Canterbury, *Acta pont.*, 363. See further Kelly, 'Some Forgeries', 365–6.

[109] John of Worcester, *a*. 1070, vol. 2.14–15, recorded that at Windsor King William gave abbeys to many Norman monks.

[110] *AL* 84–5; Woodruff, 'Some Early Professions', 60.   [111] *AL* 87–9.

[112] Woodruff, 'Some Early Professions', 61.

[113] King William I released Odo from imprisonment on his deathbed in 1087: Orderic Vitalis, 7.16, vol. 5.96–101.

impunity or of being treated as fugitives.[114] Prudence and hunger led most to return to their abbey forthwith; they were made to swear fidelity and obedience to Abbot Guy over the body of St Augustine.[115] Lanfranc seized the rest and divided them amongst English monasteries until they were compelled to profess obedience. He made a special example at Canterbury of a monk named Ailred and his associates who plotted harm to Abbot Guy by submitting them in fetters to rigorous imprisonment; when they were coerced into subjection he had mercy and allowed their return to Canterbury. Even such severe measures did not quieten opposition to Guy. Later in 1088, a group led by a certain Columbanus secretly plotted harm against the abbot. When Columbanus appeared before Lanfranc, the archbishop asked him whether he would have killed his abbot. 'If I had been able', came the answer, 'I certainly would have killed him.' Lanfranc ordered him to be tied up outside the gate of St Augustine's and in the presence of a lay crowd flogged on his naked skin;[116] he was then unfrocked and driven from the city. 'Thereby,' commented the *Actus Lanfranci*, Lanfranc 'by the fear that he struck crushed the disturbance of the other monks for so long as he lived.' Only by such repression did Lanfranc manage to suppress for a time the hostility that his attempt to impose Abbot Guy had aroused.

It has been suggested that the principal reason for Lanfranc's problems with the monks of St Augustine's was racial: the monks were largely if not entirely English, and they resisted any attempt to impose Norman authority.[117] Such resistance was probably a factor; its named leaders had English names, and apart from Abbot Scotland there was no such leaven of Norman choir monks and no such connections with Norman monasteries as was the case at Christ Church. But during Lanfranc's last years he was associated with other events that were unpalatable to St Augustine's. Lanfranc's foundation in 1085 of St Gregory's priory may have been seen as an infringement of the abbey's burial rights, with their accompanying fees. This is not proven, but the dedication to St Gregory implied a claim to Canterbury's early past of which the abbey felt itself to be the principal custodian. Much more seriously, it cannot have been without Lanfranc's knowledge and complicity that, some two years later, the clerks of St Gregory's brought, not from Minster-in-Thanet but from Lyminge, what they claimed to be the relics of St Mildrith and the next abbess of Minster, St Eadburg. The relics were buried at St Gregory's, which thus challenged the authenticity of the cult of Mildrith that had been established there since 1030. Tracts were quickly written to support the claim of St Gregory's to possess the true relics;[118] after Goscelin of Saint-Bertin came to St Augustine's in 1089 he wrote a critical and effective demolition of the claim in his *Libellus contra*

---

[114] For the treatment of fugitives, see Lanfranc, *MC* cap. 101, pp. 152–5.
[115] Despite the prohibition of oaths in *RSB* cap. 4.27, vol. 1.458–9.
[116] The severity of the punishment that Lanfranc imposed was not greater than was prescribed at Cluny according to Bernard's chapter *De fugitivis*: 1.58, pp. 252–5, which Lanfranc may have had in mind. In Bernard, a monk who offended outside the monastery was to be publicly stripped before a crowd of local people and severely beaten (*publice . . . exuetur et horribilitere verberabitur*): p. 254.
[117] See Knowles, *The Monastic Order*, 115–16; but for a wider explanation, cf. Gibson, *Lanfranc*, 189–90.
[118] See esp. the *Vita sanctorum Aethelredi et Aethelberti*.

inanes S. Mildrethae usurpatores.[119] According to the St Gregory's story, the bodies of the two saints were brought from Lyminge at Lanfranc's order and interred by Bishop Gundulf of Rochester with great solemnity.[120] Goscelin claimed that the supporting literature was the work of an unnamed Christ Church monk (*unus fratrum aecclesiae domini*).[121] But Goscelin also referred to Lanfranc as seeking to quieten the rivalry that followed the coming of the relics. At Abbot Scotland's request, he instructed the clerks of St Gregory's to celebrate St Mildrith with due restraint and reverence (*modeste*); for a while they complied, and probably did so until after Lanfranc's death.[122]

It appears likely that the tensions and conflicts of Lanfranc's last years were more the result of his high-handed imposition of Abbot Guy and of the dispute about the relics of St Mildrith than of endemic ill-feeling between English and Norman monasticism and personalities. During Abbot Scotland's lifetime the two communities could come together. When Lanfranc arrived at Canterbury in 1070 he was solemnly welcomed by the convent of Christ Church to whom were joined that of St Augustine's led by Scotland, the abbot-elect.[123] Eadmer later recalled that, soon after, he had been there when, with a great concourse of Canterbury people, both communities again came together for the first translation of St Dunstan's relics; Scotland was present.[124] Scotland later witnessed from his own garden the descent of St Dunstan to keep his vigil with the monks of Christ Church; he saw it with the appearance of satisfaction.[125]

There are indications that Lanfranc was on occasion helpful to St Augustine's in the defence of its revenues and property. The Domesday Book relates that Lanfranc and Odo of Bayeux together put a stop to the injustice of one Bruman the reeve in taking tolls from foreign merchants on the land of Holy Trinity (Christ Church) and St Augustine's; henceforth both churches were to possess the customary dues on their land under the judgement of the king's judges (*barones*) who held the plea.[126] Again, in a writ datable to 1077 and witnessed by Odo of Bayeux, the king charged Lanfranc and others to reseise Abbot Scotland with the *burgus* of Fordwich and with all lands lost under the fugitive Abbot Ethelsig; all violently misappropriated properties were to be recovered.[127] On the other hand, it is now believed that

---

[119] See Colker, 'A Hagiographic Polemic', for discussion and an edition of the texts.

[120] *Vita sanctorum Aethelredi et Aethelberti*, cap. 21, p. 108.

[121] Goscelin, *Libellus*, cap. 21, pp. 89–90. For an attractive suggestion that the monk was Osbern, see Rubenstein, 'The Life and Writings of Osbern', 33–4.

[122] Goscelin, *Libellus*, cap. 1, pp. 70–1.   [123] *AL* 84.

[124] Eadmer, *Ep. ad Glastonienses*, in: *Reliquiae Dunstanianae*, 413–14. Scotland's presence is confirmed by a miracle story told by both Osbern and Eadmer: two of Lanfranc's knights had broken the king's peace by killing two other knights who were Scotland's relatives; those guilty grasped Dunstan's feretory and asked for pardon which Scotland would not grant without punishment; next night Dunstan appeared to Scotland with a warning of dire consequences unless he granted forgiveness, which he now did: Osbern, *Mirac.*, cap. 17, pp. 142–3; Eadmer, *Mirac.*, cap. 14, pp. 232–3. Cf. another story in Osbern according to which he had talked to a knight in Thanet whom Dunstan had upheld against Scotland in a secular lawsuit: *Mirac.*, cap. 24, pp. 156–8. These stories suggest that secular issues involving their Norman lay dependants had their part in colouring relations between Christ Church and St Augustine's.

[125] Eadmer, *Mirac.*, cap. 15, pp. 233–4.   [126] *DB Kent*, no. 2.8, fo. 2^r.

[127] *Regesta WI*, no. 83, pp. 348–9, see also no. 88, pp. 356–7.

the vast work at St Augustine's of forging documents to establish its freedom may not have progressed during the later eleventh century so far as has been thought.[128] There is much to suggest that, for all the problems in relations between Christ Church and St Augustine's, Lanfranc and Abbot Scotland established a *modus vivendi* that lasted until the latter's death. This is clearly indicated by Lanfranc's restraining hand upon the clerks of St Gregory's in their promotion of St Mildrith.[129] It is also apparent in Goscelin's remark in his obituary of Scotland that the latter died amongst abundant almsgiving and with Lanfranc overseeing his obsequies (*famosissimo archipraesule Lanfranco omnem ordinem servicii persolvente*).[130]

Nevertheless, upon Lanfranc's death it was speedily apparent how fragile was a peace that rested too much upon a resolute archbishop's repression of the turbulent and sparing of the unwillingly submissive. According to the *Actus Lanfranci*, the monks openly resisted Abbot Guy and incited citizens of Canterbury to seek his life. There were deaths on both sides but Guy fled unharmed to Christ Church. King William II provided Bishops Walchelin of Winchester and Gundulf with an armed force to restore order. The bishops judged the monks' actions to be culpable and inexcusable. Under the bishops' direction they were sentenced to corporal discipline. In response to a plea of the prior and monks of Christ Church, this was administered not publicly but in the abbey of St Augustine. Those guilty were then dispersed amongst the monasteries of the kingdom; they were replaced by twenty-four monks from Christ Church, from where a new prior was also introduced. The citizens involved who could not purge their guilt had their eyes put out.[131]

By such drastic action, which involved a substantial replacement of expelled monks by others from Christ Church, the stability of St Augustine's was restored. Abbot Guy whom Lanfranc had appointed remained in office until his death; so soon as 1091 he was able to arrange the impressive festivities that marked the translation of St Augustine in the newly completed church.[132] Goscelin of Saint-Bertin was able to recount the fifty-year rebuilding without reference to the upheavals of Guy's early years, although he implied that the ceremony of 1091 was an occasion of reconciliation.[133]

So far as Lanfranc's dealings with St Augustine's are concerned, it seems clear that the abbey's antiquity, prestige, and wealth made it very difficult for him to do more than react piecemeal to circumstances; he had no *point d'appui* for more than occasional intervention. In the time of the capable Abbot Scotland there was a sufficient will on the part of both monastic communities to maintain harmony and co-operation; Lanfranc and Abbot Scotland established a working *modus vivendi* that was to the advantage of both. In choosing as Scotland's successor a monk, Guy, from another community, Lanfranc probably did not consider himself to be acting beyond the precedents of the introduction of the Winchester monk Wulfric by Stigand or of the Norman monk Scotland by King William I or the papal legates of 1070; both choices had been beneficial. In the event, the probable resentment by

---

[128] See Kelly's discussion: *Anglo-Saxon Charters*, 4, pp. lxii–lxxi.   [129] As above, n. 122.
[130] Goscelin, *Hist. trans.*, 2.41, col. 46.   [131] *AL* 88–9.   [132] As n. 106.
[133] Goscelin, *Hist. trans.*, 1.13, col. 19. Goscelin addressed his tract to Archbishop Anselm.

English monks against Normans combined with the recent controversy about St Mildrith and aspirations at St Augustine's for the freedom and autonomy of the abbey to release the violence that followed Guy's arrival. Lanfranc's reaction was heavy-handed and repressive, merely driving the monks' opposition underground until violence recurred after his death. The measures taken by the bishops of Winchester and Rochester were such as Lanfranc himself might have imposed: they were drastic but, in their own terms, effective. Abbot Guy remained actively in office and the great celebration of 1091 demonstrated the prosperity and achievement of the abbey. But underlying problems were not mitigated, let alone resolved, save in so far as many former St Augustine's monks were removed and replaced from Christ Church. A campaign of forgery reinforced the claims of St Augustine's to autonomy, and the arrival of Goscelin of Saint-Bertin furnished it with fresh resources in the debate about St Mildrith. Future archbishops were left with a situation that was essentially unchanged, save that the cathedral monastery of Christ Church was greatly enlarged and invigorated both as a monastic community and as a primatial church.

11.5 SEVERITY AND MERCY

Lanfranc's dealings with the monks of St Augustine's who resisted his choice of the external monk Guy to be their abbot were characterized by a severity which to the modern mind suggests that his character included a streak of harshness, even though it was mitigated by a degree of mercy towards those who were coerced into compliance. A reading of Lanfranc's monastic constitutions reinforces the impression of severity by the repeated prescriptions of severe corporal punishment and penance.[134] Some further appraisal of Lanfranc's exercise of severity and mercy within the monastic order may be attempted as it is illustrated by those of his letters that do not concern monasteries so far considered; although the letters are few in number and can represent only a small part of his correspondence, they are sufficient to provide an indication of his practice.

They illustrate how a successful eleventh-century monastic ruler governed, and might be seen to govern, according to Virgil's epitome of the ruling skills of ancient Rome: 'to impose good custom upon peace, to spare the submissive, and to subdue the proud (*pacique imponere morem, parcere subiectis, et debellare superbos*)'.[135] As Lanfranc said in no uncertain terms to Abbot Odo of Chertsey whom he deemed to have been lax in allowing a monk to travel about, he expected an abbot to show strictness and not to act with a naivety (*simplicitas*) that undermined monastic order; Lanfranc remedied the abbot's weakness by summarily ordering the monk back to his monastery.[136] If, as seems probable, Lanfranc's letter of advice to an

---

[134] See above, p. 157.
[135] Virgil, *Aeneid*, 6.852–3. Thus, Pope Gregory VII used approvingly to call Abbot Hugh of Cluny (1049–1109) 'blandus tirranus' because he saw him as 'sevis leonem mitibus agnum' and 'haud ignarum parcere subiectis et castigare superbos': Gilo, *Vita s. Hugonis*, 1.7, p. 57.
[136] *Letters*, no. 48, pp. 154–5.

Abbot Thurstan was addressed to the abbot of Glastonbury whose use of his lay knights to repress a rebellion of his monks over a new style of liturgical chanting led to the killing of several monks in the abbey church, then he was very restrained in his counsel to an abbot who had exercised his punitive authority with unwarrantable severity.[137] Perhaps more characteristic of Lanfranc in his insistence upon the upholding of monastic discipline was his letter to Bishop Maurice of London asking him to end a quarrel between the abbess and prioress of Barking. Under the Rule of St Benedict, they were to show the mutual command and obedience that were canonically proper within an ordered community. If either refused, she must be sternly rebuked and constrained with due severity to good conduct. If all else failed, Lanfranc would himself visit the guilty person with rigorous discipline.[138] Even if they were monastic rulers, offenders were to be firmly subdued for the health of their communities.

Lanfranc's concern for the good order of communities was complemented by a care for individual monks within them. He could behave with restraint and tactfulness about a misdirection of his own. When a monk whom he had caused to be admitted to the New Minster at Winchester proved to be a source of difficulty, he left its resolution to the authorities at Winchester, remarking only upon his aversion to pride: 'I do not want to nourish pride, which I wish to be far removed from every sort of men, and especially from our monastic order.'[139] A letter to Abbot Adelelm of Abingdon shows that, when gravely offending monks who had fled their monastery had duly repented and submitted to his reproof, he was willing to entreat their abbot in the spirit of St Paul's Epistle to Philemon to restore them fully to their places in their monastery.[140] Lanfranc also sought to secure good treatment from his abbot for a monk who had incurred the king's disfavour—in Lanfranc's view unjustly.[141] King and archbishop concurred in the view that English women who had taken refuge in a monastery from fear of the French invaders should be free to depart.[142] Lanfranc was much concerned for the spiritual and monastic progress of individual monks, such as his own nephew Lanfranc and his confrère Guy at Bec, about whom he wrote to their abbot, Anselm, and mentor, Gilbert Crispin.[143] His concern extended to physical health; when counselling a sick monk about his spiritual disposition he appended advice that he take as a remedy the herb *marrubium* (white horehound), sending a supply and detailing the dose.[144]

Such evidence as may be gleaned from Lanfranc's letters suggests that he exhibited a combination of severity arising from an insistence upon authority and obedience with a pastoral care for the duly subject which arose from mercy and charity. He thus met contemporary expectations of those with oversight of monks and

---

[137] Ibid., no. 57, pp. 172–3; for the events referred to at Glastonbury, see *ASC* E, *a*. 1083, p. 160; *Ann. mon. de Wintonia*, *a*. 1083, p. 33; John of Worcester, *a*. 1083, vol. 3.38–41; William of Malmesbury, *GP* 2.91, p. 197, *GR* 3.270, vol. 1.498–9, and *The Early History*, ed. Scott, cap. 78, pp. 176–9; Orderic Vitalis, 4, vol. 2.270–1.
[138] *Letters*, no. 59, pp. 174–5.   [139] Ibid., no. 55, pp. 168–71.   [140] Ibid., no. 28, pp. 112–15.
[141] Ibid., no. 58, pp. 172–5.   [142] Ibid., no. 53, pp. 166–7.
[143] Ibid., nos. 18–20, pp. 96–103.   [144] Ibid., no. 21, pp. 102–5.

monasteries. When the Peterborough chronicler recorded Lanfranc's death, he described him as 'the reverend father and consoler of monks'.[145] Monastic writers regarded him personally with deep reverence. Thus, for the Canterbury monk Osbern, an Englishman, he was a venerable man who was at once the holiest and the wisest of all in the country during his age.[146] Goscelin of Saint-Bertin addressed him as one 'filled with all wisdom from God'.[147] John of Worcester accumulated superlatives—most learned, most skilled, most prudent—to describe his abilities in both spiritual and secular affairs;[148] the *Vita Lanfranci* extolled his monastic virtues, placing first his wisdom.[149] His fatherhood towards monks both as an order and as individuals was also affirmed. He himself wrote that bishops and abbots had in common a fatherly care over their subjects that was exercised in the name of Christ.[150] His monk Eadmer wrote of him as having excelled in authority and manifold knowledge; he praised Lanfranc's prudence and fatherly oversight of his community at Canterbury as well as of his renewal of religion through all orders of the kingdom.[151] When applauding the many virtues of *pater Lanfrancus*, William of Malmesbury singled out his almsgiving, by which he bountifully helped needy clerks and monasteries.[152] Lanfranc's reputation for such bounty is well illustrated by a letter of Anselm about a moneyer of Arras whose debts Lanfranc had expressed willingness to relieve in the sum of 200 shillings and perhaps more, in order that he might become a monk: the moneyer should not hesitate to take advantage, 'for the reverend archbishop is a man of the utmost mercy, and especially towards the salvation of souls; and he is greatly given to alms and sufficiently abounds in gold and silver'.[153]

Such eulogies of Lanfranc must mainly be tested from the evidence gathered in the foregoing sections of this chapter. They find support above all in Lanfranc's rule of the monks of whom he was ex officio abbot at Christ Church, Canterbury; in his gradual introduction of stricter monastic life; in his programme of rebuilding; and in his pastoral care of individual monks. His monastic constitutions stand as testimony to his skill in regulating the round of divine service and the administration and discipline of a black-monk house. He exercised a firm oversight of the interests of other monasteries, especially in face of the claims of bishops. He was vigilant and effective in assisting the recovery of lost possessions and in the securing of present ones. All in all, his concern for the monastic order was central to his exercise of the office of archbishop, and it was on balance highly beneficial in its effects.

[145] *ASC* E, a. 1089, p. 168.
[146] Osbern, *Mirac.*, cap. 17, p. 142; see also his letter to Anselm: Anselm, *Epp.* no. 149, vol. 4.10.
[147] Goscelin, *Vita s. Edithae*, Pref., 34–5.
[148] John of Worcester, a. 1070, vol. 3.14–15. [149] *VL* cap. 17, p. 714.
[150] Lanfranc, *MC* cap. 1, pp. 4–5. [151] Eadmer, *VA* cap. 30, p. 1.30; p. 50; *Hist. nov.*, 1, pp. 12–13.
[152] William of Malmesbury, *GP* 1.43, pp. 68–9. [153] Anselm, *Epp.* no. 15, vol. 3.120.

12

Lanfranc and the English

'But I am a new Englishman (*Ego tamen novus Anglus*) and still almost ignorant of English matters save in so far as I gather them from others': thus Lanfranc wrote in 1072 to Pope Alexander II.[1] The phrase *novus Anglus* may have had some currency as used of churchmen from Normandy who were given high office in England, with regard both to their positions in the ancient provinces of the English church and to the problems set by their encounters with the laws and customs of that church.[2] In Lanfranc's case, the process of learning and accommodation is said to have taken some years. On Eadmer's evidence, when Anselm of Bec made his first visit to England in 1079 Lanfranc was still imperfectly schooled as an Englishman (*Erat . . . quasi rudis Anglus*): certain usages that he had found there were not as yet approved in his mind—accordingly he had changed many of them, sometimes fortified by good reason and sometimes by the decision of his sole authority; again, it was as a new citizen of England (*sicut novus Angliae civis*) that Lanfranc submitted for Anselm's advice the problem of St Elphege's commemoration.[3] The phrase *novus Anglus* seems to signify Lanfranc's identification of himself with his English as well as with his French subjects, much as he had identified himself with those amongst whom he had settled in Normandy. But his identification was to be a considered one, established over ample time and duly tested by his informed judgement and authority.

There has been considerable debate amongst historians about the process by which Lanfranc established his ultimate view of English saints. It has involved the wider question of the attitude of Norman abbots to the traditions and observances of their English subjects. In a much-discussed paragraph, Dom David Knowles numbered among the grievances of English monks the outrage that they often felt in face of their abbots' disrespectful attitude towards the old English saints.[4] He particularly cited Lanfranc's nephew, Paul of St Albans, who destroyed the tombs of his predecessors whom he called *rudes et idiotae*,[5] and Walter of Evesham, who on Lanfranc's advice examined his abbey's relics, putting doubtful ones to a kind of ordeal

---

[1] Lanfranc, *Letters*, no. 2, pp. 36–9.

[2] Thus, Lanfranc referred to Archbishop Thomas of York's initial refusal of a profession of obedience accompanied by an oath as the response of a 'novus . . . homo et Anglicae consuetudinis penitus expers'; William of Malmesbury wrote that Thomas claimed jurisdiction over the diocese of Worcester 'seu quod novus Anglus esset seu aliquorum susurrio persuasus': Lanfranc, *Letters*, no. 3/1, pp. 40–1; William of Malmesbury, *VW* 2.1, p. 24.

[3] *VA* 1.30, pp. 50–2. Brooke argues that Lanfranc's meeting with Anselm might be dated earlier than 1079: Lanfranc, *MC* pp. xxix–xxx; but it is plausible that Lanfranc at that date still felt himself a novice and at sea with the English calendar, and so expressed himself to Anselm.

[4] Knowles, *The Monastic Order*, 118–19.   [5] See above, p. 164.

by fire,[6] amongst several other cases. Knowles extended his illustrations to Lanfranc himself, who, when Anselm of Bec visited him in 1079, 'deplored the English cult of worthies of questionable sanctity, alleging St Aelfheah [Elphege] as a case in point'.[7] Only at length did Lanfranc come to appreciate some, at least, of his saintly predecessors.

Such a view, which has been widely followed,[8] in part owed its propagation to a comparison made by the nineteenth-century liturgist Edmund Bishop between the calendars in the Bosworth Psalter, now British Library, MS Addit. 37517, a late Anglo-Saxon manuscript which he assigned to Christ Church, Canterbury,[9] and in the Arundel Psalter, BL MS Arundel 155, which he regarded as a post-Conquest source embodying the then calendar of Winchester; Lanfranc introduced it at Canterbury in place of that previously followed there. The second calendar omitted many saints and feasts that appeared in the first; Bishop deemed the omissions to reflect Lanfranc's liturgical reformation at Canterbury during his early years there.[10] But it is now recognized that MS Arundel 155 was written at Christ Church between 1012 and 1023;[11] it is not evidence for Lanfranc and his time.

There has, accordingly, been a strong tendency amongst recent scholars to question whether Norman churchmen in general disparaged the sanctity of the English men and women whom they found to be venerated in their churches, and whether in particular Lanfranc, at least to begin with, purged the Canterbury calendar of many English saints and reduced or suspended the recognition of his predecessors as archbishop, Dunstan (959–88) and Elphege (1006–12).[12] For present purposes, four points may be made about the newer view.

First, a significant addition to the evidence for the observance of Christ Church, Canterbury, has been made by the recognition that the calendar in Oxford, Bodleian Library, MS Addit. C. 260 probably provides the earliest evidence for the post-Conquest calendar of the cathedral.[13] Although the manuscript probably dates from the 1120s, there are reasons for dating the basic entries of the calendar to the 1090s and so to a date very soon after Lanfranc's death. The calendar thus invites comparison with the pre-Conquest Christ Church example in Arundel 155 and also with appropriate calendars in Normandy, especially as connected with Bec. Such

---

[6] *Acta proborum virorum* and *Vita s. Wistani*, in Appendix to *Chron. abb. de Evesham*, 323–4, 335–6.
[7] As n. 4.
[8] e.g. Stenton, *Anglo-Saxon England*, 664; Gibson, *Lanfranc*, 171–3; Barlow, *The English Church 1066–1154*, 191; Rollason, *The Mildrith Legend*, 59; Klukas, 'The Architectural Implications'.
[9] The Bosworth Psalter is now considered to be from St Augustine's: Orchard, 'The Bosworth Psalter'.
[10] Gasquet and Bishop, *The Bosworth Psalter*, esp. 27–34. The calendars are edited by Wormald in *English Kalendars before A.D. 1100*, no. 5, pp. 58–69 (Bosworth), 13, pp. 169–81 (Arundel).
[11] See Pfaff, 'Lanfranc's Supposed Purge', 96–8, and 'Eadui Basan'.
[12] The most convincing statement of the revised view remains Ridyard, 'Condigna veneratio'. See also Rollason, *Saints and Relics*, 215–39; Pfaff (as n. 11); Gibson, 'Normans and Angevins', esp. 42–4. Rollason and Gibson somewhat modify their earlier views: see n. 8; Gibson in 1978 wrote that 'Initially both Dunstan and Elphege were removed from the kalendar': *Lanfranc*, 171. For a recent view which again emphasizes the radical and distinctive character of Lanfranc's work, see Rubenstein, 'Liturgy Against History'. For further surveys, see Crook, *The Architectural Setting*, 176–81, 206–9, and Brooke, in *Lanfranc, MC* pp. xxviii–xxx, xxxvi–xxxviii.
[13] See Heslop, 'The Canterbury Calendars'; he edits the text at pp. 70–7.

comparison indicates that Bec provided the basis of the post-Conquest Canterbury calendar.[14] As with his monastic constitutions so with his calendar, Lanfranc did not follow pre-Conquest English usage but looked across the Channel for his models. The brevity of the calendar in MS Addit. C. 260 tends to confirm that Lanfranc curtailed the observances of Christ Church. Nevertheless, the evidence is strongly that he did so with no special prejudice against English saints. Of twenty-seven feasts present in Arundel 155 but omitted in Addit. C. 260, only eight are of English saints; those omitted had little or nothing to do with Christ Church. Overall, the omissions seem to be of feasts unfamiliar at Bec and to the Bec monks who came to Canterbury; they were not discarded merely because they were English. Only a very few additions were made to the Canterbury calendar—perhaps not more than five, while some twelve of the twenty-one feasts originally in Addit. C. 260 but not in the calendar of Bec were of an insular character.[15] If, as seems likely, Addit. C. 260 indicates the full extent and character of Lanfranc's purge of the pre-Conquest calendar, it points to a break with the past which was major and radical but which was not directed against English saints and festivals. The purpose was to remove saints having little national or local significance and drastically to reduce those not familiar at Bec. No attempt was made to introduce commemorations that would be uncongenial to English monks. There was little by which local sensitivities might justly be offended.[16]

Second, Norman abbots like Paul of St Albans were manifestly sometimes insensitive and even offensive in their words and actions regarding their English predecessors. But it has not always been noticed that, for the most part, they had in view earlier abbots rather than the saints, and especially the major saints, of their houses. When English saints were called in question and their relics put to the test of ordeal, by current standards appropriate pieties and procedures were observed and saints whose relics survived the test continued to receive honour and commemoration. The case of Evesham may serve as an example.[17] When Walter of Cerisy became abbot in 1077, he felt serious doubts about the saints of the abbey, including Wistan and the little-known Credan. In putting their relics to the test of fire, he took steps to proceed with due solemnity and authority. As a preparation, he appointed a three-day fast and took the advice of Archbishop Lanfranc. During the testing, the seven penitential psalms and appropriate litanies were chanted. When the relics were abundantly warranted by their testing, they were restored to due honour; indeed, those of St Credan were translated to a place of greater dignity. It was expressly remembered that Walter sought to avoid seeming to dishonour the English by thus proceeding (*ne Anglicorum agitatus invidia haec agere videretur, et quia timor Dei super omnes est, triduanum fratribus indixit ieiunium . . .*).[18] One may detect in the records a strong note of resentment on the part of the English that their saints should be put into question. But Walter clearly considered their sensibilities and honoured the saints of the abbey when they were duly tested.

---

[14] Ibid. 55–6, with Table 1, p. 78.   [15] Ibid., Table 3, p. 81.
[16] Heslop's conclusions are summarized in ibid. 59, 62, 66–8.
[17] As n. 6. See further Ridyard (as n. 12), 204–5.   [18] *Vita s. Wistani* (as n. 6), 335.

For, third, it has been impressively argued that nationality was not of more than secondary importance in determining the attitude of Norman bishops and abbots towards English saints and their relics; the view that Norman churchmen were radically sceptical of them is a myth. In a society deeply disordered by the Norman conquest and its aftermath, the protection of generally acknowledged saints was essential in order both to safeguard authority and discipline within monastic communities and to protect the property, rights, and interests of those communities from ecclesiastical and lay interventions and depredations. In established monasteries, the most effective patrons were likely to be those already in place. Therefore there was a pressure upon Norman churchmen to be sure of their authenticity, especially when the saints concerned were hitherto unfamiliar to them, when relics might seem to be insufficiently authenticated, and when there was a dearth of hagiographical literature. So the testing of relics as at Evesham was indicated, not in order to discredit but to accredit them; and the Norman period in English history was prolific in the writing of saints' Lives and the compilation of collections of miracle stories, especially concerning English saints.[19]

Fourth, it is important not to be misled by the language that Norman churchmen sometimes used of their English subjects on account of its modern connotations. This is especially the case with the noun *barbari* and its cognates. In 1073, for example, when Lanfranc wrote to Pope Alexander II with a request that he be allowed to resign his see, he said that the excuse of an unknown language and of barbarous peoples (*excusatio incognitae linguae gentiumque barbararum*) had not availed in 1070 to prevent his appointment.[20] Anselm from Bec commended to his monk Herluin his confrère Maurice who was at Canterbury 'so that he might be glad to have found a brother amongst the *barbari*'.[21] Writing in 1077 to the monk Paul upon his preferment to be abbot of St Albans, Anselm commented that he was promoted to rule over *barbari* (*barbaris vestra praelata sit sanctitas*) whom he could not teach by words on account of the diversity of languages.[22] Such references to *barbari* should be understood in the light of the vocabulary of the Latin Bible. There, St Paul used it of speaking an unintelligible language (1 Cor. 14: 11) and of what is alien, without pejorative connotation (Rom. 1: 14, Col. 3: 11; cf. Acts 28: 1. 4). In a Psalm, it occurs once to express positive racial otherness (Ps. 133: 1); with a strong connotation of alien and hostile, indeed sinful, it appears only in 2 Macc. 2: 22; 10: 4. The prevailing sense is of otherness and contrast, especially in respect of spoken language. It was in such a sense that Anselm used it in his counsel to Paul of St Albans: whatever he could not convey to his monks by speech he must convey by quality of life and example, by pastoral care, and by being loved for mildness and mercy rather than feared on account of severity.[23] Paul did not act entirely within the spirit of this advice.[24] But

---

[19] See esp. Ridyard's fundamental study (as n. 12); she examines the cases of Ely, Bury St Edmunds, St Albans, Abingdon, Malmesbury, Durham, and Evesham with particular effectiveness.
[20] Lanfranc, *Letters*, no. 1, pp. 30–1.   [21] Anselm, *Epp.* no. 35, vol. 3.143.
[22] Ibid., no. 80, vol. 3.203.   [23] There is no advice about learning the English language.
[24] See above, p. 164.

Osbern's account of Lanfranc's own early dealings with his young monks in the Egelward incident suggest a concern to treat them in accordance with it.[25]

If the evidence, slight and difficult to interpret though it is, for Lanfranc's attitude to the saints of Canterbury, especially Dunstan and Elphege, is reviewed in the light of these considerations, it points to no radical hostility or even scepticism on his part, but only to a desire to be sure about how they should be commemorated and to consolidate the position of Christ Church within the church of Canterbury. At the very outset of Lanfranc's archiepiscopate, Eadmer's recollections of his preparation for the rebuilding of his cathedral church convey a strong intimation of the honour that he accorded to his predecessors Dunstan and Elphege. Writing to the monks of Glastonbury c.1120, Eadmer attested that when Lanfranc first removed Dunstan from his place of burial he did so with great solemnity. He appointed a fast of all the people of Canterbury. On the day of the translation, the monastic communities of both Christ Church and St Augustine's were assembled for the opening of the tomb; a throng of men and women accompanied the body to its new resting-place with joyful chanting, and many miracles added to the solemnity and joy of the occasion.[26] Eadmer had the ulterior purpose of proving to the monks of Glastonbury the authenticity of Dunstan's relics; but his case would have been undermined if his recollection could be shown to be false. And Eadmer had also remembered in his tract on St Ouen that, in Lanfranc's day, he had witnessed the exhumation of Dunstan and Elphege, the principal fathers of Christ Church, along with many other saints.[27]

If Lanfranc recognized the greater and lesser saints of Christ Church as signally as Eadmer recalled, it is difficult to envisage that, during his early years, he made any drastic purging of its calendar or that he suspended the prominent observance of Dunstan and Elphege. While there is some evidence for a post-Conquest discontinuance of external visits to Dunstan's resting-place,[28] there is no positive trace of a cessation of the feasts of Dunstan, Elphege, or major English saints.[29] Instead, there seems to have been a gradual and case-by-case review which was not incompatible with continuing observance while matters were still *sub iudice*. This is indicated by Eadmer's depiction of Lanfranc's slow testing of English customs and of his changing some with good reason and some by his mere authority.[30] Two factors may have

---

[25] See above, pp. 151–3.

[26] Eadmer, *Ep. ad Glastonienses*, in *Reliquiae Dunstanianae*, 413–4; cf. Osbern, *Mirac.*, 17, pp. 142–3. See above, pp. 79, 170.

[27] Eadmer, *De reliquiis s. Audoeni*, in Wilmart, *Opuscula*, 366.

[28] Thus, the Norman Conquest led to a cessation of the annual visit by Glastonbury monks to honour the saint's festival: Eadmer, *Ep. ad Glastonienses*, in *Reliquiae Dunstanianae*, 421–2. But there is no implication that the feast itself was discontinued; the ruinous state of Christ Church after the fire of 1067 and difficulties of travel in the aftermath of the conquest could be reasons why the Glastonbury monks no longer came.

[29] It is not proved by Osbern's remark about Lanfranc in a letter of 1093 to Anselm that 'novimus sanctissimum praedecessorem tuam multa primo adventus sui tempore ordinasse, quae omni tempore sibi postmodum displicuere': Anselm, *Epp.* no. 149, vol. 4.6–10, at p. 10: although Lanfranc may have come to regret early decisions about some matters relating to the calendar.

[30] Eadmer, *VA* 1.30, pp. 50–1.

contributed to Lanfranc's doubts about saints honoured at Canterbury and also have protracted the process of their resolution. First, there was uncertainty about the authenticity of the relics of even some major saints. Eadmer recalled how, after Lanfranc's death, the monk Osbern had told him of the archbishop's order that the reliquaries of Christ Church should be opened and their contents investigated. But this was done only in part: out of fear, one was left alone; only later did Osbern surreptitiously open it so that relics of Pope Gregory the Great and St Ouen were duly attested by their parchment labels.[31] Second, besides the problem of unauthenticated relics, there was sometimes a dearth of written records upon which, according to a Canterbury tradition, Lanfranc set weight. According to Gervase of Canterbury, it raised doubts in his mind about the sanctity of Archbishops Bregwine (761–4), Ethelheard (793–805), and Elfric (995–1005) that it was not attested by reliable writings.[32]

It is against the background of Lanfranc's apparent initial recognition of Dunstan and Elphege, and of the gradualness and uncertainty of his subsequent dealings about the saints of Christ Church, that his much-discussed exchange of 1079 with Anselm about the sanctity of Elphege must be considered.[33] Eadmer's account leaves little room for doubt that Lanfranc was perplexed not about the fact of Elphege's sanctity but its degree. For liturgical purposes there was a gradation of saints according to which martyrs ranked higher than confessors or virgins. It was altogether possible for Lanfranc to be thus troubled in his own mind while in public worship Elphege was being without challenge accorded the honour of sanctity. Eadmer introduced Lanfranc's private consultation of Anselm by having the archbishop reflect that, when he turned over in his mind some whom the English honoured as saints, he could not suppress his doubts about the quality (not the fact) of their sanctity: *de sanctitatis eorum merito*. About Elphege he could not but wonder that the English venerated him not only among the saints but also among the martyrs, when he was admitted to have been killed by the Danes not for confessing Christ but for refusing to redeem himself by money, thereby pauperizing his own men. Anselm replied philosophically that Elphege died for truth and justice, which was to die for Christ; after Anselm's lengthy argument, Lanfranc affirmed that, taught by his solid reason, he would henceforth celebrate and honour Elphege as indeed a great and glorious martyr of Christ. His rank among the saints had been made clear.

An interpolation of Eadmer's own into the story is further evidence that Elphege's rank of martyr was the point at issue.[34] Before embarking upon Anselm's philosophical case, he commented that if the matter were regarded from a historical viewpoint (*historialiter*) a more fundamental case was to be found. It was remembered that he had not only refused to buy his life with money but had suffered

---

[31] Eadmer, *De reliquiis s. Audoeni*, in Wilmart, *Opuscula*, 367–8.
[32] Gervase of Canterbury, *Acta pont.*, 377.
[33] Eadmer, *VA* 1.30, pp. 50–4; whence *VL* cap. 16, pp. 712–13 and (with some added material) Gervase of Canterbury (as n. 32).
[34] Eadmer, *VA* 1.30, p. 52: 'At tamen causam . . . examinatione occisus.'

a cruel death for defending the innocent citizens of Canterbury from pagan atrocities and for seeking to convert the pagans from their infidelity. One may detect in Eadmer's aside an undertone of hurt that Lanfranc had not been convinced by such historical memories of Elphege's martyr status. But Lanfranc may have been reluctant because there was insufficient written attestation.[35] Anselm's philosophical case therefore seemed to him to be decisive.

At all events, Lanfranc was thereafter convinced of Elphege's status as a martyr. According to Eadmer he commissioned the monk Osbern to write an appropriate Life and Passion of the martyr and to compose and set to music a metrical version for liturgical use.[36] Thereby, Eadmer commented, Lanfranc added no small glory to the martyr's name. In Lanfranc's monastic constitutions, the *festivitas sancti Aelfegi martyris* occurs among the feasts of second solemnity.[37]

Lanfranc's measures for the actual liturgical commemoration of St Dunstan raise problems that are more intractable, indeed perhaps insoluble. Inquiry is made difficult by three silences in the evidence. First, despite their fullness of liturgical detail, Lanfranc's monastic constitutions make no express reference to Dunstan. This silence must be considered with another problem posed by the constitutions. Lanfranc listed five principal festivals of Christ Church, naming finally the *festivitas loci* and added detailed provisions that were common to them all;[38] he then named seventeen feasts of second solemnity, putting last the *Dedicatio aecclesiae*, for which he prescribed special liturgical arrangements.[39] There is no clue as to what he meant by either 'the festival of the place' or 'the dedication of the church'. Despite the dedication of Lanfranc's new church on Palm Sunday 1077, any reference to Palm Sunday can be excluded, if only because incompatible provisions were made for the processions after terce.[40] A reference to Trinity Sunday is also improbable. Despite Lanfranc's addition of the Holy Trinity to the dedications of the cathedral, the monastic constitutions made only modest provisions for the Sunday in the octave of Pentecost; by contrast with both the *Regularis concordia* and the Cluniac Customs of Bernard upon which Lanfranc drew, no mention occurs of that Sunday as Trinity Sunday.[41] As an observance of the church at large, Trinity Sunday was still in its infancy; in Lanfranc's day the added dedication left no discernible trace within the Christ Church community.[42] There is a little more to be said for the *festivitas loci* being that of St Dunstan (19 May), for Lanfranc followed a similar list of five

---

[35] There was no pre-Conquest Life and Passion. The accounts in the Anglo-Saxon Chronicle of Elphege's death and burial in London and of the transfer of his body to Canterbury, ASC C(DE), aa. 1011–13, DE(F), a. 1023, pp. 91–2, 99–100, did not attest martyrdom as Lanfranc understood it; nor did the largely mythical report, which he is unlikely to have known, in Thietmar of Merseburg, *Chron.*, 8.42–3, pp. 398–401.

[36] In fact Osbern first wrote the hymn; the Life followed some time later: Osbern, *Vita s. Elphegi*, col. 376.

[37] Lanfranc, *MC* cap. 66, pp. 88–9. [38] Ibid., caps. 62–5, pp. 82–9.

[39] Ibid., caps. 66, 72, pp. 88–9, 96–7.

[40] The Palm Sunday procession as detailed in ibid., cap. 25, pp. 39–41, could not be reconciled with the procession detailed in cap. 72, pp. 96–7.

[41] Ibid., cap. 56, pp. 80–1; cf. *Regularis concordia*, cap. 90, pp. 135–6, and Bernard, 2.25, pp. 333–4.

[42] See above, p. 107.

festivals at Cluny which included that of the abbey's patrons St Peter and St Paul (29 June);[43] at Christ Church, Dunstan was the equivalent. But the Cluniac list, and also Lanfranc's lists with the exception of the *festivitas loci* and the *Dedicatio aecclesiae*, are in chronological order. It must be presumed that the exception was deliberate; it may be that Lanfranc did not intend to be precise about the long-term identification of the festivals concerned.

A second silence in the evidence may now be considered. In the early stages of Lanfranc's rebuilding of the church, reference was made to the removal of Dunstan's body with due solemnity, first to the oratory of the Virgin and then to the monks' refectory;[44] but nothing whatever is known of the location of the body of Dunstan (or that of Elphege) in Lanfranc's cathedral after 1077. In the light of a general remark of Eadmer, it has plausibly been suggested that Dunstan's body was placed with those of other archbishops in wooden chests in the gallery of the north transept.[45] If it remained there for a long period, perhaps even until the building of Anselm's choir where shrines of Dunstan and Elphege were built near the high altar, this may have been because Lanfranc was uncertain about the permanent location of the two archbishops' bodies just as he was uncertain about the *festivitas loci* and the *Dedicatio aecclesiae*. He left both matters open, possibly for a related reason.

What the reason may have been can only be a matter for speculation, but it may arise from a third silence in the evidence: that which concerns when, how, and with what immediate result Lanfranc added to Christ Church a dedication to the Holy Trinity. There is a plausible reason why he may have made the addition. Deeply though Lanfranc and the community of Christ Church venerated Dunstan, his memory did not rival that of St Augustine, whose body indisputably rested in the nearby abbey of his name. To make clear the primatial status of Christ Church,[46] an indisputably more exalted *festivitas loci* was desirable.[47] Prompted, perhaps, by Bernard's provision at Cluny for the honouring of the Trinity,[48] Lanfranc may have contemplated making the Sunday in the octave of Pentecost the major festival of Christ Church. If so, he may have encountered resistance from the monastic community who wished to retain the pre-eminence of Dunstan and he may have found it necessary to respect this wish.

However this may have been, there is no reason to postulate a suspension of Dunstan's cult; there are many indications that, in the 1080s, it gained strength both with Lanfranc and amongst his monks. Eadmer's (unfortunately undatable) story of Abbot Scotland's vision of Dunstan's descent in glory to keep his vigil with the monks of Christ Church while all its bells were ringing testifies to the solemnity of the commemoration, which gave great joy to the monks.[49] Lanfranc's commitment to Dunstan is more than hinted at, especially during his latter years. When, c.1080,

---

[43] Bernard, 1.50, p. 244.   [44] See above, p. 105.
[45] See above, p. 106; cf. Ramsay and Sparks, 'The Cult of St Dunstan', 314.
[46] Cf. the phrase 'propter primatem sedem': Lanfranc, *MC* cap. 1, pp. 2–3.
[47] The dedication to Christ the Saviour offered no occasion; the Lateran basilica at Rome, which the dedication followed, had its major festival on St John the Baptist's day.
[48] As n. 41.   [49] Eadmer, *Mirac.*, cap. 15, pp. 233–4.

Goscelin of Saint-Bertin wrote his Life of the English king's daughter St Edith of Wilton, he prefaced it by a long dedication to Lanfranc to whom he referred as Dunstan's most capable vicar (*eficacissimus vicarius*), thus affirming Lanfranc's perceived bond to him.[50] Goscelin also referred in his letter to the Dunstan bell of the cathedral, which according to Osbern was said to have been cast by Dunstan himself and the sweet tone of which could summon the whole city;[51] it was doubtless also a regular reminder of Dunstan to the archbishop and to the community. At the council of Gloucester of Christmas 1080, when the king and Lanfranc probably heard a dispute between the abbots of Muchelney and Glastonbury, Lanfranc's comment that he would not wish to harm the nurse of blessed Dunstan (i.e. Glastonbury) indicates regard for Dunstan.[52] The Canterbury monk Osbern wrote his *Vita* and *Miracula* of Dunstan very soon after Lanfranc's death, and he was concerned to make clear how important Dunstan had been for the late archbishop. Thus, in five consecutive chapters of the *Miracula* he appears concerned to assert (as it has been well said) 'that it was by Dunstan's help that Lanfranc was so successful as archbishop'.[53] When about to rebuild the cathedral, Lanfranc treated with reverence the body of Dunstan, who appeared to win mercy for knights who were involved in homicide (cap. 17). At Penenden Heath, Lanfranc sought and received Dunstan's help in defending the rights of his church (cap. 18). Osbern gave Dunstan prominence in his version of the Egelward incident (cap. 19). Lanfranc himself was healed from seemingly mortal illness after an appearance of Dunstan (cap. 20), who at the same time caused one of Lanfranc's chaplains to recover from a prolonged fever (cap. 21).

To judge by such indications as there are, Lanfranc always and increasingly held Dunstan in high regard; there is no reason to suppose that Dunstan, any more than Elphege, was ever not accorded high liturgical honour, even though its final definition, like the placing of the archbishops' shrines, may not have been settled during Lanfranc's lifetime. It is probably significant that a Canterbury *laudes regiae* text which is to be dated to about the time of Lanfranc's death named as intercessors for the archbishop and his clergy St Augustine, St Dunstan, and St Elphege, with Dunstan's name in capital letters to indicate special honour.[54]

Other examples confirm that Lanfranc was not hostile to English saints as such, provided that their sanctity was properly attested and the authenticity of their relics duly proved. Lanfranc's counsel that the relics of Evesham should be attested and the upshot of their being restored to veneration is significant of his approach.[55] Goscelin's dedication to him as vicar of St Dunstan of a Life of St Edith indicates the

---

[50] Goscelin, *Vita s. Edithe*, 34–9.   [51] Cf. Osbern, *Mirac.* cap. 11, p. 138.
[52] See above, p. 126.
[53] caps. 17–21, pp. 142–53; see Gibson, *Lanfranc*, 218–19. (Gibson also cites cap. 22, pp. 153–5, but it is not more than marginally relevant to Dunstan.) Especially when compared with Eadmer's treatment of the material, Osbern's presentation of Lanfranc's indebtedness to Dunstan may be double-edged: he doubtless wished to depict a genuine indebtedness that Lanfranc acknowledged; but if there was uncertainty about Dunstan's ultimate resting-place and about the *festivitas loci* at Christ Church, Osbern may have been concerned in face of Lanfranc's uncertainty to vindicate Dunstan's pre-eminence.
[54] Cowdrey, 'The Anglo-Norman Laudes regiae', 73.   [55] See above, p. 177.

author's confidence that he accepted such an English saint.[56] Bishop Gundulf of Rochester would hardly have translated the relics of St Ithamar, a saint of Kentish birth, with special solemnity unless he had Lanfranc's approval.[57] When Lanfranc was assured of the sanctity of St Aldhelm, he ordered that his cultus should be observed throughout England.[58] Lanfranc's dealings towards the end of his life as regards the relics of St Mildrith also testify to his acceptance of the sanctity of an English princess and abbess.[59] It can scarcely have been without his sanction that her supposed body was brought from Lympne to his new foundation of St Gregory at Canterbury. According to Goscelin of Saint-Bertin, when the newly arrived relics were claimed by the monks of St Augustine's to be inauthentic, they were tested in the time of Abbot Guy by an ordeal by cold water in which a boy was bound and cast into water, which in this case refused every effort to submerge him, thus proving the St Augustine's case.[60] Since Goscelin, who probably came to Canterbury in 1090, knew of the ordeal by hearsay, it may well have been held during Lanfranc's lifetime and with his knowledge. If so, it provides further evidence that recourse to the testing of relics implied no disparagement of the saint concerned, however inconvenient the alleged outcome.

For Lanfranc's wider dealings with his English subjects there is a virtually total absence of evidence. In particular, it is not known whether, and if so how far, he learnt the English language. He will have come into close contact with the English and their language, both as a royal justice and in the shire courts, and in the course of his itineration of his diocese and manors after the manner of every medieval bishop.[61] Like other sources, his *obit* referred to his many acts of charity.[62] But beyond this there is no more to be gathered about how Lanfranc communicated with his English subjects.

---

[56] See above, p. 183.

[57] *Vita Ythamari*, cited in *The Life of Gundulf*, 40 n. For Ithamar, see Bede, *Eccles. Hist.* 3.14, 20, pp. 256–7, 278–9.

[58] William of Malmesbury, *GP* 5.269, p. 428.   [59] See above, p. 170.

[60] Goscelin, *Libellus contra inanes*, cap. 20, pp. 87–9.

[61] Lanfranc's expectation that he would itinerate in his diocese is made clear in *Letters*, no. 30, pp. 116–19. His healing by Dunstan as reported by Osbern took place on his manor of Aldington: Osbern, *Mirac.*, cap. 20, p. 151.

[62] Gibson, *Lanfranc*, 228.

13

Lanfranc and King William I

There can be no doubt that, like most leading churchmen of his time, Lanfranc favoured strong kings who provided peace and justice in a violent world, not least for churches, monks, and all grades of clergy. Royal power was the more effective when exercised in collaboration with the spiritual authority and with the apparatus of church councils. The Lombardy of Lanfranc's birth had witnessed the Emperor Henry II and Pope Benedict VIII acting together at Pavia in 1022, while Lanfranc had himself been present at Mainz in 1049 when Pope Leo IX held a synod in the presence of the Emperor Henry III.[1] As archbishop, Lanfranc expressed his expectation of Christian kings with especial force to those in Ireland over which he claimed primatial authority:

God bestows no greater mercy upon countries than when he advances lovers of peace and justice to the government of souls or bodies, and especially when he commits the kingdoms of this world to be ruled by good kings. For thence peace arises, discord is quietened, and (to put it all in a phrase) the observance of the Christian religion is established.[2]

To the queen of Scotland, who was a princess of the English royal line, Lanfranc further showed that he shared current ideas of royalty by praising her own descent from a royal stock (*stirps regia*), her consequent royal education, and her noble marriage to a noble king.[3] King William of England had no such credentials in his own right and only a few through his queen. There is no direct evidence as to how Lanfranc viewed the basis of his regality. But it is a fair assumption that Lanfranc fully underwrote the Norman view that William inherited royalty in the fullest degree as the designated successor of King Edward the Confessor, and that William's victorious and prosperous rulership set upon his royalty the stamp of divine attestation and approval. Such an assumption is consistent with Lanfranc's early comment upon his rule to Pope Alexander II:

I beseech you to ask the divine clemency that he should grant a long life to my lord the king of the English, that he should make peace for him against all who resist him, and that he should incline his heart to love of him and his holy church always with spiritual devotion. For while he lives we have peace of a kind; but after his death we expect that we shall have neither peace nor anything that is good.[4]

---

[1] See above, pp. 2–3, 40.
[2] Lanfranc, *Letters*, no. 10, pp. 70–3, cf. no. 9, pp. 66–9. See above, pp. 145–6.
[3] Ibid., no. 50, pp. 160–1.
[4] Ibid., no. 1, pp. 34–5.

13.1 ARCHBISHOP AND KING

During the seventeen years of their working relationship as archbishop and king, Lanfranc and William I undoubtedly maintained a harmony and collaboration that have few if any parallels in the history of medieval Europe. In Henry I's reign, a monk of Battle Abbey commented that men of their day used to say that no two such figures were to be found together in one land as were King William and Lanfranc his archbishop.[5] William of Poitiers wrote that in Normandy before the conquest of England, Duke William respected Lanfranc whom he admitted to his close familiarity, taking him as his spiritual guide and as a watchman over church life in the duchy.[6] Nevertheless, the sources suggest certain aspects of light and shade in the collaboration of archbishop and king, especially in relation to the borders between what may broadly be called spiritual and secular affairs.

It should be said at the outset that Lanfranc was no court prelate in the usual understanding of that term. Such evidence as the witnessing of charters suggests that he was not habitually at court even when the king was in England, save at the Christmas, Easter, and Pentecost crown-wearings when his presence was necessary for liturgical reasons and when ecclesiastical business was often transacted. Nor are there indications that Lanfranc allowed any compromising of his capacity either as a monk-archbishop or as a spiritual monitor of kings as contemporary expectations of his role required him to be. Lanfranc himself sought expressly to fulfil this role in his letters to Irish kings. His exhortations to Christian kingship were such as other prominent churchmen, including Pope Gregory VII, addressed to rulers about their personal lives and government. They were part of the expectation of rulers themselves, even when strongly and sharply expressed.[7] Moreover, in England, King William I gave Lanfranc a special part in the upbringing of his younger sons. William was brought up in his household, and he carried out the knightly investiture of both William and Henry.[8]

The sources testify to William's unique receptivity to Lanfranc's admonitions in spiritual matters. For Eadmer, Lanfranc was acceptable to the king before all other men; he always sought to make the king devoted to God. William held Lanfranc, as he held Anselm as abbot of Bec, in deep familiarity (*sacratissima familiaritate*). In matters relating to their office (the qualification is significant), he took especially close counsel about what should be done; Eadmer instanced the frequent mitigation of his severity and the benefits to monasteries and churches that were the result.[9] William of Malmesbury, too, noticed William's deference to Lanfranc, and also his exceptional amiability and civility. But the king's help was especially noted in relation to Lanfranc's charitable works, and Lanfranc's influence for good upon

---

[5] *The Brevis relatio*, cap. 8, p. 34.   [6] William of Poitiers, 1.52, pp. 84–7.
[7] Cf. the story of William's listening to the censure of his rule by Guitmund of la-Croix-Saint-Leufroi: Orderic Vitalis, 4, vol. 2.270–81. Whatever the truth of the story, it illustrates William's reputation for listening quietly to censure by a holy man.
[8] William of Malmesbury, *GR* 4.305, vol. 542–3; Orderic Vitalis, 8.1, vol. 4. 120–1.
[9] Eadmer, *Hist. nov.*, 1, pp. 12, 23.

the king was demonstrated by his prompting the king to a work of mercy in resisting the profitable trade in slaves to Ireland.[10] An anecdote in the *Vita Lanfranci* well illustrates Lanfranc's role as moral mentor of the king. At the banquet that followed one of William's crown-wearings, the king was sitting crowned and bejewelled with Lanfranc at his side. A jester (*scurra*) exclaimed in tones of adulation at this sight 'Behold, I see God! Behold I see God!' Lanfranc warned the king not to tolerate words which were not proper for man but only for God; William complied with Lanfranc's charge that the jester should be severely thrashed for his blasphemy. Yet it was explained that Lanfranc's concern was less for the jester's blasphemy than for the king's pride: Lanfranc had in mind the fate of King Herod Agrippa I (Acts 12: 21–3) who, at a comparable ceremony, listened to words of adulation; he was smitten by an angel and consumed by worms.[11] In moral and spiritual matters, such boldness of speech was not only allowed to a religious archbishop but was expected of him.

In matters of this world it was otherwise; the king's word and judgement must be deferred to. This is made clear in Lanfranc's own letters. 'Against the king's command I presume to ask nothing and to order nothing': so he wrote to an abbot whose monk, one Ulric, who enjoyed the archbishop's favour, was being so severely punished by the king for an unspecified offence that in Lanfranc's eyes he was suffering persecution for righteousness' sake. Lanfranc merely commended him to his abbot's fatherly kindness as an agent of the mercy of God.[12] Writing to Bishop Gundulf of Rochester about English women who had sought refuge in nunneries for fear of the French, Lanfranc rounded off his decisions by saying: 'And this is the king's judgement and ours.'[13] Again, Lanfranc assured an Abbot Thurstan—perhaps of Ely or Glastonbury—who had incurred the king's displeasure only of his own prayers to God for him. He advised him to offer satisfaction to the king through other intermediaries; if the king spurned it, he should trust in the providence of God.[14] Even in the affairs of the monastic order, when the king's political interest was involved Lanfranc did not press his own counsel or judgement against the king. He was no less deferential to the king in the affairs of the church at large. Most conspicuously, Lanfranc's councils did not proceed with sensitive business which did not have the royal approval. Thus, when the council of London (1075) met during the king's absence across the sea on a military campaign, the consideration of the transfer of episcopal sees from rural locations which lacked his approval was postponed for his personal hearing.[15] There are, indeed, some signs of difference and even tension between Lanfranc and William. The fact that no further transfers of sees took place may be owing to their divergent views about the use of existing monasteries as support for sees that were transferred.[16] More seriously, at the beginning of Lanfranc's archiepiscopate William's refusal to allow him to receive an oath from Archbishop Thomas of York was a major reason for his failure to secure the primacy of Canterbury with the completeness that he urgently desired.[17]

---

[10] *GR* 3.269.2, vol. 1.496–7; *GP* 1.44, p. 72.
[11] *VL* cap. 13, pp. 708–9.   [12] Lanfranc, *Letters*, no. 58, pp. 172–5.
[13] Ibid., no. 53, pp. 166–7.   [14] Ibid., no. 57, pp. 172–3.   [15] canon 3, *CS* no. 92, vol. 1/2.613.
[16] See the cases of Bath and Bury: above, pp. 162, 165.   [17] See above, pp. 90, 99, 102.

Such evidence as has been reviewed indicates that the collaboration of Lanfranc with William, though cordial and fruitful, was not without its complexities. There was a balance between spiritual and moral matters, in which William was deferential to Lanfranc according to the conventions of the age and genuinely aspired to practise Christian kingship, and secular and political affairs in which, though Lanfranc was a valued counsellor and agent, William's mastery was overriding. In face of this mastery, Lanfranc had sometimes to differ in silence and occasionally to come to terms with invincible resistance. Lanfranc's skill and achievement lay in his ability to acknowledge the balance involved and in his knowing when to defer to the king as supreme. His success owed much to the bonds of respect and understanding that united the two men and to their mutual sense of their authority and power.

13.2 LANFRANC AS ROYAL DEPUTY AND ROYAL JUSTICE

The relationship of archbishop and king was the closer and more fruitful by reason of the active part that Lanfranc took in the government and administration of the English kingdom. It should be remembered that, besides being a mentor of and collaborator with the king in his ecclesiastical capacity as archbishop, Lanfranc was also committed to the royal service in a temporal way as a tenant-in-chief of the crown who, as such, owed suit to the king's court and such counsel and aid as the king might rightly require of him. Lanfranc's secular service of the king has sometimes been stated in excessive terms, as when the *Vita Lanfranci* wrote that

When the glorious King William was staying in Normandy, Lanfranc was chief and guardian of England (*princeps et custos Anglie*). All magnates were his subjects and helpers in matters pertaining to the defence and governance or peace of the kingdom according to the laws of the country.[18]

There is no evidence to confirm that Lanfranc's position anticipated the justiciarship as it was to emerge in the twelfth century; in the Conqueror's day such viceregal functions as Lanfranc performed were occasional, while during his years as archbishop Odo of Bayeux was more often active in a comparable role and Geoffrey of Coutances was so occasionally.[19]

Lanfranc came nearest to acting as the *Vita Lanfranci* outlines in 1075 during the rebellion of the earls which occurred in the king's absence, as noted in the canons of the council of London.[20] The place given to Lanfranc's part in dealing with the rebellion in his letter-collection is an indication of his prominence in what was an exceptional event.[21] The principal leader of the rebellion was Ralph 'de Gael', who possessed a lordship in the Breton marches and whom the Conqueror had made

---

[18] *VL* cap. 15, p. 711. [19] See Bates, 'The Origin of the Justiciarship', esp. 2–6.
[20] See above, p. 125.
[21] Lanfranc, *Letters*, nos. 31–6 and perhaps 37, pp. 118–29. The other principal sources are: *ASCDE*, *aa.* 1075–6, pp. 156–8; *Chronica monasterii de Hide*, 294–5; John of Worcester, *aa.* 1074–5, vol. 3.24–9; William of Malmesbury, *GR* 3.253, 255, vol. 1.468–71, 472–3, *GP* 4.182, pp. 321–2; Orderic Vitalis, 4, vol. 2.310–23, 344–51.

earl of Norfolk. Ralph was joined by Roger, earl of Hereford, a son of the king's sometime loyal supporter William fitzOsbern. They were joined by the Englishman Waltheof, whose high standing in the king's favour was marked by his holding the earldom of Huntingdon and by his marriage to a niece of the king. The causes of the rebellion are obscure,[22] but it began at a feast held near Newmarket to celebrate the marriage, which the king had sanctioned,[23] between Earl Ralph and a sister of Earl Roger. It was made the more serious when the rebels appealed for help to the Danes. But it was suppressed without undue difficulty. In the west, the English churchmen Bishop Wulfstan of Worcester and Abbot Ethelwig of Evesham acted with the help of Norman forces to prevent Earl Roger's supporters from joining those of Earl Ralph. In East Anglia, Bishops Odo of Bayeux and Geoffrey of Coutances with other Norman magnates contained Earl Ralph who, after suffering a military setback near Cambridge, returned to Norwich whence he returned to Brittany. His wife thereafter defended Norwich castle during a siege of three months, after which it was surrendered. A Danish force achieved nothing except a raid upon York and the country returned to peace. When the king returned to England late in 1075 he visited the severest sanctions for their treason upon Earls Roger and Waltheof: according to the law of Frenchmen, Roger suffered life incarceration and the forfeiture of all his goods; according to the law of Englishmen, Waltheof was beheaded. His body was buried at Crowland Abbey. To lesser conspirators the king showed no mercy.

As regards Lanfranc's role in relation to the rebellion, the meagre evidence suggests three matters for discussion. First and most clearly, there is Lanfranc's dealings with the three earls who were mainly involved. For Ralph of Norfolk he showed no concern. He was Ralph the traitor (*Rodulfus traditor*), whose whole army was ultimately routed; his departure from England rated no express mention by Lanfranc, who doubtless subsumed it in God's merciful purging of William's kingdom from Breton scum (*spurcicia Britonum*).[24] Roger of Hereford, by contrast, was of a Norman family well known at Bec. With him, Lanfranc's dealings were long and initially amicable. Their basis was pastoral; Lanfranc presented himself not as a royal agent acting under feudal law but as a bishop who followed canonical procedure. When he eventually excommunicated Roger and his adherents, he did so by canonical authority, and by his pastoral authority as primate he extended his sentence through the whole of England. Lanfranc regarded two earlier letters to Roger as constituting the initial summonses required by canonical practice.[25] In the first he exhorted Roger as his most dear son to remember his duty as a royal vassal and to be worthy of his distinguished and prosperous father; Lanfranc offered to travel anywhere in order to discuss his own and the king's business.[26] A second letter was

---

[22] Lanfranc indicates that, in the case of Hereford, friction had arisen from the impact of the king's sheriffs upon supposed comital rights and that the king had declared himself willing upon his return to investigate: Lanfranc, *Letters*, no. 31, pp. 118–21.

[23] The evidence of *ASC* is here to be preferred to that of John of Worcester.

[24] Lanfranc, *Letters*, nos. 35–6, pp. 124–7.   [25] Ibid., no. 33A, pp. 122–3.

[26] Ibid., no. 31, pp. 118–21.

written in fuller knowledge of Roger's misconduct, and Lanfranc summoned the earl to seek him; but the tone remained friendly.[27] Once Lanfranc had excommunicated him, Roger could be absolved only if he sought the king's mercy and did proper satisfaction.[28] When Roger asked to see Lanfranc, the archbishop expressed himself most willing, but he feared the royal anger if he did so. However, he would inform the king about Roger's penitence, humility, and pleas; he would help Roger in all ways compatible with his own fidelity to the king.[29] In Roger's case, Lanfranc was evidently concerned to do what he could to secure the king's mercy for a penitent subject. Only under the temporary constraint of canonical necessity was his love for Roger changed to aversion of mind and just severity.[30] Waltheof is not mentioned in Lanfranc's letters, but from the chronicle sources it seems that he withdrew from the rebellion at an early stage.[31] According to John of Worcester, he resorted to Lanfranc who absolved him from his oath to the other rebel earls. Lanfranc advised him to go straightway to William in Normandy, to give him a full account of the conspiracy, and to surrender himself to the king's mercy. But the king was in no mood for mercy either in Normandy or when he returned to England: for all Lanfranc's persuasion that Waltheof was truly penitent and despite his reputation for conversion of life, the king insisted upon his execution.

The second matter for discussion is what in a year of crisis the king expected of Lanfranc. It must be remembered that the rebellion seems to have begun unexpectedly when William had been for some time in Normandy; there was no special briefing of Lanfranc or anyone else for the contingency that arose. When it did arise, Lanfranc's letters indicate that the king regarded Lanfranc as providing a prime channel of communication and of information in both directions across the sea; this was partly because Lanfranc had at his disposal messengers who could not only carry written messages but, more important, could reliably convey verbally larger amounts of military and political intelligence.[32] This implied that Lanfranc should have an overview of affairs which could scarcely be merely passive but which involved a degree of control and initiative. Thus, one of the king's first reactions on hearing of the rebellion was, through Lanfranc, to call on all his faithful subjects of whom Lanfranc was one to do all in their power to prevent the king's castles from being handed over to his enemies; for this Lanfranc declared his support, and his concern to secure the loyalty of Roger of Hereford was part of his response.[33] In the absence of further evidence, it can only be said that the king continued to look for Lanfranc's active counsel and aid for so long as the emergency lasted.

Third, there is the question of what Lanfranc himself sought to do. He did not lead or accompany armies in the field nor did he take a direct part in the defence or investing of castles; there is no evidence that he exercised overall military command or leadership. He nevertheless did not serve only as a messenger and channel of communication. At the outset, he declared himself anxious to discuss with Roger of

---

[27] Lanfranc, *Letters*, no. 32, pp. 120–1. [28] Ibid., no. 33A, pp. 122–3.
[29] Ibid., no. 33B, pp. 122–3. [30] Ibid., no. 33A, pp. 122–3.
[31] See John of Worcester and William of Malmesbury, *GP*.
[32] Lanfranc, *Letters*, nos. 31, 33B, 34, pp. 121–5. [33] Ibid., no. 31, pp. 119–20.

Hereford the earl's affairs and those of the king.[34] His ostensible reason for asking William to postpone his return to England—that it would be a grave insult to 'us' if the king's assistance were seen to be required in subduing the defeated rebels whom 'our men' (*nostri*) were victoriously pursuing—implies that Lanfranc was himself active on the king's behalf.[35] Lanfranc received from Bishop Walcher of Durham a letter about the peace of his region which he found reassuring after the many adverse reports that he had received; because the Danes were indeed coming as the king had warned, Lanfranc ordered Walcher to be vigilantly careful that Durham castle was fortified with men, arms, and provisions.[36] Here was Lanfranc raising morale and organizing defence.

Lanfranc's view of his own role is perhaps best approached by way of the addresses of his letters to the king: 'Domino suo Anglorum regi Wil. fidelis suus L. fidele servitium et fideles orationes'; 'Gloriosissimo domino suo Anglorum regi W. fidelis suus L. fidele servitium cum orationibus'.[37] These addresses defy translation because of the ambiguity of the adjective *fidelis*, with its spectrum of meanings from religious faith and an archbishop's spiritual capacity to feudal loyalty and the temporal obligations of a tenant-in-chief.[38] There can be little doubt that Lanfranc's repeated use of the adjective was studied. In face of the rebellion he sought to act in a way that drew upon both his spiritual and his temporal authority and loyalty, and that in effect fused them together. Thus he sought to deal with Roger of Hereford, and perhaps also with Waltheof, pastorally as a spiritual father who acted by canonical authority; against 'Breton scum' and marauding Danes he brought faithful temporal service on behalf of his lord the king.

Given this complexity in Lanfranc's conduct, it is worth exploring the possibility that he sought a resolution of the crisis presented by the rebellion by means analogous to the procedure of surrender (*deditio*) as widely understood in eleventh-century Europe. It aimed not only at the submission and punishment of the guilty but also at the restoration of peace and the renewal of human relationships. It involved the turning of the wrath of an offended ruler so that he followed the course of mercy.[39] So far as individuals were concerned, Lanfranc's treatment of Roger of Hereford and Waltheof is reminiscent of such conventions, especially in his concern for their spiritual absolution and in his advice that they should seek out the king in hope of mercy. Lanfranc's attempt to control the political situation is also significant, especially in his attempt to postpone the king's return to England.[40] His real, as opposed to his declared, reason seems to have been that the king should not return to England until peace had manifestly been restored by those already in the country; then the king would have less cause to persist in his anger and to withhold his mercy. Thus, he eventually represented to the king that the whole disorder was the fault of the traitor Ralph of Norwich and the other 'Breton scum' of whom the

---

[34] Ibid. 120–1. [35] Ibid., no. 34, pp. 124–5.
[36] Ibid., no. 36, pp. 126–7. [37] Ibid., nos. 34–5, pp. 124–5.
[38] Ibid. 5–6; but Dr Gibson's translation of *fidelis* as 'loyal' inevitably obscures the ambiguity.
[39] For comment on the conventions, see Cowdrey, *Pope Gregory VII*, 160–1.
[40] Ibid., no. 34, pp. 124–5.

English kingdom was now well rid, while by God's mercy all din of warfare was silenced there.[41] Lanfranc evidently thought that such pacification could best be achieved in the absence of a wrathful king; once it was a *fait accompli* the king might be inclined to mercy, particularly to the penitent Earls Roger and Waltheof.

It was the tragedy of Lanfranc's position that, when the king returned, he showed no mercy but, despite Lanfranc's advice to the penitent rebels, visited extreme severity upon them. As Lanfranc had warned Roger, he must in the end defer to the will of the king, not least to avoid drawing the royal anger upon himself.[42] Yet Lanfranc's desire to restore human relations was not only true to an archbishop's duty to press the claim of mercy; it was also politic. It is not prudent to create martyrs. Orderic Vitalis and others show that Waltheof, whom Lanfranc vainly directed to seek the king's mercy, became the centre of a cult at Crowland; moreover, according to Orderic many came to see in his execution a turning-point in the king's reign: by God's just judgement in retribution on William he never again in thirteen years won a battle or stormed a fortress.[43] There can be little doubt that archbishop and king differed in their response to the rebellion of the earls or that the archbishop sought to keep a wrathful king at a prudent distance. But when the king's wrath prevailed, Lanfranc no less prudently accepted the situation. Yet, if a letter of Lanfranc assuring Bishop Remigius of Lincoln of the king's confidence in him and inviting him to a discussion of his position is related to the aftermath of the rebellion, it is further evidence for Lanfranc's concern for healing and reconciliation in all dimensions.[44]

In a significant, but not a numerous, range of connections, Lanfranc is recorded as having been involved in matters of royal administration and justice. In the Norman polity of William I, Lanfranc seems soon to have understood that such involvement was not only inescapable but for the benefit of the church. Thus, for example, very early in Lanfranc's archiepiscopate an assembly at the royal manor of Petherton headed by the king and Lanfranc took a stand against the claims of Archbishop Thomas of York with regard to the see of Worcester.[45] At Penenden Heath, Lanfranc received an object lesson in the value of the shire court and the testimony of local witnesses to the law of Edward the Confessor's day in defending the possessions and liberty of churches, and in the effectiveness of the royal will as exercised through such a figure as Bishop Geoffrey of Coutances in directing such means to resisting predators upon churches.[46] Again, while Lanfranc was strenuously concerned to propagate canon law as he understood it, the means whereby the separate hearing of ecclesiastical pleas was most conspicuously promoted was a royal writ expressing the common counsel of the king and his ecclesiastical and lay magnates.[47] In procuring the good order of the church and of churches, the king's will and the legal and governmental inheritance from the Old English state were significant alongside the demands of canon law and of ecclesiastical order. Not only the obligations of a tenant-in-chief of the king but also the dependence of the church

---

[41] Lanfranc, *Letters*, no. 35, pp. 124–7.   [42] Ibid., no. 33B, pp. 122–3.
[43] Orderic Vitalis, 4, vol. 2.350–1.   [44] Lanfranc, *Letters*, no. 37, pp. 128–9.
[45] See above, p. 93.   [46] See above, pp. 109–15.   [47] See above, pp. 132–4.

upon the king for good order and for justice drew Lanfranc to playing a part in royal government and administration.

The benefit to bishoprics and monasteries of strong secular authority of which churchmen were among the agents is well illustrated by a royal writ, probably of 1077, addressed by name to Lanfranc and Geoffrey of Coutances amongst the bishops and to the laymen Count Robert of Eu, Richard fitzGilbert, and Hugh of Montfort, and also to the king's other leading men in the English kingdom. By the king's order and on his behalf, they were to summon his sheriffs and instruct them to restore to his bishoprics and abbeys (*episcopatibus meis et abbatiis*) all demesne lands which his bishops and abbots (*episcopi mei et abbates*) had given them whether from carelessness, fear, or greed or which they had seized; such alienations were resolutely to be restored.[48] No evidence survives by which it can be judged how far this writ led to a general and systematic restitution of church property. But a writ addressed to four of the named persons, including Lanfranc, concerning the restoration of lands of St Augustine's abbey at Canterbury seems to be related to it, as do other writs in which Lanfranc is not named.[49] The royal will and command were evidently a considerable resource for the protection of churches.

It is, therefore, not surprising that a significant, though not a large, number of William I's genuine writs should be addressed to Lanfranc, whether solely or, more often, as first amongst a plurality of named persons or groups of persons.[50] In three cases, Lanfranc's name is followed by a list entirely or mainly comprising local magnates or shire officials in regions or shires where royal grants had been made.[51] More frequently, those named after Lanfranc are figures of greater than local importance: sometimes one other, like Bishop Odo of Bayeux[52] and Bishop Geoffrey of Coutances;[53] in connection with the Ely land-pleas of the 1080s, these bishops are both named together with Count Robert of Mortain.[54] To such names might be added a general clause such as 'and all my barons of all England'.[55] William might also address Lanfranc and a wide definition of his subjects, such as 'his bishops, abbots, and sheriffs, and his other faithful subjects, French and English'.[56] Writs which included an address to Lanfranc might simply be notifications of royal grants or judgements. But they might also initiate pleas,[57] and in one case which is especially revealing of Lanfranc's participation in processes of secular justice, William in Rouen restored to St Augustine's abbey at Canterbury eight prebends at Newington (Kent) according to the witness of the shire court of Kent at which Lanfranc had been present; the recipients of the writ were charged with the securing of the abbey's rights.[58] Other duties might be imposed, as when Lanfranc and Geoffrey of

---

[48] *Regesta WI*, no. 129, pp. 443–4. The writ survives only in a 13th-century copy in the archives of Christ Church, Canterbury.

[49] *Regesta WI*, no. 83, pp. 348–9; cf. nos. 42–3, 310, 330, pp. 210–11, 922, 964.

[50] The address-clauses of William I's writs are importantly discussed by Bates, *Regesta WI*, 55–7, to which the following discussion is greatly indebted.

[51] Ibid., nos. 4–5, 265, pp. 115–17, 796.   [52] Ibid., no. 102, p. 378.

[53] Ibid., nos. 285, 347, pp. 862, 993–4.   [54] Ibid., nos. 120–1, 123–5, pp. 423–7, 431–5.

[55] Ibid., no. 134, pp. 457–8.   [56] Ibid., nos. 190, 231–2, pp. 616, 707–9.

[57] Ibid., nos. 123, 125, pp. 431–2, 434–5.   [58] Ibid., no. 88, pp. 356–7.

Coutances were to give livery of certain lands to the Norman abbey of Saint-Martin at Troarn.[59]

But it is clear that, where executive action was prescribed, Lanfranc was not necessarily expected to carry it out himself where this was not expressly required: this might be the duty of the second addressee. Thus, when Lanfranc and Geoffrey of Coutances were to attend to a dispute about jurisdiction between Bishop Wulfstan of Worcester and Abbot Walter of Evesham, it was Geoffrey alone who in the king's place was to see that Wulfstan had his right.[60] Similarly, Bishop Odo of Bayeux alone dealt with a plea relating to lands of Evesham Abbey which the king had notified to both Lanfranc and Odo.[61] When royal writs naming Lanfranc are viewed overall, it is significant that a large proportion date from the years after 1076, when the king was frequently overseas. They suggest that, because of his position as archbishop and of his personal qualities, Lanfranc over the years played a role in administrative and judicial matters which was similar to that which he played in the political crisis of the rebellion of the earls.[62] He was the head and superior of a group of ecclesiastical and lay persons who were the king's trusted agents. He was the principal medium of royal information and command who knew of and oversaw the executive actions of others but who only occasionally and exceptionally took such actions himself, either at the king's instance or on his own initiative.

Whether the king was in England or in Normandy, known instances when Lanfranc himself acted as a royal justice are rare. The two recorded instances concern the abbeys of Bury St Edmunds and Ely in especial relation to the rights over them of diocesan bishops. In the case of Bury, the king dispatched Lanfranc to settle by local testimony drawn from nine shires the abbey's dispute with the East Anglian bishop Herfast about his rights there.[63] Pleas relating to Ely punctuated the reign of William I, and they raise problems which in some respects remain unresolved and perhaps unresolvable.[64] Three matters were at issue: the abbey's recovery of extensive estates and properties lost in the aftermath of the Norman conquest; the local jurisdictional rights of the abbey; and, ultimately, the jurisdictional claims of Bishop Remigius of Lincoln over the abbey, and especially his claim to consecrate its abbot. So far as Lanfranc's known involvement is concerned, there is no assured evidence before the election as abbot in 1081/2 of Simeon, the brother of Bishop Walchelin of Winchester. He is not referred to in connection with the meeting of several shires at Kentford which preceded Simeon's election. Nor, perhaps because the king was still in England, does his name appear in a writ to Geoffrey of Coutances and Robert of Mortain which dates from after Simeon's election and orders the summoning of the demesne tenants of the abbey so that, after appropriate inquiries, the abbey might have its lands as they were at Edward the Confessor's death.[65]

---

[59] *Regesta WI*, no. 285, p. 862.
[60] Ibid., no. 347, pp. 993–4.
[61] Ibid., nos. 134–5, pp. 457–9.
[62] See above, pp. 188–92.
[63] See the discussion above, pp. 164–7, esp. p. 166.
[64] The principal evidence is the series of royal writs edited and discussed in *Regesta WI*, nos. 117–27, pp. 410–39, mostly preserved in *Liber Eliensis*, 2.116–27, pp. 198–207. For further discussion, see Miller, 'The Ely Land Pleas'; Blake, in: *Liber Eliensis*, 426–32; Bates, *Bishop Remigius of Lincoln*, 28–9.
[65] *Regesta WI*, no. 119, pp. 421–2.

With King William overseas, seven further writs which with near certainty date from Simeon's abbacy have Lanfranc as the first or only addressee. Whatever the uncertainties about their dates and relative order, when studied in respect of their subject-matter they seem to reveal differences, and perhaps a crescendo, in what the king called upon Lanfranc to do. When the subject was the abbey's lands or possessions and its local jurisdiction, there is no clear evidence of a call for Lanfranc's direct intervention; as in the earlier writ from Simeon's time, that may, as was usual, have been left to Geoffrey of Coutances alone or with Robert of Mortain.[66] An exception may have occurred when Bishop Remigius of Lincoln claimed new customs within the Isle of Ely itself: the king instructed Lanfranc, Geoffrey, and Robert to allow Remigius only such customs as his predecessor had in the Confessor's day; Remigius must prove that what he was claiming was so sanctioned. The express requirement that his plea should be heard in the addressees' presence (*et placitum istud sit in presentia vestra*) suggests that Lanfranc was to be himself involved.[67] When the issue was who should perform Simeon's abbatial consecration, Lanfranc was certainly himself to act. At first, indeed, the king seems to have seen no problem: he ordered the same three addressees to see that Simeon was consecrated without delay and that he possessed his rightful lands and customs.[68] But when Bishop Remigius claimed right of consecration, the king seems to have called on Lanfranc alone to inform him by letter as to whether Remigius had established that his predecessors had rightfully consecrated abbots of Ely; meanwhile, Simeon's consecration must be postponed.[69] The respective rights of the diocesan bishop and the abbots of Ely seem to have emerged as being far from clear. A final surviving writ, addressed to Lanfranc alone, suggests that the king was increasingly anxious about the uncertainties of the situation at Ely. He imposed several tasks upon the archbishop: Lanfranc was to examine the abbot's charters; if they said that the abbot might be consecrated wherever the king ordered, Lanfranc was himself to consecrate Simeon; he was to have the bridge at Ely repaired without further excuse; he was to inquire through Bishop Geoffrey of Coutances, Bishop Walchelin of Winchester, and others who had been involved in investigating the lands of Ely about what they had established and by what means, and to have it set out in writing. William ended upon a note of urgency: 'See to it that I speedily know through a letter of your own the truth about this, and let an envoy of the abbot come with it.'[70] Such demands by William for action by Lanfranc himself may have been infrequent and occasional; but when they came, they were urgent and demanding. And, especially when the king was out of England, much more was done with Lanfranc's knowledge, by his authority, and subject to his oversight and advice.

[66] Ibid., nos. 120–1, 124, pp. 423–7, 433.
[67] Ibid., no. 123, pp. 431–2.   [68] Ibid., no. 125, pp. 434–5.
[69] Ibid., no. 126, pp. 436–7. The name of Bishop Geoffrey of Coutances as an addressee may be a later insertion.
[70] Ibid., no. 127, pp. 438–9. The result of any action by Lanfranc is not directly known; but a story that Bishop Walchelin of Winchester eventually persuaded Simeon to be consecrated by Remigius without prejudice to the position of future abbots suggests that the legal position was not settled in Lanfranc's lifetime: *Liber Eliensis*, 2.118, pp. 201–2.

The occasional nature of Lanfranc's action in affairs of secular government and justice may help to account for the silence of the sources about him in relation to some of the major events of the Conqueror's reign, and particularly to the Domesday survey of the kingdom. The land pleas about Canterbury property at and after the meeting on Penenden Heath and the protracted Ely inquiries which had eventually led to the king's requiring Lanfranc to provide an urgent and detailed written report are two indications of Lanfranc's interest in promoting a detailed and definitive national inquiry into the facts and rights of the tenurial situation. Given the potential benefit to churches, it is scarcely conceivable that Lanfranc should not have taken part in the deep thought and speech about these matters that the king had with his council after the Christmas court at Gloucester in 1085.[71] But there is no evidence for his part in it; he, like Archbishop Thomas of York, took no known active part in the inquiries that followed. A single letter of Lanfranc's seems to bear upon them.[72] Addressed to 'a dear and faithful friend' who was evidently an official of the Domesday circuit comprising Norfolk, Suffolk, and Essex, it assured him that Lanfranc had no demesne holdings in the shires concerned, where all Christ Church's lands were for the support of the monks. Lanfranc made clear his own hope for benefit from the greater certainty to be anticipated from the survey by confidently beseeching his friend to act as effectively in his affairs (*rebus nostris*) in the current business as opportunity was given to him from on high;[73] Lanfranc prayed that God would be his friend's vigilant helper against every evil work of those who might seek to subvert his inquiries.[74] Lanfranc's positive approval of the Domesday inquest seems clear. His non-participation may simply have been a result of his age; more probably, it arose from a long-standing agreement of archbishop and king that Lanfranc's prior concern was with the correction of the lives of men and with ordering the condition of the church.[75] In temporal matters, it was his province to know, to advise, and to direct others, but only occasionally and for particular reasons was it to act, whether in such a political contingency as in the rebellion of the earls or in such a judicial impasse as the question of episcopal rights at Ely.

---

[71] *ASC*, E, *a.* 1085, pp. 161–2; for Lanfranc's presence at Gloucester see *AL* 87.

[72] Lanfranc, *Letters*, no. 56, pp. 170–1.

[73] The words *tibi desuper data* recall John 19: 11. The biblical echoes in this letter tend to support the view that its recipient, referred to only as S., was a clerk.

[74] The evil works seem to be of those at large who might seek to mislead the Domesday inquiry rather than (as Dr Gibson suggested) Domesday officials themselves: Lanfranc, *Letters*, 171, n. 2. With the words *ab omni opere malo*, cf. 2 Tim. 4: 18.

[75] Cf. *VL* cap. 9, p. 692.

14

Lanfranc and the Gregorian Papacy

14.1 LANFRANC AND POPE GREGORY VII

Lanfranc's loyal and collaborative service of King William I in both ecclesiastical and temporal affairs stands in contrast to the coolness and distance that he showed towards the great reforming pope who from 1073 to 1085 was his contemporary in office, Gregory VII.[1] Lanfranc's attitude is the more remarkable in view of his familiarity in Italy with the early stirrings of papal reform under the Tusculan popes Benedict VIII and John XIX, his close and approving observation of the papacy especially under Leo IX, Nicholas II, and Alexander II, and above all the cordial working relationship between the apostolic see and the English church that was adumbrated in Lanfranc's early dealings as archbishop with Pope Alexander II. Neither from Lanfranc's side nor from that of Gregory VII does the evidence show clearly and expressly why Lanfranc from the outset showed such reserve. Nevertheless, the foregoing chapters suggest four reasons which, severally and together, may have contributed to it.

First, the surviving letter of Gregory while still Archdeacon Hildebrand to Lanfranc which is preserved in the latter's letter-collection somewhat curtly refused him the papal privilege that he desperately needed in order to settle the issue of the primacy of Canterbury unless he came in person to Rome for proper discussion.[2] As a consequence, since Lanfranc never again came to Rome, the primacy of Canterbury was not fully secured; in so far as it was settled, the means was a royal constitution.

Second, with regard to the exercise of papal authority in general, Hildebrand's letter contained sentences which may have put Lanfranc on his guard when its author became pope: Hildebrand thought it necessary for Lanfranc to come to the threshold of the apostles and there more effectively discuss and settle with Hildebrand and others both the issuing of a privilege and other matters; moreover, if 'our' legates should come to Lanfranc, he should hear and act on their words 'as beseems a most dear son of the holy Roman church and a dutiful (*religiosum*) bishop'.

---

[1] This chapter summarizes and revises discussions in Cowdrey, 'Pope Gregory VII and the Anglo-Norman Church', esp. 85–98, 107–14; id., 'The Papacy and the Berengarian Controversy', esp. 120–33; id., 'The Gregorian Reform in the Anglo-Norman Lands', esp. 334–47; id., 'Lanfranc, the Papacy, and the See of Canterbury'; id., 'The Enigma of Archbishop Lanfranc', esp. 136–41; id., *Pope Gregory VII*, esp. 459–67.
[2] For Hildebrand's letter, see Lanfranc, *Letters*, no. 6, pp. 58–9.

In November 1073, in the matter of the exemption of Bury St Edmunds from the jurisdiction of Bishop Herfast of Elmham, Gregory forcibly reminded Lanfranc of the universal jurisdiction of the apostolic see and of the right of access to it.[3] Recourse to the apostolic see had, indeed, been an increasing phenomemon in the western church, including England, under the earlier reform popes. But, by and large, the initiative had been local and the role of the apostolic see reactive; under Gregory that role became more proactive and directed towards intervention. At the same time, by his councils, letters, and exercise of the primacy, Lanfranc showed himself more proactive at home and interventionist than his Old English predecessors had been. There was at least the possibility of difference and conflict between papal and archiepiscopal claims and actions which made Lanfranc wary and even defensive, even though Gregory in practice seems to have been restrained in his demands upon him.[4]

A third reason was almost certainly William I's masterful rule over the English kingdom as over the Norman duchy. Indebted to Gregory though he was for supporting his invasion of England and for recognizing his kingship to be divinely blessed and prosperous, William had no intention of surrendering control of the church which was a major support of his royal power. Eadmer later asserted that all things, divine and human alike, depended upon his will. He gave as examples William's unwillingness for anyone in his dominions to acknowledge a pope save according to his own command or to receive his letters unless they had been at first (*primitus*) shown to him;[5] the archbishop of Canterbury as primate might decree or prohibit at a general council nothing save what was pleasing to the king's will and had been previously been laid down by him; no bishop might visit excommunication or any other spiritual censure upon a baron or minister of the king save by his command.[6] Comparison with a letter of Anselm to Pope Paschal II, which Eadmer seems to have known and which referred to the position under William I's sons, suggests that Eadmer may have somewhat overdrawn the position in Lanfranc's time.[7] But Gregory VII believed that fear of William I was a cause of his bishops' reluctance to come to Rome as Gregory thought that they should.[8] Lanfranc is unlikely to have done other than concur with the king in such a matter.

Fourth, Lanfranc may have felt himself to be distanced from Gregory, and even slighted by him, on account of their contrasting attitudes to Berengar of Tours and his eucharistic doctrine. Before becoming archbishop, Lanfranc had shown himself to be of one mind with Cardinal Humbert in the ultra-realist oath which he drew up

---

[3] *Reg.* 1.31, pp. 51–2.

[4] As is indicated by the fact that only three letters in Gregory's Register are addressed to Lanfranc: *Reg.* 1.31, pp. 51–2, 6.30, pp. 443–4, 9.20, pp. 600–1.

[5] By *primitus*, Eadmer probably means 'at first' in the sense of the critical first letter of a new pope the reception of which implied recognition, not 'first' in the sense that the Conqueror expected to be shown every letter, even one so routine as Gregory VII's letter to Bishop Remigius of Lincoln about the treatment of a priest guilty of homicide: *Reg.* 1.34, p. 55; see also Lanfranc, *Letters*, no. 29, pp. 114–15. In any case, the king's absences abroad would hardly have allowed for his seeing every incoming papal letter.

[6] Eadmer, *Hist, nov.*, 1, pp. 9–10.   [7] Anselm, *Epp.* no. 210, vol. 4.106.

[8] *Reg.* 7.1, p. 459; cf. 6.30, p. 443.

for the reluctant Berengar to take at Rome and in his strong condemnation of Berengarian teaching; Archdeacon Hildebrand by contrast had been uncertain and had looked for further inquiry. If Hildebrand saw the copy of Lanfranc's *De corpore et sanguine Domini* that Pope Alexander II asked him to send to Rome, there is nothing to suggest that it had any impact upon him. For several years as pope he continued to be hesitant and to leave the Berengarian question open. When in 1079 he at last condemned Berengar, he did so in terms that did not fully match those of Humbert and Lanfranc, and Lanfranc in a letter gave what may be a hint that he was less than satisfied by the pronouncement that Berengar was now required to make.[9] Gregory's conduct and proceedings in what was for Lanfranc so weighty a matter cannot have given him confidence.

When Gregory became pope, he took the initiative in seeking to establish good relations with Lanfranc. He very quickly addressed a letter to him as his most dear brother in Christ informing him about his election, entrusting its bearer verbally with some of his more private thoughts, and seeking the continual prayers of Lanfranc and his monks. He concluded the letter by urging Lanfranc especially to correct the moral abuses of the Irish in abandoning and even selling their wives and to be vigilant for such abuses elsewhere in 'the island of the English'.[10] The letter thus tacitly countenanced Lanfranc's claim to a primacy over the whole of the British Isles. Gregory's sharper letter of November 1073 centred upon Lanfranc's duty towards Bury St Edmunds as a monastery that enjoyed special apostolic protection; Gregory referred to what he recognized as Lanfranc's common purpose with him.[11]

As time progressed, Gregory's most insistent complaint against Lanfranc was his failure despite repeated summonses to fulfil the duty of coming in person to Rome. Gregory's first surviving reproof was in a letter to him of March 1079. Gregory would already have confronted such unexpected heedlessness had he not been held back by apostolic mildness and by the pledge of ancient love—evidently their friendly acquaintance in the time of earlier popes. Gregory attributed Lanfranc's negligence partly to dread of the king but more to his own fault. Let Lanfranc forestall possible sanctions against the king by suitably admonishing him and let him himself obey Gregory's wishes and commands that he come to Rome.[12] In the following November Gregory instructed his legate Hubert to order and invite at least two bishops from each of the English and Norman archdioceses to attend his next Lent synod or at least to be in Rome after Easter 1080.[13] It is virtually certain that none came. But when, probably later in that year, the legate Hubert came to William I to discuss his doing of fealty and the payment of Peter's Pence, he brought to Lanfranc a letter from Gregory about his visiting Rome—perhaps the letter registered in the previous March but probably another letter, now lost, that

---

[9] See above, p. 67.   [10] Lanfranc, *Letters*, no. 8, pp. 64–7.   [11] *Reg.* 1.31, pp. 51–2.
[12] *Reg.* 6.30, pp. 443–4. Gregory alluded to frequent earlier commands that may have been communicated verbally or by letter.
[13] *Reg.* 7.1, p. 460.

was more strongly worded.[14] Lanfranc's very cool reply survives. He gave no hint that he would or might come to Rome. He wrote that he could not see what bodily presence or physical distance or even high promotion had to do with the real issue:

For my mind is subject to your precepts in all things and through all things according to the precepts of the canons. And if by God's help I were able at some time to speak with you face to face, I would show less by words than by very deeds that I have increased in loving while (if I may be allowed to say so) you have in no small part fallen away from your former love.[15]

From Gregory's point of view, such words verged on the contumacious. The year 1080, which witnessed his second excommunication and deposition of King Henry IV of Germany and Henry's choice of Archbishop Guibert of Ravenna to be anti-pope, was an unfavourable time for pursuing matters with Lanfranc. But in the summer of 1082 Gregory returned to them. In a letter to Lanfranc he now made no mention of the king as restraining him from visiting Rome: it was Lanfranc's own pride or negligence that had led him to delay and to abuse Gregory's patience. Putting aside all excuses and vain fear, he must come to Rome by All Saintstide (1 November) and make amends for his past offence. If he were disobedient, he would be suspended from his entire episcopal office.[16] The letter had no known sequel;[17] there is no likelihood that Lanfranc went to Rome; given the perilous situation of the Gregorian papacy, Gregory could not afford to alienate the Anglo-Norman kingdom. But Lanfranc's ambivalent attitude to Gregory in his final years may well have been in part a consequence of Gregory's unwelcome insistence that he should visit Rome.[18]

When the papal legate Hubert came to England bringing Gregory VII's letter to Lanfranc about his remissness in not visiting Rome, he had other important business as well. He may have brought three letters dated 8 May 1080 and addressed to members of the royal family, all of which warmly praised William's kingship: to King William, Gregory couched in Gelasian terms an exhortation to continue in exemplary Christian kingship; he applauded Queen Matilda's sterling virtues; and he exhorted their eldest son, Robert Curthose, for the future to be dutiful to his father as beseemed his son and intended heir.[19] Gregory was evidently concerned to fortify the king's goodwill. Items in Lanfranc's letter-collection are the sole evidence for two matters about which the legate was to prompt the king verbally, using Lanfranc's good offices to broach them: William should do fealty to Gregory and his successors, and he should give better attention to the regular payment to the Roman church of Peter's Pence. William's written reply was terse and decisive:

---

[14] This is clear from Lanfranc's reply: *Letters*, no. 38, pp. 128–31. That Hubert brought a further letter is suggested by the lapse of time, by Lanfranc's statement that practically its whole length was devoted to rebuking Lanfranc with no reference to the king, and by Lanfranc's referring to points not made in *Reg.* 6.30, e.g. the deterioration in Lanfranc's devotion to the Roman church after he became a bishop.

[15] The last phrase takes up the 'pledge of ancient love' of *Reg.* 6.30.   [16] *Reg.* 9.20, pp. 600–1.

[17] Unless the alleged visit to Rome in 1082, upon the king's order, of Bishop William of Saint-Calais to seek papal sanction for the introduction of a monastic chapter at Durham cathedral was intended as a gesture of conciliation to Gregory: see *De iniusta vexacione*, 73–4; Symeon of Durham, *Libellus*, 4.2, pp. 226–9.

[18] See below, pp. 202–4.   [19] *Reg.* 7.25–7, pp. 505–8; cf. 7.23, pp. 499–502.

'The one [Peter's Pence] I have allowed; the other [fealty] I have not allowed.' Each decision was firmly but courteously explained.[20]

Lanfranc's known part in the exchange between Gregory and William has three aspects. First, he was himself able to assure Gregory that he had done his best to put the pope's case to William and to leave further explanation of the king's stance to Hubert:

> I presented to my lord the king to the best of my ability the words of your legatine message together with the legate; I put the case but I did not prevail (*suasi sed non persuasi*). And why he has not in all ways consented to your will, the legate himself is making known to you both by word of mouth and by a letter.

Second, the letter referred to was that from King William to Gregory that appears in Lanfranc's collection. Both its place there and its terse and skilful drafting suggest that, in form and substance, it is deeply influenced, if not written, by Lanfranc himself. It begins and ends cordially. The greeting *salutem cum amicicia* may carry the overtone that friendship, not fealty, governed the relations of king and pope. The concluding sentence was in harmony with Gregory's approving letters to William: 'Pray for us, for we have loved your predecessors and we wish sincerely to love and obediently to hear you above all men.' In the body of the letter, the firm refusal of fealty was counterbalanced by an admission that there had been laxity in sending Peter's Pence while the king had been in France; now he had returned this would be put right, and Hubert would bring a first instalment of the arrears. The letter is eloquent of Lanfranc's diplomatic skill in dealing with the papacy. Third, the letter included the king's promise that the balance of Peter's Pence would be sent when opportunity arose 'by messengers of our *fidelis* Archbishop Lanfranc'. The word *fidelis* was an implicit reminder of where Lanfranc's loyalty lay. But there is also evidence of Lanfranc's care in general in collecting Peter's Pence in his own diocese.[21] Lanfranc sought to balance the claims of king and papacy as he thought them to be fairly and judiciously made.

With respect to the pope's approaches to the king about doing fealty and to himself about visiting Rome, Lanfranc showed finesse in warding off papal requirements without pressing matters to crisis point. Gregory's letters to and about the king made clear the value that he placed upon William's strong and prosperous rule and his care for the church which, even though it had aspects to which Gregory objected, was to be welcomed and encouraged. He was better treated with amicable mildness than by the severity and rigour of righteousness.[22] Lanfranc could be confident that Gregory would not readily impose sanctions upon him that would alienate the king whose *fidelis* he was. Lanfranc was also adept at turning aside papal wrath. Thus, his letter which answered back in almost contumacious terms Gregory's summons that he should soon come to Rome ended with a declaration that he had, to the best of his ability, advocated to the king Gregory's request for fealty but the king had not been persuaded; he left to the legate Hubert whom he had

---

[20] Lanfranc, *Letters*, nos. 38 (last paragraph), 39, pp. 130–3.
[21] *The Domesday monachorum*, 80.   [22] *Reg.* 9.5, p. 580.

supported the task of explaining the king's refusal to Gregory. In the matter of Peter's Pence, when the pope's demand had traditional authority, Lanfranc signalled his co-operation. If Lanfranc's conduct towards Gregory was cool and distant, it was also well calculated and skilfully pursued. He astutely judged the limits of prudent opposition.

14.2 LANFRANC AND THE ANTI-POPE

Lanfranc showed similar qualities and attitudes in the papal schism which began in 1084. On Palm Sunday (24 March), after King Henry IV of Germany had entered Rome and taken control of St Peter's, Archbishop Guibert of Ravenna, the anti-pope whom Henry had chosen in 1080, was enthroned in the Lateran, taking the name of Clement III. On Easter Sunday (31 March) Clement crowned the victorious Henry as emperor. Some three months later Gregory VII found it necessary to depart from the city into exile at Salerno. So far as the Anglo-Norman lands are concerned, there is no reason to suppose that King William I was other than entirely loyal to Gregory. The continuing confidence in him of Gregory's circle is clear from a letter to him from Gregory's standing legate in Lombardy, Bishop Anselm II of Lucca, to be dated c.1085. Anselm warmly praised William's victorious and just kingship, thanked him for unspecified but tangible benefits that he had received, and in a postscript confidently called upon him to help the Roman church and to deliver it from its enemies' hands.[23]

Lanfranc, however, was soon in touch with a partisan of the anti-pope. The evidence for this is a letter in his letter-collection which, as preserved, bears only the salutation 'Lanfrancus Hu.'[24] In all probability, 'Hu.' was Hugh Candidus, cardinal-priest of S. Clemente, who for some ten years had been Gregory's bitter enemy and who had been the only Roman cardinal to have supported Henry IV's naming of Archbishop Guibert as prospective anti-pope in 1080. At the beginning of his letter Lanfranc referred to a previous letter that he had sent to 'Hu.' and to an answer to which he was now replying. His reply, a masterpiece of suspended judgement, was non-committal. The view of papal authority that Lanfranc had expressed in his tract on the eucharist is helpful towards understanding his detached standpoint. In comment upon Christ's words to St Peter about the foundation of the church and the power of the keys (Matt. 16: 18–19), Lanfranc held that, while some understood them of the pastors of the church, the weight of tradition understood them of the Roman church itself.[25] Lanfranc's view left him with latitude to judge the words and credentials of those who exercised or claimed papal authority without prejudice to the overriding authority of the Roman church itself.

[23] *Die Hannoversche Briefsammlung*, 1: *Die Hildesheimer Briefe*, no. 1, in Erdmann and Fickermann (eds.), *Briefsammlungen*, 15–17.

[24] Lanfranc, *Letters*, no. 52, pp. 164–7. The summary address may be a calculated attempt on the compiler's part to conceal the identity of 'Hu.'. The *terminus a quo* for the letter is 24 March 1084, when Guibert assumed the papal name Clement.

[25] *DCSD* cap. 16, col. 426; see above, pp. 4, 43.

Hence, Lanfranc replied to 'Hu.' with guarded circumspection. He found things in his letter of which he disapproved: his vituperation of Pope Gregory (Lanfranc used both his title and his papal name); his referring to Gregory as 'Hildebrand' (his given name); his calling Gregory's legates 'thorns in the flesh (*spinosulos*)':[26] his excessive laudation of Clement (Lanfranc used his papal name without title). Lanfranc commented that scripture forbids a man's being praised or disparaged by his neighbour during his lifetime. Thus far, Lanfranc's letter tended to be discouraging to 'Hu.'; but he next made a more encouraging observation: Henry IV—despite his renewed excommunication and deposition by Gregory in 1080, Lanfranc called him *gloriosus imperator*—would not have taken in hand without good cause so great a matter (as the installation of Clement at Rome), nor would he have achieved so signal a victory, without great help from God. Having struck this balance, Lanfranc left 'Hu.' in suspense:

I do not approve that you should come to the land of England unless you first receive licence to come from the king of the English. For our island has not yet rejected the former [Gregory], nor has it made known a decision whether to obey the other [Clement]. When the case on both sides has been heard, if it should so happen, it will be possible to perceive more clearly what should be done.

While not in any way committing himself or compromising his position, Lanfranc left himself with freedom to react to whatever the future might hold about who would be vindicated as pastor of the Roman church.

There is no known direct sequel to Lanfranc's letter to 'Hu.', but three letters survive which Clement himself addressed to him as part of his energetic endeavour to secure wide support throughout Latin Christendom.[27] They are preserved because they were copied into the end of Lanfranc's copy of his *Collectio canonum* after the colophon about his purchasing it from Bec.[28] It is not certain whether they were entered during his lifetime or with his knowledge. They are of differing dates; the first two could be from after a date in late 1084 and seem to be from soon after, though they were probably not sent together; the third was sent after Clement knew of King William II's accession in September 1087. In each of the three letters Clement besought Lanfranc in fulsome terms to visit him in Rome. In the second and third he asked for Peter's Pence to be sent, and in the third he charged Lanfranc with prompting King William II to restore to the nuns of Wilton land that they had lost in his father's day. The long third letter praised and flattered Lanfranc in extravagant terms.

The letters should probably not be regarded as implying a positive or open approach by Lanfranc and the English kingdom to the anti-pope Clement III after the death in 25 May 1085 of Gregory VII.[29] There is no suggestion that Lanfranc

---

[26] For a note on the rare word *spinosulus*, see Lanfranc, *Letters*, p. 165, n. 2. The legates may be those dispatched widely from Salerno by Gregory VII in 1084; see Cowdrey, *Gregory VII*, 231–2.

[27] For the letters, see Liebermann, 'Lanfranc and the Antipope', 330–2; for Clement's wider campaign, see Ziese, *Wibert*, 134–77, with discussion of England at pp. 134–42.

[28] See above, p. 139.

[29] As argued by Kehr, 'Zur Geschichte', 356–60; cf. Ziese, *Wibert*, 138–41.

sought or replied to any of them; the silence of the third letter about a reply suggests that he did not. The request for Peter's Pence and the approach on behalf of the Wilton nuns do not imply any even de facto recognition of Clement by the English authorities: requests for Peter's Pence, and for the archbishop of Canterbury to visit the pope, seem to have been common form in initial papal letters;[30] whoever represented the nuns may have approached Clement not by their direction but because upon arrival in Rome Clement was the pope whom they encountered. Above all, Clement's letters were not well calculated to impress Lanfranc. The eulogy of him was undiplomatic as addressed to one who had reminded Clement's partisan 'Hu.' of the scriptural prohibition of praising a man during his lifetime; the prolixity of Clement's letters and the undertones of insecurity, self-distrust, and lack of authority are more likely to have confirmed Lanfranc in his hesitation about Clement than to have drawn him to take up his cause.

Several considerations indicate that until the end of his life Lanfranc maintained the attitude of cautious non-commitment towards Clement and of non-renunciation of Gregory and his successors that he expressed in his letter to 'Hu.'. First, the continuing approval of Anselm of Bec, who like the province of Rouen and the rest of the French church did not recognize Clement, would be unthinkable if there were any public knowledge of Lanfranc's favourable dealings with the antipope. Anselm visited England in 1086, when he could scarcely not have heard about any rumours that were current; there is no hint that he felt in any way uneasy.[31] When in 1089 he heard of Lanfranc's illness, he declared his life to be necessary for the whole church and prayed for his recovery as one whose holy living was pleasing to God.[32] He had clearly not compromised himself in Anselm's eyes. Second, a letter of Lanfranc to Abbot Rodulf of Saint-Vanne at Verdun if authentic suggests that he was regarded with respect by Gregorians further afield. In 1085 Rodulf was driven from his abbey by his imperialist bishop and took refuge with other monks in Saint-Bénigne at Dijon, the abbey of the staunchly Gregorian Abbot Jarento. His conscience was perplexed about whether, having vowed stability at Saint-Vanne, he might again take such a vow at Dijon. According to Lanfranc's letter, the point of conscience was put to the archbishop on his behalf. Arguing as if in his own case, Lanfranc replied that where, as with Rodulf, it was a matter of escaping from sowers of discord and pride, a fresh vow was justified.[33] Lanfranc was thus consulted by Gregorians and gave an answer from a corresponding standpoint.[34] Third and

---

[30] See Urban II, *Ep.* 3, *PL* 151.286–7.

[31] See Anselm, *Epp.* nos. 108, 115–21, vol. 3.241, 250–62.   [32] Ibid., no. 124, vol. 3.264–5.

[33] For the letter, which is not in Lanfranc's letter collection, see *Ep.* 66, Lanfrancus, *Opera*, ed. Giles, 1.80–1; for its background, see Hugh of Flavigny, *Chron.*, 2, pp. 472–3; see also p. 407 for Abbot Richard's favour with the Norman dukes.

[34] The authenticity of the letter has been denied, e.g. by Gibson, *Lanfranc*, 243; eadem, *Lanfranc, Letters*, 94, n. 6, 184–5. But Lanfranc's defence of monastic stability in *Letters*, no. 17, pp. 94–5, scarcely excludes his position in the letter to Rodulf: it was one thing to uphold it against a visionary within a monk's community, but another to sanction taking a second vow when a monk's former monastery was compromised by schism. Lanfranc's device of arguing in his own person may recall his own early dilemma when he despaired of the standard of monastic life at Bec: see above, pp. 13–15. Even if

most important, when Urban II became pope in 1088 he wrote cordially to Lanfranc announcing his election. He gave no hint of doubting the loyalty of Lanfranc and the English kingdom, and he named as a legate Roger, a cardinal-subdeacon of the Roman church.[35]

All in all, the evidence suggests that, whatever dealings Lanfranc had with partisans of the anti-pope and whatever communications he received from him, he remained cautiously non-committal. There is no evidence of either private or public debate in England about whom to recognize as pope.[36] It is highly probable that the established habit of deference to Gregory VII persisted after his death until Urban II was chosen to succeed him.

spurious, the letter is of some evidential value as showing that the circles within which it was written did not doubt Lanfranc's public loyalty to Gregory.

[35] *EP.* 3, *PL* 151.286–7.

[36] Though the grave of Bishop Godfrey of Chichester (d. 25 Sept. 1088) contained a lead cross inscribed with a papal absolution: Mayr-Harting, *The Bishops of Chichester*, 1–2, 21, Plate 4. No papal name is given, but a specific pope seems to be envisaged; some involvement of Urban's agent Roger is possible.

15

External Concerns

As archbishop of Canterbury, Lanfranc was the ecclesiastical head of an English church that consisted of the provinces of Canterbury and York; he claimed a primacy over the British Isles, that is, also over Wales, Scotland, and Ireland. His canonical authority stopped short at the English Channel. Normandy formed the province of Rouen which was part of the French church; in 1079, indeed, Pope Gregory VII confirmed the province of Rouen as being subject to the primacy of Lyons.[1] After returning to England from Rome with his *pallium* in 1071, Lanfranc's only known journey from its shores was in 1077, when he travelled to Normandy to visit the king who was there throughout the year, and was present at the consecration of the churches of his two former abbeys, Saint-Étienne at Caen and Bec. Nevertheless, on account of his own past career and present reputation, Lanfranc continued to be considerably concerned with persons and problems both in the duchy of Normandy and beyond its frontiers.

15.1 LANFRANC AND NORMANDY

Lanfranc's Norman concerns centred upon the abbey of Bec and its two leading figures—Herluin, abbot until his death in 1078, and Anselm, prior until that date and afterwards abbot. With Herluin, Lanfranc had a particularly strong mutual bond, the intensity of which was manifest when in an unknown year Herluin came to Canterbury for no other apparent reason than to visit Lanfranc.[2] In his Life of Herluin which is the sole source, Gilbert Crispin painted a vivid picture of his visit which sheds light upon Lanfranc's public self-presentation as archbishop. Gilbert enlarged upon the godly contention in mutual submission between the two men in which the great archbishop made himself subject to his sometime abbot as would any ordinary monk. Except at masses, Lanfranc always took second place to Herluin, whose hand Lanfranc tried to kiss whenever he received anything unless the abbot snatched his hand away.[3] Lanfranc's deference went beyond the usual monastic manifestations, such as inviting a guest abbot to preside in chapter, which reflected St Paul's precept about mutual deference—'in honour preferring one

---

[1] See Cowdrey, *Pope Gregory VII*, 602–4.
[2] *VH* caps. 84–96, pp. 100–2, 201–3; whence *VL* cap. 7, pp. 608–9.
[3] Lanfranc's—to the modern mind exaggerated—gestures of humility to Herluin are reminiscent of Archbishop Thomas of York's exaggerated words of deference to Lanfranc: Lanfranc, *Letters*, no. 12, pp. 78–81; see above, p. 101. They are evidence of the familiar conventions of Lanfranc's day.

another (*honore invicem praevenientes*)' (Rom. 12: 10), which St Benedict enjoined for monastic dealings.[4] Lanfranc also made it a spectacle for everyone, especially the English, who wondered that an archbishop of Canterbury should thus subject himself to any mortal man. The more crowded his court and the greater the dignity of those of all social orders who came there, so much more obsequious was Lanfranc to Herluin in their presence. Such a voluntary yoke of obedience was a pattern of humility for all subjects who showed contempt to those set in authority over them. Lanfranc's pointing of the virtue of humility is a counterpart to the lesson that he was reputed to have brought home to the king in the incident of the court jester.[5] It had social as well as individual edification in view. It illustrates Lanfranc's conviction that, as archbishop, he had a duty by word and by gesture to impress moral precepts upon every order and grade of society.

It was Herluin's earnest desire that Lanfranc should consecrate the abbey church at Bec that he had begun to build. This followed in 1077, a, year which saw four consecrations of major Norman churches—the cathedrals of Bayeux (14 July) and Évreux, and the abbey churches of Saint-Étienne at Caen (13 September) and Bec (23 October). Some later sources give information about Lanfranc's presence and participation which is doubtful. He is not likely to have been present at Bayeux or Évreux; it is no less unlikely that, as Orderic Vitalis wrote, the dedications were all performed by Archbishop John of Rouen in Lanfranc's presence, for in mid-July John suffered a permanently incapacitating stroke that left him dumb.[6] But Lanfranc was certainly present at Caen with a large attendance that included the king and queen;[7] his being the chief consecrating bishop at Bec is established by Gilbert Crispin's long and detailed account.[8]

According to it, Lanfranc's visit to Bec fell into two parts. Upon crossing the Channel he went straight there. Gilbert presents him as showing a visible humility to the abbot and community which renewed that which he exhibited when Herluin came to Canterbury. Laying aside his pontifical eminence (*pontificali amota celsitudine*), he shared the life of the ordinary choir monks. His so doing was well remembered at Bec: the *Vita Lanfranci* added the details that, except when celebrating mass, he did not wear his episcopal ring and that he insisted upon occupying the prior's stall, thus reverting to his position in the community. Only under the compulsion of the whole community did he overcome his unwillingness to perform the pontifical function of consecrating the church. When he left for the king's court, he obtained the monks' leave as one of their number would have done. (Lanfranc similarly obtained their leave to depart for England three days after the consecration.) His business with the king was twofold: first, to settle the secular and ecclesiastical affairs that had brought him to Normandy, and second, now, to secure permission

---

[4] See *RSB* caps. 63.15–17, 72, vol. 2.646–7, 670–1. [5] See above, p. 187.
[6] Lanfranc's presence at Bayeux is virtually excluded by the terms of William's writ of 14 July, addressed to Lanfranc and others, about lands of St Augustine's abbey at Canterbury: *Regesta WI*, no. 83, pp. 348–9. For notices of the consecrations, see *Ann. Beccenses*, 3; Orderic Vitalis, 5.2, 3, vol. 3.10–13, 18–19.
[7] *Regesta WI*, no. 46, pp. 220–1.
[8] *VH* caps. 109–27, pp. 104–8/206–9; whence *VL* cap. 8, pp. 690–2 (with additions).

to proceed to the consecration which he knew to require the king's edict and concurrence. Lanfranc later returned to Bec to consecrate the church in the presence of a huge concourse of clergy and laity from the duchy and beyond, though not of the king and queen who were unavoidably detained from coming. The consecration was performed with the greatest solemnity and was followed by the dispensing of abundant hospitality. As Gilbert Crispin presented it, as performed by Lanfranc it enabled Herluin to say a *Nunc dimittis* to his own life's work.

Lanfranc's dealings with Herluin were personal and marked by an exceptional warmth and admiration. His dealings with Anselm were not without these characteristics, though they were more concerned with matters of business.[9] The principal source is the numerous letters that survive in Anselm's letter-collections, together with a few in Lanfranc's collection. As abbot, Anselm at least twice came to England during Lanfranc's lifetime.[10]

Anselm's letters raise a problem about the course of his personal relations with Lanfranc. For several years they continued in a spirit of particular cordiality which arose from the memory of their years together at Bec when Lanfranc was prior and Anselm his pupil.[11] It found expression in Anselm's letter to Lanfranc upon his becoming archbishop. Anselm greeted him as 'frater ANSELMUS suus totus (wholly his)' and dwelt upon their complete unity of soul and works.[12] In future letters written while Anselm was prior, the *suus totus* formula was developed into *suus quod suus* ('his own as owing his own self to him').[13] Anselm addressed this phrase to no one else, but at a certain point he suddenly ceased using it to Lanfranc.[14] The discontinuance calls for an explanation. It has been associated with Lanfranc's reservations about Anselm's treatise, the *Monologion* (written 1075/6), when Anselm submitted it to him: henceforth, a phrase that had arisen from a complete unity of soul and works was not appropriate; although the two men continued to address each other with affection and respect, there was a parting of the ways.[15]

Such a view perhaps calls for qualification. Attention has been drawn to Anselm's Letter 57 to Lanfranc, which cannot be precisely dated but which may pre-date the submission of the *Monologion* for Lanfranc's comment; there is no allusion to it in the letter.[16] Nor is the *suus quod suus* formula with which it opens under discussion;

---

[9] Lanfranc's dealings with Anselm are fully discussed by Southern, *Saint Anselm and his Biographer*, esp. 12–26, 51–2; id., *Saint Anselm: A Portrait*, esp. 39–66.

[10] There is uncertainty as to whether Anselm visited England twice or three times. He certainly came in 1079 and 1086; the evidence for a further visit in 1080 is inconclusive. For his visits, see *VA* 1.29–31, pp. 48–57; *VL* cap. 16, pp. 712–13; Anselm, *Epp.* nos. 98, 108, 115–24, vol. 3.228–9, 241, 250–62.

[11] See above, pp. 11, 21.   [12] Anselm, *Epp.* no. 1, vol. 3.97–8.

[13] See ibid., nos. 23, 25, 27, 32, 49, 57, 66, vol. 3.130, 132, 134, 142, 162, 171, 186.

[14] See ibid., nos. 72, 77, 89, 90, 103, 124, vol. 3.193, 199, 215, 217, 236, 264.

[15] Southern, *Saint Anselm: A Portrait*, esp. 59–62, 65–6, 113–27.

[16] Since the letter raises problems of translation and interpretation, it may be desirable to offer an English version:

To his lord and father, the reverend Archbishop Lanfranc, brother Anselm: his own as owing his own self to him (*suus quod suus*).

Just as, to commend the authority of his prophecy, Zechariah the prophet repeats throughout practically every verse: 'These words says the Lord', so to convey who speaks, to whom, and in what spirit indeed, Anselm's comment that he bore Lanfranc's stamp engraved inwardly in his mind tends to confirm it. The letter is probably to be read as reflecting the convention of *humilitas* that Lanfranc and Herluin acted out at their meetings: if Lanfranc was indeed Anselm's lord and father, humility—and logic—required that the reply should be addressed to servant and son. And that is all: Anselm addressed to Lanfranc, probably with no serious expectation that he would comply, a learned *jeu d'esprit* which suggests that relations between them were relaxed and cordial.

When and why, then, did Anselm discontinue using the *suus quod suus* formula in his letters to Lanfranc? It is absent from the letter in which Anselm first asked Lanfranc to examine his book and so before Lanfranc had expressed an opinion;[17] Anselm was not, therefore, responding to criticism. Perhaps a formula suggesting an identity of mind was omitted as seeming to prejudge the issue. It is also absent from Anselm's letter of reply to Lanfranc's comments.[18] He wrote as 'brother Anselm, in subjection Lanfranc's servant, in affection his son, in doctrine a disciple'—terms reminiscent of Letter 57. But his wish for Anselm, *quod melius potest* ('the best that he can'), may hint at a certain disappointment. Nevertheless, Anselm replied to Lanfranc's entreaty that his love would not cool by reason of Lanfranc's criticisms which were made in a spirit of love; Anselm declared that he received them in the spirit in which they were given; Anselm received Lanfranc's fatherly admonition gratefully and put forward his answer humbly.

Leaving aside the discontinuance of the *suus quod suus* formula, there is nothing to suggest that the parting of the ways in doctrinal matters precluded the full continuance of personal and official relationships in the spirit of this exchange. From September 1078 Anselm was abbot of Bec. It should not escape notice that in future surviving letters to Lanfranc he usually wrote in association with his monastery at Bec, so that the words *suus quod suus* would have been inappropriate; *quod sui* ('what those who are his own owe to him') became the habitual equivalent.[19] When Anselm came to Canterbury in 1079 he was cordially received by Lanfranc, whom he advised about the sanctity of St Elphege; he associated with the community as Lanfranc had associated with the community at Bec in 1077; he was granted spiritual confraternity with the monks of Christ Church—a grant that must have had

[cf. the phrases in the address as above] it pleases me that very often our letters that I dispatch to your fatherly eminence should exhibit blazoned upon their forehead 'To a lord and father (*domino et patri*)' and 'his as owing his own self to him (*suus quod suus*)'. For I would not say that I know how to depict a cypress [cf. Horace, *Ars poetica*, lines 19–21—i.e. outwardly and as mere routine], but that I have so engraved it upon my mind [i.e. inwardly] that whatever I might suggest when beginning our salutation [by the words *domino et patri*], the same should be apparent as being expressed in its completeness [including it the words *suus quod suus*]. Since, therefore, I so often write to you with this superscription, I earnestly inquire why you never write back to me [who am your servant and son] but to I know not whom—to your 'lord and father (*domino et patri*)' designated by the first letter of the alphabet [A]! Or if you *are* writing to your servant and son [i.e. to me], why do you endeavour to undermine by a relative opposition ['*domino et patri*'] what you cannot destroy by an opposite negation ['*non servo et non filio*']? [For the two types of opposites, see Aristotle, *Categories*, 11a17–33; 12b5–16, 13a36–7, 13b27–35.] I therefore ask that, whenever I in future receive your excellency's letters, either I may see to whom you are writing, or else at least that I may not see to whom you are not writing!

[17] Anselm, *Epp.* no. 72, p. 193.   [18] Ibid., *Epp.* no. 77, pp. 199–200.   [19] As n. 14.

Lanfranc's approval.[20] When Lanfranc died, Anselm is said to have composed his epitaph.[21] While Anselm's continuing disuse of the *suus quod suus* formula cannot be shown not to have been influenced by Lanfranc's criticism of the *Monologion*, a more likely explanation, in view of their mutual resolve to keep their relationship unaffected, is that it was deemed inappropriate when Anselm was an abbot. As Anselm's Letter 57 illustrates, it implied a subjection to another man which was not compatible with the duty of one who, according to the Rule, bore a title whose very meaning was 'father' and who was Christ's representative in the monastery (*Christi enim agere vices in monasterio creditur*).[22] Such an explanation must at least be seriously entertained.

In intellectual terms, the *Monologion* undoubtedly revealed a gap between the thought of Anselm and Lanfranc, although there is a danger of exaggerating it. The gap is clearly revealed in Eadmer's brief notice of it:

> He also wrote a little book which he has called the *Monologion*. For in it he speaks alone and with himself, and, leaving aside all authority of divine scripture, he seeks and finds by reason alone what God is; and he proves and demonstrates by invincible reason that what true faith holds concerning God is indeed so and cannot be otherwise.[23]

Such a leaving aside of authority, scriptural and also conciliar and patristic, in order to investigate Christian truth by invincible reason alone was poles apart from Lanfranc's insistence on tradition and on the province of reason as being solely to clarify and expound what ancient authorities declared. Despite this gap, Anselm sent his composition to Lanfranc at Canterbury for his examination. In his accompanying letter to Lanfranc, Anselm expressly envisaged only two possible outcomes: either Lanfranc would approve it much as it stood, in which case Anselm asked him to give it a title; or else he would radically disapprove, in which case the manuscript should be destroyed. But in a letter sent at the same time to the monk Maurice who had urged him to write the book, Anselm envisaged that Lanfranc might propose more substantial corrections.[24]

Lanfranc neither approved nor destroyed the book, to which he neither now or later gave a title;[25] but he advised substantial revision and was evidently disturbed by Anselm's lack of reliance on authorities. His response has not survived, but Anselm in due course wrote again to him.[26] After agreeing that their personal relationship should not be impaired, Anselm claimed that he had been true to tradition: he had written only what he knew he could defend from canonical writings and especially from St Augustine's *De trinitate*. Anselm still awaited Lanfranc's word as to whether his book should survive or be destroyed; he was ready to make necessary corrections under Lanfranc's direction. He ended by taking up Lanfranc's comment that a

---

[20] *VA* 1.29–30, pp. 48–54. For Anselm's generous response to radical criticism, see *VA* 1.19, p. 31.
[21] See Orderic Vitalis, 8.8, vol. 4.170–1; also the text of Lanfranc's epitaph in *PL* 158.1049–50.
[22] See *RSB* cap. 2.1–2, vol. 1.440–3.   [23] *VA* 1.19, p. 29.
[24] Anselm, *Epp*. nos. 72, 74, vol. 3.193–4, 196.
[25] For the title, see Anselm, *Epp*. nos. 100, 109, vol. 3.232, 241–2.
[26] Anselm, *Epp*. no. 77, vol. 3.199–200.

conference between them about the book would be advantageous; would that this might happen about it and about certain other things!²⁷

Thus matters were left in suspense, and there is no clear evidence whatever of any sequel. But in 1077 Lanfranc twice visited Bec;²⁸ it is scarcely thinkable that he then had no further discussion of the book with Anselm and with those monks of Bec who, as the sources testify, had pressed Anselm to write it.²⁹ While there is no certainty, it is likely that a further letter of Anselm to Lanfranc about the book is to be associated with Lanfranc's visits to Bec. It was not included in any collection of Anselm's letters, but was preserved at the head of some manuscripts of the *Monologion*. In it, Anselm seeks Lanfranc's verdict upon the work, but its tone and substance are significantly different from those of Anselm's first approach.³⁰ The tone is less personal and more formal. As if to show that past events had caused no breach, Anselm placed great emphasis on his debt to Lanfranc. He would choose him before all others as a counseller in things doubtful, a teacher in things unknown, a reprover when he went too far, an approver when he did rightly: the phrases seem to be coloured by Lanfranc's first response to the *Monologion*. Anselm ended his letter by saying that he returned to his especial counsellor: *ad singularem meum recurro consiliarium*; the verb *recurro* may imply a resubmission of the work. Anselm did not in this letter write of its possible outright acceptance; he now only envisaged its suppression or its correction. These features of the letter are pointers to further consideration, perhaps after face-to-face talks between Anselm and Lanfranc at Bec. If this were so, the most likely outcome that can be envisaged is that Lanfranc, perhaps in deference to the wishes and needs of a new generation of monks at Bec, conceded a *nihil obstat* to a suitably amended text without giving positive approval. It would be consistent with this that Anselm is not known to have submitted to him any further writing, even the *Proslogion* which was composed c.1077/8,³¹ but that personal relations seem not to have suffered. In any case, it should not upon the surviving evidence be presumed that discussion and reconsideration ceased.

However this may have been, the spiritual and material benefits which association with Bec brought to the English church in general and to the church of Canterbury in particular were too great for Lanfranc to allow that association to be weakened. Abbot Herluin's visit to Canterbury and Lanfranc's visits to Bec in 1077, as well as Anselm's many letters to Lanfranc, illustrate the archbishop's commitment to his former abbey and his care for it. At Canterbury, monks from Bec, including Prior Henry, formed the basis of the Norman implantation at Christ Church which enabled Lanfranc to renew and to expand the cathedral community

---

²⁷ 'Quapropter quod de eodem opusculo vobiscum conferendo dicitis, utinam secundum benignam voluntatem dei fieret, ut et de illo et de quibuscumque vellem liceret!'
²⁸ See above, pp. 207–8.
²⁹ Anselm, *Epp.* no. 74, vol. 3.196; letter to Lanfranc and Prologue, Anselm, *Monologion*, 6, 7.
³⁰ Letter to Lanfranc, Anselm, *Monologion*, 5–6.
³¹ But the *Proslogion* may have been among the 'certain other things' that Anselm wished to discuss with Lanfranc; see n. 27.

in order to meet his needs. Bec was also important to Lanfranc as a source of the books that he required, both as archbishop and for his monastic community.[32] The case of the Canterbury monk Osbern, whom Lanfranc sent to Bec for correction and whom Anselm as prior received and guided with conspicuous wisdom and success, illustrates the value to Lanfranc of the close link with Bec.[33] In the early problems that arose at Canterbury between Archbishop Lanfranc and Prior Henry, both Abbot Herluin of Bec and Anselm as his prior acted to relieve them, drawing upon Henry's sense of loyalty to his former abbey of Bec. Thus, Anselm communicated Herluin's plea that Henry should obey Lanfranc as he would obey himself, for the archbishop was their common lord and father.[34] Again, in 1073 Lanfranc's difficult nephew and namesake was professed at Bec. Lanfranc corresponded with Anselm about his headstrong ways and his training, and pardoned his nephew's recalcitrance after the mediation of Anselm, 'whom', wrote Lanfranc, 'I desire to obey as if God'. Anselm as prior wrote of the younger Lanfranc's progress with warmth, but his ill-health led the archbishop to summon him to Canterbury for a time to receive the best medical care.[35] These are examples of the advantages to Archbishop Lanfranc of a continuing close relationship with Bec.

The advantages to Bec and, through Bec, to others in Normandy were also great. Anselm's letters show that he had a continuing care for monks from Bec who joined the Canterbury community; close contact with Lanfranc was necessary for its effectiveness. Bec also needed his help in more tangible ways and found it to be generously forthcoming. This is well illustrated by Anselm's last letter to Lanfranc, in which he said that he was sending a monk to England in view of Bec's necessities; Anselm asked Lanfranc to respond with the generosity that was customary with him.[36]

Anselm's letters show that, over the years, this had indeed been the case. Lanfranc's help might take the form of approaching the king in England. A letter from Anselm shows that an approach might be made in order to enter a plea for mercy such as was proper amongst monks. Abbot Vitalis of Bernay had written to Abbot Herluin of Bec about a man of Vitalis who, having offended against Lanfranc, had been put in chains by the king and was under threat of mutilation. Herluin was diffident about approaching Lanfranc as the offended party; Anselm, therefore, spoke on his behalf to ask Lanfranc to take the opportunity of performing a work of forgiveness and mercy in addressing the king.[37]

In many other ways Lanfranc showed bounty to Bec, its interests, and those associated with it. Anselm wrote of him that 'this reverend archbishop is most merciful (*misericordissimus*), and especially with regard to the salvation of souls; and he is greatly devoted to almsgiving, and he sufficiently abounds in gold and silver.'[38]

---

[32] See above, pp. 150–1.   [33] Anselm, *Epp.* nos. 39, 66–7, vol. 3.150, 186–8.
[34] Ibid., nos. 63, 73, vol. 3.178–80, 194–5.
[35] Lanfranc, *Letters*, nos. 18–20, pp. 96–101; Anselm, *Epp.* nos. 4, 7, 25, 30–2, 39, 66, 72, 75, vol. 3.105, 109–10, 132, 137–40, 149–50, 186, 194, 197. For further difficulties after Archbishop Lanfranc's death, see Southern, *Saint Anselm: A Portrait*, 184, 192.
[36] Anselm, *Epp.* no. 124, vol. 3.264–5.   [37] Ibid., no. 27, vol. 3.134–5.
[38] Ibid., no. 15, vol. 3.120.

Anselm was addressing Gerard, a moneyer of Arras in Flanders, who was seeking to enter the Bec community but was hindered by indebtedness. Anselm directed him to Lanfranc, who provided 100 shillings in English money to assist him to solvency. He was thereafter professed at Bec, where despite some further difficulty he remained as a monk.[39] Lanfranc was conspicuously generous to Bec itself. His visits in 1077 were the occasion of munificent gifts.[40] Anselm's letters yield evidence of donations of a pall and of gold,[41] and more remarkably of money. While Anselm was still prior, a knight brought to Bec 120 shillings, twenty of which were to be spent as Lanfranc ordered.[42] But it was in Anselm's early years as abbot that Lanfranc's subvention became critical. After Herluin's death, Bec was reduced to dire financial straits, partly by the need to buy pulse and oats at a high price, partly by the purchase of lands, and partly by injudicious expenditure on the recasting of bells and other undertakings. Lanfranc came to the rescue with a gift of twenty pounds, followed as it would seem by further help.[43] At the same time, Anselm was writing to Lanfranc and to others in England to secure the oversight of the monks who came from Bec at Lanfranc's instance to set up the priory of St Neots (Huntingdonshire) which was being founded by Richard of Clare and his wife Rohais; Anselm commended the monks, whose way of life quickly gave rise to reports of serious indiscipline, to Lanfranc's supervision.[44] All in all, many and powerful ties and necessities bound Lanfranc as archbishop to Bec and to its abbots and monks, especially Anselm.

Of contact by Lanfranc with other Norman abbeys, very little is known. This is so even in the case of Saint-Étienne at Caen. A single letter from Lanfranc survives in which he replied in some detail to the request of his successor as abbot, William Bona Anima, for advice about who should succeed as prior after Gundulf's departure for Canterbury in 1070. Lanfranc's preferred solution, that Ernost should come from Bec, was with Abbot Herluin's leave adopted.[45] Lanfranc's advice was evidently pressingly sought and carefully given. The number of abbots who in following years came from Normandy to England, no doubt upon Lanfranc's advice, suggests that he retained an interest in and knowledge of Norman monastic affairs.[46]

So far as the Norman secular church is concerned, the principal evidence for Lanfranc's interest is the five letters in his collection that are addressed to John of Avranches as archbishop of Rouen.[47] They are written in tones of mutual regard and friendship, and of an expressed spirit of concord and charity; there is also repeated reference to the need to guard against those who would set them at variance.[48] The

---

[39] For Gerard, see Anselm, *Epp.* nos. 14–15, 23, 98, 164, vols. 3.119–21, 130–1, 229, 4.37.
[40] *VH* cap. 112, pp. 105/206–7; whence *VL* cap. 8, p. 691.
[41] Anselm, *Epp.* nos. 14, 90, vol. 3.119, 217–18; for Prior Henry of Christ Church's gift of gold, see no. 58, vol. 3.172.
[42] Ibid., no. 66, vol. 3.187.   [43] Ibid., nos. 89–90, vol. 3.215–18.
[44] Ibid., nos. 90–4, 96, vol. 3.217–23.   [45] Lanfranc, *Letters*, no. 61, pp. 176–9.
[46] See Knowles, *The Monastic Order*, 111–12.
[47] Lanfranc, *Letters*, nos. 14–17, 41, pp. 82–95, 134–7.
[48] Ibid., nos. 14 lines 67–70, 15 lines 20–6, 41 lines 8–22, pp. 88–91, 134–5.

cultivation of harmony between the archbishops of Canterbury and Rouen was evidently part of Lanfranc's purpose within the Anglo-Norman kingdom under William I. The subject-matter of Lanfranc's letters covered four main areas. The first was correctness in liturgical practice, with particular regard to the sacred vestments. John had written a book *De officiis ecclesiasticis*,[49] and he claimed authority in such matters; Lanfranc had always been a keen observer of them who was concerned for correctness. John had raised points about which he thought that he and Lanfranc differed; Lanfranc answered amicably and judiciously, and at length when he thought necessary. About the use of the stole, Lanfranc saw no difference between them; about the contentious subject of episcopal vesture at the consecration of churches, he claimed himself to be entirely correct; about the conferring of the maniple in ordinations, he considered that further thought was necessary though ancient authorities seemed to support his own view.[50] Second, while Lanfranc was a monk, John had been a secular clerk. On strictly monastic questions—monastic stability and the case of a monk who met death unpreparedly because struck by lightning—Lanfranc therefore gave expert rulings.[51] In monastic as in liturgical matters, his reliance upon authorities, whether papal practice as he had observed it, best custom as he found it in the pontificals of which he had a collection, or the deliverances of ancient writers and the Rule of St Benedict, was characteristically paramount. Third, Lanfranc was at pains to dispel rumours that he had been critical of John's measures, which had been strict,[52] to enforce clerical chastity, saying that John had misunderstood the rulings of the ancient fathers and had misapplied ecclesiastical discipline. Lanfranc claimed that his words had been twisted and that he had said nothing offensive about John; on the contrary, his own legislation against married canons had partly been encouraged by John's example. (If, as seems to be the case, Lanfranc referred to his ruling at the council of Winchester in 1076, he kept a prudent silence about his concession to currently married priests in villages and townships.)[53]

Fourth, Lanfranc involved himself deeply in John's dispute with the monks of Saint-Ouen at Rouen in ways that in some respects anticipated his own dealings in his last years as archbishop with St Augustine's abbey at Canterbury.[54] In either case the issue was monastic exemption. At Rouen, Saint-Ouen claimed freedom from the archbishop's jurisdiction; John was determined to exercise it. Matters came to a head in 1073, when on the feast of St Ouen (24 August) John attempted to celebrate mass at the high altar, only to be resisted and expelled from the church.[55] There was much violence. In two letters,[56] Lanfranc expressed his condemnation of the monks in extreme terms. His support for John was total. In uncharacteristically extravagant phrase, he grieved for John's having experienced what no bishop was on record as having experienced since pagan times. In face of it, John's letters to Lanfranc

---

[49] *Le 'De officiis ecclesiasticis'*, ed. Delamare. [50] Lanfranc, *Letters*, no. 14, lines 18–64, pp. 84–7.
[51] Ibid., no. 17, lines 24–42, pp. 94–5. [52] See above, pp. 127–8.
[53] Lanfranc, *Letters*, no. 41, pp. 134–5. [54] See above, pp. 168–9.
[55] The fullest account of events is in *Acta archiep. Roth.*, cols. 279–80.
[56] Lanfranc, *Letters*, nos. 16–17, pp. 90–5.

showed clearly that he had exhibited the duty of a bishop alike in his patience and innocency towards those set against him and in his facing up to the abominable and culpable temerity of a most abandoned congregation of monks. Lanfranc did not stop at words: he was in duty bound to write to the king in the confidence that as the times had been darkened by the enormity of such wickedness, so light might be restored by the severity of proper punishment; for to punish such an outrage was a royal duty.[57] Rouen was outside Lanfranc's primatial jurisdiction; nevertheless, as mentor of the king his function of securing the correction of monastic sin knew no boundaries;[58] nor did the mutual duty of archbishops in England and Normandy to foster the well-being of the Anglo-Norman realm, to cultivate concordant outlooks, and to give each other support.

Of Lanfranc's relations with William Bona Anima when he followed John as archbishop nothing whatever is known. No conclusions about them can be drawn from an at first sight surprising letter that Lanfranc addressed to the archdeacons of Bayeux, evidently after the king's imprisonment of Bishop Odo in 1082.[59] Lanfranc directly gave advice and guidance about the penance and future employment of a priest guilty of homicide. But the approach to Lanfranc was made by Bishop Geoffrey of Coutances, upon whose vill in the diocese of Coutances the priest lived. Geoffrey had taken Lanfranc's advice as an expert canonist; hence his becoming involved.

15.2 LANFRANC AND THE FRENCH CHURCH

Lanfranc's known concern with matters arising in the French church beyond the duchy of Normandy is limited to two of his letters. At some time before the deposition of Archbishop Manasses I of Rheims in 1080, Lanfranc wrote to him commending the cause of a vassal of King William and of himself who had suffered some kind of material injury within Manasses's jurisdiction. The man concerned had already secured from Pope Gregory VII the excommunication of the robbers unless they restored his property and an injunction to Manasses to provide justice for him.[60] Lanfranc also wrote at some length in the 1070s to Abbot Reynald of Saint-Cyprien at Poitiers and others who had approached him about the persistent allegations of Berengar of Tours that St Hilary of Poitiers had held erroneous views about the Trinity and especially about the incarnation of the second Person of the Trinity. Lanfranc declined the request of Reynald and his colleagues that they visit him, but he sent a thorough and sophisticated defence of Hilary. He first demonstrated Hilary's authority with Pope Gelasius I, in canon law, and with the orthodox fathers such as Augustine. Then he took up the matter in dispute and gave a clear theological exposition of the true faith. Lanfranc characteristically ended by

---

[57] For Lanfranc's references to the king, see ibid., nos. 16, lines 22–5; 17, lines 19–23, pp. 92–3, 94–5.
[58] The king ordered the offending monks to be sent to monastic prisons in Upper Normandy: *Ann. S. Steph. Cadom.*, 1017–18.
[59] Lanfranc, *Letters*, no. 51, pp. 162–5.   [60] Ibid., no. 25, pp. 108–11.

insisting upon the urgency of vigilance against the error that surrounded and threatened his correspondents: 'I beseech you, by every means be watchful, because schismatics and their abettors are around you and among you. Resist them with the shield of the fear of God, assailing them with the darts of the divine oracles.'[61] It is a reminder that the imperative to defend Christian truth remained an important part of Lanfranc's conception of the episcopal office.

[61] Lanfranc, *Letters*, no. 46, pp. 142–51.

16

The Last Years

16.1 THE SUCCESSION OF KING WILLIAM II

In the summer of 1087 King William I invaded the Vexin and sacked and burnt the town of Mantes. He returned from the campaign in poor health and great pain; on 9 September he died in a suburb of Rouen.[1] Eadmer as an eyewitness wrote of the intense grief of Lanfranc when he received the news. As regards the succession to William, it is likely that uncertainty prevailed until a very late stage in his illness.[2] More than once over the years he had named his eldest son, Robert Curthose, as duke of Normandy; but the naming had been undefinitive, and by 1087 Robert had been associating with King Philip I of France and other of William's enemies. There were few clear guidelines about the succession both to the duchy that William had inherited and to the lands that he had acquired. Perhaps reluctantly and under pressure from his leading Norman subjects, William provided that Robert should inherit Normandy, that William Rufus should receive the kingdom of England, and that Henry should have a generous sum of money.

It seems that, even before the old king was dead, William Rufus set out for England; according to Orderic Vitalis, his father addressed and sealed a letter to Lanfranc about setting up a king (*de constituendo rege*), and Rufus learnt of his father's death while at Wissant. At all events, Rufus made all haste to Lanfranc, who accompanied him to London and on 26 September anointed him king in Westminster abbey. He did so with due solemnity;[3] according to Henry of Huntingdon, the new king at Christmas held a court at London which was very well attended by bishops headed by Lanfranc. It was a remarkable display of episcopal solidarity with

---

[1] The principal sources for the Conqueror's death and for the succession are: *ASC* E, *a.* 1087, pp. 163, 165–6; *AL* 87; John of Worcester, *a.* 1087, vol. 3.46–7; Orderic Vitalis, 7.14–8.1, vol. 4.76–111; Eadmer, *Hist. nov.*, 1, pp. 23–6; William of Malmesbury, *GR* 3.282–3, 4.305–6, vol. 1. 510–13, 542–7, and *GP* 1.44, p. 73; Henry of Huntingdon, 6.40, pp. 406–9; *The Brevis relatio*, cap. 9, pp. 35–6, whence William of Jumièges, 8.2, vol. 2.202–5.

[2] For the problems raised by the succession, see esp. Le Patourel, 'The Norman Succession' and *The Norman Empire*, 181–4; Barlow, *William Rufus*, 53–60.

[3] It has been suggested that a coronation *ordo* preserved in British Library, MS Cotton Claudius A iii, fos. 19ʳ–29ᵛ, may have been the work of Lanfranc and used at the coronation of 1087: *The Claudius Pontificals*, ed. Turner, pp. xxxix–xlii, text at pp. 115–22. Turner's attribution has been doubted, e.g. by Gibson, *Lanfranc*, 243, and Nelson, 'The Rites', 384–5. If Lanfranc was the compiler, it is unlikely that it dates from the hectic month of Sept. 1087; Nelson fairly points out, against Gibson, that the provision for a queen has little force against Lanfranc's authorship since he would have prepared it when the succession was uncertain and the contingency of a married king must be envisaged. But Nelson shows how uncertain the attribution to Lanfranc is. The matter is best left open.

the king, no doubt intended to communicate to him the advantage of doing well by the church.

In his *Gesta regum* William of Malmesbury extolled Rufus's youthful promise, not least as being a loyal son of his father, and referred to the welcome that he received from his new subjects; it was led by Lanfranc, 'the greatest force behind events (*maximum rerum momentum*)', who was bound to him because he had educated him in his household and had knighted him. But, especially in his *Gesta pontificum*, William of Malmesbury also wrote as did Eadmer, who presented Lanfranc as from the start guarded in his approach. According to Eadmer, Lanfranc showed some hesitation in welcoming Rufus. Well aware that Lanfranc had the right to crown him, Rufus made lavish sworn promises to the archbishop in order to secure the crown—of justice, mercy, and equity in all affairs of the kingdom; of peace, liberty, and security to its churches; of thoroughgoing obedience to Lanfranc's precepts and counsels. But when established in the kingdom, he quickly forgot his promises. When mildly rebuked by Lanfranc, he angrily replied: 'Who is there who can fulfil everything that he promises?' Thereafter, according to Eadmer, Rufus could not look Lanfranc straight in the eyes; however, in some things to which his will inclined him he restrained himself during Lanfranc's lifetime out of respect for him.

Lanfranc continued to be a positive supporter of the king; the strong evidence of the sources that William of Saint-Calais, the bishop of Durham, was the king's intimate counsellor (*quem rex a secretis habuerat*) needs not mean more than that he retained the position that he had latterly had under William I;[4] Lanfranc had been less often at court than he. When Lanfranc needed William II's backing in his dealings with St Augustine's abbey at Canterbury, it was forthcoming.[5] The advantages for William and Lanfranc of their collaboration are particularly apparent in the course of and sequel to the rising against the king which occurred during the spring and summer of 1088.[6] Its purpose was to replace William Rufus as king by his brother, Robert Curthose, duke of Normandy, and so to reverse the Conqueror's dispositions for his inheritance. The leader of the rising was Odo of Bayeux, whose leading supporters included his brother Count Robert of Mortain, Robert of Montgomery, earl of Shrewsbury, and Bishop Geoffrey of Coutances. They were rich and powerful men, but they did not attract deep-rooted support; many Normans and most of the English remained loyal to William Rufus.

The course of events is complex and differently reported in different sources. But hostilities were widespread. Odo established his headquarters at Rochester, which was a key centre of communication between the Kentish ports and London, especially if Robert Curthose crossed to England. However, Rufus was able to gather forces near London and to proceed to the successful besieging of Rochester

---

[4] See also Symeon of Durham, *Libellus*, 4.8, pp. 242–3.   [5] See above, pp. 168–9, 171.
[6] The principal sources for the rising are: *ASC* E, pp. 166–8; John of Worcester, *a.* 1088, vol. 3.48–57; William of Malmesbury, *GP* 4.306, vol. 1.544–9; Orderic Vitalis, 8.2, vol. 4.122–35; *Lib. mon. de Hyda*, App. *aa.* 1087–8, pp. 298–9. For a modern account, see Barlow, *William Rufus*, 70–82.

castle. Upon its surrender, Odo was compelled to leave the country; the rebellion had failed.

Lanfranc's part in events is not well documented but was nevertheless clearly of the utmost importance for Rufus in frustrating the conspiracy against him. Lanfranc was an especial object of Odo's enmity, not only because of his ecclesiastical dignity and territorial power in the south-east, but also because Odo regarded him as the Conqueror's adviser who in 1082 had urged his imprisonment. While Odo controlled Rochester Lanfranc's lands were severely ravaged. Lanfranc himself was with the king, notably when he was gathering his forces near London; he was a leading adviser and mentor of the king in securing widespread support. With the important exception of William of Saint-Calais, bishop of Durham, the bishops preserved the loyalty and solidarity that they had foreshadowed at the Christmas court of 1087. According to John of Worcester, almost all of the leading men (*optimates*) of the south-east were with Lanfranc at London. The king owed to Lanfranc the consolidation of his supporters; Lanfranc owed to the king the defeat of Odo, who had become his dangerous enemy.

16.2 THE TRIAL OF WILLIAM OF SAINT-CALAIS

The involvement in the rebellion of Bishop William of Saint-Calais and the trial of the bishop to which it gave rise are of especial interest because of a source, known as the *De iniusta vexacione Willelmi episcopi*, which appears to embody a detailed and immediate account of the bishop's misfortunes as observed by a close partisan and supporter. The text comprises brief passages, of later compilation, which give biographical details about the bishop (3–28, 644–68),[7] and between them a long account of events between March and December 1088. Its authenticity has been, and remains, a matter for debate, but there are powerful arguments in its favour. In particular, its authenticity as an eyewitness account of the bishop's trial is strongly suggested by the complete silence about the debate during the three junctures at which the bishop and his entourage withdrew (318, 349, 383). In general and in detail, the state of canon law in England during the late 1080s, when Pseudo-Isidorian ideas had been given currency by the dissemination of the *Collectio Lanfranci*, is exactly reflected. The characteristic and developing positions and language of the leading characters are convincingly presented, especially as regards such legal concepts as the *exceptio spolii* and such vocabulary as *feudum* and *episcopatus*. Problems that have been rightly noticed with respect to personal names are usually explicable in terms of later scribal error.[8] The text may reasonably be used with substantial though not absolute confidence as a contemporary, partisan account to record the harassment of the bishop by King William II, which was deemed to be unjust partly

---

[7] In this section, figures in the text in brackets refer to the lines of the *De iniusta vexacione*, ed. Offler.
[8] Amongst many discussions, the authenticity of the *De iniusta vexacione* has been strongly challenged by Offler, 'The Tractate'; see also his edition, pp. 60–5. For further review of the case in its favour, see Cowdrey, 'The Enigma', 142; Philpott, 'The *De iniusta vexacione*'.

because the bishop had done only limited wrong and partly because he was denied due respect for his episcopal order and canonical trial only by his spiritual peers.

The time, detail, and gravity of the bishop's offence against the king are far from clear, and other sources do little to clarify them. According to the *De iniusta vexacione*, they allegedly involved perjury and infidelity—the breach of oath and of fealty to the king (e.g. 147). According to the prosecution at the trial, the bishop had at first counselled the king to resist Odo of Bayeux and his associates and had undertaken to support him with armed men, but he had subsequently fled from the king without permission, taking his followers with him (280–8); speaking later in his own defence, the bishop claimed to have been initially even more serviceable to the king (480–92). It was not, however, denied that he had of his own will given comfort to the king's enemies and that thereby he had violated his oath and fealty to the king.

The account of his harassment in the *De iniusta vexacione* opens on 12 March with the king's disseising him (as it was said) of his lands and those of his church and capturing all of his men and as much of his goods as he was able (29–31), whereupon the bishop escaped to Durham (31–2). His lands in Yorkshire were taken and divided between Odo, count of Champagne and lord of Holderness, and Alan, count of Brittany and lord of Richmond (70–3). In June or July the king and the bishop met, presumably in the south-east, but without result (111–25). After an interval the king sent an expedition to the north and ravaged the bishop's lands (149–51). The upshot was that, on 8 September, a sworn *conventio*, or agreement, was concluded with the bishop by the same Counts Odo and Alan, who were now associated with Count Roger *le Poitevin*, third son of Roger of Montgomery, earl of Shrewsbury (154–94). The *conventio* was complex, but it was remarkably favourable to the bishop. For understanding later events, three points about it call for notice. First, the *conventio* opened with the three counts pledging their faith to the bishop that they would conduct him safely with all his men to the king's court on the understanding that, if the king would not agree to justice for the bishop according to the law for a bishop and through such judges as should rightly judge a bishop, they would escort him unharmed back to Durham (154–60). Second, if certain contingencies should arise in which the bishop wished to appeal to Rome, in each case appropriate provision for his security and safe conduct were made (160–76). Third, in an addition to the *conventio* which was deemed to be part of it, seven of the bishop's men by his order swore to Count Roger, who acted on the king's behalf, that if the bishop should refuse rightful justice as provided for at the beginning of the *conventio* and choose to cross the sea, they would surrender Durham castle to the king (187–90).[9] It was envisaged that the bishop would come to the king's court by 29 September (185–7); but, for reasons unknown, both parties—the king and the bishop—agreed to a postponement until 2 November (209–10). Meanwhile, on 11 September the bishop was forced to leave Durham (649–50); nothing further is

---

[9] The seven here referred to appear to be the same as the seven knights referred to hereafter at lines 285 and 346–7.

known of his fortunes until November. As for Lanfranc, nothing emerges about his part in matters relating to William of Saint-Calais since the royal disseisin of 12 March, save that, like Thomas of York and other bishops, Lanfranc would not accede to the bishop's request for counsel during his summer meeting with the king, who forbade such contact (115–123); this was no doubt in order not to compromise the bishops when they acted as judges (cf. 211–15, 339–46).

On 2 November the bishop of Durham's case was heard at Salisbury (Old Sarum) at a well-attended meeting either in the cathedral or, more likely, in the castle. The *De iniusta vexacione* offers a long account of the proceedings as its author viewed them (210–543). When the meeting assembled, William of Saint-Calais asked the two archbishops whether he and the other bishops should be robed in order to mark the canonical status of the occasion. Lanfranc dismissed the request: 'We can very well debate concerning the king's business and yours clothed as we are, for clothes do not hinder the truth' (216–24). It was a critically important assertion that the meeting was one of the king's court dealing with the king's business.

Such was certainly the king's view. He presided over the meeting, and in the previous months he had made clear his view that the bishop of Durham should be tried *laicaliter*—as a layman would be tried (112–13, 137–8). He was not an inactive president, but as the trial progressed he became primarily concerned to secure the submission of Durham castle (441–1) and such other practicalities as the safety of his ships if they conveyed the bishop across the English Channel (508–10). At the beginning of the trial it was clear that in matters of law Lanfranc would be the voice of the king (225–7). It was an important assertion of his authority in the court as a whole.

Bishop William of Saint-Calais presented his case with skill, basing it upon the canon law of the Pseudo-Isidorian decrees in which he had schooled himself, probably by way of the *Collectio Lanfranci*; the book of 'the Christian law' that was in his hand during the trial may have been the copy, now Cambridge, Peterhouse, MS 74, that Lanfranc had sent to Durham (456–61). The bishop had an initial advantage in the favourable terms of the *conventio* agreed in the previous summer with the three counts, and especially of its first provision with its reference to justice 'according to the law for a bishop' and of its second about the right of recourse to Rome (398–404). His tactical skill is a reminder that he was appealing to canon law as a means to evade judgement in England, not because of a conscientious zeal for the liberty of the church as the Gregorian papacy proclaimed it.[10]

He deployed three lines of argument, all of them well grounded in canonical texts.[11] The first was an appeal to the rule known as the *exceptio spolii*—that a defendant, especially if a bishop, who has been despoiled of his possessions must have them restored to him before judicial proceedings might begin (*spoliatus ante omnia restituendus*). The bishop's opening plea was that the king should return to

---

[10] Cf. his opposition to Archbishop Anselm at the council of Rockingham (1095): Eadmer, *Hist. nov.*, 1, pp. 59–65.
[11] For fuller references and further discussion, see Cowdrey, 'The Enigma', 143–5.

him his episcopate (*episcopatus*) which he had some time before taken from him without a judgement (225–6, cf. 29–31); the implication was that until what had been entirely confiscated had been entirely restored there could by canon law be no further proceedings against him. His use of the word *episcopatus* is significant. There was at no time a question of William's being personally deposed from the see of Durham. But throughout his trial he refused to speak of his fief (*feodum*) as a body of lands and temporal rights that ecclesiastical tenants-in-chief held of the king on the same terms as their lay peers. He spoke of an *episcopatus*, or *episcopium*, that comprised in addition spiritual rights that placed jurisdiction in the canonical, not the temporal, forum (324–7, 369–72). Second, therefore, despoiled or not, William absolutely refused to be subject to lay judgement (274–8); as a bishop he should be judged only by bishops and by the canon law that applied to them (268–70, 350–1). He repudiated lay judgement (274–8); no doubt reflecting his view, the author of the *De iniusta vexacione* scornfully mocked the meeting from which the bishop and his advisers had withdrawn as a rump of 'the king with his bishops and earls and sheriffs and reeves and huntsmen and others of suchlike duties' (318–20). Third, when justice failed at home, by the canons it might be sought at Rome (361–6); at a point of climax in his trial, William enlarged upon the failure of justice in his trial where he was treated falsely and unjustly; he would take his case to Rome for proper hearing: 'Asking the help of God and St Peter, I shall go to Rome' (382–96).

Such was the case with which Lanfranc was confronted; his task was not made easier either by Bishop William's use of his own canonical collection or by the substantial concessions made to the bishop in the *conventio* as guaranteed by the three counts. Lanfranc built up a reply in stages. He began with the *exceptio spolii*. He argued that the king's seizure of his property was neither so definitive nor so complete as he asserted (225–6). The king had taken away nothing of his 'episcopate', and Lanfranc had seen no royal writ disseising him of it (226–9). The bishop was forced to concede, with some prevarication ('Roger [Ralph] Paynel . . . by the king's order has disseised me of my whole episcopate which I have in Yorkshire'), that steps taken against him had been local, partial, and sporadic (239–48). Lanfranc thus undermined the bishop's contention that, by the *exceptio spolii*, the king must be the first to do justice by restoring his property. Lanfranc built upon his advantage by asserting that the king and his barons had summoned the bishop to do right to the king, not vice versa: 'First do right to him,' he told the bishop, 'and afterwards ask of him what you are asking now' (249–52). The laity present rallied to Lanfranc with an enthusiastic endorsement of this advice (255–9), as did the king (265–7). Lanfranc established a position as the trusted voice of the laymen who were present. (There is no evidence of episcopal support for the bishop of Durham's arguments.) Soon after, he upheld the competence of the whole meeting by resisting a suggestion that it should rise in face of lay hostility to the bishop while a committee of bishops and abbots with lay observers reviewed the legal position. If the bishop of Durham and his party wished for separate discussion they must withdrew; 'It is not for us to rise, but let the bishop and his men go out, and let us who remain, clerks and laymen alike, consider on an equal basis what we should in justice do about this matter.' His advice elicited further lay support (297–317).

Lanfranc was now able to set out his case against the bishop more expressly. The bishop had probably made a tactical error in speaking of his *episcopatus* or *episcopium* rather than of his *feodum*: as he used the first two terms, they were unfamiliar to Anglo-Norman ears and lumped together spiritual and secular possessions and rights; especially in the England of Domesday, everyone knew what a fief was, with its similar implications for ecclesiastical and lay tenants-in-chief. Fortified by the full support of the king and of the laity as well of the bishops, Lanfranc insisted that the meeting was of the king's court, that the case against Bishop William was wholly secular, and that judgement should be passed according to the law of the land; the canon law of Pseudo-Isidore and of the *Collectio Lanfranci* that the bishop had in his hand was not relevant to settling it. Lanfranc told the bishop that: 'We are judging you not concerning your *episcopium* but concerning your fief (*feodum*), and in this manner we judged the bishop of Bayeux before the father of the present king concerning his fief; and in that law-case the king did not call him bishop but brother and earl' (366–6, cf. 372–4).[12] So the king's court judged that, because the bishop had refused to answer the charges against him and had sought to take his case to Rome, he forfeited his fief (382–6).

Bishop William played into Lanfranc's hands by refusing to surrender his castle to the king, appealing to the terms of the *conventio* (397–421). Lanfranc advised the king that, if the bishop continued to deny him his castle, he had the right to seize him under the terms of the *conventio*; Lanfranc evidently had in mind the oath of the seven that, if the bishop refused justice as stipulated and chose to cross the sea, they would surrender Durham castle to the king (422–6, cf. 187–90). With the laity who were present, Lanfranc struck the right note; led by Ranulf Peverel, they unanimously cried, 'Seize him, seize him, for this old master of the hunting-field (*iste vetulus ligaminarius*) says well!' (426–8).[13] Upon a strict interpretation of the *conventio*, Lanfranc's advice to the king might be questioned: the seven had sworn to deliver the castle, not the person, of the bishop to the king; though the first clause had referred to the king's court, it had also referred to trial according to the law of a bishop (154–60). So, when the three counts who were its guarantors heard the lay outcry, they all expressed a fear that to concur would be for them to break faith with the bishop (428–42). Lanfranc assured them that by offering the bishop full justice he had released them from their obligation (442–6). When the bishop tried to protract matters by referring to his appeal to Rome, Lanfranc insisted that the case was settled: William must either accept it or show good legal reason for now challenging it (447–54). With the settling of a day for the surrender of the castle, proceedings

---

[12] According to William of Malmesbury, Lanfranc in 1082 advised King William I privately to capture and imprison Odo: 'You will not be seizing the bishop of Bayeux but putting under guard the earl of Kent': *GR* 4.306, vol. 1.544–5 (though at *GR* 3.277, vol. 1.506–7, Lanfranc is not mentioned in connection with Odo's arrest, and Orderic Vitalis is also silent about him: 7.8, vol. 4.47–8).

[13] For the meaning of the otherwise unknown noun *ligaminarius*, see Cowdrey, 'The Enigma', 146, and Offler's note *ad loc.*: *De iniusta vexacione*, 89–90.

were effectively complete (465–7). In the rest of the day's discussions Lanfranc urged William to accept the judgement of the court and plead for the king's mercy; if he did so, Lanfranc would gladly throw himself at the king's feet in his support; but the bishop persisted in his intention to go to Rome (468–507). Lanfranc showed a similar concern for mercy in advising against the pressing of further charges against him (532–43). In the secular forum, Lanfranc's victory had been complete; the way must now be open for the bishop's eventual restoration. There was no need for Lanfranc to assert himself in the further fortunes of the bishop before he left England at about the end of the year (544–642).

For the bishop had been dispossessed of his entire fief. At home, it would be an act of injustice to implead him further (538–42). And Lanfranc could view his recourse to Rome with equanimity in the knowledge that, since William was now completely despoiled, he could not present his case to the pope unless his property had been restored. A letter of Pope Urban II to King William confirms this by the pope's request that that the bishop should receive back his *episcopatus* as the condition of his being heard at Rome along with any legal accusers.[14] In the event, Bishop William did not travel to Rome.[15] He was received honourably in Normandy by Duke Robert Curthose, who used him prominently in the government of the duchy (*a Roberto ... honorifice susceptus tocius Normannie curam suscepit*) (643–5).[16] After three years he was reconciled to King William II and restored to his see and to the faithful service of the king (645–9). It was an outcome that Lanfranc would certainly have welcomed and for which he had, indeed, prepared the way by representing the claims of mercy to the dispossessed bishop in the last stages of the trial.

Especially as thus seen through the eyes of a clerk of William of Saint-Calais, Lanfranc's part in the bishop's trial at Salisbury was a masterpiece of forensic skill. He gradually undermined the bishop's arguments and built up the support of the lay elements of the king's court until he was in a position to press successfully for a sentence of the court against the bishop in his capacity as a lay tenant-in-chief of the king; having secured a sentence according to what he claimed as justice, he assumed the role of his spiritual office in seeking to secure the operation of mercy and eventual reconciliation. He exhibited a mastery alike of canon and secular law in respect both of their substance and of their operation. His performance gave no sign of indebtedness to early legal training and practice in the Lombard courts of Pavia. Rather, Lanfranc showed a mastery of law and of affairs which sprang from his ability to respond at each stage of his career to the circumstances in which he was currently called upon to act.

---

[14] For Urban's letter, which survives in *Collectio Britannica*, see Somerville, *Pope Urban II*, 153–5. It is not known whether the letter came to the king.

[15] In all probability Bishop William knew as well as Lanfranc that the operation of the *exceptio spolii* effectively precluded his case from being heard at Rome; his appeal to the pope was more a means of obtaining safe passage from England than of procuring papal justice. Despite Lanfranc's offer of mediation with the king, he deemed it best to withdraw to Normandy until the king's anger had subsided and better terms might be available.

[16] This seems preferable as an interpretation of the surprising Latin phrase than that he 'was looked after by the whole of Normandy': *English Lawsuits*, 1.105.

16.3 DEATH AND BURIAL

When Lanfranc took part in the trial at Salisbury he was well advanced in the eighth decade of his life and within seven months of his death. According to William of Malmesbury, he had confided to his household his wish to die of some dysentery or fever, because these illnesses neither disturb the memory nor impair speech. His wish was fulfilled: although he was wearied by William Rufus's disregard of his promises of good government, he died of a fever, postponing medication until he made confession and received the viaticum.[17] He died at Canterbury on 28 May 1089,[18] and was buried in the nave of the cathedral, to the west of the choir screen.[19]

---

[17] William of Malmesbury, *GP* 1.44, p. 73.

[18] For the various dates given on the sources for Lanfranc's death, see Macdonald, *Lanfranc*, 250, n. 4; Gibson, *Lanfranc*, 227–9. News of Lanfranc's illness quickly reached Bec, from which Anselm and the monks sent a letter of sympathy which does not add to the evidence for the nature and duration of Lanfranc's illness: Anselm, *Epp.* no. 124, vol. 3.264–5.

[19] See above, pp. 105–6.

17

Conclusion

It is not possible to form a balanced overall picture of Lanfranc as a person. This is partly because from reticence he was reluctant to reveal his inner self. His biblical commentaries, treatise on the eucharist, canonical collection, and monastic constitutions disclose but little about himself; unlike John of Fécamp and St Anselm, he left no devotional outpourings. His letters are, for the most part, terse and businesslike, with only occasional self-revelation. The writings of other people sometimes shed shafts of bright light upon him and his actions, but there is little overall illumination. When it is forthcoming, it is sometimes surprising to modern minds. For example, the sources often refer to his great diligence and generosity in many kinds of almsgiving as a cornerstone of his activity; at his episcopal consecration, the customary random consultation of the Bible yielded as a keynote of his ministry Christ's words: 'Give alms, and behold! all things are clean for you' (Luke 11: 41).[1] Again, Lanfranc is shown to have taken great care for the spiritual and physical welfare of individuals for whom he had a special responsibility. The case of the monk Egelward illustrates this within the Canterbury monastic community. Similarly, a letter to a sick monk urging him to self-examination and to consideration of his last hours ended with a gift of herbal medication and directions for taking it.[2] His letter in which he agreed to be the spiritual director of Queen Margaret of Scotland struck a note of personal warmth:

> I am not what you think, but may I be so because you think it. Lest you remain deceived, pray for me that I may be a father worthy to pray to God and to be heard on your behalf. Let there be between us a mutual exchange of prayers and good works. To be sure, I have little to contribute; but I am sure that I shall receive far more. Henceforth, therefore, may I be your father; and as for you, be my daughter.[3]

The pronounced emotional warmth of this letter should be noticed. For it is not infrequently possible to detect in Lanfranc's words an emotive intensity which, perhaps unexpectedly, was a trait of his personality and a feature of his judgements and actions. Especially within the monastic order, he could have close and lasting emotional ties with those with whom he had most to do, particularly his abbot at Bec, Herluin, and his nephew Paul, abbot of St Albans, whom he treated with great generosity and loved so much that some said that Paul was his natural son. There are passages in his *De corpore et sanguine Domini* that show his eucharistic theology to be grounded in deep spiritual feeling.[4] Conversely, his revulsion against

---

[1] *VL* cap. 15, p. 712. [2] See above, pp. 151–3, 173.
[3] Lanfranc, *Letters*, no. 50, pp. 160–1. [4] e.g. *DCSD* cap. 15, cols. 405–6.

Berengar's teaching was of such intensity that he could see nothing of value in it; its author was to be summarily dismissed as *scismaticus ille, Berengarius*. On the adversaries of authority, Lanfranc was habitually thus summary and severe. The Bretons vanquished in the rebellion of the earls in 1075 were dismissed as 'Breton scum' after whose banishment the English kingdom enjoyed exceptional tranquillity. Lanfranc's letters to Archbishop John of Rouen about the resistance of the monks of Saint-Ouen to his episcopal authority well illustrate the emotional polarity of his approach: whereas the archbishop was virtually a martyr-figure, patient to his adversaries and himself blameless, Lanfranc spared no obloquy in condemning the abominable and culpable temerity of a most abandoned congregation of monks. An aspect of this polarity was Lanfranc's pronounced liability to be relatively mild in his attitude towards those in authority who had caused offence, such as the Abbot Thurstan who had fallen into the disfavour of King William I,[5] but to be severe towards offending subjects, such as the monks of St Augustine's abbey at Canterbury when they refused to accept Abbot Guy. Lanfranc's tendency towards severity was mitigated somewhat by his recognition that, in a ruler, justice must be tempered by mercy. In the case of the revolt of the earls, he pressed it strongly but unsuccessfully upon the king in respect of Earl Waltheof, and when he had brought about the conviction of Bishop William of Saint-Calais at his trial, he turned to seeking his reconciliation and pardon. But, especially where monks and clerks were concerned, Lanfranc was resolute in securing the claims of justice even to the point of severity before those of mercy came into play. The advantages of Lanfranc's firm stand for justice and order were widely appreciated; the Peterborough chronicler seems to have spoken for many in calling him 'the reverend father and consoler of monks'.

Such an epitome of his life testifies to importance of his being a monk-archbishop. He was so not only because of his background as monk and prior of Bec and then abbot of Saint-Étienne at Caen, but also because he was ex officio abbot of the cathedral monastery at Canterbury. As well as legislating for the monastic community and overseeing its expansion and rehousing, so far as he could he shared in its life and liturgy. When the king was in England attendance at the king's court was a necessity, especially at the crown-wearings of Christmas, Easter, and Pentecost. But Lanfranc was no court prelate, and although he was a trusted royal counsellor he left no perceptible mark on the ways and means of royal administration or upon such an enterprise as the Domesday survey. If he abandoned his study and teaching of the liberal arts when he assumed the cure of souls, his long doctrinal letters show that he retained and nourished his knowledge of Christian teaching. He was said also while archbishop to have continued to be assiduous in sacred study and in correcting biblical and patristic texts as well as service books.[6] He brought to bear on his work as archbishop the cumulative learning and skills of each stage of his life. Lanfranc was evidently a man of great, sustained, and well-directed industry who balanced well the claims of study and of activity.

[5] Lanfranc, *Letters*, no. 57, pp. 172–3.   [6] *VL* cap. 15, p. 711.

The practical result that he sought was well defined in his *Vita* as the correction of men's morality and the setting in order of the condition of the church (*ad mores hominum corrigendos et componendum ecclesie status*).[7] His letters to Pope Alexander II and other confidants in which he deplored his lack of visible progress in raising the morals of society, clerical and lay, and dwelt upon his consequent sense of unprofitability testify to the urgency of his concern. The basis of his ordering of the condition of the church was the holy scriptures and the Pseudo-Isidorian tradition of canon law, especially as excerpted and circulated in the *Collectio Lanfranci*, chiefly implemented by means of the holding of church councils. Papal and patristic authority was thus fundamental; as archbishop, Lanfranc had above all in mind the popes, fathers, and councils of the pre-Carolingian past. He had, indeed, been familiar with and sympathetic to the eleventh-century reform popes from Leo IX to Alexander II, but towards Gregory VII he was reserved and distant; Gregory's long deferring of judgement upon Berengar of Tours was probably a principal reason. If so, however, he differed from Gregory because in this matter the pope appeared to lag behind current trends of thought such as had been represented by Cardinal Humbert. It is a salutary reminder that, far from having been nourished and established in the traditions of a pre-reforming age, Lanfranc—like the king-duke William I—was not at odds with many of the religious currents of the later eleventh-century church; he was, if on his own terms, in harmony with them.

If Lanfranc promoted canon law and the setting of the church's order and government under the authority of its own traditions, thus tending to advance the freedom of the church, he well understood the need for the resources of secular law and government to be brought to bear if the freedom and security of the church were to be secured. The trial on Penenden Heath was probably critical in determining Lanfranc's view. It was made clear that, in an often disordered and predatory society, the property, rights, inviolability, and even freedom of churches were not to be secured by canon law and tradition alone. They needed to be strongly complemented by the customary law and witness of the men of the shire that were the legacy of the Old English to the Norman order. If there was a need for church courts and church councils and synods in order for the church to be properly free, so, too, royal and customary courts had a part to play which was no less essential. At Penenden there was probably established in Lanfranc's mind the distinctness but also the mutual complementarity of the spiritual and canonical and of the temporal and feudal aspects of society that he proclaimed in the trial of Bishop William of Saint-Calais. This perception is likely to have been confirmed when, by means of a royal writ, the king laid down that no bishop or archdeacon should hold pleas in the hundred, nor should they bring to be judged by secular men a case that pertained to the cure of souls.

Such an outlook underlay Lanfranc's relationship with the kings that he served, especially William I. It has been written of him that he was 'the perfect second-in-command, given a commander whom he could respect and admire.... He emerged

---

[7] *VL* cap. 9, p. 692.

as the perfect subordinate to carry out the ecclesiastical policy of a reforming prince.'[8] This is a fair judgement so long as certain complexities in their relationship are observed. As archbishop with a duty *ad mores hominum corrigendos*, Lanfranc was a mentor even of the king, as is shown by his use of the incident of the *scurra* to impress upon the king the virtue of humility; when the monks of Saint-Ouen erred by their rebellion against their archbishop, Lanfranc called upon the king to correct their transgression. Even in a matter of politics, Lanfranc could attempt to act upon his own appraisal of the situation. At the end of the rebellion of the earls, he evidently thought that it would be better for the king to remain in Normandy: it would be preferable for the archbishop to show mildness and to seek reconciliation with such a figure as Earl Waltheof than for the king to act in wrath and with severity, thus prolonging the effects of the rebellion. But when the king thought and acted differently, Lanfranc's loyalty and service were not perceptibly diminished. They had not been diminished in 1072, when the king's refusal to let him receive an oath from Archbishop Thomas of York contributed to his failure to settle permanently the matter of the primacy. If to seek the absence of the king in order to implement in his name a milder policy, and to defer to him without rancour when overruled, are marks of a perfect second-in-command, Lanfranc merits the title.

At all events, whereas in matters of morality Lanfranc was the king's mentor who was heard by William I but disregarded by William II, in all public and political matters the king was master. This was the case in ecclesiastical no less than temporal affairs. Lanfranc was keenly aware that the peace and order that were to be desired for both church and lay society were best guaranteed by a strong and effective king whose will was obeyed; all the resources of the kingdom, spiritual and temporal, should be at his disposal. With William I, a strong and masterful king who according to his lights was a Christian man and who valued a well organized and directed church as a support for his rulership, Lanfranc could establish a fruitful and harmonious working relationship. He probably supported William Rufus rather than Robert Curthose to succeed him because, of the two, Rufus as a good soldier was the more likely to provide peace and order. By being serviceable to him, as in the rebellion of 1088 and in the trial of William of Saint-Calais that followed, he could hope to bring him to a better way of life. It was the tragedy of Lanfranc's last months that the new king did not so respond in either his personal or in his public capacity.

Lanfranc's lasting achievement was in the government and organization of the English church, both monastic and secular. In the monastic order, Lanfranc's background and training in the revitalized monasticism of the Norman duchy brought fresh impetus to English monasteries which, although not devoid of due observance, had largely lost the vitality that had characterized the age of Dunstan, Ethelwold, and Oswald. Lanfranc's own direct contribution was most manifest at Christ Church, Canterbury, and in the increase in the number of monastic cathedrals during the Norman period, so that by Henry I's reign more than half of the English

---

[8] Barlow, 'A View', 175/235.

cathedrals had monastic chapters. The coming of, on the whole, capable and committed Norman monks to become abbots was accompanied by a rapid increase in the number of monks and of monasteries, and to a wider distribution of monasteries throughout the kingdom. Lanfranc's example as a rebuilder of monastic churches and offices was widely followed.

The Old English secular church had had little structure, organization, or common institutions; in these respects, Lanfranc's years as archbishop marked a major turning-point in English church history. He did not succeed in permanently and institutionally establishing the primacy of the see of Canterbury as he envisaged it; nevertheless, he asserted its archbishop's position as primate of all England. The series of ecclesiastical councils that were a salient feature of his archiepiscopate were councils of the whole English church, at the centre of which was a settled hierarchy of bishops of both provinces of which the archbishop of Canterbury was president while others present, including the archbishop of York, sat with him.[9] Within the dioceses episcopal synods at the same time grew in importance, while episcopal laws were to be applied not in the hundred courts but in places that the bishops determined. It would be premature to see in Lanfranc's day the emergence of a structure of church courts and jurisdiction or even of a separation of spiritual and temporal courts. But the developments that have been described under Lanfranc were the necessary conditions for the momentous development of church courts and jurisdiction that marked the twelfth and thirteenth centuries. Lanfranc's inculcation of the study of canon law and dissemination of the *Collectio Lanfranci* further assisted this development.

It would likewise be anachronistic to assign to the time of Lanfranc the establishment of a general structure extending downwards from archbishops and bishops through archdeacons and rural deans to a universal basis in territorial parishes such as came to characterize the later medieval and the modern English church. But, again, Lanfranc's period in office, with the development of councils, synods, and the separate hearing of spiritual pleas, formed the matrix of its consolidation in later decades. The papal legates of 1070 had already enjoined the appointment of archdeacons and 'other ministers of holy order'. Lanfranc's years saw the definitive emergence of the archdeacon as an official of consequence within the dioceses; it was a critical step towards the long-term organization of the English church. In intention if not in ultimate fulfilment, it was given impetus as part of Lanfranc's programme *ad mores hominum corrigendos et componendum ecclesie statum* of which his *Vita* spoke.

Viewed in this light, Lanfranc's years as archbishop went far to determine the internal structure and organization of the English church for centuries to come; indeed, many of the features that it retains to this day, for example, the constitution of the diocese, arose from Lanfranc's initiatives: his work was fundamental and long-lasting. It was also ambivalent. It was so, first, because within the Anglo-Norman

---

[9] See the record of the council of London (1075): *CS* no. 92, vol. 1/2.612 = Lanfranc, *Letters*, no. 11, pp. 72–5.

kingdom the effect of Lanfranc's work was at once to embed the church deeply in the new feudal order with its demands and loyalties and also to place fresh emphasis upon the canonical separateness of the ecclesiastical order with its contemporarily developing claim to freedom. Second, it was so because the burgeoning ecclesiastical jurisdiction and the consequently emergent structure of church organization could remain an insular development for so long as an archbishop like Lanfranc was cool towards the claims of the papacy of Gregory VII and worked in concert with a king like William I, who was a reform-minded ruler and who was determined to be master of the spiritual as well as the temporal affairs of his kingdom. But William I and Lanfranc were preparing an order in the English church which, in other times and circumstances, was well prepared for development upwards to the papal curia (as it was named from Pope Urban II's time) at Rome and for the full implications of the Gregorian call for the freedom of the church to be brought to bear in England. In this connection, Lanfranc was preparing the way for the conflicts between Anselm and William II and Henry I and between Thomas Becket and Henry II, and for the drawing of the English church into the papal and canonical order of western Christendom during the remainder of the Middle Ages.

These were developments that Lanfranc could not have foreseen. Considered in terms of his own life and achievement, which were part of the earlier world of the eleventh century, his exceptional stature as archbishop of Canterbury is apparent. In particular aspects of an archbishop's life and work in church and kingdom, others would excel him: Anselm in theological profundity and range, Hubert Walter as an administrator, Thomas Becket and Edmund of Abingdon in sanctity as the Middle Ages envisaged it, are examples that come readily to mind. But in the succession of archbishops from Augustine to the present day, only Theodore of Tarsus approaches his high competence in each of the main concerns of his office, his skill in human and political relationships, and above all the enduring character and benefit of his government of the English church both in itself and as an aspect of national life.[10]

---

[10] Cf. the considered, if in some respects rather severe, judgement of Knowles, *The Monastic Order*, 142–3.

Bibliography

SOURCES

Acta archiepiscoporum Rothomagensium, PL 147.275–80.
ADHEMAR OF CHABANNES, *Epistola de apostolatu Martialis*, PL 141.89–112.
AL: Acta Lanfranci, in *The Anglo-Saxon Chronicle, MS A*, ed. Bately, 84–9.
ALGER OF LIÈGE, *De sacramentis corporis et sanguinis Domini*, PL 180.727–854.
Anglo-Saxon Charters, 4: *Charters of St Augustine's Abbey Canterbury and Minister-in-Thanet*, ed. S. E. Kelly (Oxford, 1995).
Anglo-Saxon Litanies of the Saints, ed. M. Lapidge, HBS 106 (London, 1991).
Annales Anglosaxonici, in *Ungedruckte Anglo-Normannische Geschichtsquellen*, ed. Liebermann, 1–8.
Annales Beccenses, in *Chronique du Bec*, ed. Porée, 1–11.
Annales monasterii de Wintonia, in *Annales monastici*, 2.3–125.
Annales monastici, ed. H. R. Luard, 5 vols., RS 36 (London, 1864–9).
Annales S. Stephani Cadomensis, in *Historiae Normannorum scriptores antiqui*, ed. A. Duchesne (Paris, 1619), 1015–21.
Annals of St Mary's Abbey, Dublin, in *Chartularies of St Mary's Abbey*, 2.241–92.
ANSELM, *Epp.*: Anselm, *Epistolae*, in Anselm, *Op.* vols. 3–5.
—— *Monologion*, in Anselm, *Op.* 1.1–87.
—— *Op.*: *S. Anselmi Cantuariensis archiepiscopi opera omnia*, ed. F. S. Schmitt, 6 vols. (Edinburgh, 1946–61).
ANSELME DE SAINT-REMI, *Histoire de la dédicace de Saint-Remi*, ed. and trans. J. Hourlier, in *La Champagne bénédictine: contribution à l'année saint Benoît*, Travaux de l'Académie nationale de Reims, 160 (Rheims, 1981), 179–297.
ANSELMO D'AOSTA, *Lettere*, ed. and trans. I. Biffi and C. Marabelli, 3 vols. (Milan, 1988–).
Aristoteles Latinus, ed. L. Minio-Paluello et al. (Bruges and Paris, 1957–).
ASC: The Anglo-Saxon Chronicle, ed. D. Whitelock, with D. C. Douglas and S. Tucker (London, 1961).
AUGUSTINE OF HIPPO, *De doctrina Christiana*, ed. G. M. Green, CSEL 80 (1963).
—— *De ordine*, ed. W. M. Green, CC 29/2/2 (1970), 87–137.
BECKER, G., *Catalogi bibliothecarum antiqui* (Bonn, 1885).
Bede's Ecclesiastical History of the English Nation, ed. B. Colgrave and R. A. B. Mynors (Oxford, 1969).
BENZO OF ALBA, *Ad Heinricum IV imperatorem libri VII*, ed. H. Seyffert, MGH SRG 65 (Hanover, 1996).
BERNARD OF CLUNY, *Ordo Cluniacensis*, in Herrgott, *Vetus disciplina*, 134–364.
BERNOLD OF SAINT-BLASIEN, *De veritate corporis et sanguinis Domini*, PL 148.1453–60; see also Huygens, 'Bérenger', 378–87.
BESSIN, G., *Concilia Rotomagensis provinciae* (Rouen, 1717).
BT: The Bayeux Tapestry, with Introduction by D. M. Wilson (London, 1985).
BURCHARD OF WORMS, *Decretorum libri viginti*, PL 140.537–1066.

Canterbury Professions, ed. M. Richter, Canterbury and York Society 67 (n.p., 1973).
Cartulary of the Priory of St Gregory, Canterbury, ed. A. M. Woodcock, CSer, 3rd ser. 88 (London, 1935).
CED: *Councils and Ecclesiastical Documents Relating to Great Britain and Ireland*, ed. A. W. Haddan and W. Stubbs, 3 vols. (Oxford, 1869–78).
Chartularies of St Mary's Abbey, Dublin, with the Register of its House at Dunbrody, and Annals of Ireland, ed. J. T. Gilbert, 2 vols., RS 80 (London, 1884).
Chronica monasterii Casinensis, ed. H. Hoffmann, *MGH SS* 34 (1980).
Chronica monasterii de Hida iuxta Wintoniam, in *Liber monasterii de Hyda*, ed. E. Edwards, RS 45 (London, 1866).
Chronicon abbatiae de Evesham, ed. W. D. Macray, RS 29 (London, 1863).
Chronicon Beccense, *PL* 150.639–90.
Chronique du Bec et Chronique de François Carré, ed. A. A. Porré (Rouen, 1883).
[CICERO], *Ad C. Herennium de ratione dicendi (Rhetorica ad Herennium)*, ed. and trans. H. Caplan (Cambridge, Mass., and London, 1954).
CICERO, *De inventione, De optimo genere oratorum, Topica*, ed. and trans. H. M. Hubbell (Cambridge, Mass., and London, 1949).
COD: *Conciliorum oecumenicorum decreta*, ed. G. Alberigo *et al.* (3rd edn., Bologna, 1973).
Consuetudines Beccenses, ed. M. P. Dickson, *CCMon*. 4 (Siegburg, 1967).
Consuetudinum saeculi X/XI/XII monumenta, ed. K. Hallinger, 4 vols., *CCMon*. 7 (Siegburg, 1984–6).
CS: *Councils & Synods with Other Documents Relating to the English Church*, 1: *A.D. 871–1204*, ed. D. Whitelock, M. Brett, and C. N. L. Brooke, 2 parts (London, 1981).
DB: *Domesday Book*, ed. J. Morris *et al.*, 42 vols. (Chichester, 1975–92).
DCSD: Lanfranc, *De corpore et sanguine Domini*, *PL* 150.307–42; excerpts in Huygens, 'Bérenger', 370–7.
De iniusta vexacione Willelmi episcopi primi per Willelmum regem filium Willelmi magni regis, ed. H. S. Offler and revised by A. J. Piper and A. I. Doyle, in *Chronology, Conquest, and Conflict in Medieval England*, Camden Miscellany 35, CSer. 5th ser. (1997), 49–104.
DELISLE, L., 'Canons du concile tenu à Lisieux en 1064', *Journal des savants* (1901), 516–21.
De nobili genere Crispinorum, *PL* 150.735–44.
De obitu Willelmi ducis Normannorum regisque Anglorum qui sanctam ecclesiam in pace vivere fecit, in William of Jumièges, 2.184–91.
Deusdedit, *Coll. can.*: *Die Kanonessammlung des Kardinals Deusdedit*, ed. V. Wulf von Glanvell, 1 (Paderborn, 1905).
Die Briefe des Petrus Damiani, ed. K. Reindel, 4 vols., *MGH Briefe*, 4 (Munich, 1983–93).
Die Konzilsordines des Früh- und Hochmittelalters, ed. H. Schneider, *MGH OCC* (Hanover, 1996).
DURANDUS OF TROARN, *Liber de corpore et sanguine Christi contra Berengarium et eius sectatores*, *PL* 143.1375–424.
EADMER, *Historia novorum in Anglia*, ed. M. Rule, RS 81 (London, 1884).
—— *Vita sancti Dunstani, Liber miraculorum*, in *Memorials of Saint Dunstan*, 162–49.
Ecclesiastical Documents, viz. I, A Brief History of the Bishoprick of Somerset from its Foundation to the Year 1174; II, Charters from the Library of Dr Cox Macro, ed. J. Hunter, CSer. 7 (1840).
EF: *Briefsammlungen der Zeit Heinrichs IV.*, ed. C. Erdmann and N. Fickermann, *MGH Briefe*, 5 (Weimar, 1950).

English Episcopal Acta, 10: *Bath and Wells 1061–1205*, ed. F. M. R. Ramsey (Oxford, 1995).
—— 14: *Coventry and Lichfield 1072–1159*, ed. M. J. Franklin (Oxford, 1997).
English Kalendars before A.D. 1100, ed. F. Wormald, HBS 72 (London, 1934).
English Lawsuits from William I to Richard I, ed. R. C. van Caenegem, 2 vols., Selden Society 106–7 (London, 1990–1).
ENNODIUS OF PAVIA, *Libellus adversus eos qui contra synodum scribere praesumpserunt*, ed. F. Vogel, *MGH AA* 7 (1885), 48–67.
Facsimiles of English Royal Writs to A.D. 1100 Presented to Vivian Hunter Galbraith, ed. T. A. M. Bishop and P. Chaplais (Oxford, 1957).
Fauroux: *Recueil des actes des ducs de Normandie (911–1066)*, ed. M. Fauroux, Mémoires de la Société des Antiquaires de Normandie 36 (Caen, 1961).
FLEMING, R., 'Christ Church Canterbury's Anglo-Norman Cartulary', in Hollister, C. W. (ed.), *Anglo-Norman Political Culture and the Twelfth-Century Renaissance* (Woodbridge, 1997), 83–155.
FOLCARD, *Vita sancti Johannis*, in *HCY* 1.239–60.
GERVASE OF CANTERBURY, *Actus pontificum*, in *The Historical Works*, 2.325–414.
—— *The Historical Works*, ed. W. Stubbs, 2 vols., RS 73 (London, 1879–80).
—— *Tractatus de combustione et reparatione Cantuariensis ecclesiae*, in *The Historical Works*, 1.3–29.
GILO, *Vita sancti Hugonis abbatis*, in Cowdrey, 'Two Studies', 45–109.
GOSCELIN OF SAINT-BERTIN, *Historia translationis s. Augustini episcopi Anglorum apostoli*, *PL* 155.13–46.
—— *Libellus contra inanes S. Mildrethae usurpatores*, in Colker, 'A Hagiographical Polemic', 68–96.
—— *Vita sancte Edithe virginis*, ed. A. Wilmart, *AB* 56 (1938), 5–101, 265–307.
GUIGUES I, *Coutumes de Chartreuse*, ed. a Carthusian, *SC* 313 (Paris, 1984).
GUITMUND OF AVERSA, *De corporis et sanguinis Christi veritate in eucharistia*, *PL* 149.1427–94.
HARMER, F. E., *Anglo-Saxon Writs* (Manchester, 1952).
HCY: *The Historians of the Church of York and its Archbishops*, ed. J. Raine, 3 vols., RS 71 (London, 1879–94).
HENRY OF HUNTINGDON: Henry, Archdeacon of Huntingdon, *Historia Anglorum*, ed. and trans. D. Greenway (Oxford, 1996).
HERMANN, *De miraculis sancti Edmundi*, in *Memorials of St Edmund's Abbey*, 1.26–92.
HERRGOTT, M., *Vetus disciplina monastica*, reissue with introd. by P. Engelbert (Siegburg, 1999).
Hinschius: *Decretales Pseudo-Isidorianae et Capitula Angilramni*, ed. P. Hinschius (Leipzig, 1863).
HOYT, R. S., 'A Pre-Domesday Kentish Assessment List', in *A Medieval Miscellany for Doris Mary Stenton*, ed. P. M. Barnes and C. F. Slade, Pipe Roll Society, NS 36 for the year 1960 (London, 1962), 189–202.
HUGH OF FLAVIGNY, *Chronicon*, *MGH SS* 8 (1848), 280–501.
HUGH THE CHANTER, *The History of the Church of York 1066–1127*, ed. and trans. C. Johnson, revised by M. Brett, C. N. L. Brooke, and M. Winterbottom (Oxford, 1990).
HUMBERT OF SILVA CANDIDA, *Libri iii adversus simoniacos*, ed. F. Thaner, *MGH Libelli*, 1.95–253.
HUYGENS, R. B. C., 'Bérenger de Tours, Lanfranc et Bernold de Constance', *Sacris Erudiri*, 16 (1965), 355–403.
—— 'Textes latins du xie au xiiie siècle', *SM* 3rd ser. 8 (1967), 451–503.

—— 'Les Lettres de Bérenger de Tours et d'Ascelin de Chartres', in Gumbert and De Haan (eds.), *Texts and Manuscripts*, 2.16–22.
JEROME, *Letters*: *Sancti Eusebii Hieronymi epistulae*, ed. I. Hilberg, *CSEL* 54 (2nd edn., Vienna, 1996).
JOHN OF FÉCAMP (Pseudo-Alcuin), *De corpore et sanguine Domini et De propriis delictis* (= *Confessio fidei*, 4), *PL* 101.1085–98.
JOHN OF WORCESTER: *The Chronicle of John of Worcester*, ed. R. R. Darlington and P. McGurk, 3 vols. (Oxford, 1995–   ).
LANFRANC, *Letters*: *The Letters of Lanfranc, Archbishop of Canterbury*, ed. H. Clover and M. Gibson (Oxford, 1979).
—— *MC*: *The Monastic Constitutions of Lanfranc*, ed. and trans. D. Knowles, revised edn. by C. N. L. Brooke (Oxford, 2002); also *Decreta Lanfranci monachis Cantuariensibus transmissa*, ed. D. Knowles, *CCMon*. 3 (Siegburg, 1967).
—— Lanfrancus Archiepiscopus Cantuariensis, *In omnes Pauli epistolas commentarii*, *Opera*, ed. Giles, 2.17–146; *PL* 150.105–406.
—— *Opera omnia*, ed. L. D'Achery (Paris, 1648).
—— *Opera quae supersunt omnia*, ed. J. A. Giles, 2 vols. (Oxford and Paris, 1844).
LAPIDGE, M., 'Dominic of Evesham, *Vita S. Ecgwini episcopi et confessoris*', *AB* 96 (1978), 65–104.
Le 'De officiis ecclesiasticis de Jean d'Avranches', ed. R. Delamare (Paris, 1923).
Leges Henrici Primi, ed. L. J. Downer (Oxford, 1972).
Liber diurnus Romanorum pontificum, ed. H. Foerster (Berne, 1958).
Liber Eliensis, ed. E. O. Blake, CSer. 3rd ser. 92 (London, 1962).
Liber legis Langobardorum Papiensis dictus, in *MGH LL* 4, *Leges Langobardorum*, ed. F. Bluhme and A. Boretius, 289–585.
Liber monasterii de Hyda, ed. E. Edwards, RS 45 (London, 1866).
Liber tramitis aevi Odilonis abbatis, ed. P. Dinter, CCMon. 10 (Siegburg, 1980).
LIEBERMANN, F., 'Drei nordhumbrische Urkunden um 1100', *Archiv für das Studium der neuen Sprachen*, 111 (1903), 275–84.
Magna vita Sancti Hugonis: *The Life of St Hugh of Lincoln*, ed. D. L. Douie and H. Farmer, 2 vols. (Oxford, 1985).
Manaresi: *I placiti del Regnum Italiae*, ed. C. Manaresi, 3 vols., Fonti per la storia d'Italia 92, 96–7 (Rome, 1955–60).
Memorials of Saint Dunstan, Archbishop of Canterbury, ed. W. Stubbs, RS 63 (London, 1874).
Memorials of St Edmund's Abbey, ed. T. Arnold, 3 vols., RS 96 (London, 1890–6).
Monasticon Anglicanum, by W. Dugdale, rev. ed. by J. Caley, H. Ellis and B. Bandinel, 6 vols. in 8 (London, 1817–30).
MSN: *Miracula sancti Nicholai*, in *Catalogus codicum hagiographicorum latinorum antiquiorum saeculo XVI qui asservantur in Bibliotheca Nationali Parisiensi*, 4 vols. (Brussels, 1889–93), 2.405–23.
MUSSET, L., 'Les Actes de Guillaume le Conquérant et de la reine Matilde pour les abbayes Caennais', *Mémoires de la Société des Antiquaires de Normandie*, 37 (Caen, 1967).
ORDERIC VITALIS: *The Ecclesiastical History of Orderic Vitalis*, ed. M. Chibnall, 6 vols. (Oxford, 1969–80).
OSBERN, *Translatio sancti Elphegi*, *PL* 149.387–94.
—— *Vita sancti Dunstani, Liber miraculorum*, in *Memorials of Saint Dunstan*, 69–161.
PASCHASIUS RADBERTUS, *De corpore et sanguine Domini*, ed. B. Paulus, *CCM* 16 (Turnhout, 1969).

PETER THE VENERABLE, *Contra Petrobrusianos hereticos*, ed. J. Fearns, *CCM* 10 (Turnhout, 1968).
PRG: Le Pontifical Romano-Germanique, ed. C. Vogel and R. Elze, 3 vols., *ST* 226–7, 269 (Vatican City, 1963–72).
PRISCIAN, *Institutiones*, ed. M. Hertz, 2 vols. (Leipzig, 1855–9).
Quellen des 9. und 11. Jahrhunderts zur Geschichte der Hamburgischen Kirche und des Reichs, ed. R. Buchner, *AQ* 11 (Darmstadt, 1961).
RATRAMNUS, *De corpore et sanguine Domini*, ed. J. M. Bakhuisen van den Brink (2nd edn., Amsterdam and London, 1974).
RCL: Berengerius Turonensis, Rescriptum contra Lanfrannum, 1: Text, ed. R. B. C. Huygens, 2: Facsimile, ed. W. Milde, *CCM* 84, 84A (Turnhout, 1988).
Regesta WI: Regesta regum Anglo-Normannorum: The Acta of William I (1066–1087), ed. D. Bates (Oxford, 1998).
Reg. Greg. I: Gregorii magni Registrum epistularum, ed. D. Norberg, *CC* 140, 140A (Turnhout, 1982).
Reg.: Gregorii VII Registrum, ed. E. Caspar, *MGH Epp. sel.* 2 (Berlin, 1920–3).
Regularis concordia Anglicae nationis, ed. T. Symons, rev. by M. Wegener and K. Hallinger, in *Consuetudinum saeculi X/XI/XII monumenta*, 3.61–147; also *Regularis concordia Anglicae nationis monachorum sanctimonialiumque*, ed. and trans. T. Symons (London, etc., 1953).
Reliquiae Dunstanianae, in *Memorials of Saint Dunstan*, 364–439.
ROBERT OF TORIGNY: *The Chronicle of Robert of Torigni*, in *Chronicles of the Reigns of Stephen, Henry II, and Richard I*, ed. R. Howlett, 4 vols., RS 82 (London, 1884–9), 4.
RODULFUS GLABER, *Historiarum libri quinque*, and *Vita domni Willelmi abbatis*, ed. and trans. J. France, N. Bulst, and P. Reynolds (Oxford, 1989).
ROLLASON, D. W., *The Mildrith Legend: A Study in Early Medieval Hagiography in England* (Leicester, 1982).
RSB: La Règle de saint Benoît, ed. and trans. A. de Vogüé *et al.*, 6 vols., *SC* 181–6 (Paris, 1971–2).
SCHOLZ, B. W., 'Eadmer's Life of Bregwine, Archbishop of Canterbury 761–4', *Traditio*, 22 (1966), 127–48.
SIGEBERT OF GEMBLOUX, *DVI: Catalogus Sigeberti Gemblacensis monachi de viris illustribus*, ed. R. Witte (Frankfurt, 1974).
SOMERVILLE, R., in collaboration with KUTTNER, S., *Pope Urban II, the Collectio Britannica, and the Council of Melfi (1089)* (Oxford, 1996).
SYMEON OF DURHAM, *Gesta regum*, in *Opera omnia*, 2.3–281.
—— *Opera omnia*, ed. T. Arnold, 2 vols., RS 75 (London, 1882–5).
—— *Libellus de exordio atque procursu istius, hoc est Dunelmensis, ecclesie*, ed. and trans. D. Rollason (Oxford, 2000).
The Anglo-Saxon Chronicle: A Collaborative Edition, 3: *MS A*, ed. J. M. Bately (Cambridge, 1986).
The Benedictional of Archbishop Robert, ed. H. A. Wilson, HBS 24 (London, 1903).
The Bosworth Psalter, ed. F. A. Gasquet and E. Bishop (London, 1908).
The Brevis relatio de Guillelmo nobilissimo comite Normannorum, Written by a Monk of Battle, ed. E. M. C. van Houts, in *Chronology, Conquest and Conflict in Medieval England*, Camden Miscellany 35, CSer. 5th ser. 10 (1997), 1–48.
The Carmen de Hastingae proelio of Guy, Bishop of Amiens, ed. and trans. F. Barlow (Oxford, 1999).
The Chronicle of Battle Abbey, ed. and trans. E. Searle (Oxford, 1980).

The Chronicle of Glastonbury Abbey: An Edition, Translation and Study of John of Glastonbury's Antiquitates Glastoniensis ecclesie, ed. J. P. Carley (Woodbridge, 1985).
The Claudius Pontificals, ed. D. H. Turner, HBS 97 (London, 1971).
The Domesday monachorum of Christ Church, Canterbury, ed. D. C. Douglas (London, 1944).
The Early History of Glastonbury: An Edition, Translation and Study of William of Malmesbury's De antiquitate Glastonie ecclesie, ed. J. Scott (Woodbridge, 1981).
The 'Expositio in Cantica canticorum' of Williram, Abbot of Ebersberg: A Critical Edition, ed. E. H. Bartelmez (Philadelphia, 1967).
The Life of Gundulf, Bishop of Rochester, ed. R. M. Thomson (Toronto, 1977).
The Life of King Edward who Rests at Westminster, Attributed to a Monk of Saint-Bertin, ed. and trans. F. Barlow (2nd edn., London, 1992).
The Letters of Saint Anselm of Canterbury, trans. W. Fröhlich, 3 vols. (Kalamazoo, 1990–4).
The Textus Roffensis, facsimile ed. by P. Sawyer (Copenhagen, 1957–62); excerpts in *The Life of Gundulf*, ed. Thomson, 17–18, 73–85.
Thesaurus novus anecdotorum, ed. E. Martène and U. Durand, 5 vols. (Paris, 1717).
The Waltham Chronicle, ed. and trans. L. Watkiss and M. Chibnall (Oxford, 1994).
The Works of Gilbert Crispin, Abbot of Westminster, ed. A. S. Abulafia and G. R. Evans (London, 1986).
The Writings of Bishop Patrick of Dublin 1074–84, ed. A. Gwynn (Dublin, 1955).
THIETMAR OF MERSEBURG, *Chronicon*, ed. R. Holtzmann and W. Trillmich, *AQ* 9 (Darmstadt, 1962).
THORPE, B., *Diplomatarium Anglicum aevi Saxonici* (London, 1865).
TURGOT, *Vita s. Margaretae Scotorum reginae*, in *Symeonis Dunelmensis opera et collectanea*, ed. J. Hodgson Hinde, 1, *SS* 51 (London, 1868), 234–54.
Ungedruckte Anglo-Normannische Geschichtsquellen, ed. F. Liebermann (Strassburg, 1879).
VA: Eadmer, *The Life of St Anselm, Archbishop of Canterbury*, ed. and trans. R. W. Southern (2nd edn., Oxford, 1972).
VH: Gilbert Crispin, *Vita Herluini*, in Armitage Robinson, *Gilbert Crispin*, 87–110; and in *The Works of Gilbert Crispin*, ed. Abulafia and Evans, 183–212.
Vita sanctorum Aethelredi et Aethelberti martyrum et sanctarum virginum Miltrudis et Eadburgis, in Colker, 'A Hagiographical Polemic', 97–108.
VL: *Vita Lanfranci*, ed. M. Gibson, in D'Onofrio (ed.), *Lanfranco di Pavia*, 661–715; also *PL* 150.28–58.
VW: *The Vita Wulfstani of William of Malmesbury*, ed. R. R. Darlington, *CSer*. 3rd ser. 40 (London, 1928).
WACE, *Roman de rou*, ed. A. J. Holden, 2 vols. (Paris, 1970–3).
WHARTON, H., *Anglia sacra*, 2 vols. (London, 1691).
WHITELOCK, D., *Anglo-Saxon Wills* (Cambridge, 1930).
WILLIAM OF JUMIÈGES: *The Gesta Normannorum ducum of William of Jumièges, Orderic Vitalis, and Robert of Torigni*, ed. and trans. E. M. C. van Houts, 2 vols. (Oxford, 1992–5).
WILLIAM OF MALMESBURY, *GP*: William of Malmesbury, *De gestis pontificum Anglorum libri quinque*, ed. N. E. S. A. Hamilton, RS 52 (London, 1870).
—— *GR*: William of Malmesbury, *Gesta regum Anglorum*, ed. R. A. B. Mynors, R. M. Thomson, and M. Winterbottom, 2 vols. (Oxford, 1998–9).
WILLIAM OF POITIERS: *The Gesta Guillelmi of William of Poitiers*, ed. and trans. R. H. C. Davis and M. Chibnall (Oxford, 1998); also Guillaume de Poitiers, *Histoire de Guillaume le Conquérant*, ed. and trans. R. Foreville (Paris, 1952).

WILMART, *Opuscula*: A. Wilmart, 'Edmeri Cantuariensis cantoris nova opuscula de sanctorum veneratione et obsecratione', *RSR* 15 (1935), 184–219, 354–79.
WIPO, *Gesta Chuonradi II. imperatoris*, ed. W. Trillmich, in *Quellen des 9. und 11. Jahrhunderts*, 504–613.
WOODRUFF, C. E., 'Some Early Professions of Canonical Obedience to the See of Canterbury by Heads of Religious Houses', *Archaeologia Cantiana*, 77 (1925), 53–72.

MODERN AUTHORITIES

AIRD, W. M., 'An Absent Friend: The Career of William of St Calais', in Rollason, Harvey, and Prestwich (eds.), *Anglo-Norman Durham*, 263–7.
—— *St Cuthbert and the Normans: The Church of Durham, 1071–1153* (Woodbridge and Rochester, NY, 1998).
ALEXANDER, J. J. G., *Norman Illumination at Mont St Michel, 996–1100* (Oxford, 1970).
ALTHOFF, G., *Spielregeln der Politik im Mittelalter. Kommunikation in Frieden und Fehde* (Darmstadt, 1997).
ARMITAGE ROBINSON, J., *Gilbert Crispin, Abbot of Westminster: A Study of the Abbey under Norman Rule* (Cambridge, 1911).
BARKER, L. W., 'Ivo of Chartres and the Anglo-Norman Cultural Tradition', *ANS* 13 (1991), 15–33.
BARLOW, F., 'A View of Archbishop Lanfranc', *JEH* 16 (1965), 163–77; repr. id., *The Norman Conquest and Beyond*, 223–41.
—— *The English Church, 1000–1066* (2nd edn., London, 1979).
—— *The English Church, 1066–1154* (London and New York, 1979).
—— *The Norman Conquest and Beyond* (London, 1983).
—— *William Rufus* (London, 1983).
BARNES, J., 'Boethius and the Study of Logic', in Gibson (ed.), *Boethius*, 73–89.
BARROW, G. W. S., *The Kingdom of the Scots: Government, Church and Society* (London, 1973).
BARROW, J., 'How the Twelfth-Century Monks of Worcester Perceived their Past', in Magdalino (ed.), *The Perception of the Past*, 53–74.
BATES, D., 'The Character and Career of Odo, Bishop of Bayeux', *Speculum*, 50 (1975), 1–20.
—— 'The Land Pleas of William I's Reign: Penenden Heath Revisited', *BIHR* 51 (1978), 1–19.
—— 'The Origins of the Justiciarship', *ANS* 4 (1982), 1–12, 167–71.
—— *Normandy Before 1066* (London and New York, 1986).
—— *Bishop Remigius of Lincoln, 1067–1092* (London, 1992).
—— 'The Forged Charters of William the Conqueror and William of St Calais', in Rollason et al., *Anglo-Norman Durham*, 111–24.
BAYLÉ, M., 'Les Ateliers de sculpture de Saint-Étienne de Caen au XIe et au XIIe siècles', *ANS* 10 (1987), 1–23.
BAZIN, G., *Le Mont Saint-Michel: histoire et archéologie de l'origine à nos jours* (new edn., New York, 1978).
BETHELL, D. L., 'English Black Monks and Episcopal Elections in the 1120s', *EHR* 84 (1969), 673–98.
BIDDLE, M., 'Seasonal Festivals and Residence: Winchester, Westminster and Gloucester in the Tenth to Twelfth Centuries', *ANS* 8 (1985), 51–72.
—— (ed.), *Winchester in the Early Middle Ages* (Oxford, 1976).
BIFFI, I., 'Lanfranco esegeta di san Paolo', in D'Onofrio (ed.), *Lanfranco di Pavia*, 167–87.

BLAIR, W. J., 'Local Churches in Domesday Book and Before', in Holt (ed.), *Domesday Studies*, 265–78.
—— 'Secular Minster Churches in Domesday Book', in Sawyer (ed.), *Domesday Book*, 104–42.
BLOCKLEY, K., with SPARKS, M., and TATTON-BROWN, T. (eds.), *Canterbury Cathedral Nave: Archaeology, History and Architecture* (Canterbury, 1997).
BÖHMER, H., *Kirche und Staat in England und in der Normandie im XI. und XII. Jahrhundert* (Leipzig, 1899).
—— *Die Fälschungen Erzbischof Lanfranks* (Leipzig, 1902).
BORGHI, R., and TIBALDI, R., 'Lanfranco "musicus"', in D'Onofrio (ed.), *Lanfranco di Pavia*, 255–80.
BOÜARD, M. DE, *Le château de Caen* (Caen, 1979).
BRESSLAU, H., *Jahrbücher des deutschen Reichs unter Konrad II.*, 2 vols. (Leipzig, 1879–84).
BRETT, M., *The English Church under Henry I* (Oxford, 1975).
—— 'The *Collectio Lanfranci* and its Competitors', in Smith and Ward (eds.), *Intellectual Life*, 157–74.
—— 'Gundulf and the Cathedral Communities of Canterbury and Rochester', in Eales and Sharpe (eds.), *Canterbury*, 15–25.
—— 'A Supplementary Note on the Charters Attributed to Archbishop Lanfranc', in D'Onofrio (ed.), *Lanfranco di Pavia*, 521–7.
BROOKE, C. N. L., 'Gregorian Reform in Action: Clerical Marriage in England, 1050–1200', *Cambridge Historical Journal*, 1 (1956), 1–21; repr. id., *Medieval Church and Society: Selected Essays* (London, 1971), 69–99.
—— 'Archbishop Lanfranc, the English Bishops, and the Council of London of 1075', *Studia Gratiana*, 12 (1967), 39–59.
—— 'The Archdeacon and the Norman Conquest', in id., *Churches and Churchmen in Medieval Europe* (London, 1999), 117–33.
—— LUSCOMBE, D. E., MARTIN, G. H., and OWEN, D. (eds.), *Church and Government in the Middle Ages: Essays Presented to C. R. Cheney on his 70th Birthday* (Cambridge, 1976).
BROOKE, Z. N., *The English Church and the Papacy* (Cambridge, 1931).
BROOKS, N., *The Early History of the Church of Canterbury* (Leicester, 1984).
—— 'The Anglo-Saxon Cathedral Community, 597–1070', in Collinson *et al.* (eds.), *A History of Canterbury Cathedral*, 1–37.
BRÜHL, C., 'Das *palatium* von Pavia und die *Honorantiae civitatis Papiae*', in id., *Aus Mittelalter und Diplomatik. Gesammelte Aufsätze*, 2 vols. (Hildesheim, 1989), 1.138–69.
BULLOUGH, D. A., 'Urban Change in Medieval Italy: The Example of Pavia', *Papers of the British School at Rome*, 34 (1966), 82–130.
CALASSO, F., *Medio evo del diritto*, 1: *Le fonti* (Milan, 1954).
CANTIN, A., 'La Position prise par Lanfranc sur le traitement des mystères de la foi par les raisons dialectiques', in D'Onofrio (ed.), *Lanfranco di Pavia*, 361–80.
CARLSON, E. G., 'Excavations at Saint-Étienne, Caen', *Gesta*, 10 (1971), 22–30.
CHADWICK, H., 'Ego Berengarius', *JTS* NS 40 (1989), 414–45.
CHIBNALL, M., *The World of Orderic Vitalis* (Oxford, 1984).
CLAPHAM, A. W., *English Romanesque Architecture After the Conquest* (Oxford, 1934).
CLOVER, H., 'Alexander II's Letter *Accepimus a quibusdam* and its Relationship to the Canterbury Forgeries', in G.-U. Langé (ed.), *La Normandie bénédictine au temps de Guillaume le Conquérant (xie siècle)* (Lille, 1967), 417–22.
COLISH, M. L., *The Mirror of Language: A Study in the Medieval Theory of Knowledge* (revised edn., Lincoln, Nebr., and London, 1983).

COLKER, M. L., 'A Hagiographic Polemic', *Mediaeval Studies*, 39 (1977), 60–108.
COLLINSON, P., RAMSAY, N., and SPARKS, M. (eds.), *A History of Canterbury Cathedral* (Oxford, 1995).
COOPER, A., 'Extraordinary Privilege: The Trial of Penenden Heath and the Domesday Inquest', *EHR* 116 (2001), 1167–92.
COWDREY, H. E. J., 'Archbishop Aribert II of Milan', *History*, 51 (1966), 1–15; repr. id., *Popes, Monks and Crusaders*, no. IV.
—— 'Bishop Ermenfrid of Sion and the Penitential Ordinance Following the Battle of Hastings', *JEH* 20 (1969), 225–42.
—— 'Pope Gregory VII and the Anglo-Norman Church and Kingdom', *SG* 9 (1972), 79–114; repr. id., *Popes, Monks and Crusaders*, no. IX.
—— 'Two Studies in Cluniac History', *SG* 11 (1987), 1–298.
—— 'The Anglo-Norman *Laudes regiae*', *Viator*, 12 (1981), 37–78; repr. id., *Popes, Monks and Crusaders*, no. VIII.
—— *Popes, Monks and Crusaders* (London, 1984).
—— 'The Gregorian Reform in the Anglo-Norman Lands and Scandinavia', *SG* 13 (1989), 321–52; repr. id., *Popes and Church Reform*, no. VII.
—— 'The Papacy and the Berengarian Controversy', in Ganz *et al.* (eds.), *Auctoritas und Ratio*, 109–38; repr. id., *Popes and Church Reform*, no. VI.
—— 'Lanfranc, the Papacy, and the See of Canterbury', in D'Onofrio (ed.), *Lanfranco di Pavia*, 439–500; repr. id., *Popes and Church Reform*, no. X.
—— 'The Enigma of Archbishop Lanfranc', *HSJ* 6 (1994), 129–52; repr. id., *Popes and Church Reform*, no. XI.
—— *Pope Gregory VII 1073–1085* (Oxford, 1998).
—— *The Crusades and Latin Monasticism, 11th–12th Centuries* (Aldershot, 1999).
—— 'William I's Relations with Cluny Further Considered', in id., *The Crusades and Latin Monasticism*, no. VIII.
—— *Popes and Church Reform in the 11th Century* (Aldershot, 2000).
—— 'Archbishop Thomas of York and the *pallium*', *HSJ* (forthcoming).
CRISTIANI, M., 'Le "ragioni" di Berengario di Tours', in D'Onofrio, *Lanfranco di Pavia*, 327–60.
CROOK, J., *The Architectural Setting of the Cult of Saints in the Early Christian West, c.300–c.1200* (Oxford, 2000).
CUSHING, K., *Papacy and Law in the Gregorian Revolution: The Canonistic Work of Anselm of Lucca* (Oxford, 1998).
DAVID, C. W., *Robert Curthose, Duke of Normandy* (Cambridge, Mass., 1920).
DAVIES, R. R., *Conquest, Coexistence and Change: Wales 1063–1415* (Oxford, 1987).
DAVIS, R. H. C., and WALLACE-HADRILL, J. M. (eds.), *The Writing of History in the Middle Ages: Essays Presented to Richard William Southern* (Oxford, 1981).
DIURNI, G., *L'Expositio ad Librum Papiensem e la scienza giuridica preirneriana* (Rome, 1976).
D'ONOFRIO, G., *Lanfranco di Pavia e l'Europa del secolo XI nel IX centenario della morte* (Rome, 1993).
—— 'Lanfranco teologo e la storia della filosofia', in D'Onofrio (ed.), *Lanfranco di Pavia*, 189–228.
DOUGLAS, D. C., 'Odo, Lanfranc and the Domesday Survey', in J. G. Edwards, V. H. Galbraith, and E. F. Jacob (eds.), *Historical Essays in Honour of James Tait* (Manchester, 1933), 47–57.
—— *William the Conqueror* (London, 1964).

DRONKE, P. (ed.), *A History of Twelfth-Century Western Philosophy* (Cambridge, 1988).
DU BOULAY, F. R. H., *The Lordship of Canterbury: An Essay in Medieval Society* (London, 1966).
DUEBALL, M., *Die Suprematstreit zwischen den Erzdiözesen Canterbury und York* (Berlin, 1929).
DUMVILLE, D. N., *Liturgy and the Ecclesiastical History of Late Anglo-Saxon England: Four Studies* (Woodbridge, 1992).
EALES, R., and SHARPE, R. (eds.), *Canterbury and the Norman Conquest: Churches, Saints and Scholars, 1066–1109* (London, 1995).
EMMS, R., 'The Historical Traditions of St Augustine's Abbey, Canterbury', in Eales and Sharpe (eds.), *Canterbury*, 159–68.
EVANS, G. R., '*Solummodo sacramentum et non verum*: Issues of Logic and Language in the Berengarian Controversy', in D'Onofrio (ed.), *Lanfranco di Pavia*, 381–405.
Fälschungen im Mittelalter. Internationaler Kongress der MGH, München, 16.–19. September 1986, 6 vols., MGH Schriften 33 (Hanover, 1988–9).
FERNIE, E., 'St Anselm's Crypt', in *Medieval Art and Architecture*, 27–38.
FLANAGAN, M. T., *Irish Society, Anglo-Norman Settlers, Angevin Kingship: Interactions in Ireland in the Late Twelfth Century* (Oxford, 1989).
FOREVILLE, R., 'The Synod of the Province of Rouen in the Eleventh and Twelfth Centuries', in Brooke *et al.* (eds.), *Church and Government*, 19–39.
—— 'Lanfranc et la politique ecclésiastique de Guillaume le Conquérant', in D'Onofrio (ed.), *Lanfranco di Pavia*, 409–23.
FRAUENKNECHT, E., *Der Traktat De ordinando pontifice*, MGH S. und T. 5 (Hanover, 1992).
FUHRMANN, H., *Einfluß und Verbreitung der pseudoisidorischen Fälschungen*, 3 vols., MGH Schriften, 24/1–3 (Stuttgart, 1972–4).
GALBRAITH, V. H., 'The East Anglian See and the Abbey of Bury St Edmunds', *EHR* 40 (1925), 222–8.
GAMESON, R., 'English Manuscript Art in the Eleventh Century: Canterbury and its Context', in Eales and Sharpe (eds.), *Canterbury*, 95–144.
GANZ, P., HUYGENS, R. B. C., and NIEWÖHNER, F. (eds.), *Auctoritas und ratio. Studien zu Berengar von Tours* (Wiesbaden, 1990).
GEM, R., 'The Significance of the 11th-Century Rebuilding of Christ Church and St Augustine's, Canterbury, in the Development of Romanesque Architecture', in *Medieval Art and Architecture*, 1–19.
GERSCH, S., 'Anselm of Canterbury', in Dronke (ed.), *A History of Twelfth-Century Western Philosophy*, 255–78.
GIBSON, M., 'Lanfranc's "Commentary on the Pauline Epistles"', *JTS*, NS 22 (1971), 86–112; repr. eadem, '*Artes' and the Bible*, no. XII.
—— 'Lanfranc's Notes on Patristic Texts', *JTS*, NS 22 (1971), 435–50; repr. eadem, '*Artes' and the Bible*, no. XIII.
—— *Lanfranc of Bec* (Oxford, 1978).
—— 'History at Bec in the Twelfth Century', in Davis and Wallace-Hadrill (eds.), *The Study of History*, 167–86; repr. eadem, '*Artes' and the Bible*, no. XX.
—— 'The Image of Lanfranc', in D'Onofrio (ed.), *Lanfranco di Pavia*, 21–8.
—— '*Artes' and the Bible in the Medieval West* (Aldershot, 1993).
—— 'Normans and Angevins, 1070–1220', in Collinson *et al.* (eds.), *A History of Canterbury Cathedral*, 38–68.
—— (ed.), *Boethius: His Life, Thought and Influence* (Oxford, 1981).
GOTTLOB, T., *Der abendländische Chorepiskopat* (Bonn, 1928).

GRANSDEN, A., 'Baldwin, Abbot of Bury St Edmunds, 1065–1097', *ANS* 4 (1981), 65–76.
GRÉGOIRE, R., 'Il diritto monastico elaborato nei *Decreta* di Lanfranco', in D'Onofrio (ed.), *Lanfranco di Pavia*, 117–29.
GULLICK, M., 'The English-Owned Manuscripts of the *Collectio Lanfranci* (s. xi/xii)', in *The Legacy of M. R. James*, ed. L. Dennison (Donnington, 2001), 99–117.
GUMBERT, J. P., and DE HAAN, M. J. M. (eds.), *Texts and Manuscripts Essays Presented to G. I. Lieftinck*, 2 vols. (Amsterdam, 1972).
GWYNN, A., *The Irish Church in the Eleventh and Twelfth Centuries* (Dublin, 1992).
HERRMANN, K.-J., *Das Tuskulanerpapsttum (1012–1046)* (Stuttgart, 1973).
HESLOP, T. A. 'The Canterbury Calendars and the Norman Conquest', in Eales and Sharpe (eds.), *Canterbury*, 53–85.
HICKS, C. (ed.), *England in the Eleventh Century* (Stamford, 1992).
HIRSCH, S., with PABST, H., and BRESSLAU, H., *Jahrbücher des deutschen Reichs unter Heinrich II.*, 3 vols. (Leipzig, 1862–75).
HOLT, J. C. (ed.), *Domesday Studies* (Woodbridge and Wolfeboro, 1987).
HOLTZMANN, R., *Geschichte der sächsischen Kaiserzeit* (Munich, n.d.).
HÜLS, R., *Kardinäle, Klerus und Kirchen Roms, 1049–1130* (Tübingen, 1977).
HUNT, R. W., 'Studies on Priscian in the Eleventh and Twelfth Centuries', *MARS* 1 (1943), 194–231.
HUNT, R. W., PANTIN, W. A., and SOUTHERN, R. W. (eds.), *Studies in Medieval History Presented to Frederick Maurice Powicke* (Oxford, 1948).
JAMES, M. R., *The Ancient Libraries of Canterbury and Dover* (Cambridge, 1903).
JOHN, E., 'The Division of the *mensa* in Early English Monasteries', *JEH* 6 (1957), 143–55.
JONES, P., *The Italian City-state: From Commune to Signoria* (Oxford, 1997).
KEHR, P. F., 'Zur Geschichte Wiberts von Ravenna (Clemens III.)', *Sitzungsberichte der preussischen Akademie der Wissenschaften, Berlin, phil.-hist. Klasse* (1921), 355–68, 973–88.
KELLY, S. E., 'Some Forgeries in the Archive of St Augustine's Abbey, Canterbury', in *Fälschungen im Mittelalter*, 4.347–68.
KÉRY, L., *Canonical Collections of the Early Middle Ages, ca.400–1140* (Washington DC, 1999).
KISSAN, B. W., 'Lanfranc's Alleged Division of Lands Between Archbishop and Community', *EHR* 54 (1939), 385–93.
KLÖCKENER, M., *Die Liturgie der Diözesansynode. Studien zur Geschichte und Theologie des Ordo ad synodum des Pontificale Romanum. Mit einer Darstellung des Pontificales und einem Verzeichnis seiner Drucke* (Münster, 1986).
KLUKAS, A. W., 'The Architectural Implications of the *Decreta Lanfranci*', *ANS* 6 (1984), 136–71.
KNOWLES, D., *The Monastic Order in England* (2nd edn., Cambridge, 1963).
—— and HADCOCK, R. N., *Medieval Religious Houses: England and Wales* (2nd edn., London and New York, 1971).
LECLERCQ, J., *The Love of Learning and the Desire for God: A Study of Monastic Culture*, trans. C. Misrahi (London, 1978).
—— and BONNES, J.-P., *Un maître de la vie spirituelle au xie siècle: Jean de Fécamp* (Paris, 1946).
LEMARIGNIER, J.-F., *Étude sur les privilèges d'exemption et de juridiction ecclésiastique des abbayes normandes depuis les origines jusq'en 1140* (Paris, 1937).
LE NEVE, J., compiled by D. E. GREENWAY, *Fasti ecclesiae anglicanae 1066–1300*, 7 vols. so far: (1) St Paul's, London (London, 1968); (2) Monastic Cathedrals (1971); (3) Lincoln (1977); (4) Salisbury (1991); (5) Chichester (1996); (6) York (1999); (7) Bath and Wells (2001).

LE PATOUREL, J., 'The Date of the Trial on Penenden Heath', *EHR* 61 (1946), 378–88; repr. id., *Feudal Empires*, no. V.
—— 'The Reports of the Trial on Penenden Heath', in Hunt *et al.* (eds.), *Studies in Medieval History*, 15–26.
—— 'The Norman Succession, 996–1135', *EHR* 76 (1971), 225–50.
—— *The Norman Empire* (Oxford, 1976).
—— *Feudal Empires: Norman and Plantagenet*, ed. M. Jones (London, 1984).
LEVISON, W., 'A Report on the Penenden Trial', *EHR* 27 (1912), 717–20.
—— *England and the Continent in the Eighth Century* (Oxford, 1946).
LEWRY, O., 'Boethian Logic in the Medieval West', in Gibson (ed.), *Boethius*, 90–134.
LIEBERMANN, F., 'Lanfranc and the Antipope', *EHR* 16 (1901), 328–32.
LOEW (= LOWE), E. A., *The Beneventan Script*, 2 vols. (2nd edn. by V. Brown, Rome, 1980).
LOYN, H. R., 'William's Bishops: Some Further Thoughts', *ANS* 10 (1987), 223–35.
—— *The English Church, 940–1154* (Harlow, 2000).
MACDONALD, A. J., *Lanfranc: A Study of his Life, Work and Writing* (2nd edn., London, 1944).
MACY, G., *The Theologies of the Eucharist in the Early Scholastic Period: A Study of the Salvific Function of the Sacrament According to the Theologians c.1080–c.1220* (Oxford, 1984).
MAGDALINO, P. (ed.), *The Perception of the Past in Twelfth-Century Europe* (London and Rio Grande, 1992).
MARABELLI, C., 'Un profilo di Lanfranco dalle sue "Lettere"', in D'Onofrio (ed.), *Lanfranco di Pavia*, 510–19.
MARENBON, J., *Early Medieval Philosophy (480–1150)* (London, 1983).
MASON, E., *St Wulfstan of Worcester, c.1008–1095* (Oxford, 1990).
MASSETTO, G. P., 'Gli studi di diritto nella Lombardia del secolo XI', in D'Onofrio (ed.), *Lanfranco di Pavia*, 61–116.
MAYR-HARTING, H., *The Bishops of Chichester, 1075–1207: Biographical Notes and Problems* (Chichester, 1963).
Medieval Art and Architecture at Canterbury Before 1220 (The British Archaeological Association and The Kent Archaeological Society, 1982).
MEYER, M. A. (ed.), *The Culture of Christendom: Essays in Medieval History in Memory of Denis L. T. Bethell* (London and Rio Grande, 1993).
MEYNIAL, E. (ed.), *Mélanges Fitting*, 2 vols. (Montpellier, 1907–8).
MILLER, E., 'The Ely Land Pleas in the Reign of William I', *EHR* 62 (1947), 438–56.
MONTCLOS, J. DE, *Lanfranc et Bérenger: la controverse eucharistique du xie siècle* (Louvain, 1971).
—— 'Lanfranc et Bérenger: les origines de la doctrine de la transubstantion', in D'Onofrio (ed.), *Lanfranco di Pavia*, 297–326.
MORRIS, C., 'William I and the Church Courts', *EHR* 82 (1967), 449–63.
MOSCHETTI, G., 'Bonfiglio', *DBI* 12.17–19.
MUSSET, L., *Normandie romane*, 2 vols. (2nd edn., La-Pierre-Qui-Vire, 1975).
NELSON, J. L., 'The Rites of the Conqueror', *ANS* 4 (1982), 117–32, 210–21; repr. eadem, *Politics and Rituals in Medieval Europe* (London and Ronceverte, 1986), 374–401.
OFFLER, H. S., 'The Tractate *De iniusta vexacione Willelmi episcopi primi*', *EHR* 66 (1951), 321–41; repr. id., *North of the Tees: Studies in Medieval British History*, ed. A. J. Piper and A. I. Doyle (Aldershot, 1996), no. VI.
OLDONI, M., 'La scuola di Lanfranco', in D'Onofrio (ed.), *Lanfranco di Pavia*, 629–58.
ORCHARD, N., 'The Bosworth Psalter and the St Augustine's Missal', in Eales and Sharpe (eds.), *Canterbury*, 87–94.

ORTENBERG, V., *The English Church and the Continent in the Tenth and Eleventh Centuries: Cultural, Spiritual, end Artistic Exchanges* (Oxford, 1992).

PAULER, R., *Das Regnum Italiae in ottonischer Zeit* (Tübingen, 1982).

PFAFF, R. W., 'Lanfranc's Supposed Purge of the Anglo-Saxon Calendar', in T. Reuter (ed.), *Warriors and Churchmen in the High Middle Ages: Essays Presented to Karl Leyser* (London and Rio Grande, 1992), 89–102.

—— 'Eadui Basan: Scriptorum princeps?' in Hicks (ed.), *England in the Eleventh Century*, 267–83.

PHILPOTT, M., 'Archbishop Lanfranc and the Canon Law', Univ. of Oxford D.Phil. thesis, 1993.

—— 'Lanfranc's Canonical Collection and "the Law of the Church" ', in D'Onofrio (ed.), *Lanfranco di Pavia*, 131–47.

—— 'The *De iniusta vexacione Willelmi episcopi primi* and Canon Law in Anglo-Norman Durham', in Rollason *et al.* (eds.), *Anglo-Norman Durham*, 125–37.

—— 'Some Interactions Between the English and Irish Churches', *ANS* 20 (1998), 187–204.

PICASSO, G., 'Lanfranco e la riforma gregoriana', in D'Onofrio (ed.), *Lanfranco di Pavia*, 425–38.

PONTAL, O., *Les Conciles de la France capétienne jusqu'en 1215* (Paris, 1995).

RADDING, C. M., *The Origins of Medieval Jurisprudence: Pavia and Bologna, 950–1150* (New Haven and London, 1988).

RADY, J., TATTON-BROWN, T., and BOWEN, J. A. (eds.), 'The Archbishop's Palace at Canterbury', *Journal of the British Archaeological Association*, 144 (1991), 1–60.

RAMSAY, N., and SPARKS, M., 'The Cult of St Dunstan at Canterbury', in Ramsay *et al.* (eds.), *St Dunstan*, 311–23.

—— —— and TATTON-BROWN, T. (eds.), *St Dunstan: His Life, Times, and Cult* (Woodbridge, 1992).

RICHÉ, P., 'L'Enseignement des artes libéraux en Italie et en France au xie siècle', in D'Onofrio (ed.), *Lanfranco di Pavia*, 157–66.

RIDYARD, S. J., '*Condigna veneratio*: Post-Conquest Attitudes to the Saints of the Anglo-Saxons', *ANS* 9 (1987), 179–206.

ROLLASON, D. W., *Saints and Relics in Anglo-Saxon England* (Oxford, 1989).

—— 'Symeon of Durham and the Community of Durham in the Eleventh Century', in Hicks (ed.), *England in the Eleventh Century*, 183–98.

ROLLASON, D., HARVEY, M., and PRESTWICH, M. (eds.), *Anglo-Norman Durham* (Woodbridge, 1994).

ROSSI, M., 'Benedetto', *DBI* 8.305–7.

RUBENSTEIN, J., 'The Life and Writings of Osbern of Canterbury', in Eales and Sharpe (eds.), *Canterbury*, 27–40.

—— 'Liturgy Against History: The Competing Visions of Lanfranc and Eadmer of Canterbury', *Speculum*, 74 (1999), 279–309.

RUUD, M., 'Episcopal Reluctance: Lanfranc's Resignation Reconsidered', *Albion*, 29 (1987), 163–75.

SAWYER, P., *Domesday Book: A Reassessment* (London, 1985).

SCAMMELL, J., 'The Rural Chapter in England from the Eleventh to the Fourteenth Century', *EHR* 86 (1971), 1–21.

SCHIEFFER, R., *Die Entstehung des päpstlichen Investiturverbots für den deutschen König*, *MGH Schriften*, 28 (Stuttgart, 1981).

SCHMIDT, T., *Alexander II. (1061–1073) und die römische Reformgruppe seiner Zeit* (Stuttgart, 1977).
SCHNITH, K., 'Die englischen Reichskonzilien 1076–1085 in Spiegel der anglonormannischen Geschichtsschrieben', *Annuarium Historiae Conciliorum*, 13 (1981), 183–97.
—— 'Wesen und Wandlungen des anglonormannischen concilium generale', in K. Seibt (ed.), *Gesellschaftsgeschichte Festschrift für Karl Bosl 80. Geburtstag*, 2 vols. (Munich, 1988), 2.22–36.
SCIUTO, I., 'Il problema della ragione in Lanfranco, Berengario e Pier Damiani in relazione all'opera di Anselmo d'Aosta', in D'Onofrio (ed.), *Lanfranco di Pavia*, 595–607.
SETTIA, A. A., 'Pavia capitale del *Regnum* nel secolo XI', in D'Onofrio (ed.), *Lanfranco di Pavia*, 31–60.
SHARPE, R., 'Goscelin's St Augustine and St Mildreth: Hagiography and Liturgy in Context', *JTS*, NS 41 (1990), 502–16.
—— 'The Setting of St Augustine's Translation, 1091', in Eales and Sharpe (eds.), *Canterbury*, 1–13.
SHEERIN, D., 'Some Observations on the Date of Lanfranc's *Decreta*', *SMon.* 17 (1975), 13–27.
SMALLEY, B., 'La *Glossa ordinaria*: Quelques prédécesseurs d'Anselme de Laon', *RTAM* 9 (1937), 365–400.
—— *The Study of the Bible in the Middle Ages* (3rd edn., Oxford, 1983).
SMITH, L., and WARD, B. (eds.), *Intellectual Life in the Middle Ages: Essays Presented to Margaret Gibson* (London and Rio Grande, 1992).
SMITH, M. F., 'Archbishop Stigand and the Eye of the Needle', *ANS* 16 (1994), 199–219.
SMITH, R. A. L., 'John of Tours, Bishop of Bath, 1088–1122', *Downside Review*, 60 (1942), 132–41; repr. id., *Collected Papers*, 74–82.
—— 'The Place of Gundulf in the Anglo-Norman Church', *EHR* 58 (1943), 257–72; repr. id., *Collected Papers*, 83–102.
—— *Collected Papers* (London, 1947).
SOUTHERN, R. W., 'The Canterbury Forgeries', *EHR* 73 (1958), 193–226.
—— 'Lanfranc of Bec and Berengar of Tours', in Hunt *et al.* (eds.), *Studies in Medieval History*, 27–48.
—— *Saint Anselm and his Biographer: A Study of Monastic Life and Thought, 1059–c.1130* (Cambridge, 1963).
—— *Saint Anselm: A Portrait in a Landscape* (Cambridge, 1990).
—— *Scholastic Humanism and the Unification of Europe*, 3 vols. (Oxford, 1995–).
SPEAR, D. S., 'Les Archidiacres de Rouen au cours de la période ducale', *Annales de Normandie*, 34 (1984), 15–50.
—— 'William Bona Anima, Abbot of St Stephen's of Caen, 1070–79', *HSJ* 1 (1989), 51–60.
—— 'The School of Caen Revisited', *HSJ* 4 (1992), 55–66.
—— 'L'Administration épiscopale normande. Archidiacres et dignitaires des chapitres', in *Les Évêques normands du xie siècle*, ed. P. Bouet and B. Neveux (Caen, 1995), 81–102.
STEINDORFF, E., *Jahrbücher des deutschen Reichs unter Heinrich III.*, 2 vols. (Leipzig, 1874–81).
STENTON, D. M., *English Justice Between the Norman Conquest and the Great Charter, 1066–1215* (London, 1965).
STENTON, F. M., *Anglo-Saxon England* (3rd edn., Oxford, 1971).
STRIK, H. J. A., 'Remains of the Lanfranc Building in the Great Central Tower and the North-West Choir/Transept Area', in *Medieval Art and Architecture*, 20–5.
STUBBS, W., *Registrum sacrum Anglicanum* (2nd edn., Oxford, 1897).

TAMASSIA, N., 'Lanfranco arcivescovo di Canterbury e la scuola pavese', in Meynial (ed.), *Mélanges Fitting*, 2.189–201.

TATTON-BROWN, T., 'The Beginnings of St Gregory's Priory and St John's Hospital in Canterbury', in Eales and Sharpe (eds.), *Canterbury*, 41–52.

TILLMANN, H., *Die päpstlichen Legaten in England bis zur Beendigung des Legation Gualas (1218)* (Bonn, 1926).

TUTSCH, B., 'Die Rezeptionsgeschichte der Consuetudines Bernhards und Ulrichs von Cluny im Spiegel ihrer handschriftliche Über lieferung', *FMS* 30 (1996), 248–93.

TWEEDALE, M. M., 'Logic (i): From the Late Eleventh Century to the Time of Abelard', in Dronke (ed.), *A History of Twelfth-Century Western Philosophy*, 196–226.

ULLMANN, W., 'Cardinal Humbert and the Ecclesia Romana', *SG* 4 (1952), 111–27; repr. id., *The Papacy and Political Ideas in the Middle Ages* (London, 1976), no. I.

VAN HOUTS, E. M. C., 'The Ship List of William the Conqueror', *ANS* 10 (1988), 159–83.

VAUGHN, S. N., 'Lanfranc at Bec: A Reinterpretation', *Albion*, 17 (1985), 135–48.

——*Anselm of Bec and Robert of Melun: The Innocence of the Dove and the Wisdom of the Serpent* (Berkeley, Los Angeles, and London, 1987).

——'Lanfranc, Anselm and the School of Bec: In Search of the Students of Bec', in Meyer (ed.), *The Culture of Christendom*, 155–81.

VIOLA, C., 'Lanfranc de Pavie et Anselme d'Aosta', in D'Onofrio (ed.), *Lanfranco di Pavia*, 531–94.

VIOLANTE, C., 'Anselmo da Baggio', *DBI* 3 (1961), 399–407.

VOLLRATH, H., *Die Synoden Englands bis 1066* (Paderborn, etc., 1985).

WATT, J. A., *The Church and the Two Nations in Medieval Ireland* (Cambridge, 1970).

WEBBER, T., *Scribes and Scholars at Salisbury Cathedral, c.1075–c.1125* (Oxford, 1992).

——'Script and Manuscript Production at Christ Church, Canterbury, after the Norman Conquest', in Eales and Sharpe (eds.), *Canterbury*, 145–58.

WICKHAM LEGG, J., and HOPE, W. H. ST J., *Inventories of Canterbury Cathedral* (Westminster, 1902).

WILLIS, R., *The Architectural History of Canterbury Cathedral* (London, 1845).

——*The Architectural History of the Conventual Buildings of Christ Church at Canterbury* (London, 1869).

WOLLASCH, J., 'Reformmönchtum und Schriftlichkeit', *FMS* 26 (1992), 274–86.

WOODMAN, F., *The Architectural History of Canterbury Cathedral* (London and Boston, 1981).

ZANATTA, F., 'L'autorità della ragione: Contributo all'interpretazione della lettera 77 di Anselmo d'Aosta a Lanfranco di Pavia', in D'Onofrio (ed.), *Lanfranco di Pavia*, 609–27.

ZIESE, J., *Wibert von Ravenna. Der Gegenpapst Clemens III. (1084–1100)* (Stuttgart, 1982).

Index

Abbreviations: a.: abbot, ab.: abbey, abp.: archbishop, adn.: archdeacon, ap.: anti-pope, b.: battle, bp.: bishop, c.: count, card.: cardinal, counc.: council, ch.: church, d.: duke, dn.: deacon, dss.: duchess, e.: earl, emp.: emperor, emps.: empress, kg.: king, leg.: legate, m.: monk, mon.: monastery, p.: pope, pr.: prior, pt.: priest, q.: queen, St: Saint, subdn.: subdeacon

Adalbert, abp. of Hamburg-Bremen 147
Adelelm, ab. of Abingdon 173
Agnes of Poitou, emps. 36
Alan, c. of Brittany and lord of Richmond 220
Albert, m. of Bec and Canterbury 151
Aldhelm, St 184
Aldred, abp. of York 79–81, 93, 103, 129
Alexander II, p. 20, 22–4, 26–8, 43–5, 64–5, 76–7, 81, 168, 175, 197, 199
   and the Norman duchy 18, 31, 35–7, 130
   and Lanfranc's move to Canterbury 78–9, 82–4, 149, 178, 185
   and the English ch. and kingdom 88–9, 93–7, 100–3, 129, 141, 150, 161, 165
Alger of Liège, m. 59
Aluric, adn. at Winchester 135
Ambrose, St, bp. of Milan 39, 51, 61–2, 73, 151
'Ambrosiaster' 51
Anacletus, p. 91
Anschitill, adn. at Canterbury 124, 136
Anselm II, bp. of Lucca 24, 202
Anselm, St, ab. of Bec, abp. of Canterbury 103, 106, 155
   enters Bec 11
   L.'s relations with while at Bec 21–2, 150–1, 173, 178
   L.'s relations with after 1070 175–6, 180–1, 204, 208–13, 225
   theological writings 50, 208, 210–11
Ansfrid, ab. of Préaux 17–18
archdeacons:
   in Normandy 27–8, 140, 215
   in England before 1066 135–6
   in England after 1066 85, 130, 132–6, 157, 230
Aristotle 48, 57
Arundel Psalter 176–7
Athelney, a. 125–6
Augustine, St, abp. of Canterbury 86, 96, 156, 167, 183
Augustine, St, bp. of Hippo 3, 39, 50–1, 61–2, 66, 72, 156
Avranches 10

Baldwin, ab. of Bury St Edmunds 80, 93, 164–7

Baldwin V, c. of Flanders 34–5
Barking, a. 173
Bath, a. 162–3
Bec, a.:
   historical traditions at 5
   entry of L. 11–12
   L. as monk and prior 14–24
   and Canterbury 150–1, 156
   L. as abp. and 206–8, 211–13
Bede 95–6
Benedict X, ap. 80–2
Benedict VIII, p. 2–4, 41, 75, 77, 185, 197
Benedict IX, p. 4
Benedict of Chiusa, m. 9
Benedict, St, of Nursia 156
   Rule of 12, 14–15, 19, 76, 125, 154–5, 158–9, 206–7, 210, 214
Berard, clerk of Bury St Edmunds 166
Berengar of Tours:
   L.'s possible early contact 9–10
   eucharistic controversy with L. 38–40, 42–4, 59–74, 198–9, 215
   piety and devotion 73
Bernard, m. of Cluny 156, 181
Boethius 3, 48
Bonfilius, Pavian jurist 7
Boniface V, p. 96
Bosworth Psalter 176
Bregwine, abp. of Canterbury 180
Bruman, reeve at Canterbury 170
Burchard, bp. of Worms 132
Bury St Edmunds, a. 164–7, 194, 198–9

Caen:
   town 25
   Saint-Étienne, a. 24–8, 35–6, 38, 207
   la Trinité, a. 24–5, 35–7
Calixtus II, p. 103
Canterbury:
   Christ Church 79, 104–7, 149–60, 179
   St Augustine's, a. 79, 134, 167–72, 179, 184, 193
   St Gregory's priory 107–9, 137, 169–70, 184
   St John the Baptist, hospital 107–9
   St Martin's ch. 118

Canterbury (*cont.*):
  St Nicholas, Harbledown, leper hospital 107, 109
Caradog ap Gruffudd, ruler of Morgannwg 148
Cassian, John 50
Charlemagne, emp. 1
Chartres 10
chastity, clerical 2–3, 30, 53, 84, 127–8, 131, 214
Chester, city and see 125, 163
Chichester, see 125, 130
chorepiscopi 118, 145
Cicero 48–9
Clememt III, ap., *formerly* Guibert, abp. of Ravenna 20, 41, 47, 200, 202–5
Cluny, a. 9, 169
  and the Norman duchy 17–18
  and the English ch. and kingdom 156
Cnut, kg. 123
Columbanus, m. of St Augustine's at Canterbury 169
Conrad II, emp. 3
Councils, synods, and assemblies 29–30, 120–31, 140
  NORMANDY
  Brionne (1050) 32, 34, 42, 62–3, 143
  Caen (?1045) 135; (1047) 123; (1061) 123
  Lillebonne (1080) 30, 123, 127–8, 132, 135
  Lisieux (1054) 29–30; (1064) 30, 123
  Rouen (*c*.1045) 30, 37; (1061) 17; (1063) 30; (1069) 29–30; (1070) 123; (1072) 30, 123; (1074) 123, 135; (1078) 123; (1079) 123
  BRITISH ISLES
  Cashel (1101) 146
  Gloucester (1080) 123, 125–6, 183; (1085) 123, 125–6, 131
  London (1074/5) 87, 123–5, 127, 133, 136, 143, 145, 160, 187, 210; (1077/8) 123, 126
  Rath Breasail (1111) 146
  Westminster (1102) 131
  Winchester (1070) 83–7, 124, 128, 131; (1072) 87, 94–5, 97–101, 123–7; (1076) 123, 125–7, 131, 133, 214
  Windsor (1070) 83–7, 124, 131, 168; (1072) 94–5, 97–101, 123–4
  York (?early 1060s) 129
  OTHER
  Constantinople (381) 68
  Chalcedon (451) 68
  Ephesus (431) 68
  Mainz (1049) 40–1, 75, 185
  Nicaea (325) 68, 118, 121, 131
  Pavia (1022) 2–3, 75, 185
  Rheims (1049) 32, 35–6, 38–41, 61, 168
  Rome: Lateran synods (1050) 31, 39, 41–2, 61, 66–8; (1059) 35, 42, 63–4, 67–8; (1060) 118; (1078) 66; (1079) 66–7; (1080) 199
  Seville II (619) 118
  Siponto (1050) 40
  Toledo IV (633) 121
  Tours (1054) 63
  Vercelli (1050) 40, 42, 61–2, 66
Coventry, a. 149, 163
Credan, St 177
crown-wearings 125, 153, 186–7, 237

De decem categoriis 50
Dijon, Saint-Bénigne, a. 9, 214
Domesday survey 115–16, 137, 196
Domnall, bp. of Munster 66, 146
Donatus, bp. of Dublin 93, 146
Dublin, Christ Church cathedral 146
Dunfermline, Holy Trinity, mon. 147–8
Dunstan, St, abp. of Canterbury 105–6, 112, 149, 151–4, 156, 170, 176, 179–84
Durandus of Troarn, m. 60
Durham, city and see 161–2, 191, 220–1, 224

Eadburga, St 108–9
Eadmer, m. of Christ Church, Canterbury 179, 198
Eadsige, abp. of Canterbury 109
Edith, St 183–4
Edmund the Atheling 147
Edward the Confessor, kg. of England 79, 114, 164, 185
Edward, m. of Christ Church, Canterbury, *formerly* adn. of London 157
Edwin, pr. of St Augustine's at Canterbury 168
Egbert, abp. of York 95
Egelward, m. of Christ Church, Canterbury 151–5, 160, 179, 183, 226
Elfric, abp. of Canterbury 180
Elfsige, ab. of Bath 162
Elfstan, ab. of St Augustine's at Canterbury 167
Elphege, St, abp. of Canterbury 106, 150–1, 175–6, 179–83
Ely, a. 193–6
Ermenfrid, bp. of Sion, papal leg. 29–30, 37, 78, 80–1, 84–6
Ernost, bp. of Rochester 21, 110, 118, 213
Ernulf, pr. of Christ Church, Canterbury 106, 151
Ethelbert, kg. of Kent 96
Ethelheard, abp. of Canterbury 180
Ethelmar, bp. of Elmham 79, 81, 84
Ethelnoth, ab. of Glastonbury 126
Ethelric, bp. of Selsey/Chichester 80, 84, 89, 110, 114, 126, 141
Ethelsig, ab. of St Augustine's at Canterbury 80, 167–8, 170
Ethelwig, ab. of Evesham 112, 189
Ethelwine, bp. of Durham 79, 84
Ethelwold, bp. of Winchester 149
Eusebius, p. 142
Eustace, c. of Boulogne 81
Evesham, a. 9, 160, 177–8, 183, 194
exceptio spolii 61–2, 219, 221–4

Florus of Lyons 51
Formosus, p. 97
Fulcard, ab. of Thorney 126

Geoffrey, bp. of Coutances 25, 27, 31, 37, 114, 124, 188–9, 192–5, 215, 218
Geoffrey Martel, c. of Anjou 34
Gerard, moneyer of Arras, m. of Bec 124, 212–13
Gervase, m. of Christ Church, Canterbury 105–6
Gilbert, c. of Brionne 34
Gilbert Crispin, ab. of Westminster 5, 19, 22, 151
Giso, bp. of Wells 79–80, 125–6, 162
Glastonbury, a. 125–6, 183
Godfrey, bp. of Chichester 205
Godric, dean of Christ Church, Canterbury 82, 150
Godwin, e. of Wessex 112
Godwine, bp. at St Martin's ch., Canterbury 118
Goldwin, m. of Christ Church, Canterbury 147
Goscelin of Saint-Bertin, m. 169–72, 182–4
Gregory I, p. 30, 50, 68, 83–4, 86, 89, 94, 96–8, 125, 128, 142, 151, 156, 167, 180
Gregory III, p. 96
Gregory VII, p., *formerly* Hildebrand, adn. 41, 161, 165, 172, 225
  and the Berengarian controversy 63, 66–7, 198–9
  and the primacy of Canterbury 101–2, 114–15, 197
  and other English affairs 197–205
Guibert, abp. of Ravenna, *see* Clement III, ap.
Guitmund, ab. of la Croix-Saint-Leufroi, bp. of Aversa, 22, 59, 186
Gundulf, bp. of Rochester 21–2, 26, 116, 118–19, 137, 151–2, 161, 170–1, 184, 187, 213
Guthric, kg. of Dublin 145
Guy, ab. of St Augustine's at Canterbury 167–72, 184
Guy, c. of Brionne and Vernon 34
Guy, m. of Bec and Canterbury 151, 173

Harold, kg. of England 80, 82–3
Harrow (Middx.) 118
Henry II, emp. 2–4, 41, 75, 185
Henry III, emp. 36, 38, 40–1, 75, 185
Henry IV, emp. 41, 200, 202–3
Henry I, kg. of England 186, 219
Henry I, kg. of France 62
Henry, m. of Bec and Canterbury 151
Henry, pr. of Christ Church, Canterbury, ab. of Battle 22, 150–3, 155, 211–12
Herbert, bp. of Lisieux 31
Herbert of Losinga, bp. of Thetford/Norwich 164–7
Herfast, bp. of Thetford/Elmham 32, 79, 81, 84, 90, 92, 130, 142–7, 194, 198
Herluin, ab. of Bec 12–16, 78, 206–8, 211–13, 226

Herluin, m. of Bec and Canterbury 151, 178
Herman, bp. of Sherborne/Ramsbury 79, 89, 160
Herod Agrippa I, Jewish kg. 187
Hilary, St, of Poitiers 65–6, 215
Hildebrand, adn. at Rome, *see* Gregory VII, p.
Holvard, m. of Christ Church, Canterbury 151, 153
Honorius I, p. 96
Honorius II, p. 103
Hubert, papal leg. 78, 85, 94, 100, 199–201
Hugh I, ab. of Cluny 156, 172
Hugh, bp. of Avranches 31
Hugh, bp. of Bayeux 31
Hugh, bp. of Lisieux 17–18
Hugh, bp. of London 142
Hugh Candidus, card.-pt. of S. Clemente 41, 202–4
Hugh the Chanter, canon of York 87–8
Hugh of Montfort 111–12, 193
Humbert, card.-bp. of Silva Candida 41, 43–4
  and papal authority 4, 77
  and the eucharistic controversy 43, 63–4, 67–8, 70, 77, 198–9

Ingelrannus, master of Chartres 10, 39
Innocent III, p. 122
Ithamar, St 184
Ivo, bp. of Chartres 22
Ivo, bp. of Sées 31

Jarento, ab. of Saint-Bénigne at Dijon 204
Jerome, St 39, 50, 61–2, 151
John, ab. of Fécamp 9, 31, 36, 60
John, bp. of Avranches, abp. of Rouen 32, 37, 43, 123, 130, 135, 140, 151, 207, 213–15, 227
John, card.-pt., papal leg. 83–5
John Chrysostom, St 51
John XII, p. 97
John XIX, p. 197
'John the Scot', *see* Ratramnus of Corbie, m.
John de Villula, bp. of Wells/Bath 162–3

Kentford 194

Lanfranc, abp. of Canterbury:
  EARLY LIFE
  birth and family 5
  life at Pavia 4–9
  study and practice of Lombard law 6–8, 13
  study and teaching of the arts 5–6
  travels to France 9–10
  encounter with Berengar 9
  conversion to monasticism at Bec 11–12
  AS MONK AND PRIOR OF BEC
  initial difficulties 13–15
  becomes prior 14
  relations with Abbot Herluin 12–14
  opens school 19–20

Lanfranc (cont.):
  pupils 20–4
  teaches liberal arts 47–9
  increasing concern with theology 20, 50, 56
  association with reform popes 20, 38–45
  the Berengarian controversy 34, 38–40, 42–4, 59–74
  and other monasteries 16–18
  and councils 32
  relations with Duke William 32–8
  WRITINGS WHILE IN NORMANDY
  on the arts 47–9
  on patristic texts 50
  on the Psalms 46–7, 50–1
  on the Pauline epistles 50–9
  on the eucharist 64–5, 67–74
  AS ABBOT OF SAINT-ÉTIENNE AT CAEN
  becomes abbot 24
  building work 26
  establishes a school 20
  relations with reform papacy 27–8, 38–45
  relations with Duke William 24–5, 29–38
  AS ARCHBISHOP OF CANTERBURY
  appointed and consecrated 78–9, 85–6
  wishes to resign 78
  as primate: Canterbury and York 87–103, 187
  as primate: the British Isles 100, 124, 144–8
  as holder of councils 123–8
  and church organization 129–38
  relations with King William I 92, 102, 128, 185–96, 228–9
  relations with King William II 217–19, 225
  relations with Pope Alexander II 141
  relations with Pope Gregory VII 101–2, 141, 197–205
  relations with the anti-pope Clement III 202–5
  Christ Church, Canterbury 104–7, 109–17, 150–60
  Monastic constitutions 154–60
  cathedral monasteries 150, 160–3
  other monasteries 163–75
  charitable foundations at Canterbury 107–9
  and the see of Rochester 117–19
  visits Bec 15, 207–8
  relations with Anselm 208–11, 217–25
  and canon law 138–43, 228
  the *Collectio Lanfranci* 44, 139–41, 203, 221–2
  as royal justice 188–95
  and the English 156, 169–70, 175–84
  correction of texts 46, 227
  death and burial 225
  CHARACTER, PIETY, REPUTATION 13, 226–7
  almsgiving 154, 174, 212, 226
  astuteness 174, 215
  care for liturgical detail 214
  charity 107–9, 173–4
  grace of tears 13, 24, 43
  humility 13, 173, 207
  pastoral care 152, 154, 173–4
  severity and mercy 160, 169, 172–4
  wisdom 174
  zeal for the monastic life 174, 227
Lanfranc, m. of Bec 173, 212
laudes regiae 29, 81, 183
Leo, bp. of Vercelli 2
Leo I, p. 142
Leo III, p. 96
Leo IV, p. 122
Leo IX, p. 30–1, 35, 37–41, 43, 45, 61–3, 67, 75–7, 82, 96–7, 168, 185, 197
Leofric, bp. of Exeter 79
Leofwine, bp. of Lichfield 84, 89
Liber Papiensis 7–8
Liemar, abp. of Hamburg-Bremen 147
Lincoln, city and see 129
Lyminge, mon. 108–9, 169–70, 184

Mainer, ab. of Saint-Évroult 16–17
Malcolm III Canmore, kg. of Scotland 147–8
Manasses I, abp. of Rheims 215
Margaret, q. of Scotland 147–8, 185, 226
Matilda, dss. of Normandy, q. of England 25, 34–6, 81, 200
Mauger, abp. of Rouen 16, 30, 32, 35, 37
Maurice, bp. of London 173
Maurice, m. of Bec and Canterbury 151, 178, 210
Maurilius, abp. of Rouen 12, 17, 21, 30, 32, 37
Mildrith, St 108–9, 167, 169–72, 184
Milo Crispin, m. of Bec 5
Minster-in-Thanet, mon. 167, 169
Mont Saint-Michel, a. 9–10, 12, 130
Muchelney, a. 125–6, 183

Nicholas II, p. 17–18, 20, 35–7, 42–4, 48, 63–4, 67, 76–7, 80, 82–3, 128, 197

Odilo, ab. of Cluny 156
Odo, ab. of Chertsey 172
Odo, bp. of Bayeux and e. of Kent 124
  as diocesan bishop 25, 27, 76
  and King William I 135, 188–9, 193–4, 215, 223
  and L. 106, 110–15, 168, 170
  and King William II 218–20, 223
Odo, c. of Champagne and lord of Holderness 220
Offa, kg. of Mercia 164
Orderic Vitalis, m. of Saint-Évroult 16, 192
Osbern, ab. of Saint-Évroult 16–18
Osbern, bp. of Exeter 93, 100
Osbern, m. of Bec and Canterbury 151, 180–1, 183, 212
Oswald, bp. of Worcester 149
Otto I, emp. 7
Otto III, emp. 2
Ouen, St 180

Parc, Norman vill 32–4
Paschal II, p. 102–3
Paschasius Radbertus, m. of Corbie 39, 60–1
Patrick, bp. of Dublin 144–5
Paul, ab. of St Albans 155, 159, 164, 175, 177–8, 226
Paul, e. of the Orkneys 147
Paulinus, bp. of York 95
Pavia 1–9, 224
Penenden Heath 102, 109–15, 119, 132, 134, 143, 167, 183, 192, 196, 228
Peter, bp. of Lichfield/Chester 147, 149, 163
Peter, card.-pt., papal leg. 83–5
Peter Damiani, St, card.-bp. of Ostia 66–7
Peter's pence 83, 199–204
Peter the Venerable, ab. of Cluny 59
Petherton, royal manor 93, 124, 192
Philip I, kg. of France 73, 217
Priscian 48–9
Pseudo-Isidorian decrees 91–2, 118, 121–2, 125, 133, 139, 221–3, 228

Ralph, bp. of the Orkneys 147
Ralph of Courbépine 112
Ralph 'de Gael', e. of Norfolk 188–9, 191–2
Ralph, pr. of Saint-Étienne at Caen and of Rochester, ab. of Battle 26
Ranulf Peverel 223
Ratramnus, m. of Corbie ('John the Scot') 39, 60–1
Regularis concordia 149–50, 155–6, 181
Remigius, bp. of Dorchester/Lincoln 81–2, 89–92, 94, 136, 192, 194–5, 198
Remiremont, a. 40–1
Reynald, ab. of Saint-Cyprien at Poitiers 65, 215–16
Reynald, bp. of Pavia 2–4
Richard II, d. of Normandy 9
Richard, e. of Clare 213
Richard fitzGilbert 193
Riwallon, ab. of the New Minster at Winchester 124
Robert, bp. of Chester/Coventry 92, 163
Robert, c. of Eu 193
Robert, c. of Mortain 193–5, 218
Robert Curthose, d. of Normandy 200, 217–18, 224, 229
Robert of Grandmesnil, ab. of Saint-Évroult 16–18, 31
Robert of Jumièges, abp. of Canterbury 80–2
Robert of Montgomery, e. of Shrewsbury 28
Rochester, city and see 117–19, 159–61, 218–19
Rodulf, ab. of Saint-Vannes at Verdun 204
Roger, e. of Hereford 189–92
Roger *le Poitevin*, c. 220
Roger, m. of Caen and Canterbury 151
Roger, Roman subdn. and papal leg. 205
Rouen, Saint-Ouen, a. 9, 214–15, 227

St Albans, a. 155, 159, 164

Saint-Èvroult, a. 16–19
St Neots, priory 213
Salisbury (Sarum), see and city 125, 160–1, 221–4
Salwio, m. of Canterbury 151
Samuel, bp. of Dublin 146
Samuel, m. of Caen and Canterbury 151
Scotland, ab. of St Augustine's at Canterbury 124, 167–8, 170–1
Sergius, p. 96
Silverius, p. 152
Simeon, ab. of Ely 194–5
simony 30–1, 40–1, 85, 127
Siward, bp. of Rochester 79–80, 118–19
Siward, bp. at St Martin's, Canterbury 118
Stephen IX, p. 82
Stigand, abp. of Canterbury 79–85, 90, 92, 103, 109, 168
Stigand, bp. of Selsey/Chichester 79, 84, 116–17, 130, 136
Suppo, ab. of Mont Saint-Michel 9
synods, *see* councils

Theodore of Mopsuestia 51
Theodoric, Ostrogothic kg. 1, 3–4
Theodoric of Paderborn 22, 64
Thierry, ab. of Saint-Évroult 16–17
Thomas I, abp. of York 89, 124, 196
  to 1070 22, 84–95, 98–102
  the primacy dispute with L. 90, 175, 187
  other dealings with L. 102, 133, 147, 165, 221
  in the diocese of York 136
Thurstan, ab. of Ely 80
Thurstan, ab. of Glastonbury 126, 172–3, 187, 227
Thurstan, abp. of York 103
Toirdhealbhach Ó Briain, kg. of Munster 145–6
Toul, St Aper, mon. 48
Troarn, Saint-Martin, a. 194

Ulric, m. 187
Urban II, p. 205, 214

Val-ès-Dunes, b. 34
Victor II, p. 43, 82
Vitalian, p. 96
Vitalis, ab. of Bernay 212
Vitalis, m. of Caen and Canterbury 151

Waichelin, bp. of Winchester 79, 84, 86, 124, 149–50, 161, 171, 194–5
Walcher, bp. of Durham 130, 142, 161–2, 191
Walter, ab. of Evesham 175, 177, 194
Walter, bp. of Hereford 79–80
Waltheof, e. of Huntingdon 130, 189–92, 227
Wells, see of 162–3
William, ab. of Cormeilles 14
William Bona Anima, ab. of Saint-Étienne at Caen, abp. of Rouen 21–2, 26, 32, 213, 215
William of Corbeil, abp. of Canterbury 103, 108

William, bp. of Elmham 92
William, bp. of London 79, 124
William II, d. of Normandy, I, kg. of England:
  AS DUKE TO 1066
  and the Norman church 16–18, 29–32
  and councils 30, 123–8
  attitude to the papacy 18, 31–2
  and Berengar 34, 62
  marriage 33–7
  AS KING OF ENGLAND
  relations with L. 78, 185–96
  and the primacy of Canterbury 88, 90, 92–6, 100, 102–3
  and ecclesiastical jurisdiction 132–4, 142–3
  and Penenden Heath 112–15
  and English monasteries 150, 164–7
  and the Gregorian papacy 197–205
  and the revolt of the earls 188–92
  death 217–18
William fitzOsbern, e. of Hereford 189
William II, kg. of England 162–4, 171, 186, 203
  crowned by L. 217–18
  subsequent relations with L. 218–19
  and the trial of William of Saint-Calais 219–24
William of Poitiers, adn. of Lisieux 30
William of Saint-Calais, bp. of Durham 125, 161–2, 200, 218–24, 228
William of Volpiano, ab. of Saint-Bénigne at Dijon 9, 29
William, ab. of Ebersberg 20–1, 23, 48
Wilton, a. 203–4
Winchester, see and city 149–50, 160–1
Wistan, St 177
Worcester, city and see 160
Wulfketel, ab. of Crowland 126
Wulfric, ab. of the New Minster at Winchester 124, 126
Wulfric II, ab. of St Augustine's at Canterbury 167–8, 171
Wulfstan II, bp. of Worcester 79–81, 84, 90, 93, 114, 130, 135, 147, 160, 189, 194

Lightning Source UK Ltd.
Milton Keynes UK
UKHW022309280223
417837UK00003B/259